Tapestry of Grace Primer Guidebook

TAPESTRY *of* GRACE

Primer

GUIDEBOOK

LAMPSTAND PRESS
KINGSPORT, TN

Tapestry of Grace Primer Guidebook

Created by Michael Somerville

Copyright © 2014 Michael Somerville

Published by Lampstand Press, 1135 N. Eastman Road
Kingsport, TN 37664

All rights reserved. No part of this publication may be reproduced or distributed in any form or by any means, or stored in a database or retrieval system, without the prior written permission of the publisher, except as provided by USA copyright law.

Cover design: David Somerville

First printing, 2014
Printed in the United States of America

ISBN 9780991571819

Contents

TAPESTRY PRIMER INTRODUCTION	11
Why Should You Care About Stories?	11
What Storyline Do We Follow?	11
What Themes Do We Emphasize Or Avoid?	12
Who Are The "Central Characters" In Our Story?	14
How Should You Use This Book?	15
MINI-UNIT 1 OVERVIEW: EDEN TO EGYPT	16
Topic 1: From The Beginning To Babel	23
Topic 2: A Chosen People	29
Topic 3: Egypt: Gift Of The Nile	37
MINI-UNIT 2 OVERVIEW: TABERNACLE AND TEMPLE	44
Topic 1: Burning Bush To Tabernacle	51
Topic 2: The Promised Land	63
Topic 3: The Heart Of The King	75
MINI-UNIT 3 OVERVIEW: DANIEL'S REVELATION	88
Topic 1: Babylon: The Head Of Gold	95
Topic 2: Persia: The Torso Of Silver	101
Topic 3: Greece: The Belly Of Bronze	109
MINI-UNIT 4 OVERVIEW: CHRIST AND THE CHURCH	120
Topic 1: Alexander The Great: Preparation For Proclamation	125
Topic 2: Imperial Rome: Backdrop To The Atonement	135
Topic 3: The Zenith Of Imperial Rome: Backdrop To The Early Church	143
MINI-UNIT 5 OVERVIEW: THE BROKEN ROAD	150
Topic 1: Collapse into Chaos	157

Topic 2: The Making Of Medieval Europe: Charlemagne	*167*
Topic 3: Popes and Princes	*177*
MINI-UNIT 6 OVERVIEW: RECOVERY AND DISCOVERY	**188**
Topic 1: Recovering Trade, Lands, and Knowledge	*195*
Topic 2: Explorers, Inventors, and Reformers	*205*
Topic 3: Roses And Reformation	*215*
MINI-UNIT 7 OVERVIEW: A NEW WORLD	**222**
Topic 1: Early New World Colonies	*227*
Topic 2: Waves Of Colonists	*237*
Topic 3: Colonists And Native Americans	*243*
MINI-UNIT 8 OVERVIEW: ONE NATION	**252**
Topic 1: French And Indian War	*257*
Topic 2: Gathering Clouds	*263*
Topic 3: Give Me Liberty!	*269*
MINI-UNIT 9 OVERVIEW: GROWING PAINS	**282**
Topic 1: Jefferson And The Louisiana Purchase	*287*
Topic 2: The Oregon Trail	*291*
Topic 3: Early Industrial Revolution	*297*
MINI-UNIT 10 OVERVIEW: A HOUSE DIVIDED	**306**
Topic 1: The Civil War (Part 1): Lincoln And The Start Of The Civil War	*311*
Topic 2: The Civil War (Part 2): Decisive Years Of The Civil War	*317*
Topic 3: The Civil War (Part 3): Closing Years Of The Civil War	*323*
MINI-UNIT 11 OVERVIEW: ENGINES OF EMPIRES	**330**
Topic 1: Reconstruction and Expansion	*335*
Topic 2: Industry and Immigration	*345*
Topic 3: Airplanes And Automobiles	*355*

MINI-UNIT 12 OVERVIEW: A SMALLER WORLD	364
Topic 1: Wired Worlds At War	*371*
Topic 2: One Small Step For Man	*389*
Topic 3: At Our Fingertips And In His Hands	*397*

Introduction

Why should you care about stories?

We know that stories have great influence on the way people view the world. Solomon used proverbs to communicate wisdom. Aesop used fables to teach morality in ancient Greece. Jesus used parables to convey timeless truths about the Kingdom of Heaven. Stories matter. They not only engage our minds, but affect our hearts and can shape our souls. Because stories have great influence, we want you to understand the storyline that we follow so that you know where we will lead you and your child as you explore this story together.

The history of the world is an amazing, rich, textured, complex story with a cast of billions that spans millennia. In simplifying this story for your young child, you will be giving him merely an introduction to its major characters and themes. We have tried to guide you by making key decisions about what to emphasize.

What storyline do we follow?

We believe that human history is a story told by an Author, and that this Author is also the Creator of humanity. We unapologetically use the Bible as our primary resource for ancient history. We follow the story of God's people from Creation through the establishment of the Church—the spiritual heirs of Abraham and the family of God. While we introduce other cultures with whom the Israelites interacted (Egyptians, Phoenicians, Babylonians, Persians, Greeks, and Romans), we do not do a global survey of ancient civilizations in *Tapestry Primer*. (By contrast, *Tapestry of Grace* does provide this deeper study over the course of a full year in the Ancient World.)

After the establishment of the Church, we follow the history of the western Church. While the Eastern Roman Empire has a rich history, and while developments were happening all over the world (and, again, *Tapestry of Grace* includes these), we stick closely to the clash of ideas that was worked out on the stage of Western Europe. Here, the gospel of Christ alternatively shaped and challenged the rulers of the day. In the West, we see the development of foundational ideas that are still influencing our world currently, and we set the stage for the American chapter of world history.

We want students to understand their place in history. Since *Tapestry Primer* is written for very young American children in the twenty-first century, our *Guidebook* takes you across the Atlantic and focus on the birth and struggles of a new nation on the continent of North America. Specifically, we focus on the British settlements. Each of the thirteen original colonies had its own story. In this introduction to colonial America, we focus more on understanding daily life and the fact that these different colonies came together to form one new nation than studying any one colony in great detail. We follow the story west as the nation expands after winning independence.

The Civil War in America was a key moment in the history of the Union, and we spend plenty of time studying that conflict. After we finish, we remain focused on American history, following America out onto the world stage as our country was pulled into world wars and launched into outer space and cyberspace. We include topics that introduce daily life during the major conflicts and events of the last century: the two world wars, the Cold War, the Civil Rights Movement, the Space Race, and increasing globalization.

But even while we introduce these events, our main focus is not on the conflicts. These may be either too difficult or too complex for younger children to fully understand. Throughout this entire program, we focus attention on daily life and on people, places, and things that helped shape the story. We believe that this gives you the ability to decide when and how to explain some of the darker moments of history to your student.

What themes do we emphasize or avoid?

The history of our world is a history of broken beauty, of a battle waged in a garden, and of God's mercy amidst necessary judgments for wrongdoing.

In the beginning, God created the heavens and the earth. He made all things good. He created mankind to live in unbroken relationship with Himself, while working, tending, stewarding, and enriching Creation as a bearer of the image of God, for God's glory.

INTRODUCTION

Mankind fell. Seeking to glorify ourselves as the bearers of God's image rather than God Himself, we pursued our own glory and pleasure—with disastrous consequences. Our fall affected all of Creation and subjected it to His righteous judgment. Yet God did not abandon or destroy His work, but promised to redeem and restore it.

God reached out to restore mankind. For a while, people humbled themselves. After humility came honor. But after honor came pride. And pride came before the fall. In history, we see this pattern repeated again and again. Mankind seeks for good outside of God and fails to find it.

Along the way, mankind has done evil; people everywhere have exercised unspeakable cruelty toward each other. We address this inescapable reality in our overviews of the stories for teachers, hopefully providing a redemptive perspective on the pain. For the children, we do not emphasize the dark chapters of history. This isn't to say that we avoid all conflict or struggle, but we don't emphasize the more tragic moments.

We do emphasize the unalterable fact that history is not random or pointless. The course of history remains in the hands of its good, wise, and powerful Creator, who will sovereignly direct history toward its conclusion in the full redemption and restoration of people so that they live in loving relationship with God, while working, tending, stewarding, and enriching the new heavens and the new earth, with Christ ruling as the King of Kings and the Lord of Lords.

But still, battles are exciting! Along the way, the clash of ideas on the world stage is a fascinating study. For teachers, we highlight the major movements and conflicts of ideas as they come and go, rising and falling in their turn. We also watch as people, made in the image of God, exercised their creative powers by inventing tools. At times, these tools have changed their world, as we'll see in the story.

Our "Topic Overviews" expand on these themes. We want to help you, as teachers, make connections and remember ideas that may have gotten a bit dim over the years. We hope that this survey course reminds you of your history in a way that surprises and intrigues you!

If you find yourself wanting more, remember that this is only a survey of the full *Tapestry of Grace* program, which offers the homeschool family a high-quality humanities education, or can simply guide you with resources that you can use to dig deeper into the fascinating story of which we are all a part. We encourage you to take advantage of it for yourself!

Who are the "central characters" in our story?

The Author

God, the Author of life, created all things. Although He delegated authority to people as His representatives, He maintains absolute authority. We trace God's actions, as seen in Creation, the Fall, and our redemption through Jesus Christ. We trace authority as power shifts over the ages.

People

People, created in God's image, are key actors in the story. We introduce young students to the great characters and stories of history that they will study again and again. We show the movements and clashes of their ideas over time.

Good

When we were created, God blessed us and called us good. We were made in God's image to do good works. Over the centuries, we have often sought to redefine good. The question, "What is good?" is often present in the story, influencing the actors.

Evil

Evil entered when we sought good outside of God's will. Sadly, we have not yet stopped finding evil when we seek good outside of God. Without emphasizing evil, we recognize that the story has a villain. Often, it is us. To God's glory, He saves us from our deception and depravity.

The Word

The Word of God, His revealed will, shapes history. God created the world by His word and revealed Himself through His Word. The Word became flesh and dwelt among us. Promise, Covenant, Law, Incarnation, and Scripture shape history as we either respond to God's Word or rebel against it.

God's Creation

Creation is the stage on which God has chosen to act out history. At times, this supporting character takes center stage. Events in history are affected by the places in which they occur. We learn to appreciate where history happened.

Man's Creation

People create tools as we exercise our role as God's image bearers. Over time, civilizations have been empowered or endangered by the tools we have made. We observe these inventions and discoveries as they occur, noting the shaping influences they have had on daily life.

INTRODUCTION

How should you use this book?

Now that you know why stories matter, the storylines that we plan to follow, what themes we emphasize and avoid, and who the central characters are, we want to give you a few brief suggestions for how to get the most out of this *Guidebook*.

The rest of this book is organized into twelve sections, one for each three-topic mini-unit in *Tapestry Primer*. Each section focuses your attention on a particular part of the story, moving choronologically from the beginning of recorded history to the end of the twentieth century.

In each section, we provide a concise summary of the entire unit as an overview for you. The summary introduces ideas and events that will be explored more fully in each topic. Take a few minutes to read this as you are planning for each new unit in order to understand what will be covered as you go.

We then explore each of the three topics in the mini-unit. In each, we seek to tell the story to you, the teacher. We hope you find this engaging and substantive without being dry or overwhelming. Most topics are less than ten pages, so we do not try to exhaustively cover every facet of history. Rather, we acquaint you with the important ideas and major characters and developments. In these sections, we have the chance to point out how events show God's active role in history. Try to allow enough time to read over each topic before you plan to teach it so that it is fresh in your mind.

If you are wondering, we do not expect you to read this aloud to your student, although you may find certain sections helpful for him as you work your way through the material. Using this *Guidebook*, we trust you will be able to retell the story for your child in ways that resonate with him. This resource will help you connect the dots and call attention to points of interest as you and your student embark on this journey through our history.

Let's get started.

Mini-Unit 1: Eden to Egypt

Remember our seven main "characters?" Note how they fit in as we study how God created and chose His people.

The Author	God created the world, gave the promise of redemption, recreated the world after the Flood, and broke language at Babel. He chose His own people, guiding the patriarchs. He orchestrated events in Joseph's life to save many and provide a place for His chosen people to grow.
People	Adam and Eve chose to pursue their own knowledge rather than obey God's Word. After the Fall, people's actions became more evil and self-serving. Different tribes began to form after Babel. God called Abraham, creating the Covenant. The Israelites were uniquely God's chosen people. As the unit ends, we see Moses growing up in the Pharaoh's palace.
Good	God defined Good as trust in His words. Satan redefined Good as pursuit of knowledge. Noah obeyed God by faith and built the Ark. Abraham believed God and did not withhold Isaac. Jacob held onto God until he was blessed. Joseph trusted God in order to interpret Pharaoh's dreams.
Evil	Satan wanted to be God and tempted people to seek Good outside of God. People did what was evil in God's sight before the Flood. After the Flood, people sought their own glory. Abraham and Isaac lied to protect themselves. Jacob was a deceiver. Joseph was arrogant. Egyptians worshipped creation rather than the Creator.
The Word	God created all things by the Word. After the Fall, God gave the promise of redemption. He gave instructions by which Noah and all life would be saved. God established His Covenant with Abraham. God blessed Jacob and named him Israel. He spoke to Joseph in dreams.
God's Creation	Creation was good, but was cursed with futility and death after the Fall. After the Flood, God's rainbow was the sign of His covenant with Creation. We study oceans and continents before focusing on Abraham's travels across the Fertile Crescent of Mesopotamia to Egypt, the gift of the Nile. The Nile replenished the soil of Egypt, while deserts protected Egypt from attack, allowing a large, specialized civilization to develop along its banks.
Man's Creation	We move from Stone Age to Bronze Age. After the Fall, people toiled to produce food. They domesticated animals, cultivated crops, made tents, forged metal, made musical instruments, built boats, preserved knowledge through written languages, built towers and cities, translated languages, traded, and amassed wealth.

Mini-Unit 1 Overview
Eden to Egypt

Introduction

Tapestry Primer guides your family on a journey through the history of the world in one (or two) years, and we start right at the beginning. As we mentioned in the introduction, we will be following seven main characters throughout our study of history. We meet each of these characters right away.

In this first unit study, we study Creation to Moses' birth in about 1600 BC. Our first topic sets the scene, covering Creation through the Flood and the Tower of Babel. The second topic follows the patriarchs (Abraham, Isaac, Jacob) as God chose them as His people and called them to the Promised Land. Finally, our third topic explains how God's people came to be living in Egypt. In Moses' day, these stories explained to Israelites living in Egypt who their one God was, why He had chosen them, and how they came to be slaves. This story mattered to the Israelites. But, before we begin the story, let's pause to remember why the story matters to us.

Why History Matters

There's an old saying: "Those who cannot remember the past are condemned to repeat it." Christians believe, in a way that other people do not, that history matters. To the atheist, history is a series of accidents and coincidences that somehow got us this far. To the Buddhist or Hindu, history is an illusion to be transcended. Jews and

Muslims believe in a God who rules over history, but only Christians believe God entered into it Himself in the form of Jesus of Nazareth. We believe that history really is "His Story."

Over the course of the year, if you believe it is appropriate, your child will be exposed to some ancient myths and legends. These myths are a part of our common culture, but they may raise troubling questions. Ancient people believed all these stories about their gods. Are the things we believe about God just myths, too?

There is a solid, satisfying answer. As you study history, mythology, and Scripture, you can see for yourself that the Bible is *different*. The myths are stories about powerful, immortal, but ultimately human-like beings who lust and lie and cheat and steal, whose love is generally selfish and selective, and who treat their creations in whimsical, self-serving ways. Even a child can see that they are made in man's image. In the Bible, by contrast, a holy God reveals Himself as Someone who is wrapped in absolute strength and beauty, unapproachable except on His own terms, yet loving generously at great cost to Himself. As it turns out, studying myths is one way to understand who God is and why He deserves our worship.

Opportunities to compare the Bible with ancient myths are part of why history matters. Through historical studies, we can begin to see who He is and what He desires of us. Let us hear the old stories with new ears as we rediscover our history along with the people of God.

Scripture is History

There are two overarching points to emphasize throughout this unit. One is that history matters. The other is that Scripture is real. We will spend this first mini-unit learning to understand the oldest history book in the world. It is called Genesis, and was authored by Moses.

Can you guess why God picked Moses to write Genesis? Why not Adam, Noah, or Abraham? We don't know for sure, but the days of Moses were certainly an important time for a history lesson. Abraham's covenant with God was a dim centuries-old memory (much longer than America has been a nation). Yet, that covenant was the basis for their identity as a culture. As we read in the Bible, the reason that God sent the Israelites into bondage in Egypt was to preserve, through the pressure of being strangers (and then slaves), their unique cultural status.

One reason that God inspired Moses to write down the Genesis account was probably to teach these Israelites their history, all the way back to the beginning. They needed to know that God is the Creator who made and owns everything. The myths of Egypt were not the truth, but there was unity of purpose in Heaven and on Earth! The Israelites needed to know about sin and disobedience, which was the true reason for strife on earth. They needed to know that God had a good plan for them—one that had been in existence from the beginning—and that they could trust Him.

From the Beginning to Babel

This story has an Author. In this mini-unit, we'll learn how God created the world by his Word. He planted the Garden of Eden and created people to work and keep it. People were created good, and to do good. This paradise didn't last long. Battle was quickly waged in the garden. Satan, who desired to injure God's glory, tempted Eve to seek good outside of God's will, relying on her own sense of good and evil. In rejecting what God defined as good, Adam and Eve fell, and sin entered the world. Cursed justly, our first parents were driven out of the Garden. All seemed lost! But, though people had fallen, God was neither defeated nor done. In the same breath as the curse, He gave us the incredible promise of future redemption.

Since Creation would not yield food easily after the curse, people had to eat by the sweat of their brows. They exercised their gifts as image-bearers of the Creator and fashioned tools to make work easier. People learned to domesticate animals, cultivate crops, make tents, forge metal, make musical instruments, construct boats, preserve knowledge through written languages, build towers, translate languages, establish trade, and amass wealth.

Yet people also continued to do evil. Cain murdered Abel, committing the first act of inhumanity toward a fellow man (and that man was his brother!). It would not be the last. As a whole, mankind became so depraved that God repented of having made it and resolved to destroy Creation and begin again.

But Noah found favor in the eyes of God. By faith, Noah built the Ark and was saved, along with his family and the seeds of a new creation. After people and animals emerged from the Ark, God promised that He would never again destroy the world with a flood. He set His rainbow in the heavens as a sign of His promise. Yet, although those who had practiced evil were destroyed, sin still dwelt in the hearts of all human beings. Before long, people would again seek their own glory outside of God's good plan, refusing to fill the earth and choosing instead to build a tower to the heavens so that they would not be divided. Ironically, God brought judgment against this arrogance by breaking their language at the Tower of Babel. After this, man's fall was complete, and people—separated by language—began to scatter over Creation in accordance with the plan of God Almighty.

A Chosen People

God created mankind to live in fellowship and relationship with Himself. Throughout the story of the Bible, we see God taking the initiative to restore and redeem what humans have broken. After mankind was divided at Babel and the separated peoples scattered, God took the initiative to call one group to be His own Chosen People.

In Genesis 12:1-3, we read that the LORD said to Abram,

> Go from your country and your kindred and your father's house to the land that I will show you. And I will make of you a great nation, and I will bless you and make your name great, so that you will be a blessing. I will bless those who bless you, and him who dishonors you I will curse, and in you all the families of the earth shall be blessed.

Abram's journey would test his faith. Childless until he was a century old, and later homeless except for his beloved wife's tomb, Abram wandered the land that God promised He would give to his descendants. Abraham believed God, and it was credited to him as righteousness. Yet, his belief was not without moments of doubt or self-sufficiency. He was not sinless. He deceived rulers about the true nature of his relationship with Sarah, and he fathered Ishmael, initiating millennia of conflict. God chose Abraham and made His covenant with him. Abraham chose to obey God, and did not withhold his only son, whom he loved. God mercifully provided a substitute so that Abraham's son would be spared. There would be no substitute for God's son.

Isaac was the child of the Promise. For a time, it seemed like God would visibly fulfill His promise in Isaac. God wonderfully provided a bride for Isaac and they quickly had twins. Certainly, God was about to fulfill His promise to make Abraham's descendants a great nation! However, the story is more complex than that.

Isaac's sons, Esau and Jacob, grew up in conflict with one another. After Jacob tricked Esau out of his birthright, Isaac's family was threatened with one brother's vow to murder the other. It might have been Cain and Abel all over again. Evil was still present in the hearts of Mankind.

Of all the patriarchs (ruling fathers), Jacob may have seemed the least likely to fulfill God's Promise. Deceitful, selfish, and manipulative, Jacob tricked almost every member of his whole extended family over the course of his life, and was himself deceived multiple times: by Laban, by Rachel, and by his own sons. Yet, God revealed

Himself to Jacob—first at Bethel and then at Peniel. After his divine wrestling match, Jacob, the trickster, was lamed and renamed Israel, which means "Triumphant with God." Jacob settled in the land of Canaan that God had promised to Abraham. Jacob's twelve sons eventually became the founders of the twelve tribes of Israel.

Egypt: Gift of the Nile

We could almost end the story there. Abraham's descendants were living in the Promised Land. God had kept His promise, hadn't He? Not quite. God promised to make Abraham's descendants a great nation, not just another nomadic tribe. To do that, they needed to grow in numbers and retain both their ethnic purity and unique religious identity. If you read Genesis closely, you'll see that Jacob's twelve sons endangered God's plan through bickering, self-centeredness, and ethical compromises. The knowledge of God was not flourishing among them!

This situation sets up an amazing story of how God the Author works for our good according to His Word, even in the midst of human sin and evil. In the story of Joseph, an arrogant young man antagonized his brothers, who then intended to kill him. Instead, though, they sold him into slavery and lied to his father (leading Jacob to believe Joseph had been killed by a wild animal), filling both Jacob and Joseph's life with sorrow. Yet, God was at work! After years of sorrow and toil, God raised Joseph to the position of the governor of all Egypt, second only to the Pharaoh. Then God sent a famine to Canaan.

Rather than use his power and authority to seek revenge on his brothers, Joseph forgave them and gave glory to God. He told his brothers, "You meant it for evil, but God meant it for good" (Genesis 50:20). (This is a fitting summary for so many events in history.)

Joseph was able to provide a place for Israel to grow, and grow they did! The Bible tells us that, because they were shepherds, they were culturally distasteful to the Egyptians, and so were given good land *and* isolation. This circumstance was a means God used to keep Israel ethnically pure.

After a couple of centuries' sojourn in Egypt, Israel had grown enough to be a serious threat to Egypt's pharaohs. A new dynasty arose between Joseph and Moses. A new Pharaoh saw the numerous, non-Egyptian Israelites as a threat and began to oppress them as slaves, hoping that hard labor and ill treatment would curtail their numbers. Instead, Hebrew slaves were resilient, and their focus was concentrated on a promised redeemer. When the pharaoh saw that enslavement had not accomplished his ends, he commanded that a whole generation of Israelites be thrown into the Nile to appease sacred crocodiles.

Our mini-unit ends with Moses being saved from the dangers of the Nile and being raised in Pharaoh's palace. In the next mini-unit, we'll follow Moses into the desert of Midian, where he encountered God in a way that would change all of history.

Mini-Unit 1, Topic 1
From the Beginning to Babel

"In the beginning... God."

This week, we begin to retell the story of how a loving God spoke the world into being, filled it with good things, and gave it purpose. It's the story of how the people God made chose to worship and serve created things, rather than their Creator. It's about how the creature wanted to be like God, with disastrous consequences. Sadly, the story of mankind is a story of flawed creatures trying to replace their flawless Creator with gods made in their own likenesses, instead of embracing their role as those who glorify and enjoy Him, bearing His matchless image and stewarding His creation.

Yet, against this pitch-black backdrop, God's plan of redemption sparkles. This week we have two wonderful examples of how God remembered mercy in the midst of deserved judgment. First, in Genesis 3, we read about God's promise of a Savior. Then, in Genesis 9, we read about God's renewed covenant with the creation after the judgment of the Flood. Already, we are being introduced to the characters, the conflicts, the climaxes, and the conclusions that we will see played out again and again in the context of history.

These chapters were written to give God's people the knowledge of who they were and where they came from. They tell a different story than the ones that the Israelites would have heard in Egypt. Just as they needed to know God's truth about their beginnings, so we and our children need to know. We also need to know who God is so that we may walk with Him.

With that brief overview, here is more background on what we're studying this week.

Background to the Exodus

Genesis was written to encourage and instruct the people of Israel. Remember, these people were not a tightly-knit nation yet. They were a rabble—a mixed multitude of Israelites and other people—many of whom had forgotten where they came from. The Egyptians, who as a people considered foreigners to be almost sub-human, probably wanted the Israelites to believe they had always been slaves.

While the Bible doesn't condemn slavery as an economic institution, slavery always comes across as a powerfully *negative* symbol in Scripture. The Old Testament is full of references to slavery, especially when Israel reaped the consequences of idolatry and apostasy. The New Testament uses the image of slavery over and over. Romans 6:20 tells us we were slaves to sin. Romans 6:22 says we are God's slaves now. In Mark 10:44, Jesus says, "Whoever would be first among you must be slave of all." Yet Galatians 5:1 says, "For freedom Christ has set us free; stand firm therefore, and do not submit again to a yoke of slavery." So, slavery is a significant biblical concept, and it is especially important to realize that when God sent Moses to bring His people out of Egypt, they were *slaves*.

Let's put the slavery of the Israelites in perspective. The Israelites were in Egypt for something around 400 years.[1] To put this in context, 400 years before 2014, the first English-speaking colonies were just being established in the New World. That's a long time ago! Some Israelite families must have passed on the stories of Abraham, Isaac, and Jacob to their children. We assume that Moses' and Aaron's parents told them all about Adam and Eve and Noah. But there were doubtless many Israelites who had forgotten their heritage, especially as they were surrounded by other beliefs.

Genesis was God's answer to that problem. It taught the mixed multitude how God created man in His own image to enjoy fellowship with Him in the world He created. It explained where sin and sorrow came from. It told how God called Abraham out of Mesopotamia, and that He promised to give him a land of his own and more descendants than the stars of the sky. It was hard for Abraham to believe that when his wife had turned ninety and he still didn't have a son, but the Israelites could see for themselves how that part of God's promise had come true. That made it easier for them to believe in the other half: the Promised Land really did lie beyond their sandy horizon.

---

1 There is lively debate among scholars as to whether to date the 400 years that Scripture mentions from the covenant God made with Abraham, or from the time when Israel went down into Egypt to live.

So, it is easy to understand why Moses wrote Genesis 11-50. We'll be studying those chapters over the next three weeks. This week, though, we want to consider why Moses wrote the first few chapters. How would those chapters particularly affect the slaves who had just escaped Egypt?

Some Lessons of Genesis 1-11

Let's take a specific example. Remember the story of Cain and Abel in Genesis 4? Cain was a farmer and Abel was a shepherd. That doesn't mean a lot to us—we mostly remember that God accepted Abel's offering and rejected Cain's. But their occupations would have mattered a lot to the Israelites. When Joseph's brothers arrived in Egypt, they told the Egyptians that they were shepherds, and Genesis 46 tells us that "every shepherd was an abomination to the Egyptians." But way back in Genesis 4, God was telling His people that He accepted them even if other peoples despised them.

What about the Flood? We've all heard the story of Noah and the ark—but we haven't heard it through the ears of people who could still remember the screams of Pharaoh's army as the Red Sea swept them all away. You can make a lot of new connections by reading Genesis with an Exodus perspective!

The Tower of Babel was another foundational story for God's new people. Egypt was one of the major centers of civilization. The Israelites would have seen and heard people from many different lands coming and going. They themselves had come from Canaan and spoke a different language than the Egyptians around them. In Genesis 11, Moses explains that the differences between the peoples were established by God. Moses also connected the Israelites to where they were in the family tree. The Tower of Babel was built by Ham's grandson, Cush. Another of Ham's sons was named Egypt. To us, they are places on a map. To the Israelites, they were people groups. Through these stories that Moses recorded, God was helping His people see themselves as He saw them—separate and holy from the other peoples around them.

God wanted the Israelites to learn some important lessons from the stories of Genesis 1:11. Here are just a few.

- ❏ God is one, not many. (There is no strife in Heaven between many gods.)
- ❏ God has a plan that has been going on since the dawn of time.
- ❏ All of nature is subject to the One who made it.
- ❏ Man is unique in all creation, made in God's image.
- ❏ God made man to be holy and happy.
- ❏ God designed people for both meaningful work and pleasant rest.

- ❏ Death (which is better defined as eternal separation from God than the cessation of physical functions) is a perversion of God's perfect plan.
- ❏ Disaster strikes when people think they can gain what is good and avoid what is evil when relying on themselves instead of their Creator.
- ❏ God preserved His chosen people even in judgment.

The Egyptians had a radically different worldview. They had their own set of ideas about deities, man, work, rest, nature, sin, and death. So do our secular neighbors. It seems likely that God gave the Israelites Genesis partly in order to give them (and us) a whole new worldview.

The Genesis Overture

The first chapters of Genesis contain a lot more than just six days of Creation. Creation matters because so much of our faith is introduced in the telling of this tale. Genesis is to history what an overture is to a musical: it introduces, in one medley, snatches of songs that will be fully expressed in the context of the story later on.

Adam and Eve enjoyed unbroken fellowship with God and with each other in the Garden. Over the course of history, we'll have lots of opportunities to study how fallen men and women interact. Men and women have treated each other badly since Genesis 3, when Eve disobeyed the clear teaching of God through her husband, and Adam tried to blame Eve for his own wrong choice.

When humans sinned, Adam's relationship with Eve changed. Genesis 3:16 says, "Your desire shall be for [this could be accurately translated as 'against'] your husband, and he shall rule over you." Before they sinned, Adam's authority over Eve was not a burden, but after the Fall, the God-ordained flow of authority was corrupted. We'll be studying different ways that sinful men have ruled over sinful subjects in culture after culture.

One of the consequences of Adam's sin was that work became a hardship instead of a joy. We'll be studying how people work through the ages. Many people view work as a curse, but if we start with Genesis, we see that meaningful work is part of God's original plan for humanity. Eden was a garden, not a resort. The curse has made human toil difficult, and sin complicates economics, but despite all this, work remains a fundamental part of what we were made for.

Conclusion

Genesis directly contradicted the Egyptian worldview. It contradicts the secular modern worldview, too. When we get to the nineteenth and twentieth centuries, we'll study one worldview after another in light of what we find in Genesis. As we work our way through the secular notions that shape how many of us view humanity today, we'll keep on seeing how relevant these first few chapters really are! Your student may not be ready to make these connections yet, but you'll appreciate seeing how God has woven His truth through all time.

Mini-Unit 1, Topic 2
A Chosen People

Introduction

In Topic 1, we saw our first Parents[1] disobey God's one command. In response, God judged humanity—He drove us out of the Garden of Eden, away from the Tree of Life. Men tried to get around that judgment by building a Tower whose top would reach to Heaven. God intervened again by confusing the tongues of humankind, dividing people by language. Thus were we divided from one another and separated from God—a bad way to start human history! Fortunately, that is not the end of the story.

This week, we'll learn how God initiated a plan of redemption that would ultimately overcome His righteous judgments of mankind's sin. Out of many fallen nations, God chose one man, Abraham, to found one holy nation through which all the peoples of the earth would be blessed.

We'll be reading a lot of Bible stories this week, and Genesis is not always G-rated. We've tried to select stories that are age-appropriate, but read through them yourself to make sure that you're comfortable discussing them with your student. We have recommended that you use an age-appropriate storybook Bible to communicate the basic point of the story and introduce the characters. Don't worry if you don't go to

---

[1] Children may ask why we today bear a sin nature because of the choices of our first parents. It is because our Parents were both our representatives before God and our progenitors. In the same way, Jesus Christ stood once for us all and bore our sin so that we would be righteous before God and receive resurrected bodies one day, if we are found in Him. (See Romans 5:12-21.)

the Bible itself at this age; remember, you'll be back.

One of our goals is to help your student understand that these were real people who lived real lives in real places. Throughout this program, we'll study a number of different cultures. Take the time to imagine what it would be like to live at this time along with your student.

Canaan

Great ancient civilizations grew up on the major river systems such as the Nile and the land between the rivers called Tigris and Euphrates. The land of Canaan has just been a blob on the map—at the most, a place set smack on a trade route from one great empire to another. That blob would become the Promised Land because God called one man out of Mesopotamia to start a whole new nation.

Abram

That man was Abram. As far as we know, he began life as a pagan. He grew up in a wealthy family in the city of Ur near the mouth of the river Euphrates. He may have been a moon-worshipper, since archaeologists believe this cult was strong in Ur, Abram's hometown. Ironically, though his name means "exalted father," at the start of our story he had no children.

Abram's father, Terah, led the family to Haran, a city far up the Euphrates River from Ur. In Genesis 12, God tells Abram to leave the land between the rivers. God made Abram a promise—actually, a whole series of promises. God said:

- ❏ He would make Abram a "great nation."
- ❏ He would bless him.
- ❏ He would make his name great and famous.
- ❏ Abram would be a blessing.
- ❏ God would bless whoever blessed Abram.
- ❏ Whoever cursed Abram would be cursed.
- ❏ God would bless all nations through Abram.

Those are seven promises—big, hard-to-believe promises. The amazing thing is that Abram responded in faith, demonstrated by leaving his home and heading off to Canaan.

Covenants

In Genesis 15, God increased His blessings on Abram. We read how God made His earlier promises into a covenant. What is a covenant, exactly? Covenants are like contracts, in some ways, but very different in others. In a contract, two people make promises to each other. I promise to you $100, for example, and you promise to paint my porch. The promises in a contract depend on each other: if you don't paint the porch, I don't owe you anything. A contract can be ended at any time if both parties agree to it.

A covenant, by contrast, consists of mutual promises that don't depend on each other. The most familiar example is a marriage—at least, an old-fashioned marriage. If a man promises to love his wife and she promises to love him, those promise are still binding even if one party or the other fails to keep them. Your spouse's failures do not let you off the hook—and vice versa. Under a covenant, your obligation to love your spouse is just as binding as it ever was even if your spouse wrongs you.

When we make marriage vows, we promise to be faithful to each other "until death do us part." Jesus prohibited divorce, with one exception: the case of adultery. Does that mean marriage is a covenant unless one person commits adultery, and then it becomes a less binding contract that can be conveniently ended by divorce? Not really—under the Old Testament law, adultery was punished by death. In the time when Jesus was teaching, Roman law didn't permit a person to be put to death for adultery (hence, divorce instead), but Jesus was speaking a way that is consistent with the Old Testament tradition that adultery is grounds for dissolving a marriage—because in Moses' day the marriage would have been dissolved anyway on account of death.

Covenants were common in the ancient Middle East. The Hebrew word for making a covenant is to "cut" a covenant, because one common covenant ritual was to slaughter an animal, cut it in half, and then both parties of the covenant would walk between the pieces of it and articulate their promises. The implication was, "May God cut me in half like this cow if I break my promises to you."

What's amazing about Genesis 15 is that God appeared in the form of a smoking firepot and a flaming torch that moved between the pieces of Abram's sacrifice while Abram looked on. God was the only one walking between the pieces of the sacrificed animals. As far as Old Testament scholars can tell, God was telling Abraham, "Let me be cut in half like this cow if I violate My promises." Verse 18 of that chapter says, "In the same day the Lord made a covenant with Abram, saying, "Unto thy seed have I given this land, from the river of Egypt unto the great river, the river Euphrates."

The Israelites in the wilderness knew this covenant-making God who appeared as a smoking firepot and a flaming torch to Abram—they followed His pillar of smoke by day and the pillar of fire by night.

Doubt

It's good news for people that a covenant is binding even if one party fails to fulfill its obligations, because Abram was far from perfect. Scattered through the book of Genesis are stories of his shortcomings. Genesis 12, 16, and 20 describe the problems his doubts caused. Just ten verses after God called Abram in Genesis 12, drought struck Canaan. Abram picked up and went to Egypt, outside the land that God was giving him. That's a problem, because God called Abram to trust in Him, not to trust in other things in other places. Later, in Genesis 20, Abraham lied to Abimelech, king of the Philistines, because he was afraid that men would kill him to get his beautiful wife. He was still trusting in human tricks, not the power of God—yet God demonstrated His power once again by revealing those tricks while still protecting Sarah.

The most lasting damage done by Abraham's doubt appears in Genesis 16, where Sarah persuaded him to take her Egyptian maid, Hagar, to bear a child for her. Hagar gave birth to Ishmael, who grew up to be a mighty chieftain, head of twelve tribes in Arabia. Ishmael's descendants are with us to this day—and the conflict between the Arabs and the Jews may well be the world's most lasting example of sibling rivalry.

Sin

When people try to make God's promises come true by their own actions and in their own preferred time frame, instead of waiting on Him or obeying Him, they sin. We're still dealing with the consequences of Eve's desire to "be like God" and Abraham's effort to make God's promises come true in the time frame he thought appropriate.

Throughout this year, we'll be following one particularly dark thread through the tapestry of time: the thread of evil, seen in man's sin. What does the word "sin" mean to your child?

We define the term "sin" broadly to include any case where men or women seek to find what is good and/or to avoid what is evil independent of God. Humans were created to be dependent on God, not independent from Him. Eve sinned by desiring to be wise apart from God. Adam sinned in seeking to avoid separation from Eve, after she had eaten the forbidden fruit but before he had eaten, by disobeying God and choosing to join her in her sin. We can point to many such examples. This definition of sin may help your student identify sin more clearly in his own life.

Given this understanding of sin, Abraham's great virtue consisted of believing God and following His direction towards righteousness. Abraham's failing consisted in trying to get hold of what he perceived as good without God's help.

Faith

We can learn a lot about sin and doubt by studying Abraham, but that's not what he's famous for. On the contrary, Abraham is famous for his faith. In Genesis 18, the Lord comes down to earth to destroy Sodom and Gomorrah. But then He said:

> Shall I hide from Abraham what I am about to do, seeing that Abraham shall surely become a great and mighty nation, and all the nations of the earth shall be blessed in him? For I have chosen him, that he may command his children and his household after him to keep the way of the Lord by doing righteousness and justice, so that the Lord may bring to Abraham what he has promised him.

If there is any one verse that fathers ought to memorize to keep on track for homeschooling, this may be it. "I have chosen him, that he may command his children and his household after him to keep the way of the Lord by doing righteousness and justice, so that the Lord may bring to Abraham what He has promised him."

Why did God want Abraham to do these things? "So that the Lord may bring to Abraham what He has promised him." God is eager to bless us—it seems He is more eager to bless us than we are eager to be blessed! But our doubt and disobedience get in the way. When we put our faith in something other than God, the promises are on hold—for God will not share His glory with another.

Isaac

Isaac was the child of promise. Isaac's birth was both miraculous and a tangible sign of God's commitment to His Covenant. Imagine how Abraham felt when Isaac was born! And, imagine how he felt when God asked him to sacrifice his one and only son! The philosopher Kierkegaard suggests in his essay "Fear and Trembling" that the reason Abraham "rose early in the morning" to take Isaac to Moriah for the sacrifice is because Abraham had been up all night, dreading the next day. Now, imagine Abraham's relief when God provided a substitute sacrifice.

After Sarah's death, God's gift of Rebekah as a wife for Isaac is a beautiful example of His providence at work. This week's lessons might offer a good chance to tell your child about your own love story, and how God led you and your spouse to find each other.

In Genesis 26, we see God clearly affirming His promise to the next generation of Abraham's descendants by speaking directly to Isaac. We also see God's clear direction that Isaac was *not* to go down to Egypt (unlike Abraham). Point out this difference as you read the stories. It's amazing how God planned the time and place where His people would enter the Egyptian world.

Jacob

God passed down His covenant to Jacob, promising to him the land that He had promised to Abraham, and foretelling that kings would descend from Jacob (Genesis 35:11-12). A good deal can be understood about the meaning of Jacob's story from the patterns in the plot.[1]

From Jacob, we learn that God is really the primary actor and initiator toward people. God foretold that Jacob would be the child of promise, and then God appeared to Jacob and gave him the promise, though Jacob had not deserved this favor or sought God. God is the one who made the sovereign choice. God chose Jacob, not Esau. In the book of Romans, Paul uses this mystery when explaining God's attitude toward those of us who have come to know Him.

> Though they were not yet born and had done nothing either good or bad—in order that God's purpose of election might continue, not because of works but because of him who calls—she was told, 'The older will serve the younger.' As it is written, 'Jacob I loved, but Esau I hated.' (Romans 9:11-12)

Jacob's story also helps us understand that sin is real. People sinfully try to oppose, distort, or accomplish God's will in their own strength, but "our God is in the heavens; He does all that He pleases" (Psalm 115:3). There is a recurring pattern in Jacob's story:

1) Sin on Jacob's part (especially trickery), which leads to …
2) Bad consequences and Jacob being in fear for his very life, followed by…
3) God intervening and drawing Jacob to himself.

---

1 Given the age of *Tapestry Primer* students, we do not read or discuss Jacob's and Laban's patterns of deception, Jacob's two wives, or Jacob's wives' slaves (concubines) in detail. It's your choice whether you want to introduce your student to these characters and concepts at this point, or cover them later when your student is older.

This happened three times, and it would seem that in the end Jacob at last learned to trust God, for he said at the end that God was his Shepherd throughout his life.

This pattern in Jacob's life is both an echo of Abraham's behavior (for instance, in trying to bring about the promised child with Hagar) and a picture of the future history of Israel—sin, God drawing the people to Himself, and the people's repentance and trust.

Another theme is that of basic morality. From Jacob's story, we learn that sinful human striving and deceit is wrong. Every time Jacob tried to get ahead by cheating or deceiving, he experienced negative consequences. As Jacob tricked his father and others, so his sons tricked the men of Shechem and Jacob himself. And we note that sinful human favoritism always causes problems in the family.

It is a right relationship with God that is good and leads to right living. After Jacob worshiped God at Bethel the second time—and made his final decision to follow God wholeheartedly—there were no more records of him cheating or deceiving others.

From Jacob's story, the Israelites would learn something about what they should value. After living most of his life valuing earthly advancement and success, Jacob at last valued God as his Shepherd and Redeemer. Also, the Israelites could learn that the value God places on people is not always according to human expectations. Isaac blessed his younger son Jacob above his older son Esau (albeit by deception), and Jacob blessed Joseph's younger son Ephraim above his older son Manasseh (purposefully). So, God lifted up Egypt's slaves to be His chosen nation.

Conclusion

Abraham is called "the father of everyone who believes," but it's not because his faith was unfailing. Perhaps he's the father of everyone who ever cried, "Lord, I believe—help my unbelief!" Abraham is a complex character, with strengths and weaknesses like our own. This is one way the Bible is so different from so many other religious books: it tells the failings of its greatest heroes as well as their strengths. God's faithful ways with Abraham provide real spiritual guidance for our children—and for us.

In the same way, Abraham's descendants were real people. While we do not dwell on their character deficiencies in detail at this level of learning, there is much that we can learn as we return to these characters in more depth over the years. Ultimately, we can see clearly that God is the Author of this story and that He is working to accomplish His purposes through His people.

Mini-Unit 1, Topic 3

Egypt: Gift of the Nile

Introduction

This week, we leave the direct Biblical accounts and transition into our study of the history of the world of Egypt. Almost everybody knows something about Egypt—think of sand and camels, pyramids and mummies, and the Nile River flowing through it. Although we all know a little about Egypt, the more you learn about it, the more amazing it is. Civilization emerged in Egypt about 5,000 years ago, around 3000 BC, and thrived for more than two millenia. It is easily one of the most enduring civilizations in history.

If all you are studying is history, Egypt can seem a little dry. Centuries roll past without a lot of changes. But if your whole family wants to integrate studies with history at the heart, Egypt is hard to beat. Remember, our emphasis with our students is on learning about daily life.

This week, we spend a lot of time on the Nile River and Egyptian geography, understanding how the story of history was played out on the stage of the created world. We'll also spend a bit of time on the history of Egypt. The key people to meet are Joseph and Moses, who had two very different experiences with two very different pharaohs, as God set the stage for the deliverance of His people (in foreshadowing of the gospel to come). This grand story was being played out against the backdrop of daily life.

Geography

Egypt is a land of stark contrasts, where geography really matters. Tell your child that it isn't hard to find, even on a globe—all he has to do is look for the big continents (Africa and Asia), and then find the place where the seas almost come together. The Mediterranean Sea comes within just a few miles of Red Sea at the Suez Canal. If your child can find that spot on a globe and then look for the big river, he's found the Nile. Find the Nile and you've found Egypt!

There's more to geography than just finding places on a map, though. Geography deals with how people interact with places. Your student can see that for himself as he traces the blue ribbon of the Nile through the African desert. That steady supply of water made human habitation possible. Interestingly, the annual floods produced by rainfall in the highlands of central Africa washed a rich soil downhill so Egyptian fields in the lower lands didn't get exhausted by continuous farming. Nowadays, we have fertilizer and understand the need for crop rotation. The Egyptians didn't, but that didn't matter. God provided for them, and they just waited for their river to rise each year. Where there's plenty of food, there will be plenty of people—and plenty of people can cause plenty of trouble.

In ancient times, walls protected people from each other. If you look around the world at ancient cities, what you'll find are city walls—because one village was often the worst enemy of the one next door. However, Egypt had very few walled cities! Egyptians had something better than walls—they had deserts that were hard for invaders to cross in large numbers. Particularly in the south, you'll want to point out the Sahara Desert. The Sahara was smaller in ancient times. Today, it is big, and it's still growing: currently, it is bigger than the United States. It stretches all the way across Africa, from the Atlantic Ocean to the Red Sea. That vast expanse of sand is broken by the ribbon of the Nile. Though it wasn't as large 5,000 years ago, it was big enough to keep out invaders from the east and west.

With a stable food supply from the river and protection from most enemies, the early Egyptians developed flourishing communities along the river. Villages grew into cities, and cities became kingdoms. When one kingdom finally became strong enough to rule the entire valley, the Egyptians enjoyed remarkable security.

The Nile

Get ready to learn along with your kids—that's the secret of full-family education. Did you know that the Nile flows "up"? It flows up the map from the south. It's the longest river in the world, at more than 4,000 miles long. The Nile is a great topic for kids with good imaginations. The Egyptians built boats out of bundles of papyrus reeds. Imagine yourself paddling downstream, past riverbanks crawling with crocodiles, as hippos snort in the shallows. Flocks of ducks and geese explode out of the marshes as lions roar in the reeds by the river. Hungry hyenas follow the lions, hoping for scraps.

Yet all this life was hemmed in on either side by hundreds of miles of desert.

Abundant Food Supply

The abundance of life near the river gave rise to one of the world's oldest, and most sophisticated, civilizations. Indeed, in the Bible, Egypt is symbolic of both the allure and the powerlessness of worldliness!

We will spend two weeks learning about Egyptian life, but this week let's just concentrate on the relationship between the river and human habitations. The river was so vital that Egypt has been called "the gift of the Nile."

Your child may not understand how important this river really was. It's easy to see that it provided drinking water, but the Nile provided something else that was just as important in the long run—mud.

It may sound crazy, but mud made Egypt great. Each year in summer, heavy rains soaked the high mountains of Ethiopia, far to the south. The saturated soil flooded into the Blue Nile, which carried the silt all the way downstream. Eventually, much of this Ethiopian soil wound up in the great Nile Delta, which bulges out into the Mediterranean.

Along the course of the mighty river, as the waters receded from Egyptian fields each year, the flood left hundreds of miles of mud. That mud was fantastic fertilizer, which caused the crops—and the population—to grow. In one sense, the mighty civilization of Egypt started with mud.

Here's a point worth noting: when the Israelites left Egypt, they wouldn't have been prepared for the challenge of farming a land that wasn't re-fertilized every rainy season. The crops in Canaan would have exhausted the soil after a few years of farming. God had something better for His people than mud and floods, though—He gave them His perfect law. In Leviticus 25:4, God commanded His people to let the land rest every seventh year. This biblical crop rotation provided wisdom the Israelites never would have learned along the fertile banks of the Nile.

Specialization

Egypt's rich food supply and stable government resulted in increasing specialization. Specialization happens when people do not have to work hard to feed themselves and have time enough to develop skills in different areas, purchasing the labor or goods from others. In ancient Egypt, there were potters, jewelers, weavers, perfumers, miners, sailors, shoemakers, butchers, and kings.

We will be learning more about the government of Egypt next week. For now, it is worth noting how many people with special skills the royal family employed. Chapter 40 of the book of Genesis tells how Joseph met Pharaoh's chief baker and butler while he was in jail. We take jobs like butlers and bakers for granted, but the division and increasing specialization of labor is a big part of what makes a civilization a civilization. In Egypt, there were a number of experts in the royal family's employment, such as architects, scribes, accountants, and musicians (just to name a few).

In addition to the Egyptians' plentiful peace and prosperity to make trade and commerce profitable, they had positional stability: they did not need to migrate to follow herds as hunters, or flocks as shepherds. All of these factors resulted in the many specialized jobs.

When people barely make enough to live on, they don't get much opportunity to specialize. Everybody is just trying to survive! When people can specialize, though, they tend to develop new tools and skills that make it easier to grow more food and keep their enemies at bay. They also create works of art and large public buildings. These endeavors lead to more people, more trade, and more specialization and production.

Throughout our study of history, we will see civilization after civilization rise— and fall—and we will keep pointing out three things you need to have a civilization: a stable food supply, a strong central government, and safety from outside enemies. Where these three things are present, civilizations tend to rise. When they cease to be there, civilizations fall.

Egypt developed scientifically, as well. With so much of their lives depending on the annual flooding of the Nile, they paid attention to the passing of the year. They realized there are just over 365 days in a year, although they had a different way of counting them than we do. (Their calendar had twelve 30-day months with five extra days tacked on at the end.) Their enormous building projects required them to come up with ways to measure areas, volumes, distances, weights, and so on. Egyptian doctors understood a lot about the human body in general, while some experts devoted themselves to one medical specialty or another. The Egyptians doctors kept records—something that was unheard of in any other culture at the time.

One special "class" in Egypt (if you can call it that) was that of slaves. The Bible gives us a front-row seat on Egyptian slavery in Genesis and Exodus. This week we will study the lives of two men who spent large portions of their lives immersed in this Egyptian culture.

Joseph

Parental guidance is needed for the story of Joseph.[1] There is foreshadowing (hinting at what will come later on) throughout Joseph's story. Besides the obvious examples of the prophetic dreams and Joseph's interpretation of them, there is also a more subtle theme: Joseph was thirty years old when Pharaoh made him the overseer of Egypt, and through him both the Jewish nation and also the Egyptian nation were saved from famine. Can you think of another Jewish man who began to minister at the age of thirty, and through whom both Jews and Gentiles were saved from a great calamity? The difference is that Joseph gave earthly bread that kept people alive during a brief famine, whereas Jesus gave His own flesh as the bread of life to save us from the greatest calamity of all: separation from God.

The foreshadowing continues at the end of the story of Joseph, when Jacob is reunited with his son in Egypt. On his death bed, Jacob prophesies, "The scepter will not depart from Judah, nor the ruler's staff from between his feet, until he to whom it belongs shall come and the obedience of the nations shall be his" (Genesis 49:10). This prophecy was fulfilled by Christ, who was born into the line of Judah and is sometimes referred to as the Lion of Judah.

The amazing truth about prophecy in the Bible is that when God foreshadows an event, He then brings it about in actual history, using real people. He is the first and greatest Author, who hints in the beginning what He will reveal at the end, giving prophecies and pictures of the coming of Christ and His triumph. Only a God of infinite wisdom and power could promise something at the beginning of time and perfectly bring it to fulfillment at the end! Equally wonderful is the fact that He has written the story for us, so we can read it and see His awesome plan unfold.

---

[1] Given the age of *Tapestry Primer* students, we leave it to you to carefully consider whether or not to read or discuss Potiphar's wife's attempted seduction of Joseph. If you want to explain how Joseph was sent to jail, you can say that Potiphar's wife accused Joseph of doing something that he did not do, and that he was wrongly imprisoned.

What Patterns or Repeated Events Are in the Story of Joseph?

On three different occasions, people in the story have dreams, which always come in sets of two, and which all come true: Joseph had two dreams about his family bowing down to him (Genesis 37:5-11), Pharaoh's two servants had dreams (Genesis 40), and Pharaoh had two dreams about the coming famine (Genesis 41:1-40).

There is a clear pattern of Joseph having favor, honor, and a degree of authority, then suffering evil when he was innocent, which God then used for good and gave Joseph favor, honor, and a degree of authority again. This pattern occurs three times.

1. Joseph was favored by his father Jacob and sent to oversee his brothers as they were tending their flocks. Joseph's brothers then sold him into slavery, but God blessed Joseph in Egypt in the house of Potiphar.

2. Potiphar put Joseph over all that he had, but Potiphar's wife falsely accused Joseph of molesting her. Joseph was then thrown into prison, but God gave him favor with the jailor.

3. The jailor put Joseph in charge of the prisoners. Joseph accurately interpreted the dreams of Pharaoh's baker and cupbearer, but the cupbearer forgot Joseph, who was left in prison for two more years. God then gave Pharaoh two dreams and gave Joseph the interpretation of the dreams. In response, Pharaoh placed Joseph over all of Egypt, and God thus used Joseph to save the Egyptians and the Israelites from the famine.

Importantly, Joseph repeatedly gave God the glory for interpreting the dreams and for providentially caring for him and his family. We'll see this echoed by Daniel in later dream interpretations. Both Joseph and Daniel refused to claim credit for their prophetic abilities.

As with Abraham and Jacob, Joseph's story has a pattern of events. Each time Joseph experienced injustice and hardship, God used them for good—both for Joseph and for others. Joseph summed up this theme in Genesis 50:20 when addressing his brothers: "As for you, you meant evil against me, but God meant it for good, to bring it about that many people should be kept alive, as they are today."

Joseph's story is different from those of Abraham, Isaac, and Jacob. Joseph spent the majority of his life outside the Promised Land. Even more noticeable is that there is no record of God speaking directly to Joseph. He revealed to Joseph the interpretations of dreams, but did not appear to Joseph or repeat His covenantal promises as He did to Abraham, Isaac, and Jacob. Finally, Joseph is significantly different from his ancestors in that he seemed to trust God wholeheartedly, consistently acted with integrity, and put God first in everything.

Again, although Joseph might be called the main character of the story, since the story documents his life, God is the main actor in the story. It is God who delivered Joseph and placed him in exactly the right place at the right time to accomplish His will—the salvation of the Israelites from the famine. God worked sovereignly as the actor and the Author of this story.

Between Joseph's faithful service to Pharaoh as governor of Egypt and the Pharaoh who would order the annihilation of a generation of Israelite baby boys were roughly 400 years.[1]

Moses

At least one of those baby boys survived. As we study this topic, we meet Moses, whose basket of reeds was providentially guided down the treacherous Nile River to arrive at the feet of Pharaoh's daughter. Moses is a great character to keep in mind as you discuss Egypt. He's the perfect person to help you visualize day-to-day life in ancient Egypt, whether you're discussing slaves or royalty—because he was both! See if your kids can look at Egypt through Moses' eyes. What did he see when he looked out his window? Young children can fill in facts like what he ate or did for fun.

While we focus on the younger students in *Tapestry Primer*, this is a good moment to point out that in the full *Tapestry of Grace* program, your whole family would study together, with middle school kids making the connections between the Bible stories and what they're learning about Egyptian culture, while teens (and parents!) ponder what Hebrews 11:26 says about Moses: "He considered the reproach of Christ greater wealth than the treasures of Egypt, for he was looking to the reward."

Conclusion

The more we learn, the more we see how it all goes together. The rains in Ethiopia fertilize the fields in Egypt where Israelite slaves groaned in bondage for centuries until God called Moses away from the palace to lead them to freedom.

We will follow threads like authority, slavery, sacrifice, and promise throughout history—for a purpose. In the end, it all comes back to the glory of God. Jesus left the glories of Heaven to be born in a stable here on Earth. He paid a higher price than Moses did to deliver us from bondage worse than anything the Egyptians could inflict.

---

1 See footnote on p. 24.

Mini-Unit 2: Tabernacle and Temple

We will learn how God rescued His people from the greatest power on earth, only to have them rebel and ask for a king generations later. Note how our seven main "characters" fit in.

 The Author	God reveals Himself as "I Am." He shows His authority over the god-king Pharaoh, false gods, and the mighty army of Egypt. God established the authority of the Law as He led His people in the desert. After giving them victory in the Promised Land, God established the authority of the Judges, and then established the authority of a king after His own heart.
 People	Moses confronted the Pharaoh and led a mob of slaves who became a holy nation. Joshua conquered the Promised Land. Judges led Israel to victory over her neighbors. Saul tried to rule in his own strength and was conquered. David followed God (mostly), and Israel's kingdom grew. Solomon started well, but his divided heart led to a divided kingdom.
 Good	Moses received the Law, which defined how a holy people should live. Joshua obeyed God's words and triumphed. Rahab kept her promise. Ruth and Boaz showed kindness. David trusted God's power and acted rightly toward Saul. Solomon chose wisdom over wealth, victory, and long life.
 Evil	Pharaoh hardened his heart against God, refused to obey, and lost his eldest son. The Israelites did what was right in their own eyes rather than following the Law and were oppressed by neighboring kingdoms. Saul acted out of fear and relied on his own wisdom. David sinned. Solomon was led astray.
 The Word	God revealed Himself by name to Moses and to the people of Israel. God gave the Law. He advanced His plan and included Rahab and Ruth in His story. God anointed David as King, foreshadowing the promised Christ.
 God's Creation	God showed His power over Creation, especially parts that the Egyptians had worshipped—the Nile, weather, health, crops, insects, etc. He showed His power over the Red Sea, the wilderness, the Jordan River, the walls of Jericho, and the sun in the sky. God's power is displayed in Creation as He brings His people into their inheritance in the Promised Land of Canaan.
 Man's Creation	As we move from Bronze Age to Iron Age, we see God's power was supreme. Egyptian magicians failed to duplicate God's acts by their "magic." Pharaoh trusted chariots. The men of Jericho trusted walls. But both were utterly defeated by God's power. David defeated Goliath's iron weapons with a sling and stone. The Phoenicians developed a written language.

MINI-UNIT 2: TABERNACLE AND TEMPLE

Mini-Unit 2 Overview
Tabernacle and Temple

Introduction

In this mini-unit, we follow God's people from Moses' ancient Egypt into the Fertile Crescent and the Promised Land. We'll follow Joshua and his armies into Canaan, see what the period of the Judges was like, and then learn about the Israelite kings: Saul, David, and Solomon.

In this mini-unit, there is so much we can learn about our holy God's personal relationship with His chosen people. From the moment when God commands Moses to remove his sandals because he is standing on holy ground to the moment when God's glory fills the Temple built by Solomon, we watch God reveal as much of His holiness as He can to His people without destroying them. God gave His people His Law, defining unambiguously what was right and what was wrong. Yet we consistently see God's people turning away.

How can a holy God live among a sinful people? We will explore that question as we study these next three topics. There are several moments in history when it seems like people hoped that Heaven was about to be established on earth. The Exodus, when God's people were led by the visible presence of God, mediated by Moses, may have seemed like the best chance we could ever have. But sin and evil were still present, turning obedience to rebellion, even on the borders of the Promised Land. Instead of being a short victory lap from Egypt to Canaan, the Exodus turned into forty years of wandering in the wilderness as God transformed His people.

How can a people who witnessed a holy God acting on their behalf so consistently forget Him and rely on their own wisdom or strength? In this mini-unit, we learn that man continued to seek good outside of God's revealed plan. There is a very predictable pattern in history that is on full display in Israel throughout this mini-unit. It goes like this:

- ❑ Israel at rest grows prosperous.
- ❑ Israel forgets the LORD and serves false gods.
- ❑ The LORD sends judgment, often in the shape of foreign armies.
- ❑ Israel repents and cries out to the LORD.
- ❑ The LORD sends a judge to lead Israel, often in defeat of her enemies.
- ❑ Israel has rest and grows prosperous. (*repeat*)

What about our supporting characters of God's creation and man's creation? In a very powerful way, God shows His authority over both. The ten plagues, the crossing of the Red Sea, God's halting the sun in the heavens, and the crossing of the Jordan River at full flood all show God's power over His creation. God's authority overpowered the magic of the Egyptian priests as they failed to duplicate the plague of gnats. God's authority overpowered the military might of Egypt as the horses and chariots of Egypt were swept away in the Red Sea. God's authority leveled the mighty walls of Jericho in a shout of praise. God's authority triumphed as David overpowered Goliath's iron weapons with a stone-age sling and unshakable faith in the name of the LORD.

Burning Bush to Tabernacle

We pick up the story when Moses chose to identify with the Israelite slaves and left Egypt after striking down an Egyptian overseer. Moses established a new life with Midianite shepherds, who grazed their flocks on the slopes of Mt. Sinai. Moses had a wife, a place in the tribe, and probably had begun to forget his life in Egypt and the suffering of the people there. But God had not. Speaking to Moses through a bush that burned (but did not burn up), God revealed Himself powerfully as the self-existent "I AM," the God of Abraham, Isaac, and Jacob. God commissioned the very reluctant Moses to lead His people out of Egypt.

Moses obeyed God and returned to Egypt to challenge the full power and authority of Pharaoh and all the gods of Egypt. Armed with a shepherd's staff and the presence of God, Moses was God's instrument of salvation and triumphed over the might and glory of Egypt.

As they journeyed to Mount Sinai, God's people had been delivered from their outward oppression, but they had not been delivered from their sinful desires to seek comfort and to grumble. It's convicting to think about how quickly our own hearts often behave the same way, grumbling and complaining when we encounter hardships. God provided for His people time and time again—even on the way to Mt. Sinai. He gave them bread from Heaven ("manna"), He defeated their enemies, and He gave them water out of a rock. More importantly, He gave them His Law and the plan for a Tabernacle where He could dwell among them, even though they were sinful and He was holy.

Holiness is a key idea in the Exodus. The word "holy" means "separate." God separated His people from Egypt, marking their houses' doorways with the blood of the Passover Lamb. Through the Exodus and years of wandering in the desert, God transformed the mob of Hebrew slaves and "others" into a holy nation that could enter into the land that God had promised their fathers. Change came slowly. Moses led a generation of slaves into the desert. One generation later, Joshua led a nation of warriors to victory.

The Promised Land

Joshua led the Israelites into Canaan, armed with bronze weapons and the power of God. From the moment that the feet of the Levites carrying the Ark of the Covenant touched the Jordan River, which bordered the land to the east, God's power and authority were on full display. God filled the hearts of the Canaanites with fear. Obeying God's instructions, Joshua fought the battle of Jericho, and the walls tumbled down! Joshua is a shining example of unwavering obedience to God's Word. In his example, we see a pattern that would be fully realized in his namesake, Jesus, who obeyed God perfectly throughout His life.

Sadly, future generations did not obey in the same way. The nation of slaves had become a nation of warriors, but not a nation of faithful-hearted people. Israel failed to fulfill her role as God's avenger against the infanticide, ritual prostitution, and other sins that characterized the Canaanite culture. Israel's near neighbors remained, and they became an ongoing snare for them.

Yet God did not forsake them. In the stories that we read from the books of Judges and Ruth, we see a glimpse of what life was like in Bronze-Age Israel for the

400 years that came between when the people took the Promised Land and when they demanded a king. The books of Judges and Ruth provide a portrait of day-to-day life in the ancient Near East. In this time, Israel was a theocracy, ruled by God under the guidance of temporary judges. God still dwelled in the Tabernacle, and there was no king in Israel. Every man did what was right in his own eyes. This led to both exemplary acts of kindness (consider the story of Boaz, Ruth, and Naomi) and appalling acts of barbarity (see the end of Judges).

The Heart of the King

When the Israelites demanded a king in order to become like all the other nations around them, God warned them that a king would ultimately exploit and oppress them. The Israelites felt they needed a king to take on the Philistines. The Philistine's Iron Age culture had weapons that could hack through the Israelites bronze weapons as if they were straw. Philistine iron chariots seemed invincible to the Israelites. It's ironic that God used a Stone Age weapon—a sling—to bring down the Philistine champion, Goliath.

We will look at the last (and one of the greatest) of the judges, Samuel, and then at the three kings of the unified Israel. We want to learn about what motivated each of these kings. Saul was a Benjamite, which meant he was of the smallest and least respected tribe in Israel.[1]

Saul's reign was characterized by fear, political calculation, and failure. From the moment when he cowered among the baggage at his coronation to the moment when he fell on his own sword in battle with the Philistines on Mt. Gilboa, Saul showed that his faith and trust were not really in God. By contrast, we learn that from a very young age, David was a man after God's own heart. In striking contrast to Saul, David trusted God. From his valiant defeat of Goliath, the Philistine champion, to his refusal to harm the LORD's anointed, Saul, to his acceptance of judgment for his sins, David revealed an unshaken faith and trust in God. It is fitting that we have so many of David's psalms that help reveal his real struggles and his victories of faith to us.

We end this mini-unit with David's son, Solomon, on the throne as Israel enters a Golden Age. While Solomon began well and asked for wisdom, over time his heart became divided when tempted by his prosperity, his many wives, and possibly even his trust in his own wisdom. Solomon's divided heart led to the division of the Kingdom. After Solomon died, Israel entered a decline that ended in the judgment and

---

[1] Read the story of how the Benjamites were almost wiped out in Judges 19-21. This is not a story that you want to share with youngsters, but it gives insight as to why Saul was insecure.

exile that had been prophesied by Moses before Israel first entered the Promised Land.

Conclusion

In the last mini-unit, we saw God make His covenant with Abraham. He promised him that He would bless him and make him a blessing, and that all the people of the earth would be blessed in him. In this unit, God made a covenant with Israel at Mt. Horeb, and with David, who wanted to build a house for God. God told him no, but that He would build David a house instead. God gave Israel the king they wanted as a foretaste; God planned to give them the King He wanted—the Son of David, King of kings and Lord of lords. We end this mini-unit with the image of the glory of God that had brightened the face of Moses filling the golden Temple built by Solomon, David's son. It is a bright image, but it is only the palest reflection of the glory of the New Jerusalem.

Mini-Unit 2, Topic 1
Burning Bush to Tabernacle

Introduction

As we study daily life in Egypt this topic, we focus on Egyptian political government. Depending on whether you are introducing the topic of idols and false gods to your child, we include optional readings on Egyptian mythology. Politics and religion were part of daily life in Egypt, and we want our students to understand that God showed His power over both as He revealed Himself to His chosen people.

Last topic, we located Egypt on the globe. We'll zoom in this week on Egypt's biggest man-made features, the pyramids, as a backdrop to the story of Moses and the Exodus. What are these mysterious monuments, really, and who are the kings who lie buried within them?

In the Bible readings this week, your student will hear about how God delivered His people from the full power of Egypt. Studying the rulers of Egypt will help your student understand that God delivered His people from the greatest nation on earth at that time. With His power, He brought them out of slavery, despite Egypt's powerful government, religious leaders, and armies. It is fascinating to realize that the ten plagues God sent on Egypt directly challenged the power of the most important of Egypt's false gods.

In Exodus, God established His supremacy and authority both politically and spiritually.

Exodus Background: Ancient Egyptian History

To understand the kings of Egypt, let's look at the Nile a little more closely: there's the Nile Delta, one distinctive region, and the Nile Valley that leads to it. These two areas were known as Lower Egypt and Upper Egypt: lower meaning "downstream," so that "Upper Egypt" lies below "Lower Egypt" on any modern map.

The first Egyptian villages that archaeologists have located appear to be more than 5,000 years old. Some villages were in Upper Egypt and others were in the Delta region. Somewhere back in the mists of time, these villages united into two separate kingdoms. We don't know a lot about these early days, but we do know the king of Upper Egypt had a crown that was a white headpiece shaped like a cone. The king of Lower Egypt had a different crown: a red cylinder.

Upper Crown
Hedjet

According to Egyptian tradition, Menes, King of Upper Egypt, conquered the area around the Nile Delta around 3100 BC. He united Upper and Lower Egypt and formed the first national government the world had ever seen. He built a new capital city, Memphis, near modern Cairo. When the two kingdoms were united the crown was united, too: the double crown of Egypt was a white cone inside a red cylinder. (See the diagrams to the right.)

Lower Crown
Deshret

After that first king died, his heirs ruled over Egypt for a long time—but theirs was only the first of more than thirty royal dynasties in Egypt's history. That's because Egypt lasted a long time. These dynasties are the most convenient way to trace a time line as long as Egypt's.

Let's take a look at the basic time line. Egyptologists identify three Egyptian kingdoms that span 1500 years: the Old Kingdom, the Middle Kingdom, and the New Kingdom. To put things into a bit of perspective, the "New" Kingdom ended before David took the throne of Israel. Egypt finished off fifteen centuries of monarchy before Israel even got started!

Double Crown
Pschent

There was a civilization of sorts in Egypt well before the Old Kingdom, and a turbulent "intermediate period" of a century or more between each of the three kingdoms. After the intermediate period that followed the New Kingdom, Egypt went through what is called its "Late Period." Things went downhill from there: Egypt wound up under foreign domination. Egypt was conquered or ruled by the Assyrians, Babylonians, the Persians, the Greeks, and the Romans in turn. But previous to that, for thousands of years, Egypt was the mightiest power in the known world—so much so that, as we mentioned before, Egypt became the Old Testament symbol for worldly pride and human achievement.

Dynasties I and II came before the Old Kingdom. The Old Kingdom began at the transition from Dynasty II to Dynasty III, in 2686 BC. It lasted for the next 500 years. This is when the Egyptians built the famed great pyramids. Dynasties III and IV were a time of great royal power, but the power of the kings began to weaken in the next two dynasties and fell apart altogether for the next five.

In 1991 BC, a new Pharaoh took charge. Amenemhet seized the throne. His successors restored Egypt's wealth and power. They conquered the Nubians to the south and established trade with Canaan and Syria. But this Middle Kingdom ran out of steam in 1786 BC, and weak rulers led Egypt for the next 120 years.

Around 1670 BC, Egypt was overrun by immigrants with powerful new weapons. The Hyksos had chariots and better bows than the native Egyptians. Hyksos kings ruled Egypt for almost a century, but they were displaced when the New Kingdom began.

Did Joseph come to Egypt during the Hyksos period? Was the New Kingdom the "new Pharaoh that knew not Joseph" that we read about in Exodus 1 and Acts 7? We don't know! Old Testament scholars and archaeologists have spent generations trying to nail down the details. What we do know is that history matters and Scripture tells us about real people: these Egyptian dynasties connect up with things we read about in our daily devotions.

It is against this backdrop that we see the story of God leading His people out by the hand of Moses. If we consider that God may well have led the Israelites out during a time when Egypt was at the height of its power, using plagues that directly demonstrated God's power over that of the Egyptian gods, it should give us a much richer understanding of God's work for His glory.

The New Kingdom lasted for 500 years, during which Egypt was the strongest power in the world. Egypt developed a permanent army with horse-drawn chariots that conquered territory as far north as modern Iraq and as far south as Ethiopia. But Egypt's power began to wane about the time Israel united twelve tribes into a nation.

Government

At different times, the Egyptians equated the Pharaoh with Ra (also spelled Re), the sun god, and Horus, the king god. As the earthly incarnation of Ra, the Pharaoh mounted back up to heaven on the rays of the sun when he died. As the incarnation of Horus, the son of Isis and Osiris, when the Pharaoh died, he supposedly turned into Osiris. Suffice it to say, he represented the gods and he could make no mistakes—thus Pharaoh was the ultimate in infallibility and authority.

In the Old Testament, Egypt is a symbol of wealth and worldly power. Pharaoh was the embodiment of this whole system: his subjects called him "Egypt." Historically speaking, Egypt sank when the kings were weak and grew stronger with good leaders. We will see this pattern over and over again as we study the history of the world. Strong leaders usually make a big difference—for good or for evil.

You Can't Take It With You?

Most of the Egyptian artifacts we have today came from their tombs. That's all the pyramids are, really: the enormous tombs of kings. The pharaohs were carefully mummified after they died because Egyptians believed they would need their bodies again. They thought that, after death, a person would be able to enjoy the things that were buried with him—but that was all they would enjoy. That's why they mummified their pets, made little clay images of servants, and painted pictures on the walls. Those magnificently decorated graves were their attempt to lay up treasures in the afterlife.

Engineering

The pyramids were engineering marvels, especially when you think about all the modern tools that the Egyptians *didn't* have! Pretend you're standing in the middle of a sandy desert. What are you going to build a pyramid with? Answer: stones. Big ones!

But, how do you get them to your building site? Many of them came from quarries near the pyramids, but the Egyptians also brought huge granite blocks almost five hundred miles down the river. The Nile was ideal for transporting great big, square blocks of rock.

Now, remember, they didn't have modern machinery or tools—not even iron or bronze ones. How were the needed stones to be mined and shaped? The hardest metal they had was copper. Try chiseling stone with a penny and see how far you get! Yet the Egyptians carved out perfectly shaped stones. The ones inside the tomb itself fit so closely that you can't slip a playing card between them.

Once you've got your blocks, what do you do with them? How do the sides of the structure arise? How do you get that last stone almost five hundred feet into the air? To this day, nobody really knows how Egyptians did it!

One surprising thing we do know is that the Egyptians didn't rely on slave labor for their pyramids, as popular movies might suggest. The Egyptian farmers worked on the pyramids during the months when the Nile's flooding made farming impossible. Experts speculate that around 100,000 Egyptians worked on the pyramids each year, and were paid (at least in food, clothing, and housing) for their work.

The Great Pyramid of Khufu was one of the Seven Wonders of the Ancient World. It was the tallest man-made structure in the world until the nineteenth century. That's 43 centuries! The engineering of pyramids is incredibly precise: each side is perfectly oriented to the compass: north, south, east, and west. The sides are exactly equal in length, with less than 0.1% error. The pyramid consists of approximately 2,000,000 blocks of stone, each weighing more than two tons. They say there are enough blocks in the three pyramids at Giza to build a stone wall ten feet high and one foot thick all the way around France.

Think about the glory of Egypt, including these pyramids—and then consider Moses. He had been a prince of Egypt before he gave it all up to identify himself with the oppressed Israelites. He killed an Egyptian slavedriver and fled to the desert, where he wound up a poor shepherd in Midian.

Only One God

In the mini-unit overview, we told about how God revealed Himself to Moses through the Burning Bush. In order to understand how shocking some of God's revelations must have been to Moses, we need to remember that he grew up surrounded by the mythology and polytheism of Egypt. Polytheism simply means that people believed in many specialized gods. (We spell polytheistic gods with a lowercase "g" to differentiate from the one true God.)

Egyptians worshipped the sun, the Nile, cats, cobras, and a host of idols, but that wasn't all they treated as divine. Pharaoh was one of the "gods" of Egypt, too, as we explained in the government section. Talk about an absolute monarchy!

Egyptian mythology included stories of the births and deaths of some of these gods. In so many ways, they were gods created in man's image. At the burning bush, Moses met the God who had created mankind in *His* image. By revealing Himself as the self-sufficient, self-existent God, the LORD was directly challenging all of the combined power of the gods of Egypt. As we know, one God is more than enough, if He is the true God (and He is!).

Judgment of God

In the Ancient World, displays of power defined the preeminence of gods. The book of Exodus pits a mixed multitude of helpless slaves against mighty Egypt. Moses, the son of a slave woman, goes up against the god-king of the greatest nation on earth. Pharaoh had an army of chariots at his command. Moses had a shepherd's staff. Moses defied Pharaoh and all the other gods of Egypt. Moses said that a God that the Egyptians had never heard of demanded the release of His people. You know the rest of the story!

It is inspiring to realize the intentionality with which God brought His wonders and judgment against Egypt. Each plague both judged the land of Egypt and displayed His superiority over specific false gods who were worshipped in Egypt.

- ❏ The Egyptians worshipped the Nile. God turned the Nile to blood.
- ❏ Heqt was the frog-goddess of childbirth. God drove the frogs out of the river, and they died in heaps.
- ❏ Thoth was the god of the magicians who admitted their defeat when God sent flies across the land.
- ❏ Hathor, the cow goddess, and Apis, the bull, were both helpless when God struck Egypt's flocks and herds with pestilence.
- ❏ Isis, goddess of healing, could do nothing about the plague of boils.
- ❏ Osiris, god of crops, could not protect Egypt's farms from hail.
- ❏ Osiris was also powerless to stop the swarms of locusts sent by the true God.
- ❏ Re, the sun-god, could not keep shining when God turned day to night.
- ❏ Pharaoh—though the Egyptians called him divine—could not protect his first-born son from the angel of death.

The gods of Egypt were helpless before the God of Abraham, Isaac, and Jacob, but Pharaoh's hardened heart did not allow him to admit defeat. His mighty armies were finally defeated when God unleashed the pent-up waters of the Red Sea that had just been parted to release His people from the final grip of Egyptian bondage.

When God delivered His people out of bondage, He put every power of the enemy to shame. Not only did His people go free, they took the spoils of Egypt with them.

Mount Sinai

The rest of Exodus tells about the year the Israelites spent at the foot of Mount Sinai, where God gave them a renewed covenant. He provided the Tabernacle: a visible means for meeting with an invisible God. He provided a whole series of festivals and holy days to remind them of their history of redemption and His ever-present providence. He gave them a perfect Law, consistent with His holiness.

Using your Bible atlas, trace the path the Israelites took from the Red Sea down to Sinai. Along the way they ran out of food and water and encountered their first pitched battle. God gave them manna to eat and brought water out of the rock for them. Manna and the Sabbath commanded by God became visible, daily reminders of Israel's dependence upon God, and His goodness to provide all that they needed.

It took three months to make the trek to Sinai, and already Moses was getting worn out by the challenge of riding herd on such a multitude. With 600,000 men on the move, Moses may well have been responsible for around two million people—and he was the only government this mob knew. Fortunately, God gave Moses a wise counselor—his father-in-law, Jethro. Jethro watched him trying cases all day long for just one day, and said, "This has to stop! You're wearing yourself out." Jethro advised Moses to choose capable judges and to write down laws for the people. This was the beginning of a new government, and with it, the Israelites began the transition from mob to new nation.

The Ten Commandments

Moses took Jethro's advice to write down the laws, but it was God who chiseled them into stone with His own finger. God appeared to the Israelites at Mount Sinai in smoke and thunder.

Exodus 19 says:

> On the morning of the third day there were thunders and lightnings and a thick cloud on the mountain and a very loud trumpet blast, so that all the people in the camp trembled. Then Moses brought the people out of the camp to meet God, and they took their stand at the foot of the mountain. Now Mount Sinai was wrapped in smoke because the Lord had descended on it in fire. The smoke of it went up like the smoke of a kiln, and the whole mountain trembled greatly. And as the sound of the trumpet grew louder and louder, Moses spoke, and God answered him in thunder. The Lord came down on Mount Sinai, to the top of the mountain. And the Lord called Moses

to the top of the mountain, and Moses went up.

God gave Moses the Ten Commandments there. These aren't the only laws God gave to people, but they are the most familiar, and it has been said that the bulk of the books of Moses form commentaries (or expansions) of these ten. Even today, they aren't out of date or irrelevant.

The Covenant

In Exodus 24, after God gave the people His commandments, Moses built an altar and sacrificed there. The essence of this exchange is expressed in Exodus 19:4-8:

> 'You yourselves have seen what I did to Egypt, and how I carried you on eagles' wings and brought you to myself. Now if you obey me fully and keep my covenant, then out of all nations you will be my treasured possession. Although the whole earth is mine, you will be for me a kingdom of priests and a holy nation.' These are the words you are to speak to the Israelites.
>
> So Moses went back and summoned the elders of the people and set before them all the words the Lord had commanded him to speak. The people all responded together, 'We will do everything the Lord has said.'

The sacred covenant that God established with Israel followed a specific form. It followed the format developed by the ancient Hittite kings, who established a covenant with the people when they took them under their dominion. These kingly covenants were radically unlike a bargain or our modern contracts. The Hittite covenants between a vassal [1] and a lord originated entirely with the superior party. The vassal had a choice: they could accept or reject the arrangement (covenants generally imply a two-way relationship), but they could not negotiate or alter the terms of the disposition in any way.

God's covenant with Israel had the same quality. The people could agree to be God's covenant people or not, but they couldn't haggle over terms. They couldn't try to bargain it down to six commandments and a couple of suggestions. As we noted before, a covenant is binding even if one party breaks their promises: God would keep His promise to be Israel's Lord even if Israel didn't obey. Israel's disobedience resulted in chastening instead of covenant blessing, but it did not change the covenant.

---

1 A vassal was a person who swore allegiance to a ruler and promised to support that ruler, often receiving delegated authority over some property. We discuss this more fully when we learn about medieval Europe in Mini-Unit 5.

MINI-UNIT 2: TABERNACLE AND TEMPLE

The Tabernacle

God's covenant relationship with Israel was uniquely expressed through His holy law, but there is more to the covenant than the Law. Galatians 3:24 says the law was our schoolmaster to bring us to Christ. The Law was always to be a means to an end—and the end of the Law was to enable mankind to be with God Himself. Exodus 25-31 spells out instructions for building and consecrating the Tabernacle, the place for meeting with God.

In a number of specific ways, the Tabernacle presented an image of Eden. It was decorated with pomegranates and cherubim—reflections of the fruit trees of Paradise and the angels that guard its gate (because of the separation that sin had made between people and paradise). The gate of Eden is to the east according to Genesis 3:24, and so was the doorway of the Tabernacle.

The people responded with amazing generosity to Moses' call for materials to construct this Tabernacle. Exodus 36:6-7 says,

> Moses gave command, and word was proclaimed throughout the camp, 'Let no man or woman do anything more for the contribution for the sanctuary.' So the people were restrained from bringing, for the material they had was sufficient to do all the work, and more.

If you ever list the greatest miracles in Scripture, it wouldn't hurt to include that verse. (We see the same phenomenon repeated when King David asked the people to contribute to the Temple.) Have you ever seen people give so much that the leaders had to tell them to stop?

Feasts and Holy Days

Knowing how easy it is for human beings to turn from Him, God gave the Israelites periodic holy days for rest, celebration, and remembrance of His goodness. On these days, no work was done, and various aspects of God's character or work were glorified.

We've already studied the Passover event, when the Israelites sacrificed perfect little lambs and spread their blood on their door posts so that the angel of death passed over them. God directed that the Passover be celebrated and remembered in a yearly ritual.

This week, your child can focus on the feast that happens every week. The Israelites call it *Shabbat*; Gentiles call it the Sabbath—God's day of rest. On this, the

Israelites, their slaves, and their animals were to have a rest from all normal work.

What does your church teach about the Sabbath? Some emphasize it, others pretty much ignore it. How does your family celebrate this holy day? We've always tried to set the seventh day apart somehow, because we want our children to believe that it's the best day of the week. No matter how busy we've been, Sunday has always been the day of the week with no other plans.

Holiness and Animal Sacrifice

After the Exodus, we find the story of God's people continued in the book of Leviticus. The fundamental theme of Leviticus is holiness. The fundamental question of the book is, "How can sinful people approach a holy God?" If that's a question that fascinates you, Leviticus is a fascinating book. If you couldn't care less, Leviticus seems dry, boring, and irrelevant.

God determines how He is to be served, and He spells out how He should be worshipped. Many people nowadays say they worship God in their own way. Does that satisfy a holy God? In Leviticus 10, Aaron's sons, Nadab and Abihu, tried to "worship God in their own way," but they were struck dead for offering "strange fire" before the Lord.

In Leviticus, God taught the Israelites that sin had consequences. Their unclean acts offended a holy God, giving them guilty consciences that needed reconciliation. Reconciliation was not cheap! It was messy, bloody, and deadly for the animals sacrificed in the place of guilty people.

The violent realities of animal sacrifice illustrated to the Israelites that sin was serious, and that they constantly fell short of God's standards. Israel had learned, even before Leviticus, that they needed to be covered from God's righteous judgment by the blood of the Passover Lamb. As we learn in the New Testament, Jesus Christ became the ultimate sacrifice—the One who died once for all, removing all need for the animal sacrifices outlined in Leviticus. But those laws were in place for many centuries, acting as both a means of atonement and a school teacher to bring us to Christ (as it says in Galatians 3:24-25).

Conclusion

The pyramids are wonders, sure enough, but in the end, they're still tombs. That tells us a great deal about the Egyptian view of life—and death. In many ways, Egypt can be illustrated by its pyramids—massive, impressive, inspiring, but ultimately a fantastic outlay of human energy and effort at what cannot be attained apart from God: real eternal life.

We've hinted at this verse before, but it really serves wonderfully to sum up God's authoritative perspective on this chapter of His story. Hebrews 11:24-29 tell us:

> By faith Moses, when he was grown up, refused to be called the son of Pharaoh's daughter, choosing rather to be mistreated with the people of God than to enjoy the fleeting pleasures of sin. He considered the reproach of Christ greater wealth than the treasures of Egypt, for he was looking to the reward. By faith he left Egypt, not being afraid of the anger of the king, for he endured as seeing him who is invisible. By faith he kept the Passover and sprinkled the blood, so that the Destroyer of the firstborn might not touch them. By faith the people crossed the Red Sea as on dry land, but the Egyptians, when they attempted to do the same, were drowned.

May we and our students learn to love and obey the one true God and to look forward to the reward of eternal life that He offers, instead of the counterfeit immortality offered by the world.

Mini-Unit 2, Topic 2
The Promised Land

Introduction

This week, we continue our study of redemptive history by reading selections from the books of Joshua, Judges, and Ruth as we look at Bronze-Age Israel. We'll study the geography of the Promised Land in some depth because it makes more of a difference to the story than you might think. We'll also meet the Canaanites, the original inhabitants of the land.

You may be wondering what happened to the stories of the Israelites wandering in the desert. While we mention them briefly, we are focusing most of our attention on the period of time between when God began to lead His people into the Promised Land by the hand of Joshua and when He gave Israel the king that they demanded in order to be like their neighbors.

This week, consider daily life for the Israelites as they conquered and settled the Promised Land. Especially, we want students to learn about Israel's relationship with neighboring kingdoms. Who were they? What was it like for the Israelites to live their lives surrounded by them? Why was there enmity between Israel and her neighbors? Also, because of that enmity, why would Israel want a king when they had God?

Preparing a Faithful People

Numbers 13 and 14 tell of the twelve spies who went into the land of Canaan. Joshua and Caleb brought back a good report. The other ten spies projected doubt and fear. As a result, the people refused to go into the land God had promised them.

In response, God asked, "How long will this people despise Me? And how long will they not believe in Me, in spite of all the signs that I have done among them?"

God was ready to wipe them out and start over with Moses, but Moses begged Him not to. God relented, but not without judging the Israelites for their sin. Every one of the men who walked out of Egypt was doomed to die in the wilderness—all but two. The two faith-filled spies, Joshua and Caleb, were the only ones who would enter Canaan.

Moses' Failure at the Waters of Meribah

Numbers 20 tells a sad story. The people grumbled because there was no water. In response, God told Moses,

> 'Take your staff, and assemble the congregation, you and Aaron your brother, and tell the rock before their eyes to yield its water. So you shall bring water out of the rock for them and give drink to the congregation and their cattle.'
>
> Moses took the staff and gathered the assembly together before the rock, and he said to them, 'Hear now, you rebels: shall we bring water for you out of this rock?' And Moses lifted up his hand and struck the rock with his staff twice, and water came out abundantly, and the congregation drank.
>
> But the Lord said to Moses and Aaron, 'Because you did not believe in me, to uphold me as holy in the eyes of the people of Israel, therefore you shall not bring this assembly into the land that I have given them.'

Wow! What a judgment, for what seems to be such a small sin! But was it really small? Moses was tasked with representing God's character to the people. God, who is long-suffering and merciful, was incredibly patient with these grumblers. He told Moses to speak to the rock, thus to reveal His power and providence. But Moses struck the rock in anger and rebuked the people. What the people saw was Moses' anger, not God's kindness.

As parents, especially for homeschooling fathers, we represent the Heavenly Father to our children. How many times have we showed them irritation or resentment instead of God's patience? What are the consequences of our impatience? Thankfully, we have a Savior who knows our weaknesses and is at work to redeem us, but this week's topic offers a helpful reminder to us to grow ever more in self-control and patient mercy, for the sake of how we represent Christ.

Joshua

Moving on from Moses, let's meet one of the great heroes of the Bible: Joshua. If you are raising sons, there aren't a lot of better role models than Joshua. God exhorted him to be strong and courageous, and he was! Throughout his life, Joshua exemplified faith in action.

Even Joshua's name is significant. The Hebrew name "Joshua" is the same as the Greek name "Jesus." The name means, "The LORD saves" or "Yahweh saves." Interestingly, according to Numbers 13:16, Joshua was originally named Hoshea (meaning "salvation"), but Moses called him Joshua, instead.

This little incident of Moses changing a man's name from "Hoshea" to "Joshua" marks the continental divide between our universal, human longing for things to somehow get better and the actual answer to the problem that we face. Humans want salvation in general; God gives us salvation in Jesus.

The Old Testament hero we know as Joshua was born at least twenty years before Moses led God's people out of Egypt. We know that "a new Pharaoh who knew not Joseph" had taken power by the time that Moses was born, which must have been fifty or sixty years earlier. For at least eighty years, then, the Israelites were groaning under the oppressive rule of a hostile power. Somewhere in the middle of this long hard time, an Ephraimite couple named their baby boy "salvation."

They didn't name him "Joshua" (which means "YHWH is salvation") because they didn't know the name of YHWH. When Moses encountered God at the burning bush, Moses asked, "Who shall I say sent me?" He did not know God's name, because God had not yet revealed it! There were millions of slaves in Egypt who were dreaming of salvation with no knowledge of their Savior.

The book of Joshua tells the story of Israel's long-awaited entry into the Promised Land. It will be very helpful to have a Bible atlas handy as you read this week. Here is another opportunity to note the importance of geography to history. The environmental conditions of a culture can determine what people eat and drink, the clothes they wear, the styles of homes they build, the number of enemies they fight, and even the results of their battles. In God's providence, nothing happens without a reason—and geography is no exception!

God's Victory over Jericho

When the Israelites left Egypt, they were a nation of slaves. By the time the next generation entered the Promised Land, the Israelites had become warriors with a few victories under their belts. Still, it was one thing to go up against unsophisticated enemies like Sihon, King of the Amorites, and Og, King of Bashan. It was another thing to go against great walled cities like Jericho. Way back in Numbers 13 and 14, the Israelite spies felt like grasshoppers when they looked at the mighty Canaanites.

Joshua sent spies into the land, just like Moses had, but his spies brought a very different report. Joshua 2 tells the story: These spies hid on top of the house of Rahab, a prostitute. She told them, "I know that the Lord has given you the land, and that the fear of you has fallen upon us, and that all the inhabitants of the land melt away before you" (Joshua 2:9). Imagine the feelings, then, with which the inhabitants of Jericho watched Joshua and his army march around their city, day after day, for a week. At the end of that time, a mighty trumpet blast—and the power of God Almighty—caused the walls to crumble and gave these warriors a serious victory!

The victory was the Lord's, and so were the spoils of victory. Joshua commanded the soldiers to bring all the loot that they found to the treasury of the Lord.

Israel Defeated by Sin

After the great victory at Jericho, things looked easy for the Israelites. The next city in their path was very small—the city of Ai. They didn't even bother sending their whole army out to deal with it. Imagine their surprise when they got trounced by the men of Ai!

There was a reason they were defeated: there was sin in the camp. A man named Achan confessed that he had coveted some gold and some beautiful cloth that had been plundered from Jericho. Achan's covetousness resulted in God allowing Israel's defeat at Ai. Israel purged the sin from their midst by destroying Achan and all that he had—but you need not get into those details with your tender child.

The main message from this story is the seriousness of Achan's crime: it forfeited God's blessing for the whole community. Without God's help, the Israelites were just another wandering mob. Without obedience to His commands, why should Israel count on God's help?

Conquest

Israel's basic battle plan was to divide and conquer. Israel swept through the middle cities of Canaan, then took southern territory before heading north. This first wave of lightning-fast victories broke the back of Canaanite opposition, but it didn't eliminate every Canaanite inhabitant in the land. The Bible says God left them in the land to keep it from reverting to wilderness until the Israelites could expand to fill it. Their presence was a temptation, however; it was easier to make peace with the people God had ordered them to drive out than to make war. At the end of his life, Joshua charged the people of God to be careful to obey His commandment. Joshua 23:11-13 says:

> Be very careful, therefore, to love the Lord your God. For if you turn back and cling to the remnant of these nations remaining among you and make marriages with them, so that you associate with them and they with you, know for certain that the Lord your God will no longer drive out these nations before you, but they shall be a snare and a trap for you, a whip on your sides and thorns in your eyes, until you perish from off this good ground that the Lord your God has given you.

Israel's Neighbors—The Canaanites

Note that the Promised Land was placed between two major highways—the International Coastal Highway and the King's Highway—that ran between Mesopotamia and Egypt, two large centers of civilization. Both Egyptian and Mesopotamian rulers sought to control Israel's Promised Land as time rolled along.

For the Egyptians, control of Palestine was an important geographical barrier that might slow down attacking enemies, as well as a source of money and goods in the form of taxes or tributes. For Mesopotamian cultures, who were not as blessed with minerals (iron, gold, etc.) or even as stable a food supply as Egypt had, control of the International Highway meant cheaper goods, tax money, maybe extra taxes on traded goods, and even extra food. (Notice how the geographical locations of these civilizations and the availability of resources affected people's choices!)

These larger, competing neighbors would influence the newborn nation of Israel. Many of us probably remember Sunday School lessons about the Canaanites, the Hittites, the Perizzites, the Hivites, and the Jebusites. Or maybe we *don't* remember much about Sunday School lessons, but those names sound sort of familiar! Israel's neighbors have often become just strange names to modern Bible readers.

As we study Israel's history, we're going to look closely at these neighbors. We will try to understand who they were (just as you might try to understand how your neighbor Smith is different from your neighbor Tzorvik), where they came from, and their roles in God's history of redemption. Each neighbor had a specific way of tempting Israel, for instance. We'll begin with neighbors that were actually living within the borders of Israel.

The Canaanites may have settled in the region sometime around 2000 BC, a few centuries before Abraham arrived. They were a Semitic people, whose language is related to Hebrew, Arabic, and other mid-Eastern tongues. By the time the Israelites arrived, their civilization was quite advanced: they lived in walled city-states, somewhat like the Greeks. The Canaanites who lived on the coastland north of Israel later became known as Phoenicians.

As we will learn, the Canaanites tempted the Israelites to doubt and abandon their God in order to serve Canaanite divinities as well as seek the pleasures of the flesh and material gain. How could the Israelites be tempted by the Canaanites, after all they had experienced in the wilderness? It was easier than you might think.

In the Ancient World, remember that power and prosperity were seen as direct evidence of the power of a person's or culture's gods. Ancients also believed that gods were localized, having authority over a region, or a city, or a mountaintop, for instance. To the nomadic Israelite shepherds, the Canaanite cities looked mighty, fortified, and wealthy. There were large buildings, beautiful carvings, abundant goods from other lands, slaves, fine clothing, and metal riches. The God of Israel was still invisible and mysterious, by contrast.

The Israelites would have been sorely tempted, especially during the long period of the judges (about 400 years), to look with envious eyes on the remaining cities of the Canaanites, and to consider adding the Canaanite gods to worship rosters in order to increase their worldly prosperity.

The Canaanites included a number of cultures that collectively surrounded Israel. Let's figure out where they were. If you stood in Israel on the shore of the Mediterranean and journeyed south, you turned right into Africa and eventually reached Egypt. If, instead, you went north, up along the seacoast in Israel, you'll reach modern Lebanon, then Turkey, and then you turn left into Europe to reach Greece. Next topic, we'll be learning about the Philistines and the Phoenicians, who traveled along these seacoasts.

In the time of the Judges, sea travel wasn't an important factor for the Israelites. They came into the Promised Land from the deserts across the Jordan (from east to west), not by the sea.

Israel was positioned like a rest stop along the interstate. Parts of the Promised Land were right on the trade route, and these were much affected by the worldly cultures of Canaan, Egypt, and Mesopotamia. Other parts of the Promised Land were off the highway, so to speak—the hill country of Judah, for example, was pretty far off the main road.

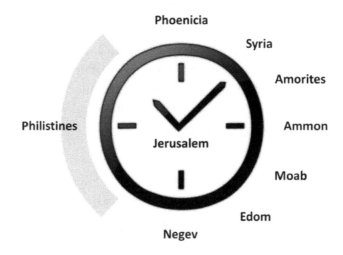

Phoenicia

If you stood in Jerusalem, due north, at twelve o'clock, were the Phoenicians, who lived along the seacoast. We'll study them in our next topic.

Syria

North-northeast, at one o'clock, lay Syria, a land peopled mostly by Arameans. Abraham was from Aramean stock, as Moses observes in Deuteronomy 26:5. The Syrian city of Damascus was a major stop on the trade routes from Mesopotamia to Egypt.

Amorites

The Arameans' area had previously been populated by Amorites. The Amorite kingdom lay south of Syria, at about 2 o'clock, but Israel soon conquered Sihon, king of the Amorites, and Moses gave those lands to the tribes of Manasseh, Gad, and Reuben. We call this Israelite territory to the northeast the "Trans-Jordan," because it was located on the far side of the Jordan River from the bulk of Israel.

Ammon

Due east of Jerusalem, at 3 o'clock, lay the Ammonites. They were descended from Ben-Ammi, the son of Lot and his daughter by incest. (Lot was Abraham's nephew.) The Ammonite capital was called Rabbat Amman, and Amman is the capital of the country of Jordan, today.

The city of Amman was on the King's Highway, an ancient trade route connecting Mesopotamia with the port city of Aqaba at the northern tip of the Red Sea. Famously, Moses wanted to lead the Israelites up this road to reach the Promised Land, but the kings of Edom and the Amorites wouldn't let them pass.

Moab

South of Ammon, at about 4 o'clock, lay Moab. The Moabites were descended from Lot's other incestuously-begotten son, Moab. Moab was separated from Ammon by a canyon carved by the Arnon River. Ruth, the great-grandmother of King David, was from Moab.

Edom

Edom lay south of Moab, at about 5 o'clock. The Edomites were descended from Esau, the brother of Jacob. Edom had rich copper and iron mines that made it a major stop on the trade routes.

The Negev

Due south of Jerusalem, at six o'clock, the land became drier and drier until it turned into the Negev Desert. Virtually no people lived here in Bible times. It is one place called "the wilderness" in Bible stories.

Philistines

The coastland to the west of Jerusalem, at nine o'clock, had been colonized, probably by those who are known as the Sea Peoples to historians. Bible readers are more familiar with them as the Philistines. Their five main walled cities were Gath, Ashkelon, Ashdod, Ekron, and Gaza.

That's where the modern name of the Gaza Strip comes from—and, of course, "Palestine" itself is derived from the word "Philistine."

Bronze-Age Israel Under the Judges

The Hebrew word we translate as "judge" means a whole lot more than the English word. Interestingly enough, this is because the ancient Hebrews had a very limited vocabulary for government. Government, for them, was not the complex technical field it is today for us. It was what happened when a man (or a woman, in the case of Deborah) rightly exercised authority. "To judge," in Hebrew, meant to make rules, decide cases, issue commands. It meant "to lead" as much as it meant "render a verdict."

In the period of the Judges, Israel had a code of laws from God. These were so good that we are still discovering new insights into justice from them to this day. But the Israelites had no other institutions of government in this period. There were no police, no standing army, no tax collectors, and no bureaucrats. Every man had only the laws of Moses and his own conscience.

In theory, it was the ideal form of government. In practice, human nature messed it up. As we described in the mini-unit overview, there was a predictable pattern of rest, prosperity, forgetfulness, judgment, appeal to God, deliverance, and rest that was repeated time and again.

Israel at this period of time may have been the world's only true example of a theocracy. In theory, theocracy means "government by God," but in practice it usually means government by humans who claim to act in God's name. When religiously-motivated people seize control of the government, it's still government by humans, not government by God.

As the period of the Judges ended, the sons of the high priest Eli tried to govern Israel, as is recorded in the first few chapters of Samuel. That's all the proof we need to know that government by priests is not the same as government by God. Eli's sons were wicked men—so wicked that God rebuked their father for not restraining them. When Eli did not act, God did. Eli and his sons all died on the same terrible day.

The leadership passed to Samuel, the prophet, who judged Israel for many years. But Samuel's sons proved to be just as much of a disappointment as Eli's had been. The Bible tells us that they took bribes, defiled sacrifices, and perverted justice. Once again, we see the difference between a true theocracy (which is government by God Himself) and a government controlled by religious officials.

There's another major theme in the book of Judges, which is repeated at least four times: "In those days there was no king in Israel" (Judges 17:6, 18:1, 19:1, and 21:25). To this, two of these passages add, "And everyone did what was right in his own eyes" (Judges 17:6 and 21:25).

Instead of a free theocracy, where each man followed God's law guided by his own conscience, rampant idolatry and anarchy took over. This, of course, was because God had not yet written His laws on human hearts, because the Savior had not yet come (2 Corinthians 3:3). Even with the salt and light of Christians, we still await Christ's return to bring true peace and freedom. Israel's wickedness routinely resulted in God's chastening, usually at the hand of a foreign foe. The saying, "If you don't rule yourself, somebody else will," held true for the Israelites.

Ruth

In this topic, we meet one person who did what was right in God's eyes in those days. Her name was Ruth, and she wasn't even an Israelite! The book of Ruth gives us an excellent glimpse of daily life in the Bronze Age. The story starts in the little town of Bethlehem, deep in the territory of Judah (which, you'll remember, was off the main road).

A famine drove a farmer named Elimelech to Moab, on the other side of the Dead Sea. He took his wife and his two sons with him, and they settled down there. Unfortunately, Elimelech died there, leaving Naomi alone with her sons. The boys grew up and married Moabite girls, but then both sons died, and Naomi was left alone with her two daughters-in-law ten years after she had left home.

It's a great read-aloud for any age: Ruth followed her mother-in-law back to Israel, saying "Your people shall be my people, and your God my God" (Ruth 1:16). It's a happy-ending romance, and it sets the stage for our next topic, because Ruth was the great-grandmother of a boy named David.

Iron-Age Philistines

The Hittites (another of Israel's neighbors, further away to the north and east) had a big but indirect impact on the Israelites. It was the Hittites who discovered how to use iron and developed fast, strong chariots. The Philistines probably learned about iron technology from them, but the Israelites didn't have iron weapons or war chariots, which put them at a serious disadvantage in the period of the judges. We'll see how the Philistines used their monopoly on iron weapons to keep the Israelites down next week. The Israelites had good reason to be afraid of iron weapons and chariots.

Conclusion

The pattern of Israel's history as recorded in the book of Judges goes like this:

- ❏ Israel at rest grows prosperous.
- ❏ Israel forgets the LORD and serves false gods (the idols of her neighbors).
- ❏ The LORD sends judgment, often in the shape of foreign armies.
- ❏ Israel repents and cries out to the LORD.
- ❏ The LORD sends a judge to lead Israel, often in defeat of her enemies.
- ❏ Israel has rest and grows prosperous. (*repeat*)

Note that while this pattern is repeated, there is also a downward spiral in the faithfulness of the judges. During this era, God was Israel's only king, but the people weren't any better at serving an invisible king than they were at worshipping an invisible God. They wanted something they could see.

Mini-Unit 2, Topic 3
The Heart of the King

Introduction

We will look at two major threads this week. We'll wrap up our study of Bronze-Age Israel by looking at David, God's anointed king. For full-family learning, it doesn't get much better than this. Everybody in the home can get something out of David's story! He was a warrior and a worshipper, a poet and a king. He was a real man that any sinner can look to because he was seriously wicked at times, and humble enough to repent when he went wrong. Yet he was also a leader that any man can admire.

This week, we briefly meet Samuel, the last of the Judges. Samuel obeyed God personally, but his failures as a father resulted in the people of Israel demanding that he establish a king for them. God agreed, and Samuel anointed Saul at God's direction. We'll look at Saul, whose fear, political calculation, and faithlessness became an excellent contrast for David's courage, commitment, and faithfulness. We will focus most of our attention on the story of David, with Samuel and Saul as key players in the early part of David's life, and his son, Solomon, as a key player at the end of his life.

We'll also conclude our study of Israel's neighbors with a look at the Philistines and the Phoenicians. The Philistines were the enemies of Saul and David. Let's understand them before looking at the major Biblical characters. Then we'll consider the Phoenicians, who were the allies of David and Solomon, at the end of this topic.

Philistines

The Philistines lived along the Mediterranean seacoast, abutting Egyptian territory. They're on the shortest road from Egypt to Israel—right on the route Moses would have taken if he had gone straight from Egypt to the Promised Land. Exodus 13:17-18 (ESV) tells us:

> When Pharaoh let the people go, God did not lead them by way of the land of the Philistines, although that was near. For God said, 'Lest the people change their minds when they see war and return to Egypt.' But God led the people around by the way of the wilderness toward the Red Sea.

The Israelites didn't conquer the major Philistine cities for centuries. Remember, God directed Joshua to come into the Promised Land from the east (the far side of the Jordan River from Philistine territory) and begin conquering from east to west, from the mountains to the coast. During Joshua's time, the Philistines held their territory against the Israelites and then grew in strength. The Philistines were bigger, stronger, and better armed than the Israelites, and they provoked a fundamental change in Israel's government. They were a threat to Israel's freedom that God used to bring about the transition to a monarchy.

Origins

Who were these Philistines? Where did they come from? There are plenty of mysteries surrounding the Philistines. Most experts agree that the Philistines who fought Saul were some of the so-called Sea Peoples who appear in Egyptian records from eleven and twelve centuries before Christ. The Egyptians refer to repeated attacks by these Sea Peoples. They apparently failed in their efforts to invade Egypt itself, but they settled the seacoast to the north and east. Some experts think the Sea Peoples were displaced Hittites. They used iron, like the Hittites, whose empire was collapsing around this time.

Whoever the Philistines were, they have strong archeological connections to Mycenean Greeks (the Greeks who fought against Troy in Homer's epics). Goliath's armor, as described in detail in 1 Samuel 17, matches the armor on a famous Mycenean artifact—the Warrior Vase—point for point. In general, Philistine pottery indicates a strong Mycenaen connection. From all the evidence we have, Goliath would have fit right in with the Greek army outside of Troy. That's not to say that Goliath was a Greek warrior—he may have been a refugee from the Minoan civilization of Crete, because the Myceneans who conquered Troy overwhelmed the Minoans, too.

Warriors

Whatever his background, when Goliath marched out as the Philistine champion to taunt the Israelites, he had two major advantages over the Israelite men who might take him up on his challenge: Goliath stood almost ten feet tall, and he had iron weapons. His spearhead alone weighed fifteen pounds, and the weight of its shaft must have been proportionate. If you have a child who is less than sixty pounds, he's probably lighter than Goliath's spear was. Goliath's iron sword could have slashed right through the bronze weapons of the Israelites, and his spear would have pierced their primitive armor as if it were paper.

This was a formidable foe, and much more dangerous than the Canaanites that Joshua had conquered! You can see why the Israelites of Saul's day would tremble. You can also see God's providence in leading Israel into the Promised Land by the "back door," so to speak.

Technology

As we said, the Philistines had picked up from the Hittites the art of iron-working, and it was a secret that they guarded closely. Iron was much harder, stronger, and more rigid than bronze, and it lasted longer. Weapons and tools made of iron were more valuable to these ancients than gold, since they could also be sharpened to a keener edge. The Philistines had also learned from the Hittites the secrets of superior chariot construction. They used iron in the wheels and framework of the chariot so that the axle didn't bend or break over rough terrain. These chariots were insuperable on the plains (except when things were muddy), but of little use in the hill country of Israel.

Scripture says there were only two or three iron swords in all of Israel. Most Israelite soldiers would have fought with slings, arrows, wooden pikes and swords, or (if wealthy) bronze swords or spear heads. Not a blacksmith could be found in the whole land of Israel, as we know because the Philistines said, "Otherwise the Hebrews will make swords or spears!" (1 Samuel 13:19). In the first great battle between Saul's troops and the Philistines, Saul and his son Jonathan had the only iron swords in entire the Israelite army (1 Samuel 13:22).

Religion

The Philistines were polytheists who worshipped many idols, but their most distinctive deity was Dagon. (The Hebrew word "dag" means "fish.") After the Philistines captured the Ark on the day that Eli and his sons died, they brought it into the temple of Dagon for the night for safe-keeping. Obviously, they thought, Dagon was stronger than YHWH, since the Philistines had prevailed!

But 1 Samuel 5:4 tells us that, in the morning, the Philistines found that the idol of Dagon had fallen down before the Ark of the Covenant. They righted it, but on the next morning, it had fallen again, and the head and hands of Dagon were broken off so that only the stump of Dagon was left to him—literally, "only the fish," in the original Hebrew. That's why biblical scholars think of Dagon as a fish-god combination, like a merman.

Saul and the Monarchy

God's long-term plan for His people has always included a kingdom: the Kingdom of God. Jesus is the King of Kings and Lord of Lords. God promised Abraham that He would make him and Sarah very fruitful. Of both of them, He said, "I will make nations of you, and kings will come from you" (Genesis 17:6, 16). In 1 Samuel, we meet Israel's first king: Saul.

1 Samuel 9-11 lists all the positive qualities of Saul. He was tall, handsome, and strong. He was diligent: he kept searching for his father's donkeys long after others might have given up. He started off with an awareness of his weakness (when chosen as king, he was hiding in the baggage). As the brand-new leader of the nation, he took effective action—the Ammonites besieged an Israelite city, and Saul got the entire nation of Israel up and moving in response. He defeated the Ammonites in battle and was affirmed as king by all the people.

Despite all these good points, Saul was not faithful to God's covenant. In 1 Samuel 13, he presumed to act as priest because he was afraid to wait until Samuel showed up to offer sacrifices, since he perceived that his soldiers were becoming impatient. Later, when God commanded him to destroy all that he took when he conquered the accursed Amalekites, he kept out the best. Samuel confronted him about it, and he said he was saving it for a sacrifice. Samuel replied:

> Has the LORD as great delight in burnt offerings and sacrifices, as in obeying the voice of the LORD? Behold, to obey is better than sacrifice, and to listen than the fat of rams. For rebellion is as the sin of divination, and presumption is as iniquity and idolatry. Because you have rejected the word of the LORD, he has also rejected you from being king. (1 Samuel 15:22-23 ESV)

For the rest of Saul's life, he would live under the cloud of God's judgment.

Ultimately, Saul was badly wounded in a hard-fought battle with the Philistines, and ended by committing suicide rather than be mutilated by the enemy.

David

Let's turn our attention to Israel's second king, David: the shepherd boy who fought the giant and became the Shepherd of Israel, God's anointed.

1 Samuel 16 tells how the prophet Samuel anointed David to be king. David's anointing foreshadowed Jesus in another way. The Hebrew word for "anoint" is "mashach," from which we get the word "Messiah." The Greek word for "the anointed one" is "Christ." David was the ancestor of Jesus, and his life foreshadowed Jesus' coming as the ultimate "anointed one." In this story, we see how God chose and anointed David to be king many years before the people accepted him. God also planned for Jesus' rule long before His coming.

The Heart of the King—Contrasting David and Saul

We've mentioned that David and Saul can be viewed in contrast. Let's explore why David was a man after God's own heart and Saul was not. Both led God's people and both were sinners.

The differences are clear. Saul was presumptuous and careless about obeying God. He didn't truly fear God. David did fear God and trusted Him, time after time. David's first priority was clearly for God's glory, not his own. Even when David sinned, his heart was soft. He loved God, even though his flesh got him into trouble.

Saul's sins revealed his heart attitudes. Saul seemed to consistently be seeking, in anxious, faithless, self-reliant ways, to know what God would do. Whether by legitimate means (through the prophet Samuel and other prophets, dreams, etc.) or by forbidden means (offering his own sacrifice and consulting the witch of Endor), Saul fruitlessly sought a means to his own ends. Saul was unquiet; he would not wait for God's work done God's way in God's time.

David is a sharp contrast for Saul: though living in the same hard times and hunted by his own king, he consistently rejected chances to do things his way or in his time. David seldom showed the same impatient fear that Saul consistently displayed. The Psalms show how David cried out to God in troubled trust, rather than in anxious demand.

David the Refugee

During Saul's reign, David tried to be a loyal subject, but his jealous king drove him out of Israel. David lived like Robin Hood, with a band of men in the desert land to the south of Judah. Time after time, Saul tried to catch him and kill him. But David repeatedly demonstrated his reverence for Saul, the Lord's anointed, even when it was in David's power to harm Saul.

1 Samuel tells us that David eventually decided Israel wasn't big enough for both him and Saul, so he fled with two of his wives and his men into Philistine territory, where he pretended to serve Achish, the king of Gath, as a mercenary (hired soldier). This is ironic, considering that the giant Goliath was from Gath!

We've seen how the Philistines had a monopoly on iron weapons. David's time in Philistine territory may have given him an opportunity to arm his men and learn new tactics. The problem, of course, was that Achish expected David to fight with him against the Israelites. David deceived Achish by attacking the other people groups that still remained in the south of Israel—pagans like the Amalakites. God had ordered the Israelites to utterly eradicate these people from the Promised Land. David made sure to leave no survivors. When David came back from such raids with booty, he lied and told the Achish that he had attacked some Israelite city—and there were no witnesses to contradict him.

Achish thus believed that David had betrayed his own people, so they weren't worried about him becoming the Israelites' new leader. In fact, Achish wanted to take David with him for the final battle with Saul, but the other Philistine kings were more cautious. David wasn't there the day the Philistines killed Saul and his sons, but he wept at the news of their deaths.

David Becomes King

After Saul's death, David wasn't instantly accepted as king by all of Israel. David's own tribe of Judah welcomed him and made him their king in Hebron, but the other eleven tribes followed the one surviving son of Saul. The Bible tells us that there was a long war between the house of Saul and the house of David. After Saul's son Ishbosheth died, the other tribes of Israel rallied around David. They came to David at Hebron to make him their king, too. Finally, David was in a position to lead all of Israel. He took swift and effective action.

David's Accomplishments

His first dramatic act was to conquer Jerusalem, a stronghold of the Jebusites. Joshua had conquered this city in the first wave of the Israelite invasion, but the Jebusites had taken it back and held it for centuries. Jerusalem was a walled city set on a high mountaintop. It seemed impregnable—the Jebusites thought they could hold it forever. However, David sent his warriors in through a water shaft under the walls, conquered it, and made the city his capital.

David's next act was to establish good relations with a friendly neighbor. Hiram, King of Tyre, was a Phoenician who saw an opportunity to trade. He sent David cedar trees and carpenters to build his new palace, which was the beginning of a long and mutually beneficial relationship.

The Philistines were not happy about these new developments. They came out in force to deal with David. Twice they mustered their troops in the Valley of Rephaim. Twice David defeated them there, relying on the Lord's direction and ending immediate threats from the Philistines.

The Ark of the Covenant

With a new capital, helpful alliances, and a cease-fire, David turned to a matter near and dear to his heart. He wanted to bring the Ark of the Covenant to Jerusalem. It had been captured by the Philistines, then returned, but it had been abandoned ever since. David took an ox-cart down to bring it up to his city. As the cart grew unsteady because of mud at one point, one of the priests, Uzzah, reached out his hand to steady the Ark on its cart. God struck Uzzah dead in an instant. That stopped David in his tracks. David was angry that God killed Uzzah. After all, Uzzah was trying to do a good thing!

The problem is, God is holy, and we are not. Moses had clearly instructed the priests to carry the Ark by hand, and on special poles, according to God's specific commandment. Putting the Ark on an ox-cart was convenient, but it fell short of God's standard of holiness.

The ark might have stayed where it was, but God showered His favor on the man who volunteered to keep it. David recovered his temper and tried again. This time, the priests carried the Ark as God had commanded, and David offered an animal sacrifice every six steps. The Ark reached Jerusalem, the place where God had chosen for His name to dwell.

Getting the Ark to Jerusalem was just the start, though. David wanted to build a house for his God. Here he was, living in a palace lined with Phoenician cedar, while the Ark of the Covenant sat out in a tent. However, God held him back. 2 Samuel 7:11-14 relates His words to David:

> … the Lord will make you a house. When your days are fulfilled and you lie down with your fathers, I will raise up your offspring after you, who shall come from your body, and I will establish his kingdom. He shall build a house for my name, and I will establish the throne of his kingdom forever. I will be to him a father, and he shall be to me a son.

This was God's covenant with David—as unbreakable as His covenant with Abraham, so many centuries before. Just as God called Abraham out of Ur and then confirmed it years later, so He anointed David and then made His eternal covenant with him.

David's Sinful Choices

David was an amazing man, but he wasn't perfect. He had several less-than-shining moments. Perhaps the best-known story relates how David sinned with Bathsheba and the terrible consequences that resulted. 1 Samuel 11-12 tells the whole sad story of David's sin and of his repentance. David coveted his neighbor's wife, committed adultery, and then lied and murdered to conceal it.

When confronted with his sin, though, he sincerely repented. He confessed his sin instead of covering it up, mourned for it, pled for God's forgiveness, and threw himself upon His mercy. After God rendered His judgment, David accepted the consequences. God forgave David, but his sin had lasting consequences.

Solomon

David's son, Solomon, became king next, and under his rule, Israel reached the height of its power. Solomon's name comes from the Hebrew word *shalom*, which means "peace." His reign was peaceful, and God allowed him to build the great Temple in Jerusalem—the one his father David had planned.

Solomon began with humility and the fear of the Lord, but he grew proud and self-reliant over time. His reign was successful by worldly standards, but he was a failure in God's eyes. How could a man who started off so right wind up so wrong?

His Situation

Solomon almost didn't become king because his brother, Adonijah, tried to seize the throne. Some of David's top advisors had been ready to help Adonijah seize the throne just before Solomon was crowned. Just in time, David heard of the plot from Bathsheba and had Solomon crowned king instead. Soon after that, David died.

This left Solomon on pretty shaky ground. His father had been a mighty warrior who had had a lot of wives. That meant there were plenty of other princes who could challenge his right to rule—and they did! Solomon was vulnerable, and he knew it. Perhaps that's why he offered 1,000 sacrifices to God at one time, early in his reign. 1 Kings 3 tells how the Lord appeared to Solomon in a dream by night, and said, "Ask what I shall give you." Solomon asked for wisdom to rule his people, and God gave him that and more!

His Empire

Let's put Solomon into historical context. Moses and Joshua lived four or five hundred years earlier, around the end of the Bronze Age. By David's time, Egypt was a major power, which is why Solomon married one of Pharaoh's daughters. It was a shrewd political alliance.

Solomon was an enormously effective king—he single-handedly transformed Israel from a farming society with a very limited government into one vast government bureaucracy. When we studied Saul, we heard Samuel say a king in Israel would be more trouble than he was worth. Solomon proved just how prophetic Samuel was!

He set up twelve overseers in the land to keep everything under control. He had 40,000 horses and 12,000 chariots. His vast court consumed nearly two thousand bushels of flour and meal every day—not to mention 30 cows a day, 100 sheep, and more. He drafted 30,000 Israelite men to work for him at his building projects in monthly shifts, 10,000 at a time. He enslaved 150,000 Canaanites in the land who had managed to survive since the time of Israel's original conquest under Joshua. Solomon's most famous building project was the Temple. The Temple was beautiful and incredibly expensive—it was literally covered with gold.

At the height of his power, Solomon's trade empire extended amazing distances. We aren't really sure about all the place names in the Bible, but it's clear that he built a fleet in the Red Sea that traded with countries bordering the Indian Ocean.

Critiquing Solomon

Your child needs to know about Solomon's prayerful beginnings, his glorious reign, and the beautiful Temple he built. However, Solomon started well, but ended badly. When he was weak and afraid, he turned to God. When he grew stronger, he was more interested in pleasing others than he was in pleasing God.

Solomon was a man of peace who built his empire with alliances (sealed through royal marriages) instead of with warfare. This helps explain why Solomon married so often: he had 700 wives and 300 concubines. However, this way of gaining peace cost Solomon more than war might have. The Bible says that his heart was turned to idolatry through his foreign wives.

In Solomon's life we see an echo of the pattern we saw over and over again in Judges and see in the world around us. He turned to God in his weakness and God answered him, and met his need. He received blessings and become prosperous. He began to rely on his own strength instead of God and started to compromise. God let him go his own way, and he discovered how weak he really was all over again. This pattern repeats itself with men and nations.

As your child considers the glory of Solomon's reign, remember that Solomon himself said in Ecclesiastes 1:2, "Vanity of vanities! All is vanity!" All of Solomon's glory—including his beautiful Temple—was in vain. Sadly, this is the always the verdict when God does not dwell in our hearts as well as our temples.

Phoenicia

As we conclude this mini-unit, let's start to turn our eyes away from Israel. Other empires would rise and fall across Mesopotamia as God prepared the world for the fullness of time, when He would reveal His answer to human sin and evil. One of these empires was an ally of Israel—Phoenicia.

History

Phoenicia was on the coastal road from Egypt to Mesopotamia, so it picked up a lot from those ancient empires. Egypt was one of its first trading partners—as far back as 2500 BC, Egyptians were importing cedars from Lebanon. A thousand years later, Phoenicia became an Egyptian province, and the two cultures mixed for a century. The Egyptians began worshipping some Phoenician idols, and the Phoenicians picked up ideas from Egypt.

Babylon had a big impact on Phoenicia, too. The Phoenicians were writing in Babylonian cuneiform by 1300 BC and used Babylonian seals for their documents. The Hittite Empire expanded to include Phoenicia briefly, around 1200 BC, but then collapsed, leaving the Phoenicians on their own.

Trading around the Mediterranean

The Phoenicians became an increasingly powerful force in the Mediterranean world. They were seafaring traders who established colonies around the Mediterranean. Their trading network was so extensive that later historians have called the Mediterranean at this time a "Phoenician lake." They grew to be a world power by the time of Roman dominion. The Latin word for Phoenician is "punic." Ultimately, there would be three great Punic wars between Rome and the Phoenician-founded city of Carthage, which started as one of their trading posts and grew very wealthy and influential over the centuries.

Here follows a quick run-down on Phoenician colonies you might know. Many of them were simple ports of call, but others grew to be major cities.

Hiram, king of Tyre, formed a trading company with the kings of Israel—first with David and then with Solomon. Near that time, Tyre planted a colony on the coast of Africa called Utica. The tin and silver mines of Spain were important points of call for Phoenician traders, who may have settled Cadiz in Spain. Cartagena, Spain, was originally named "Cartago Nova," meaning New Carthage, a Phoenician colony. Phoenicians established trading posts on the Italian peninsula and French mainland at places like Genoa and Marseille. They were influential on many of the islands of the Mediterranean: they had ports on the major Italian islands of Sicily, Corsica, and Sardinia. There is also evidence of Phoenician settlements on Cyprus, Malta, and the Balearic islands.

The Phoenicians weren't limited to the Mediterranean Sea. They went through the Strait of Gibraltar and traded along the Atlantic coasts of Africa. The Greek historian Herodotus says that Phoenicians sailed around the bottom Africa in the 600s BC, some 2,000 years before the Portuguese repeated that feat in 1497 AD. Phoenicians went up the Atlantic coast of Europe, too, and may have mined for tin in Cornwall, in southwestern Britain.

This is not to say that Phoenicians really colonized these places. Their settlements were mostly trading posts, not real cities. The Phoenicians were interested in going places and trading things, not in settling down and digging in. The Greeks, by contrast, who also colonized significant regions of Mediterranean lands, tended to leave home when they ran out of farmland. Their overseas colonies typically grew into substantial new cities.

Technology

Phoenicians were famous for their technologies. They blew glass, made purple dye, and, of course, had sailing ships that criss-crossed the Mediterranean. The dye was made by crushing snails, and their cloth was so precious (expensive) that purple has been the color of royalty ever since. The Greek word for purple, "phoinix," was the basis for the word that foreigners called the area where they lived—Phoenicia. Today, this is modern Lebanon and the coastal regions of Israel.

Our alphabet came from Phoenicia. They scratched out primitive alphas and betas possibly in the city of Byblos, which came to mean "book" and gave us the word "Bible." The Greek and Latin alphabets are derived from Phoenician symbols. So was Hebrew, originally—the Hebrew alphabet started as a form of Phoenician writing, but they changed their alphabet when the Babylonians conquered Israel.

Conclusion

David was an amazing man—and God's covenant with David was even more amazing. David represents the ideal of a king who fears God and leads a people to do things they could never accomplish on their own. His story also demonstrates that a king is not above the law—when David sinned, there were real consequences. The Bible's account of David is that though he was a sinner, he was a man after God's own heart, and God's lovingkindness never abandoned him. Indeed, his name means "beloved."

As we consider Saul, David, and Solomon, we see how important it is to keep watch on our own hearts, especially in light of the pattern of peace, prosperity, wandering, and judgment that we see throughout Israel's history. The root cause of the problem is that our hearts are prone to seek good outside of God. Like us, Saul, David, and Solomon needed their hearts to be changed, and that is what God always planned to make possible.

MINI-UNIT 2: TABERNACLE AND TEMPLE

TAPESTRY OF GRACE PRIMER GUIDEBOOK

Mini-Unit 3: Daniel's Revelation

We will learn about ancient empires that God used to accomplish His purposes and advance His plan of redemption. Note how our seven main "characters" fit in.

The Author	God judged His people and sent them into exile (but did not forsake them) in Babylon. God showed His power and authority in the palace of the Emperor. It was foretold that God's plan was for Babylonian, Persian, Greek, and Roman empires to rise and rule the world.
People	Nebuchadnezzar conquered Jerusalem, taking Daniel into captivity. The Babylonians were conquered by the Persians. Cyrus the Persian sent the Jews home. Esther saved her people. The Greek civilization developed on the Ionian Peninsula as a loosely connected alliance of city-states who defended themselves against the full might of the Persian Empire.
Good	Daniel obeyed God in the midst of a pagan culture. He trusted God, served well, and prospered. Daniel, his friends, Esther, Ezra, and Nehemiah obeyed God, even at the risk of their lives. In contrast, we learn about the Greeks, who defined good using myths and morals, mixed with a belief in a dooming Fate. Aesop captured Greek morality in his fables.
Evil	Nebuchadnezzar's pride led to his humiliation. Jealous Persian presidents tried to trap Daniel and were destroyed. Haman tried to destroy the Jews and fell into his own trap. Ezra and Nehemiah were attacked by the jealous people around him and by the selfishness of their own people. The Persians tried to enslave the Greeks and were defeated.
The Word	Jeremiah's letter to the exiles, Isaiah, and Nebuchanezzar's dream show that God is at work in the events of history. The revelation of the statue with the head of gold, chest and arms of silver, belly and thighs of bronze, legs of iron, and feet of iron and clay are central. God's plan for empires was to establish a kingdom not made by human hands. The promise of redemption would soon be fulfilled.
God's Creation	Persians ruled a sprawling empire that spread from Africa to India, yet they were defeated by the Greeks, who were kept safe from Persian invasion by mountains and seas. Geography defined and isolated the Greek city-states and played a major role in the defense of Greece.
Man's Creation	Persians developed an effective bureaucracy and a network of roads to communicate across 127 provinces, joined by the Royal Road. The Greeks used relied on well-armed, disciplined citizen-soldiers to hold back the invading Persians. They were saved by the "wall of wood" (their ships) at the battle of Salamis.

Mini-Unit 3 Overview
Daniel's Revelation

Introduction

Welcome to a new mini-unit! We have a lot to cover in the next three topics, and Nebuchadnezzar's dream of the statue that is smashed by a rock will be an image that we keep revisiting. Through this dream and Daniel's prophetic interpretation of it, we learn that God has planned each event in history and is the ultimate authority over all rulers. In this mini-unit, empires rise and fall as the world is prepared for Christ's Kingdom, which will never end.

Our story resumes on a melancholy note. After Solomon's rule, his kingdom was divided into north and south. The Northern Kingdom, which included the majority of tribes and territory, was known as Israel and had Samaria as its capital. From the inception of this kingdom, apostasy was rampant. The Lord was patient with them for centuries, but eventually the Northern Kingdom was conquered by the Assyrians, who were brutal conquerors. They habitually sought to subdue new domains by relocating entire people groups. Israel's ten tribes were permanently scattered in exile around the Mediterranean Sea and Asia Minor, while the Assyrians imported a genetically mixed multitude of Middle Eastern people from Babylon, Cuthah, Avva, Hamath, and Sepharvaim (2 Kings 17:24). These tribes were put in the cities of Samaria instead of the people of Israel, and became the Samaritans whom Jesus famously interacts with in the New Testament.

The Southern Kingdom (called Judah, with Jerusalem as its capital) lasted a bit longer than its northern counterpart. Judah experienced times of revival, and had some outstanding kings who led in righteousness. Furthermore, though there were coups that changed the genetic dynasties of the Northern Kingdom, the Southern Kingdom's line of kings from David was unbroken. However, despite warnings through prophets and periodic revivals, the overall reality was that God's people needed more than the Law and the prophets—they needed God's Spirit to reside in their hearts. As they were, they were unable to remain faithful, and they grew in rebellious apostasy, as had their northern brethren.

Our story for this mini-unit (and your child) resumes at the point where God's righteous judgment of Judah's continued rebellion, evil, and sin has come to fruition. God sent Babylon to conquer and demolish Jerusalem. Like the Assyrians, the Babylonians deported conquered people groups, so God's people were taken into captivity in the capital city of the empire, where they would remain for seventy years.

Eventually, in accordance with God's promise, a remnant of Israelites from Judah returned to Jerusalem to build a pitifully small replacement temple on the site where Solomon's golden and grand temple had once stood. The older refugees, who had known the original Temple, wept at how small the new one was, while all the younger folks cheered because they had a temple again.

As we follow the Israelites through this part of the story, empires rise and fall around them. This is another unit where it really pays to take a long, hard look at maps. We'll be covering territories from Spain to India and back. Before we go further, let's remember the story of Nebuchadnezzar's dream, which Daniel interpreted for him in a Spirit-granted prophecy.

In Daniel Chapter 2, Nebuchadnezzar dreams of an enormous statue. The king saw a great statue with a golden head, a silver torso, a bronze belly, legs of iron, and feet of iron mixed with clay. God told Daniel both the dream and the interpretation of the dream.

The head of gold was the Babylonian empire. The torso of silver was the next empire that would follow—the Persians. The belly of bronze and the legs of iron were empires, too—and all of them were brought down in an instant by a rock not cut by human hands, which ground them all to powder and then grew into a mountain that filled the earth.

In the Bible, we learn that God granted the Apostle John a vision of the end times in the Book of Revelation. Although we may have different interpretations of the Book of Revelation, it is clear to all who read it that God has a planned, settled, orderly purpose for the future. We know that God's authority will determine each phase in order. For Daniel, Nebuchadnezzar's dream must have seemed like the Book of Revelation does to us. It foretold God's good plan.

Babylon: The Head of Gold

As we said, the Northern Kingdom of Israel had been defeated previously by the Assyrian Empire, who scattered the Israelites around the Mediterranean and across Asia Minor. Before this, God had sent the prophet Jonah to the Assyrian capital of Nineveh to warn them of their sins and invite them to repent. (This would have been like God sending one man into Munich during Hitler's ascendency to tell the Nazis to repent!) Shockingly, the Ninevites listened to Jonah's warning, but the repentance must have been brief, because after they had done God's will in judging the Northern Kingdom, the Assyrians fell suddenly (and surprisingly) to the Babylonians.

The Babylonians crushed the Assyrians—and Judah, too. They demolished Jerusalem, deporting most of its population in a series of removals. We know a lot about the Jewish experience in the Babylonian Captivity—the prophets Jeremiah and Ezekiel spoke God's words to God's people during this terrible time, explaining why things were happening and giving hope for the future.

The Babylonians seized the prophet Daniel when he was only a boy and took him off to learn their language and literature in one of the earliest deportation waves. Everybody loves the Bible stories about Daniel and his friends, Shadrach, Meshach, and Abednego, who were true to the Lord despite serious trials and temptations!

Daniel served in the courts of the Babylonian kings. The Book of Daniel describes the rule of several powerful Babylonian rulers, especially those of Nebuchanezzar and Belshazzar. Through Daniel's eyes, we learn something about what life was like in Babylon, a great city that was home to one of the wonders of the Ancient World: the famous Hanging Gardens of Babylon.

In Daniel 5, we read of God's continued revelation of His authority. The handwriting was on the wall for Babylon (literally). As Belshazzar threw a drunken revelry for his lords, his wives, and his concubines using the holy silver and gold vessels that had been taken from Solomon's Temple by Nebuchadnezzar, fingers of a human hand appeared and wrote "Mene, Mene, Tekel, Upharsin." The king was greatly alarmed at the vision, and even more so when none of his magicians and enchanters could tell him what it meant.

Then the queen advised the king to call Daniel, who gave the correct interpretation. God had numbered the days of Babylon and brought them to an end. The Babylonians, in all their glory, were weighed on a scale and found wanting. Their kingdom was to be divided and given to the Medes and the Persians. That very night, Belshazzar the Chaldean king was killed, and Darius the Mede received the kingdom.

Persia: The Torso of Silver

Daniel served the kings of Babylon and now he served the king of Persia, too, but things didn't start off smoothly when the Persians took over. Daniel's rivals at court set him up—they persuaded the new king to make a new law that said everybody had to pray to the king, and only the king, or be thrown into the den of lions. That's the way it was with the laws of the Medes and the Persians—Queen Esther ran into the same problem when evil Haman persuaded her husband, King Xerxes of Persia, to pass a law allowing everybody to kill Jews for a day. But though Daniel was thrown into that pit, God saved Daniel, and He saved Esther and the entire Jewish nation, too!

The Persians conquered east into India, and south and west as far as Ethiopia. Assyria and Babylon had risen in their day, but then had fallen relatively quickly. Persia, by contrast, lasted a long, long time. Be sure to take a look at a map and imagine the size of this empire and the challenges of administration it faced in ancient times.

The modern nation of Iran is what is left of the Persian Empire, more than two thousand years later. The Persians were effective administrators and built a network of roads across their empire that enabled them to communicate quickly. They also understood delegation of authority, and they formed provinces with governors who reported to the king. The Persians also allowed many cultures to maintain local autonomy under the ultimate authority of the Persian Emperor. The Persian army was vast, but it was mostly made up of forced conscripts from across the empire.

With massive territorial holdings in Asia and Africa, the Persians pushed west and got as far as modern Turkey, where they bumped into the Greeks, just across the thin body of water called the Hellespont that separates Asia from Europe. The Persians didn't think that these tiny, squabbling city-states of Greece could possibly take on a mighty empire with 127 provinces. But the Greeks were too fiercely independent to surrender to Persian rule without a fight. The Persians invaded Greece repeatedly—and ultimately lost!

Greece: The Belly of Bronze

Who were the Greeks, and how were they able to withstand the onslaught of the Persians? We will learn about the Greeks to understand who they were and what happened when they met the Persians. As background for you, here's some basic information.

There were four Greek cultures that developed during the Bronze Age. Eventually, these combined and re-combined to give rise to individual and isolated Greek city states on the hilly, poor-soiled lands of the Balkan Peninsula up into Macedonia. Related Ionian Greeks colonized the eastern shores of the Aegean Sea (on the coast of modern Turkey). It was here that the famed Trojan wars were fought. These colonies eventually came into contact with the Persian Empire.

The geography of Greece played a major role in shaping the Greek identity. Mountains and seas carved Grecian populations into small, relatively isolated pockets. In these limited spaces, the Greeks developed free and independent city-states that shared trade, a common language, and many religious traditions with their neighbors. But, these city states also had their own local deities, and their own (often very different) approaches to daily life and government.

As the Persians and the Greeks clashed, the Persians learned that small groups of free, motivated, well-armed warriors could defeat masses of conscripted slaves. For this mini-unit, we end with the defeat of the Persians in what became known to the Greeks as the Persian Wars. It's an exciting story that your child should really find interesting! In the next mini-unit, we will learn about the Golden Age of Greece, and later, how one Greek general defeated the mighty Persians and carved out of their ruin an empire of his own—for ten years—and thus further prepared the world for a Savior.

Mini-Unit 3, Topic 1
Babylon: The Head of Gold

Introduction

This is another exciting week for students! A lot of threads come together this week. Way back in Genesis 11, Abram left "Ur of the Chaldees" to begin a life of wandering. In our story this week, we learn that those same Chaldeans conquered the city of Babylon, grew, and then conquered the hitherto invincible Assyrian empire, eventually leveling Jerusalem. In many ways, they were the head of gold.

Assyria and the Babylonians

Babylon comes back into the Bible story during the time when the Assyrians wiped out the Northern Kingdom of Israel. 2 Kings 17:24 tells us that the king of Assyria brought people from Babylon, among other places, to repopulate the cities of Samaria (northern Israel). At that point, Babylon was nothing to write home about: it was one more victim of Assyrian power, just like everybody else in the region.

God raised up the Assyrians to do His will, and then He put them down. The invincible Assyrian armies had been held off by Hezekiah's ragtag Hebrew army—and driven off by an angel that killed 185,000 of their soldiers in one night. After the Assyrians left Jerusalem, the city of Babylon sent envoys to celebrate Hezekiah's success. In II Kings 20, we are told that Hezekiah showed everything he had to these visitors. The prophet Isaiah heard about it, and said,

'Behold, the days are coming, when all that is in your house... shall be carried to Babylon. Nothing shall be left, says the Lord.' Hezekiah said, 'The word of the Lord is good.' For he thought, 'Why not, if there will be peace and security in my days?'

Hezekiah couldn't imagine how a third-rate power like Babylon could be a threat anytime soon. But the Middle East at this time was very unstable. At one moment, Assyria was the world's greatest empire. Then, in the blink of a historical eye, it was gone, and Babylon took over. The peace that Hezekiah dreamed of didn't last long after his death!

Neo-Babylonians

Who were these Babylonians, then, who wiped out the mighty Assyrians? Historians refer to these new conquerors as the Neo-Babylonians, or Chaldeans. Chaldea was a region south of the city of Babylon, near the shores of the Persian Gulf. Over time, the Chaldeans took over Babylon, merging the populations, and then took on Assyria.

In Abraham's day, a thousand years before the period we are now studying, Babylon had been a major city in the land between the Tigris and Euphrates rivers. Scholars call that the Fertile Crescent and often deem it the Cradle of Civilization—that's where the Bible says the first cities were after the Flood. Remember the Tower of Babel in Genesis 11?

There were about four hundred years from Abraham to Moses. Another four hundred years passed again before David took the throne. Now, after a few more centuries, the Babylonians knocked David's descendants off that throne. Here is the sequence of events:

1. God called Abraham out of Ur of the Chaldeans.
2. God led Moses out of Egypt and led Joshua into the Promised Land.
3. God established David as the king of all Israel in Jerusalem.
4. God sent the Babylonians to enslave Judah and destroy Jerusalem.

Babylon rebelled against Assyrian rule in 626 BC. Fourteen years later, the Babylonians teamed up with the Medes, who live in modern-day Iran. Their combined forces sacked Nineveh, the capital of Assyria. After conquering the Assyrians, the Neo-Babylonian Empire was huge, but it was short-lived. Within another generation, the Medes and Persians sacked Babylon and seized its empire virtually intact.

While in power, the Babylonians annihilated Jerusalem—but not all at once. There were three separate waves. The first was in the time of King Jehoiachin, around 597 BC. In that first defeat of Jerusalem, the Babylonians took much of the treasure from the Temple and deported more than 3,000 of the upper-class, leading citizens.

Judah agreed to pay tribute, but formed an alliance with Egypt and tried to revolt eleven years later. This time, the Babylonians razed the city and deported more people. Finally, five years later, the last and poorest of the people were deported. The prophet Jeremiah tells how the ones who weren't carried off to Babylon fled to Egypt out of fear, only to die there.

Jeremiah

Jeremiah was the only prophet of the time who was not deported in the first or second waves. He was an eyewitness to the whole tragedy and wrote the book of the Bible that bears his name, plus another, shorter book that is heartbreaking—the Book of Lamentations. Tradition has it that he died in Egypt, where he went with the last of the exiles after warning them against such flight.

Lamentations is tragic, but beautiful. It is short—only five chapters—and well worth reading aloud. Chapter 3 is particularly powerful, because after detailing great pain and sorrow and feelings of being both abandoned and attacked by God, the speaker declares:

> But this I call to mind, and therefore I have hope:
> The steadfast love of the Lord never ceases;
> His mercies never come to an end;
> They are new every morning;
> Great is your faithfulness.

God's people had plenty of opportunities to see His faithfulness and steadfast mercy at work as God worked out His plan for the exiles of the Babylonian captivity.

Daniel

Daniel was just a youth when he was caught up in the first wave of deportation. The King of Babylon was looking for intelligent and healthy young men like Daniel to learn the literature and language of the Chaldeans, which was similar to Hebrew. (This makes sense when we remember that the area of Chaldea was where Abraham originally came from! In fact, several chapters of the Old Testament are actually written in Chaldean Aramaic.)

Nevertheless, there was a lot for Daniel to learn. The Chaldeans were famous astrologers. In Daniel 2, King Nebuchadnezzar had a very bad dream, so he called for "the magicians, the enchanters, the sorcerers, and the Chaldeans." Then the Chaldeans said to the king in Aramaic, "O king, live forever! Tell your servants the dream, and we will show the interpretation."

But Nebuchadnezzar wouldn't tell. The ancients believed that dreams were messages from the gods, and this one dream concerned Nebuchadnezzar enough that he wanted to make sure he got the message right. Rather than have people around him tell him what he wanted to hear, he wanted them to tell him the dream first, so he would have a reason to believe their interpretation. When they couldn't, he was going to kill all the wise men of Babylon—until Daniel stepped up. God revealed the dream to Daniel, and Daniel told the king what it meant.

As you know from this mini-unit's introduction, Nebuchadnezzar had dreamed of a great figure with a head of gold, a torso of silver, a belly of bronze, and legs of iron. Its feet were made of iron mixed with brittle clay—until a stone that was cut by no human hand struck it on the feet and ground the whole statue to powder. That stone then became a mountain that filled the earth. Daniel told the king that the statue represented the empires of the earth: Babylon was the head of gold, and the empires that would follow were the torso of silver, the belly of bronze, etc.

Conclusion

Nebuchadnezzar's dream is the script for the rest of this mini-unit and part of the next. We've started on a roller coaster ride of empires that rise and fall—but the next major phase of our study ends with the coming of a Kingdom that is not of this world, and a King who rules forever.

A stone is coming that will cause many to stumble—and empires to fall—and it grinds the powers of this world to powder. It is awesome to realize that we are part of Nebuchadnezzar's dream. Your family is part of the mountain that is filling the earth!

This is a good opportunity to pause so that we can appreciate God's sovereignty over all things. It is quite easy for us to look back with the perspective of history and marvel over the specific prophecies that God gave to Daniel and Jeremiah. God revealed His plan to them through His words. With hindsight, we can now connect the dots of Daniel's revelation and see that the steadfast love of the Lord never failed and that His mercies never came to an end. We can see God's goodness to His people, even when they were under the authority of conquerors who worshiped idols, demons, power, and wealth. As we look back on this chapter of history, it is good to remember that God has made unfulfilled promises to us. How are we at trusting that God will undertake to guide the future as well as He has the past?

Mini-Unit 3, Topic 2
Persia: The Torso of Silver

Introduction

This week, we leave Babylon behind and turn to the torso of silver from Daniel's revelation: the empire of the Medes and Persians. The Assyrian and Neo-Babylonian empires rose and fell and vanished away. Nineveh and Babylon are ruins in the sands of Iraq.

Persia, by contrast, has never really gone away. The Persians have been defeated in battle and their empire has been taken over now and then, but descendants of the people we will study this week are still making headlines in the twenty-first century. God described the Persians to Daniel as the chest and arms of silver. The Persian Empire was the heart of the Ancient World for a time, with arms that stretched from India to Africa.

We will take a look at daily life in the Persian Empire through the eyes of God's people who were in exile—especially Daniel and Esther.

Conquest of the Babylonians

The city of Babylon fell to the Medes and Persians in a single night, and with it, the entire Babylonian Empire. The book of Daniel tells how the last Babylonian king, Belshazzar, made a great feast for a thousand of his lords.

> Belshazzar, when he tasted the wine, commanded that the vessels of gold and of silver that Nebuchadnezzar his father had taken out of the temple in Jerusalem be brought, that the king and his lords, his wives, and his concubines might drink from them. Then they brought in the golden vessels that had been taken out of the temple, the house of God in Jerusalem, and the king and his lords, his wives, and his concubines drank from them. They drank wine and praised the gods of gold and silver, bronze, iron, wood, and stone. Immediately the fingers of a human hand appeared and wrote on the plaster of the wall of the king's palace opposite the lampstand. And the king saw the hand as it wrote. (Daniel 5:2-5)

They brought in Daniel, who had served Belshazzar's father. Daniel said,

> O king, the Most High God gave Nebuchadnezzar your father kingship and greatness and glory and majesty. And because of the greatness that he gave him, all peoples, nations, and languages trembled and feared before him. Whom he would, he killed, and whom he would, he kept alive; whom he would, he raised up, and whom he would, he humbled. But when his heart was lifted up and his spirit was hardened so that he dealt proudly, he was brought down from his kingly throne, and his glory was taken from him. He was driven from among the children of mankind, and his mind was made like that of a beast, and his dwelling was with the wild donkeys. He was fed grass like an ox, and his body was wet with the dew of heaven, until he knew that the Most High God rules the kingdom of mankind and sets over it whom he will. And you his son, Belshazzar, have not humbled your heart, though you knew all this, but you have lifted up yourself against the Lord of heaven. And the vessels of his house have been brought in before you, and you and your lords, your wives, and your concubines have drunk wine from them. And you have praised the gods of silver and gold, of bronze, iron, wood, and stone, which do not see or hear or know, but the God in whose hand is your breath, and whose are all your ways, you have not honored. (Daniel 5:18-23)

The words on the wall were: "mene, mene, tekel, upharsin." If you knew Babylonian, you'd recognize those as the names of common coins. It's like saying "nickels, nickels, dimes, and quarters." But words can have multiple meanings—"quarter" means a fourth of a dollar, but "to quarter" means to cut something into fourths. In the same way, the words "mene," "tekel," and "upharsin" meant something more to the Babylonians.

Here's how Daniel spelled it out for King Belshazzar:

- ☐ Mene: God has numbered the days of your kingdom and brought it to an end.
- ☐ Tekel: You have been weighed in the balances and found wanting.
- ☐ Upharsin: Your kingdom is divided and given to the Medes and Persians.

And so it was: that very night, Belshazzar the Chaldean king of the Neo-Babylonian Empire was killed.

Medes and Persians

All these ancient empires may look a lot alike to us today, but there was quite the contrast between the Babylonians and the Persians. For the Jewish people, the difference couldn't have been bigger. The Babylonians killed the last Jewish king, but the Persians made Esther their Queen. The Babylonians wiped out Jerusalem and destroyed their Temple, whereas the Persians rebuilt both. Isaiah the prophet rebuked King Hezekiah for showing the Babylonians around his city, but Isaiah 44:28 says of the Persian king Cyrus, "He is my shepherd, and he shall fulfill all my purpose'; saying of Jerusalem, 'She shall be built,' and of the temple, 'Your foundation shall be laid.'"

Ezra, Nehemiah, and Esther all tell of the favor the Jews experienced under Persian rule. There were problems, of course—the Jews were almost wiped out by an arch-enemy, Haman—but he was no match for the quiet sovereignty of God, as demonstrated in Esther's story. To this day, the Jewish people celebrate the destruction of their enemies at that time with the annual festival of Purim.

If you're looking for a good read-aloud, you can't beat the book of Esther. It's a great story! In fact, reading it aloud is part of the Purim tradition. Jewish kids love the traditions that go with it: dressing up in costumes and rattling noisemakers during the Esther play so they can drown out the word "Haman" every time his name is read. The story is easy to act out—so let your kids ham it up, whether you read it out loud or let them act it out for you. This is another great way to make these stories come alive for your student!

Daniel and Persian Administration

The Persians developed a whole new system for running empires. Whereas the Assyrians and Babylonians were ferocious warriors who were good at building empires by conquering nations, the Persians mastered the art of maintaining an empire through good administration.

In Daniel, we learn that Darius set 120 satraps (or provincial governors) over the affairs of his empire. These satraps were overseen by three high officials (or presidents), of whom Daniel served as one. Daniel excelled in this role, and the king planned to set him over the whole kingdom. Daniel 6 tells us that this was because an excellent spirit was in him. It is interesting to see how certain themes in history seem to be repeated. Can you recall another exile that rose to the stewardship of a vast empire? Joseph did— and he was also described as having the Spirit of God in him.

In Babylon, some of the other high officials did not welcome the prospect of Daniel's promotion. They manipulated the king and sought to use Daniel's faithfulness to God as a weapon against him. This is why Daniel was sent to the lions' den! But God intervened: Daniel was spared, and the men who maliciously accused Daniel suffered the fate that they had assigned to him. God did not intervene to spare them! The Persian emperor had not wanted to hurt Daniel, and at the happy turn of events, he published a decree throughout all his royal dominion giving thanks and praise to the Living God.

Darius was able to publish decrees throughout his royal dominion because of another hallmark of Persian administration. They built roads and established an amazing courier system for carrying the mail, with teams who would relay messages at record speeds. We see mention of these roads in the Bible: they enabled word of both Haman's plot to kill the Jews and of Esther and Mordecai's counter-decrees to be spread quickly throughout the entire Empire.

The Greek historian Herodotus was impressed. He wrote the famous lines, "Neither snow, nor rain, nor heat, nor gloom of night stays these couriers from the swift completion of their appointed rounds."[1] New Yorkers recognize these lines—they are carved over the entrance of the central post office there.

Persian administration wasn't limited to good communication. They had the knack of keeping their subjects loyal. Part of this was their people skills—they allowed those they dominated more latitude than had their predecessors. The Persians certainly treated the Jews well, and with good results. Cyrus the Great fulfilled Jeremiah's prophecy and allowed exiles to return to Jerusalem. Many of those who did were eager to prove themselves loyal Persian subjects.

Opposition and God's Sovereignty over Bureaucracy

The returning Israelites' neighbors, on the other hand, were eager to get them in trouble. Ezra 4 contains a letter from those neighbors to Artaxerxes the Persian king, King Darius, in Susa. It warned him that the Jews were rebuilding Jerusalem. These

---

1 United States Postal Service Motto. Accessed 10 February 2014. Retrieved from <http://about.usps.com/who-we-are/postal-history/mission-motto.pdf>.

informers told him to look in the historical records, because the Persians were strict about precedent laws. They told the king that there he would find that,

> This city is a rebellious city, hurtful to kings and provinces, and that sedition was stirred up in it from of old. That was why this city was laid waste. We make known to the king that if this city is rebuilt and its walls finished, you will then have no possession in the province Beyond the River. (Ezra 4:15-16)

Darius found that mighty kings had ruled over Jerusalem in the past. So he ordered the building to stop until he made a decree to the contrary. Despite the king's order, the prophets Haggai and Zechariah urged the Jews to rebuild the Temple. The people listened to the prophets, and went back to work on the Temple.

This enraged their enemies. They demanded, "Who gave you a decree to build this house and to finish this structure?" (Ezra 5:9)

The Jews answered,

> We are the servants of the God of heaven and earth, and we are rebuilding the house that was built many years ago, which a great king of Israel built and finished. But because our fathers had angered the God of heaven, he gave them into the hand of Nebuchadnezzar king of Babylon, the Chaldean, who destroyed this house and carried away the people to Babylonia. However, in the first year of Cyrus king of Babylon, Cyrus the king made a decree that this house of God should be rebuilt. (Ezra 5:11-13)

The Jews turned the tables on their adversaries. This time, they were the ones who asked the king to search the archives:

> Let search be made in the royal archives there in Babylon, to see whether a decree was issued by Cyrus the king for the rebuilding of this house of God in Jerusalem. (Ezra 5:17)

Then King Darius made a decree, and the search was made in Babylonia. Sure enough, they found the record. Here's what it said:

> In the first year of Cyrus the king, Cyrus the king issued a decree: Concerning the house of God at Jerusalem, let the house be rebuilt. (Ezra 6:3)

So King Darius wrote to the enemies of Jerusalem:

> Let the work on this house of God alone. Let the governor of the Jews and the elders of the Jews rebuild this house of God on its site. Moreover, I make a decree regarding what you shall do for these elders of the Jews for the

rebuilding of this house of God. The cost is to be paid to these men in full and without delay from the royal revenue, the tribute of the province from Beyond the River! ... Also I make a decree that if anyone alters this edict, a beam shall be pulled out of his house, and he shall be impaled on it, and his house shall be made a dunghill. (Ezra 6:7-8, 11)

Isn't that satisfying? Some people have trouble believing that God can do miracles—but the book of Ezra proves that God can even work them through bureaucrats!

Judaism

The new Temple was completed, but it wasn't much to look at. Ezra tells us that the when the foundations were laid, some of the people shouted for joy, while older people—who had seen Solomon's Temple—wept aloud at how small it was. Things sure were different.

The Babylonian exile changed Jewish life forever. Before the Exile, people were pretty casual about the Law of Moses. While they had a beautiful Temple, they worshipped God—or idols!—on top of every high hill. When they were free to govern themselves, they pretty much ignored God's law. It was only after God wiped out their beautiful Temple and took away their freedom that they began to be scrupulous about keeping His laws.

During the Captivity, the absence of the Temple brought synagogue worship into being. These houses of prayer were places where young Jewish boys learned to read and write in Hebrew, and where the holy Scriptures were stored and preserved. Synagogues also served as houses of prayer. But the Israelites had longed to return and rebuild their Temple so that ritual sacrifices could resume.

After their return from exile, the priest Ezra had a big influence on the process of reestablishing religious practices in Israel. He helped shape Judaism as we know it today. Under Ezra, the Jewish people finally got serious about worshipping one God and Him only. They put away their idols, preserved their racial purity and cultural isolation, and once and for all strove to live according to God's Law.

Zoroastrianism

As the Jews witnessed God's mighty acts on their behalf, and as they rededicated themselves to God, they did so amidst a culture with a very different understanding of divine power.

The Persians had a distinctive religion, Zoroastrianism, which held that there are two equally mighty gods. In this "dualistic" religion ("duo" being a word for "two"), one god is the source of everything good, while everything evil is caused by the other god. Ormuzd was their god of peace, love, and light, while Ahriman was responsible for conflict, hatred, and darkness.

Isaiah contradicts this idea. Isaiah 45:7 (ESV) says, "I am Jehovah, unrivalled: I form the light and create the dark. I make good fortune and create calamity, it is I, Jehovah, who do all this."

This is a hard word for some Christians to accept—but the alternative is dualism, which simply isn't compatible with Scripture. The Bible teaches there is one God, not two. Though there is a Devil, YHWH is the sovereign Lord of history—even the hardest parts of history.

Conclusion and the Seeds of Conflict with the Greeks

In this topic, we have learned about events that happened in the heart of the Persian Empire. In the stories of Daniel in the lions' den, Ezra, Nehemiah, and Esther, we saw both God's power and His providence on display. As you close this topic, review the different promises that God made to His people that were kept, even though they were captives and exiles outside of the Promised Land. God's steadfast love never failed, and His mercies never came to an end. When the Jews were faithless, God remained faithful.

Next topic, we'll see that the Persians were looking towards the West. As their enormous empire expanded from India to Ethiopia, the Greek cities on the coasts of Turkey blocked their pathway into Europe. At first, the Greeks submitted to Persian rule, but then Athens urged them to rebel! Who were the Greeks, why would they rebel, and what would happen when they did?

Mini-Unit 3, Topic 3
Greece: The Belly of Bronze

Introduction

It's time to meet the Greeks! This topic, we'll learn about where they came from, what their culture was like, and how they came to live in various parts of the Mediterranean world. After a bit of background, we'll learn what happened when the Greeks encountered the Persian Empire. You just can't beat the Persian Wars for action, adventure, and impact. It's great material: the enormous world-spanning empire takes on the little-bitty city-states of Greece—and the little guys won! Bronze was the toughest metal of the day, and the Greeks (the statue's belly and thighs of bronze) were nothing if not tough.

Geography

First, let's locate Greek civilizations on the world map. Just above Egypt is the Mediterranean Sea. The northeastern part of the Mediterranean is the Aegean Sea. The Aegean Sea is bounded today by modern Greece to the west, Balkan nations to the north, and modern Turkey on the east. It is home to various large and small islands as well, which were settled by ancient seafaring peoples. Several of them were centers of Aegean culture thousands of years ago.

The early Greek cultures were all seafaring people, and no wonder! The Balkan (Greek) peninsula is surrounded by the Aegean Sea to the east, the Ionian Sea to the west, and the Mediterranean to the south. God fashioned it to be a peninsula with deep bays formed by smaller outcroppings of land, so that no part of Greece is more than 85 miles from the sea, and much of it lies within sight of the water.

One important center of ancient Greek civilization was the Peloponnesus, the large peninsula with small valleys and rugged mountains and coastlines, which forms the southern part of the Balkan Peninsula. A very narrow isthmus (land bridge) joins this area to the rest of the Balkan Peninsula. (The city of Corinth was built on that isthmus.)

The Balkan Peninsula's terrain affected the development of Greek government, which in turn affected the history of the world. Most of Greece was rocky, with the fertile land limited to small valleys or along the coast. Where other great civilizations began in the fertile plains beside major rivers, the Greeks established each city-state around a fortified hill called an acropolis. Walls surrounded some cities to protect them from invaders. At the center of each city was the *agora*—an open area that served as a marketplace and meeting place. It was in these isolated city-states that very different forms of Greek government developed—democracy among them!

Geography forced the Greeks out of their comfort zones. With limited food and natural resources at home, they had to learn how to trade for what they needed. Limited room for growth also led to colonization as numbers exceeded resources. The Greeks eventually planted cities along the shores of the Mediterranean Sea and the Black Sea. Still later, major colonies were planted in southern Italy and on the island of Sicily. These latter two areas became the most successful. Indeed, this area became known as Magna Graecia—Greater Greece. But, before we learn what happened to these colonies, let's go back to consider the beginnings of Greek civilization.

Ancient Greece

The Bronze Age in the Aegean was a time of great advances in architecture, painting, and crafts. There is no written history from this time, although there are some records on clay tablets.

We know a lot about them, though, because their stories have been handed down from ancient times. Homer's great epic poems, the *Iliad* and the *Odyssey*, provide us with a great deal of detail about life in the Greek Bronze Age. (Remember, the Bronze Age is roughly around the time when David was fighting the Philistines.)

In the early days, there were four basic "flavors" of Greeks that became layered on top of each other over time. The earliest was called the Cycladic culture, which flourished on a number of islands in the Aegean Sea. The Cycladic people mostly subsisted by fishing. They grew grapes for wine and sailed around the Aegean to trade with other people. We know about them because they created pottery and carved distinctive stone figurines. After 1900 BC, however, the distinct Cycladic culture declined. What came next were the Minoan, Mycenaean, and Trojan cultures.

The Minoan Culture

The Minoan culture flourished on the island of Crete. From most artifacts and archeological findings, it seems that this was a peaceful, cultured society. They were great traders with surrounding civilizations, and they built several beautiful palaces on their roomy island. They also gave us one of the greatest of the Greek legends.

Apparently, King Minos of Crete conquered Athens, which then had to send seven maidens and seven youths every nine years as sacrifices for the Minotaur—a monster that was half-man and half-bull, and lived in a labyrinth (a maze) designed by Daedalus, then famed as the world's greatest inventor.

Things went along this way for a while, with the Minotaur eating young Athenians every nine years, until Prince Theseus, son of King Aegeus of Athens, volunteered to be one of the sacrificial victims. He told his father he would kill the Minotaur, and promised that if he succeeded, he would change the black sails of mourning into white sails to signal his success.

After several adventures (too numerous to relate here in detail), Theseus came home victorious. But in the excitement he forgot to change his black sails to white. King Aegeus was so overcome with grief that he flung himself from the cliff where he had waited and watched every day since his son departed in the ship. The sea has been called the Aegean Sea ever since.

It turns out that the story of the Minotaur had some basis in truth. In 1900, Sir Arthur Evans discovered a palace at Knossos in Crete with many underground passageways that resembles the labyrinth. We don't know if there was ever a minotaur, but the Minoans did invent the dangerous sport of "bull-dancing." Wall frescoes found at Knossos show bulls and bull-baiting games as part of their religious worship.

The Minoans laid some major foundations for later Greek civilizations. They traded with people as far away as Egypt. They developed a base ten number system and invented an undeciphered form of writing known as "Linear A."

The Minoan civilization was wiped out, possibly by a great fire or series of earthquakes, after about 1450 BC. There are no remaining traces of Minoan culture after the mid-1100s BC.

The Mycenaean Culture

The Mycenaen Greeks lived on the Greek mainland, on the Peloponnesian peninsula. Nobody knows where the Mycenaens came from, but scholars think they were the ancestors of the Greeks. Their civilization began there around 2,000 BC, and the Mycenaen culture spread as far as Athens and Thebes.

The Mycenaeans took over the ruins of the Minoan civilization (and may have caused its demise) and used Minoan architecture as a model for their palaces, building them like fortresses made of huge stone blocks. By 1500 BC, the Mycenaeans had grown so powerful and influential that they dominated later Greek culture.

The Mycenaean civilization collapsed sometime after 1200 BC. Some legends say the Mycenaeans were invaded by the Dorians, a people from northwestern Greece, but no one really knows what happened, except that the Mycaenaean culture was destroyed. Whether or not they were the conquerors of the Mycenaeaens, the Dorians ultimately replaced them.

The Trojan Culture

The geography of the Aegean is blended into Greek mythology. For example, consider Troy (built on the western coast of modern Turkey), which the mainland Greeks besieged for ten years allegedly because Helen, the most beautiful woman in the world, had run away from her husband, the King of Sparta, to marry a prince of Troy. (Sparta was located on the Peloponnesus.)

Troy was near the entrance to the Dardanelles, the waterway that leads from the Mediterranean to the Black Sea. That's also where the mythical Jason sailed his legendary ship, the Argo, to get a Golden Fleece. Odysseus, another hero of Greek mythology who supposedly fought at Troy, sailed his ship between Scylla and Charybdis, which are suspiciously similar to the dangers of the straits of Messina between Italy and Sicily.

In the nineteenth century, man named Heinrich Schliemann decided that the legends must contain some elements of history. He reasoned that the great epics of the Trojan War couldn't all be myth. He started looking for Troy, using the legends for a guide. In 1870, he found the ruins of Troy! Other archeologists started following up on other myths and discovered more ruins that matched some details of Greek stories.

Since Heinrich Schleimann rediscovered Troy, archaeologists have uncovered the remains of nine cities on its site. Each successive city was built on the ruins of the one before it. "THE" city of Troy of the famed Trojan War seems to have been built during the early 1200s BC. It was set afire and destroyed in the mid-1200s BC. If there is any truth to the legends, Troy was conquered and burned by Mycenaean invaders from the mainland of Greece.

The legendary Trojan War was described in two great epic poems, the *Iliad* and the *Odyssey*, both written by a Greek named Homer. Scholars estimate that these were written in 800 BC, about four hundred years after the probable date for the historical war of Troy. Homer's great epics have been imitated and echoed ever since they were written. The first and most obvious mimic was the *Aeneid*, written by a Roman poet named Virgil a few decades before the birth of Christ.

The Trojan War, by all accounts, took place sometime around 1200 BC. (And, as we mentioned last mini-unit, there is some evidence to suggest that the Philistines whom David fought against were close descendants of Trojans who fled from their ruined city.) It wasn't long after this date that all the Bronze Age civilizations of the Aegean collapsed.

Within a century of the war, the Greeks had lost the ability to read and write. They lacked the resources to build great structures. Most trade ended. The next 300 years were the Greek Dark Ages. All that was left behind were the stories of their heroes and their gods, which they carried with them. These stories eventually became so intertwined with those of Rome that we now often speak of "Greco-Roman" mythology as one thing.

Grecian Governments

Most of the other ancient cultures we have studied had one leader of a central government, like the Pharaoh of Egypt or the king of the Persian Empire. The Greek communities were different: they were organized into city-states. A city-state consisted of a city or town and the farmland around it. Greek city-states were fiercely independent and often warred against one another. This diversity had its disadvantages, of course, but it also had some strengths—patriotism and citizenship were key values for the Greeks.

This led to many innovations in the field of government—in fact, the Greeks seem to have invented the study of government (though, of course, not government itself).

City-states began to develop distinctive patterns of government during the Greeks' Dark Ages, sometime between 1200 BC and the time of Homer. At first, these communities were ruled by kings, but by 750 BC or so, the nobles in most city-states had overthrown the kings and become rulers. This shift from a monarchy (rule by one) to an aristocracy (rule by "the best") was crucial to the new forms of government.

The city-states were divided, both from each other and within themselves. Not every resident of a city was a citizen; citizenship was a privilege. Only citizens could own land or take part in government, and only citizens were expected to fight for their homes. Women and slaves weren't citizens, nor were the serfs (a peasant class, tied to the land) or foreigners. Citizens who fell on hard times could fall into debt and slavery—and lose their citizenship.

Even though the Greeks never united into a single nation, they were united in other important ways. They shared the same religion, language, and culture. They came together for athletic competitions at the Olympic Games and regional religious events, including a Greek invention called "Theater." (Theater developed at the annual religious festival called "City Dionysia," where men wrote and performed plays in competition for a prize.)

Daily Life for the Ancient Greeks

We focus less on the study of daily life for the Greeks in this unit than we have for other cultures this year, but don't worry: we'll get back to more of that when we study the Romans. The full *Tapestry of Grace* program spends weeks on the Greeks, and even offers directions for putting on a full-length Greek play!

Even in our cursory glimpse at the Greeks, however, there are many variations to note, since each city-state had its own unique characteristics. This week, we spend time learning about some of the things that united the Greeks.

We spend time reading Aesop's Fables aloud. One of the major cultural elements that made the Greeks "greek" and not "barbarian" was their shared language. Imagine children across Greece hearing simple stories like these and growing up knowing to persevere because of the story of the Tortoise and the Hare, or learning to value diligence in imitation of the ants (instead of being lazy like Grasshopper), or appreciating small acts of kindness because of the story of the Lion and the Mouse.

Your child will also learn about the Olympic Games. With so many different city-states, Greek men must have loved the chance to show who was the strongest, fastest, and best. Events like this helped the Greeks unite in order to face threats like the attacks of the Persian Empire. If you're lucky, you'll be studying this material during a year when our nation is participating in the modern version of the Olympic Games. Maybe you have a favorite memory associated with an Olympic event that you can share with your child.

Sparta and Athens

Sparta and Athens were rivals for decades during the Persian Wars, and then fought each other on the battlefield for most of the next thirty years during the Peloponnesian War.

The two leading cities of ancient Greece could not have been more different—Sparta was a rigid, disciplined, military commune, while Athens was a fluid, inquisitive, and sometimes chaotic democracy.

The Spartans were into simplicity and warfare. They did everything they could to stamp out individuality in their culture. Even their money was made of huge bars of rusty iron (hard to transport and ugly to look at), for the expressed purpose of keeping their people from getting too materialistic. Two centuries before the Persian Wars, Lycurgus the lawgiver had drastically revised Spartan laws and customs to stamp out any shred of individuality. Everything from marriage to money to meals was regulated with the goal of cultivating a communal identity and obliterating personal ambitions. Spartans were warriors—and nothing else. Sparta was an armed camp.

Athens, by contrast, was a zoo! Through trial and error, it had moved from being a monarchy to becoming an oligarchy (ruled by a few elites) to a tyranny (rule by a strong man) to a democracy (where each citizen had one vote—but remember, not all people were citizens). This last development came in 508 BC, just a few years before the Persian Wars began. There were significant weaknesses in pure democracy—it can become mob rule. Older students using the full *Tapestry of Grace* curriculum will read Plato's "Apology," which tells of the trial and execution of the philosopher Socrates. Socrates was put to death by majority rule for the crime of annoying his neighbors with constant questions and "corrupting the youth of Athens."

Both of these city-states played key roles during the Persian Wars and in the general course of history on the Grecian mainland.

The Persian Wars

All of this is background to explain how the Greeks developed to the point where they came into conflict with the Persians. The threat of Persian conquest forced these fiercely individual city-states to unite, at least temporarily. When the allied Greeks went up against the Persian Empire, it became a history-shaping series of conflicts known as the Persian Wars.

The Persians Wars were one of the greatest "David and Goliath" conflicts of all time. Let's review the size of "Goliath" here: the Persian Empire reached into Asia—all the way east to India. It extended all the way south to Ethiopia. The Persian giant was ready to extend its grasp into Europe. Nothing stood in its way but the squabbling little city-states of Greece and their colonies.

As we've learned, the Greeks had colonies all around the coastlines of the Mediterranean because they were sailors, traders, and colonizers. The Ionian Greeks had built cities up and down the coast of modern-day Turkey, and that's where the Persians first ran into them. During the 500s, the Persian Empire overran these little cities and made them pay tribute. In 499 BC, however, the cities started to rebel. With a lot of help from Athens, across the Aegean on the Greek mainland, they spent the next five years in a state of revolt. King Darius I of Persia (who is part of the story told in the book of Daniel) eventually crushed their rebellion, and then he sent an army to punish Athens.

The Persian Wars were packed with providential events. One of the more amazing acts of providence was the fact that Athens and Sparta were able to work together. Athens and Sparta forgot their rivalries in order to fight Persia, but it was a little like the United States and the Soviet Union joining together to fight Hitler during World War II. It never would have happened without the greater threat to both of them, given their differences.

There are three major battles of the Persian Wars to which we want to pay special attention. These are the battles of Marathon (won by the Athenian army), Thermopylae (a heroic delaying action in which King Leonidas' brave Spartans fought to the death to give the rest of the Greeks time to prepare their defense), and Salamis (in which the Greek city-states were finally saved from Persia by a "wooden wall").

Battle of Marathon

The first Persian army to invade Greece was huge. As soon as it reached the Greek mainland, the Athenians sent a messenger to Sparta to beg for their help. He ran almost 150 miles in under two days! But the Persians were coming on too fast—they reached the plains of Marathon, 26.2 miles from Athens, before the Spartans arrived. The Athenian army launched a surprise attack against the vastly larger Persian forces. The well-trained, well-equipped, patriotic Greek hoplites (foot soldiers) triumphed over the hordes of Persian conscripts.

There is a legend that the victorious Greeks sent a runner to Athens to carry the news. He ran so hard that he barely reached the city. He said, "Rejoice, we conquer," then fell to the ground and died. The distance from Marathon to Athens is the length of a marathon race today.

Battle of Thermopylae

The Athenians had fended off the first big Persian attack at Marathon. The next battle came ten years later, when Xerxes I, the son of Darius, led another huge army to Greece. This is the same Xerxes, by the way, who married Queen Esther! This time, the Persians tried to come around from the north. That meant they had to go through the mountain pass of Thermopylae. King Leonidas of Sparta had about 5000 men under his command. They were to defend Greek territories against a vast Persian fighting force. The Greek historian Herodotus claimed the Persian force was over five million men!

When one Spartan soldier, Dienekes, heard there were so many Persian arrows that they blotted out the sun, he said, "So much the better, we shall fight in the shade."[1] King Xerxes told Leonidas to surrender his arms. Leonidas retorted, "Come and take them!"

The Greeks formed a phalanx (a battle formation where each man's shield protected his neighbor) across the narrow pass. The Persians were thus faced with a solid wall of shields and spear points. No matter how many Persians there were, they could only get so many into the pass at one time. The Persians attacked and attacked, but got nowhere. Persian soldiers were commanded to march over the bodies of their dead comrades, only to join them in death. According to one source, the first 10,000 Persians died without killing more than two or three Spartans. Xerxes sent officers with whips to drive the next 20,000 soldiers into the fray, with no more success. Fifty thousand more Persians attacked on the second day of battle, but they were driven back.

With reinforcements, the Greeks might have fought forever—but a local man betrayed them. He led the Persians through a mountain path behind Greek lines. King Leonidas dismissed most of his forces, but he stayed behind with his guard of 300 Spartans and 700 Thespian volunteers. It was a suicide mission and they all knew it, but it allowed the rest of the allied Greek army to escape and defend Greece from the Persians.

Leonidas and his men fought until their spears broke, and then fought with their short swords. They fought till their swords broke, and then they fought with teeth and fists and nails. Leonidas fell, and the remaining Spartans defended his body so fiercely that the Persians were afraid to try to take them in hand-to-hand combat. The last

1 Herodotus, *Histories*, 7.226.

Spartans were killed by a rain of arrows.

A thousand Greeks died at Thermopylae. Nobody knows how many Persians fell. Some historians think it was 20,000—the Greeks who were there said it was 50,000. This had a serious effect on Persian morale!

Battle of Salamis

The Spartans held off the Persians, but they couldn't stop them. The Persians were loose on the Greek mainland, and they burned and sacked every city that did not surrender, including Athens. Some Athenians put their hope in a word from the Oracle at Delphi, which said that the island of Salamis would "bring death to women's sons," but that the Greeks would be saved by a "wall of wood." They barricaded the entrance to the Acropolis with a wooden wall, fencing themselves in. The wooden wall was overrun, they were all killed, and the Athenian Acropolis was burned down.

The Athenian leader Themistocles had a different take on the oracle's words, however. He thought that the wooden wall was the Greek fleet of ships. He urged the Athenians to retreat to the island of Salamis, saying it was the Persian women's sons who would die there.

The Greeks had been routed on the mainland, but they still had about 360 ships. By contrast, the Persians had started with more than 1,200 ships! A lot of Persian ships had been lost by this time, but they still had somewhere between 650-800. The Greek ships were bottled up in the harbor of Salamis when the Persians started closing in. This was the fight for everything!

The Greek ships used wind and weather brilliantly. Ship-to-ship combat, at this time, consisted of ramming ships to cripple them, and then leaping over the sides to fight by hand. The otherwise-deadly Persian archers were thrown off by the motion of the waves, so Greek short-swords had an advantage. The Persian admiral was killed early in the battle, throwing their entire fleet into confusion. The only Persian captain with any skill turned out to be a woman—Artemisia, whose ship rammed nine Greek ones.

The battle of Salamis has been called the most significant single battle in human history. It marked the farthest reach of Persian power. Without that wall of wooden ships, Europe might have become a Persian province. What we know as Western civilization might not have survived.

Conclusion

The Persian Wars almost wrap up our focus on the empires of the ancient near east—almost. We'll study one more enormous empire in this unit. A little over 100 years after the conclusion of the Persian Wars, Alexander the Great exploded out of Greece to take over everything that the Persians had controlled, and he accomplished it in just ten years. He founded new cities (and renamed others) after himself as he campaigned, and he left Greek overseers in charge in them. He then died, at the age of 32, and his empire was subsequently split between three of his generals. Thus, Alexander's empire rose and fell faster than any of them—but the Greek language and culture that he spread throughout the known world had tremendous influence.

TAPESTRY OF GRACE PRIMER GUIDEBOOK

Mini-Unit 4: Christ and the Church

We will learn how the fullness of time arrived and as we reach the climactic unfolding of God's plan of redemption. Note how our seven main "characters" fit in.

 The Author	Alexander the Great thought he was a god, conquered his world, and died without an heir. Rome conquered Alexander's divided empire and crushed the Mediterranean under an iron boot. Meanwhile, in a stable in Bethlehem, ultimate authority came. Pilate claimed authority over Jesus, while he was told that his secular power was given by God. Jesus gave up His life. Miracles, teachings, and resurrection proved all authority now and forever belongs to Jesus Christ, the Son of God.
 People	Alexander the Great and Julius Caesar were mighty conquerors. Caesar Augustus became the first Emperor of Rome. Most importantly, Jesus Christ walked among us, His life marking the central point of history.
 Good	Alexander sought to do good by pursuing his ambitions like one of the Greek heroes. Julius Caesar refused the crown of Rome. Pontius Pilate asked what truth was. Meanwhile, Jesus changed the world, redefined good and evil, and offered His own perfect righteousness to all people.
 Evil	Alexander's pride spurred him to pursue glory. Julius Caesar's closest friends betrayed and murdered him. Herod murdered a generation of Jewish baby boys. The Sanhedrin condemned one man to die on behalf of the nation. Pilate condemned an innocent man to death. The Son of God took the sin and evil of the entire world, and He conquered it.
 The Word	The Word became flesh and made His dwelling among us. Daniel's revelation came to fruition in the fullness of time as the Kingdom of Heaven came. The Holy Spirit came, filling His people with His power. The Church began to spread through the world, proclaiming the Kingdom of Heaven.
 God's Creation	Creation reacted when Jesus was crucified. The centurion who watched Jesus die said, "Surely this man was the Son of God." The world was plunged into darkness. Jesus and the apostles showed that God's power prevailed over sickness, storms, shipwrecks, and even death itself.
 Man's Creation	Romans invented crucifixion, but also connected their empire with safe roads and trade routes. Romans engineered aqueducts, public works, marble cities, and established peace and stability (called the *Pax Romana*) using their military strength.

Mini-Unit 4 Overview
Christ and the Church

Introduction

We've been retelling the story that God authored, and we have seen His authority in action. However, even when it seemed as if God's promise had triumphed and the relationship between God and mankind was restored, human wickedness and evil still prevailed. Human sin ruined the fellowship between God and Man, and our choice to pursue good as we defined it rather than as God defined it has affected every part of the story.

In this mini-unit, we reach what the Apostle Paul referred to as the "fullness of time." We'll see how God's preparations came to fruition as God Himself became Man, forever defeating evil and redefining good. The Word that had spoken Creation into being became a created being. The One who caused trees to take root and clap their hands for joy as the morning stars sang together would hang on a tree as the sun clothed itself in darkness. In this mini-unit we reach the climax of history: we count the years themselves down to this point. After the Incarnation, we begin to count the years up, marking the time since then. This is a big deal historically. As we retell this story, let's pause to appreciate how God authored events so Jesus arrived at just the right time.

Alexander the Great: Preparation for Proclamation

As we mentioned, Alexander led the Greeks to carve out an empire of their own, and his campaign lasted ten years. In Macedonia, a province of northern Greece, Alexander the Great inherited the throne at the age of twenty. By the time of his sudden death at the age of 32, he had conquered Greece, Turkey, Egypt, Babylon, and Persia. His empire represents the bronze belly and thighs of Nebuchadnezzar's statue, and there is some indication that Alexander knew it. On his tour of conquest through Judea, he spared Jerusalem after learning of the prophecy.

He swept on through Afghanistan and India, and would have gone after China, too, if his men had not rebelled! They forced him to turn back to the West. He then died in Babylon without leaving a will or an established heir, so his generals divided his empire into three parts. Decades before the birth of Jesus, the power vacuum was filled by the last of the four empires revealed in Daniel's interpretation of Nebuchadnezzar's dream: Imperial Rome.

Imperial Rome: Backdrop to the Atonement

We end our study of the Ancient World with the rise and fall of one of the great civilizations of all time—ancient Rome. If you've never studied Roman history before, you may be surprised how much seems familiar. On the other hand, even if you're a history buff, you may be amazed at how much you still have left to learn!

Rome seems familiar because it's such a part of our cultural traditions. It's hard to comprehend the many ways that Rome still affects us. As one simple example, over half of the English dictionary comes from Latin, the Roman language.

You can't miss Rome's influence on the New Testament. Because the Romans oppressed the Jews, the Jews wanted Jesus to be a king who would defeat Rome. Because Jesus had a more important mission to accomplish and refused to be the kind of king they wanted, the Jews were angry with Him. Also, because the Jewish leaders feared Rome's reaction to what Jesus was doing, they were that much more eager to put Him to death! After Jesus' ascent into Heaven, Rome continued to play a major role in unintentionally helping spread the gospel through the known world.

Returning one more time to Nebuchadnezzar's statue, we Christians know that Jesus was the rock that was not made by human hands, and the Church that He established would become a mountain that filled the whole earth and crushed empires down through the centuries, even when those empires worked hard to stamp out Jesus and His Church.

The Zenith of Imperial Rome: Backdrop to the Early Church

To review: the Assyrians, the Babylonians, the Persians, the Greeks, and the Romans all played crucial roles in preparing for the spread of the Good News. As you know, the Assyrians conquered the Northern Kingdom of Israel, forcibly exiling the ten tribes. The Babylonians conquered and unified most of the ancient Near East, deporting the Southern Kingdom of Judah and beginning what is known as the Diaspora (meaning dispersion or scattering). The Persians took over the Babylonian empire and built roads that connected people from India to Ethiopia. The Greeks, under Alexander the Great, conquered much of Asia and Northern Africa in a shockingly short amount of time, upending centuries of custom and tradition. Over the next two centuries or so, different powers warred with each other and created political and religious havoc in Israel.

The Romans filled the power void left by Alexander as the Roman Empire was firmly established under its first emperor, Augustus Caesar, in 27 BC. Rome had already conquered Jerusalem in 63 BC, making it a Roman province. Roman governors provided capable and relatively tolerant administration, ushering in a period of comparative peace and stability. Indeed, the ascendency of Roman rule brought relative peace all around the Mediterranean Sea, and their roads and patrol of the sea made travel throughout the Empire safe as well as comparatively quick and easy. Thus, as the disciples of Jesus were persecuted by Jewish authorities or sent out on missionary journeys, they traveled across the Mediterranean World, taking the message of the gospel with them.

The gospel proclaimed good news to the poor and to the oppressed. There were many of these under Roman rule! We will get to study this and other aspects of daily life in Roman society. These poor ones were the people who would have heard for the first time that God had become man in order to redeem not only His chosen people, but people of every language and nation!

Conclusion

In this mini-unit, our emphasis will be on enjoying the amazing ways that God timed the arrival of His Son and the proclamation of the Kingdom of Heaven. As you study the means that God used to accomplish this end, you'll understand more clearly how the Church was a new thing in history—a movement not made by human hands. We'll study how the ripple effects of Jesus' death on the cross and His resurrection began to spread through society and affect entire nations as the early Church grew.

Mini-Unit 4, Topic 1
Alexander the Great: Preparation for Proclamation

Greece After the Persian Wars

The greatest moments in Greek history may have been the Spartan defense of Thermopylae or the Athenian victory over the Persian fleet at Salamis. These desperate battles came at incredible cost—the death of the Spartan heroes, to the last man, and the burning of Athens to the ground—but the heroic Greek defense held back the Persian juggernaut (overpowering force) and set the stage for a golden age in Greece. Athens burst into full bloom: building beautiful temples, writing plays, planting colonies, developing philosophical language, and experimenting with democracy. Sadly, the passing of the Persian threat also opened the door for the leading Greek city-states of Athens and Sparta to renew the rivalry between themselves, which became a series of battles known as the Peloponnesian War. It lasted for thirty years, off and on, and ended with the decline of Athens.

The Golden Age of Classical Greece

Athens' Golden Age saw an explosion of Greek art and architecture. Athenian playwrights wrote tragedies and comedies (many of which are still performed today) as part of religious festivals. Sculptors carved masterpieces that crown the world's great museums today. Architects built the famous Parthenon on the Acropolis, as well as many lesser buildings of beautiful grace and proportions. It was during this era that a philosopher named Socrates lived (and died for his "crimes").

Socrates

The crime of Socrates was simple—he made his neighbors look dumb. In a pure democracy, anything can be deemed a crime if a majority of the citizens say it is. And it wasn't hard to offend a majority of the Athenians, since they were quite puffed up with knowledge. All Socrates had to do was needle them a little to let all the hot air out. If this had been a hobby, he might have survived it all—but to him it was a religious mission. He believed that a god had commanded him to question his neighbors in this way.

It all started with the Oracle at Delphi. The oracle told his friend Chaerophon that no man was wiser than Socrates. Socrates found this hard to believe—he knew he wasn't wise! But then he started talking to his neighbors, and he realized that he just might be wiser than they were, in this one way: he knew that he knew nothing, while they all thought they knew everything.

Socrates engaged his neighbors in dialogues, asking them question after question about what they thought they believed, instead of putting his own opinions on display. This technique is very effective at making people think, or showing that they haven't yet thought deeply about a subject. Today, we call that teaching technique the Socratic Method because, like Socrates, the teacher uses questions (as opposed to lectures) that challenge students to think deeply as the teacher guides the discussion.

There's a problem with showing proud people that they are really fools: you make a lot of enemies. Socrates was put on trial for his life. He could have run away from Athens, even after he was tried and convicted. He didn't, though. He argued that he had accepted all the benefits of citizenship in Athens, and it would be unjust of him to run away from the burdens of citizenship. How would other nations receive him if he flouted the laws of Athens? What would happen to him after death if he set himself above the laws?

According to his biographer, Plato, Socrates was not afraid to die. As far as he knew, death was just the door to the next great adventure! He said,

> I don't know what is on the other side of death, but I do know what is on this side. I know that injustice and disobedience to a better, whether God or man, is evil and dishonorable, and I will never fear or avoid a possible good rather

than a certain evil.[1]

So Socrates accepted the death penalty of Athens. He obeyed what he believed was the voice of a god, telling him to keep questioning. He ended his life saying, "As I fear the god, whether these men of Athens acquit me or not, whatever they do, understand that I shall never alter my ways, not even if I have to die many times."[2]

Pericles

During its Golden Age, Athens reached the pinnacle of its power and prosperity. Because of its pure democracy, the people voted on everything, but Athenian government was led by elected politicians. Chief among these was Pericles, who led Athens for more than thirty years.

Pericles made great changes to Athens. He was the first to introduce salaries for public officials. He changed the constitution so that common people could finally serve in office.

Pericles had big ambitions for Athens. He wanted his city to be the most powerful state in Greece. He urged the Athenians to plant colonies around the Mediterranean, and he backed up this peaceful expansion with more violent means. At his urging, Athens fought battles of conquest in Egypt, the Greek mainland, and the islands in the Aegean Sea. Some of Pericles' ventures were successful; others were disastrous. Though he was always considered a great man, his ambitions led to rivalry with other Greek city states, and these ultimately led to Athens' downfall.

Peloponnesian War

Athens, with her great navy and wealth, spread her influence farther and farther abroad. This meant trouble—Sparta became jealous of her growing power.

If the high point of Greek history was the Greek alliance against the Persians, the low point may well be what came afterwards. As allies, Sparta and Athens stopped the invincible Persian army and sunk the enormous Persian fleet. But their alliance fell apart soon after peace was won.

The naval battle of Salamis ended the Persian threat in 480 BC, and the Athenians formed a new alliance three years later. This collection of city-states was called the Delian League, named after the island of Delos. The Spartans responded by heading a rival organization, the Peloponnesian League. It was a lot like the situation after World

---
1 Plato, *The Apology of Socrates*.
2 Plato, *The Apology of Socrates*.

War II: the US formed NATO and the USSR formed the Warsaw Pact after they had beaten Hitler together. In the modern version, two armed camps battled in a (mostly) Cold War of ideologies and threatening postures. But in ancient Greece, Athens and Sparta clashed with weapons and bloodshed.

The Peloponnesian War officially started when the Spartans attacked Athens. Athens sort of provoked this, though. Under Pericles' leadership, they started building walls to connect the city of Athens with the port of Piraeus, which was about seven miles away. These "long walls" would have made Athens well-nigh invulnerable to attack by land—and since the Athenians already dominated the sea, it would have given them a permanent advantage over their rivals. Sparta wasn't going to let this happen!

The first phase of the war was called the Archidamian War. Archidamus, the Spartan king, attacked Athens once a year for ten years running. Athens beat back these attacks, relying on their city walls. Pericles persuaded the people to abandon their farms and villages around Athens, surviving on sea power alone. Athens wasn't built to handle so many refugees, however, and a plague broke out inside the crowded city. Pericles himself died in the plague in 429 BC.

Nicias, an Athenian leader, finally persuaded both sides to agree to a peace that lasted the next eight years. This broke down when Alcibiades persuaded Athens to launch attacks against Spartan-controlled territory in 418 BC, followed by an attempt to conquer the island of Sicily three years later.

The Spartans couldn't beat Athens at sea, so they turned to their old enemy Persia for help. With Persian resources, Sparta build an impressive navy and took Athens by surprise. Over the next nine years, the Spartans won more and more battles, and Athenian power dwindled. Sparta finally conquered Athens in 404 BC, banned democracy, and set up a new, Spartan-controlled government called "the Thirty Tyrants." The Greek experiment with self-government was over.

Alexander the Great

Onto the stage of history stepped Alexander the Great, who was born in 356 BC. This man was amazing—he was like a bulldozer, leveling everything in his path. As we've said, he conquered his world in ten years, but then died at age 32 without a will. His only child was born a few months after Alexander died, but the child was murdered while young, leaving no heir. Alexander's empire rose and fell incredibly quickly, but he paved the way for the world we know today.

Alexander's Youth

Alexander's father was Philip of Macedon, ruler of a small mountainous region in northern Greece. The New Testament cities of Thessalonica, Philippi, and Berea are in this area. Mount Olympus was in this area, too, but aside from that, Macedonia was never much to write about before Alexander.

As a youth, Alexander showed signs of impressive courage, boldness, and presence of mind. Plutarch [1] records an incident when Philip turned down the chance to buy a magnificent but untameable horse. The thirteen-year-old Alexander asked if he could have the horse if he could tame it. When Philip said he could, Alexander fearlessly grabbed the horse and turned him toward the sun so that the horse would not be spooked by his own shadow. Alexander also removed his cloak, which was flapping and startling the horse. That was the beginning of a long partnership. This horse, Bucephalus, became Alexander's favorite warhorse and served him well in many battles. When Bucephalus finally died, Alexander founded and named a city after him. But all of this came later in the story.

King Philip brought in a famous tutor from Athens for his young prince—the philosopher Aristotle. And while Aristotle is just a footnote in Alexander's life, we'll be bumping into him quite often during our tour through human history.

Aristotle was a student of Plato at the School of Athens. As we mentioned before, Plato was a student and biographer of Socrates, and popularized his Socratic Method. Aristotle invented formal logic as we know it, and he laid the foundations of many of our modern disciplines. He wrote about everything—physics, metaphysics, poetry, ethics—and was held in high esteem during his own lifetime for his knowledge. By the middle ages, Aristotle was simply known as "the" Philosopher.

Alexander probably learned a lot from his tutor, but he wasn't famous for being a great philosopher. He was a warrior. He was only sixteen when he got his first chance to show his skill. His father was leading the armies far away from home when soldiers from the neighboring kingdom of Thrace attacked. Alexander rounded up men and took them on—and beat them! Alexander and his father Philip soon conquered all of Greece.

But there was trouble brewing—Alexander's mother filled her boy's head with the idea that he was the son of a god, not a man. Then, Philip divorced Alexander's mother and took a new queen—but shortly after the wedding, Philip died under suspicious circumstances! Alexander was only twenty, but he held onto the throne. From then on, he was on his own.

---

[1] Plutarch. *Life of Alexander*, 6. See also *Arrian*. Anabasis Alexandri V.19.

Greek Mythology and Superstition in Alexander's Life

Why would Alexander believe that he might be the son of a god? Actually, this idea was not uncommon in Greek mythology. Greek "gods" were more human than divine in many ways, and the Olympians assumed human shapes in many stories. In addition, many Greek stories featured heroes who were half-god, half-man.

Teachers, you may or may not want to introduce mythology to your young student. If you don't, we wanted to explain why we take time to retell a few of these Greek myths in a curriculum that looks at history from the perspective of a biblical worldview. If you do, we want you to do so with an awareness of the greater purpose.

We introduce Greek myths for several reasons: to learn about a major influence on Western literature, to learn more about ancient Greek culture, and to take the opportunity to examine these influential myths from a biblical perspective.

We have found that a child who has been trained to spot the petty lies and jealousies of the mythological deities as portrayed in Greek stories typically finds the Bible more credible, not less, as a result of studying these tales. The Bible is unique in portraying a God who is real, personal, and active, yet radically unlike sinful humans.

The Greek gods, by contrast, appear all too human. They display lust, jealousy, and anger. The most important gods were supposed to live on Mount Olympus. Zeus and his wife, Hera, were king and queen of Olympus. Some other major idols were Aphrodite, goddess of love; Apollo, god of music and light; Poseidon, god of the sea; Hades, god of the underworld; Ares, god of war; and Athena, goddess of wisdom. These so-called gods lusted, cheated, squabbled, gossiped, and betrayed each other on a grand scale. They also played with the lives of mortals for their own glory or simply for their own amusement. Created in man's image, they reflect the chaos and sin of a fallen world.

Like many other polytheists, the Greeks were very superstitious. They believed that their deities could foretell the future, and they went to shrines called oracles to consult priests and priestesses. The most important oracle was at Delphi (a Greek city that was central to many other city-states on the Greek mainland).

Greeks also believed three goddesses (the Fates) determined the course of every mortal life. Seers and soothsayers looked for omens of good or bad luck. Greek priests and priestesses were known to go into trances and deliver oracles—prophetic sayings that had to be interpreted and often did more harm than good.

The Greeks also had a complex picture of the afterlife. They believed that when a person died, Hermes, the messenger god, would meet the soul and guide it into the Underworld, where he had to cross the River Styx. Charon, the ferryman, took the dead man across if he had a coin to pay him. Those who did not were forced to wander the banks of the Styx for 100 years.

Once across this great river, the soul had to pass a horrible three-headed dog, Cerberus, whose job it was to stop the living from entering the Underworld—and the dead from getting out.

After this peril was passed, the soul then had to be judged by three gods named Minos, Rhadamanthys, and Aeacus, who would decide whether the soul should be punished or rewarded for the life he had led on earth. (Notice that for Greeks, salvation was based upon human works, which would only have been good enough if the standard for human behavior was drastically lowered from what the one true and holy God requires.)

Hades was king of the Underworld, and Persephone was his Queen. The afterlife was very different for different people, depending on how they had lived or what they knew. If the soul had led a good and pious life, or if the person was a member of certain cults, then he was sent to the sunny and joyful Elysian Fields. If the soul's life on earth was neither very good nor very bad, it was sent to the Asphodel Fields, where everything was grayish and dull. There was nothing for such a soul to do but drift and wait for offerings from its loved ones back on earth to cheer it up. Most people came here. If the soul had been wicked and sinful, then it was sent to Tartarus, a place of excruciating pain and eternal torment.

Like many other false religions, the Grecian system developed an understanding of right and wrong that was based on man-centered definitions, not God's definition. The Greeks created gods in their own image that reflected the petty factions, jealousies, and vices that they practiced.

Even in their mythology, the Greeks wrestled with the problem that "good" people do bad things, and many of the most famous myths include heroes who must perform acts of penance to redeem themselves from the consequences of their actions. Greeks told stories of gods and heroes but had no understanding of a substitutionary Savior. Yet, even in their religion, they were grasping toward the Unknown God, and even built an altar to him in the heart of Athens.

This was the religious climate in which Alexander was raised, and it must have fueled his opinion of his own invincibility and his quest for personal glory, like the heroes in the myths he was told.

Alexander's Conquests

Greeks actually started Alexander's world conquest by rebelling against this boy-king. Thebes led the revolt, and Alexander crushed it ruthlessly. He flattened the whole city except for one house—that of Pindar, the poet, who his teacher Aristotle had praised. Soon Alexander had re-conquered Greece. Then he took on their old enemy, the Persians.

City after city fell as Alexander marched into Turkey. When he finally came face to face with the main Persian army, he found himself up against more than half a million men. Alexander's men were terrified, but that didn't stop him. He attacked the weakest point of the Persian line and made straight for King Darius—who fled before him! With the leader out of the way, the army fell.

Alexander took a little field trip over to Africa, where the Egyptians welcomed him as a liberator and crowned him as Pharaoh. The Egyptians flattered his vanity, and after a long march through the desert to the temple of Zeus-Ammon, he left Egypt even more convinced that he was the son of a god, not a man. He left orders to build Alexandria, a city named for him, and then headed back towards the heart of Persia, where Darius was waiting.

This time Darius was ready for Alexander. He knew Alexander's methods, and he chose his own ground. It could have gone very, very badly for Alexander, that day, but the Persians wound up literally falling into their own traps. Their chariots ran head-long into the booby-traps that they had set for Alexander's men. Once again, Darius fled for his life.

Alexander swept through Babylon and headed for Persopolis, the capital of the Persian Empire. If you recall the Persian Wars, you'll remember how a huge Persian army was held up at the pass of Thermopylae until a local Greek betrayed King Leonidas and showed the Persians a way around the mountain pass.

This time, it was the Greeks who got held up on their way to the capital city of Persia. Their enemies defended a narrow mountain pass known as the Persian Gates. A local shepherd boy told them about another path, right over the top of the mountain. Alexander led his men up the steep and dangerous path in the dead of night and took the Persians by surprise on the other side the next morning.

The Macedonians took Persopolis, looted it, and burned it to the ground. Alexander set himself up in style as a Persian king, but it didn't sit well with his men. Success had gone to his head—he honestly believed he was the son of a god, not a man. He went on to conquer the wild lands of modern Afghanistan and then went on to India.

He would have gone on to China, but his Macedonian troops finally refused. Angry and sulking, he marched them back through the deserts, which killed more of his men than any enemy ever did, and arrived back at Persia, only to find rebellion brewing.

Alexander was a brilliant conqueror, but he did not bring lasting peace. He died at 32, struck down by a fever. His bride, Roxane, gave birth to a son a few months after his death, but instead of ruling his father's empire, the boy was murdered along with his mother a few years later.

So Alexander died without a functional heir. His generals fought over his empire, and it was split into several territories. Antipater took the old homeland of Macedonia and Greece; Antigonus took Phrygia (in modern Turkey); General Ptolemy took Egypt; and General Seleucus had what was left, which stretched all the way out to India. The Ptolemies and Seleucid dynasties battled over Judea for years to come, and some of the other territories had changing borders and masters for decades.

The Septuagint

Alexander didn't leave a unified empire, but he established Greek culture everywhere he went. Thanks to Alexander and his successors, Greek became the common tongue throughout the known world. Greek is unique for its expressions of nuance, and its vocabulary of words that relate to the meaning of life. Such were characteristics developed during its Golden Age. It was in this language that God chose to express the message of the gospel and the glory of His Son.

The Jewish Bible (the Old Testament books, and some others not included in all Old Testament renderings) was translated into Greek during this Hellenistic Era by a team of 72 scholars in Alexandria. This translation was known as the Septuagint, from the Greek word for "seventy."

Without the Septuagint, many would never have known the Jewish vision of one Holy God. Even the Jews weren't speaking Hebrew by the time of Jesus—they spoke Aramaic. The Greek translation of the Old Testament made it possible for any educated ancient man to read the Law of Moses, sing the Psalms of David, or see the visions of Ezekiel. It prepared the world for its Savior!

This Greek translation included some books that were never in the Hebrew Bible—books like Maccabees and the Wisdom of Ben Sira. It also included some new chapters of Daniel and Esther. These books and chapters were accepted as Scripture by the Greek Orthodox and Roman Catholic churches, but were excluded by Martin Luther and other Reformers from the Protestant Bible.

Hanukkah

Greek culture affected the Jewish people as much as anybody else. One Seleucid king, Antiochus IV Epiphanes, set up an altar to Zeus in the Jewish Temple in Jerusalem! The priest Mattathias revolted and fled into the wilderness with his five sons. Mattathias soon died, but his son Judas Maccabaeus led a rebel army to victory. After defeating the Seleucids, "Judah the Hammer" (as he came to be known) entered Jerusalem in triumph and cleansed the Temple, restoring the worship of God. The Jewish holiday that we know as Hanukkah celebrates one incident from this period.

According to the story, there was only enough purified oil to light the holy lamp in the Temple for one day. This was a problem: God had commanded the lamps to be lit continuously! According to the Talmud, the lamp miraculously burned for eight days, the time needed to prepare a fresh supply of oil. To this day, Jews celebrate this event by lighting a special menorah with eight branches each December.

Conclusion

Like the Babylonians, Alexander and the Greeks may not have left an empire, but they left a mark on history. Alexander was a king who thought he was the son of a god, but he paved the way for a very different kind of king who really *was* the Son of God!

MINI-UNIT 4: CHRIST AND THE CHURCH

Mini-Unit 4, Topic 2

Imperial Rome: Backdrop to the Atonement

Introduction

We will spend the next few topics studying ancient Rome. We'll see what it was like to be a conquered people under Roman rule, and we'll learn about the everyday life of a Roman citizen in the Empire.

Our primary text for this topic is very familiar: it's the New Testament!

Let's start with a broad overview of the Roman Empire and then zero in on the province of Judea.

In *Tapestry of Grace*, we follow the history of Rome from its very humble beginnings to its final collapse. In *Tapestry Primer*, we pick up its story when Rome had defeated most of her major enemies, won control of the Mediterranean, and established the *Pax Romana* (the "Roman peace") under the first emperors.

Rome didn't start off as anything special—just a cluster of shepherds' huts on the hills around a swampy spot by an Italian river. Its early history was similar to that of other cultures: little squabbling wars between small tribes went on until, eventually, leaders arose who were strong enough to unite the groups into one.

When Rome grew powerful, those humble beginnings didn't seem impressive enough, so the Romans made up legends about their roots—Romulus, the founder of Rome, was supposedly the son of Mars, god of war. Later on, the Romans added even more to the story—their poet Virgil, in his epic *Aeneid*, made the mother of Romulus a descendant of Aeneas, prince of Troy from the legendary story of the Trojan War. Romulus was the first of seven kings who ruled before 510 BC. The last king, Tarquin the Proud, was driven out in an uprising of the people that led to the world's first republic.

The Roman Republic lasted from about 510 BC to 27 BC—nearly 500 years. Rome proved to be very good at a number of things, one of which was conquering her neighbors. Another was ruling them. The Romans had a simple three-step plan to victory.

First, they teamed up with friendly allies to make a big army to defeat the enemy. Next, they promised defeated leaders they could live in peace as long as they sent soldiers to Rome and paid their taxes. This then made conquered enemies into allies! Last, they gave defeated leaders and their families the gift of Roman citizenship. This gave them a stake in the overall success of the Republic.

As Rome grew more powerful, its neighbors decided it was a whole lot smarter to be part of Rome's winning team than to be enslaved. This went on until all of Italy was united under Roman rule. Then Rome ran into a neighbor that didn't want to become Roman: Carthage.

Carthage was a Phoenician trading city across the Mediterranean Sea, on the north coast of Africa. According to legend, it was founded by a Phoenician named Dido, a former Queen of Tyre, who fled from Phoenicia to Africa after her husband was murdered.

By the time of their showdown, called the Punic Wars, Carthage and Rome were evenly matched: Rome's armies ruled the land, but Carthage's navy ruled the seas. It took Rome three wars and 100 years to conquer Carthage. In the process, Rome ceased to be a solid society built on middle-class values, having instead become a split society where patricians grew rich from the spoils of war while small farmers were plunged into poverty, lost their homes, and moved to the city. Self-government gave way to rule by whichever man could best please the homeless mob.

The final years of the Republic were rough. Rome enjoyed unbroken victories abroad but suffered unending troubles at home. The Republic was designed to serve a single city-state, but Rome's foreign wars of conquest changed the dynamics of power. The governor of a Roman province had more power than most kings, and governors increasingly used their power to achieve their own goals. Wars of conquest brought tribute and treasure to Rome and glory to the generals who led them, but Rome wasn't big enough for all those egos. During the final century before Christ, Rome endured twelve civil wars in sixty years.

No republic can survive that kind of internal struggle. Julius Caesar achieved complete control with an army at his back, and became a *de facto* (in practice, but not necessarily in law) monarch of the Republic when the Senate voted him "Dictator for Life." However, he was assassinated by men who still believed in self-rule. His heir, Octavian, finished what Julius had begun—he was proclaimed "First Citizen" in 27 BC. The world's first republic then entered the first phase of becoming the world's greatest empire. As its unchallenged leader for about forty years, Octavian was also known as Caesar Augustus.

It was this Caesar Augustus that we read about in the book of Luke. He declared that all of the world should be taxed, which led a young couple to leave Nazareth and go to Bethlehem. This brings our survey of the Bible up to the New Testament. But before we turn our focus to Judea, let's meet the first few Emperors of Rome who were members of the family named Caesar.

The First Five Caesars

Julius Caesar made the family name famous, but, as we saw, he actually wasn't the first true Emperor of Rome. That is to say, he refused the title. Remember that it was his great-nephew and heir, Octavian, who gathered up the reins of power after Julius Caesar's assassination and first ruled as a true emperor of Rome. Let's look at the next five Caesars now, since the events recorded in the New Testament all unfolded under Roman rule. Jesus was born during the reign of Augustus and killed in the reign of Tiberius Caesar, his heir. Simon Peter was executed by Emperor Nero, the last of the direct heirs of Julius Caesar.

The first five emperors of Rome were:

- ❏ Octavian, who took the name Caesar Augustus. He ruled Rome longer than any other emperor, and died when Jesus was a youth, in 14 AD.
- ❏ Tiberius, his stepson, ruled for the next 23 years; he was the emperor when Jesus was crucified around 33 AD.
- ❏ Octavian's grandnephew Caligula took the throne in 37 AD and ruled for four short years.
- ❏ Caligula was succeeded by his uncle Claudius, who stayed in power for thirteen years, until 54 AD.

❏ When Claudius died, his seventeen-year-old-grandnephew Nero took over. Nero lasted fourteen years as emperor, until 68 AD.

Let's take a closer look at the first and last of these five men.

Augustus

Augustus Caesar was highly respected by the Romans, both during his life and long after his death. As we said, civil wars and uncertainty had been the norm before Augustus won his right to rule. Once he took over, Rome began to flourish at a whole new level.

There were no major wars or uprisings during his era—Augustus' reign marked the beginning of the *Pax Romana* (the Roman Peace), which lasted two centuries. In this era, Rome's legions concentrated on keeping the peace instead of propelling favored generals to power. Safe travel enabled commerce, arts, architecture, and learning to flourish. It also paved the way for the gospel to spread like wildfire throughout the Roman world.

Nero

Nero, the last emperor of Julius Caesar's dynasty, stands in stark contrast to Augustus. By the time Nero killed himself while hiding out from the Roman Senate, he had managed to get himself hated by just about everyone.

Sophisticated Romans shuddered at his attempts to style himself a great artist. Nero became increasingly self-consumed as his reign progressed. His cruelty was legendary: he murdered his wife and his mother, as well as many noble rivals. Nero fled, then killed himself before he could be caught. He is usually known as the madman who set Rome on fire so that he could write an epic poem about it and rebuild the city in the way he wanted it. He is also known as an emperor who persecuted Christians. As legend has it, he blamed the Christians for the fire in Rome. He persecuted them in many ways, putting them to death and even feeding them to lions in the Circus for the mob's entertainment.

The Senate decided that Nero was a public enemy in 68 AD, and proclaimed General Galba emperor in his place. They then sent soldiers to find and execute Nero.

Persecution

Jesus commanded His followers to love their enemies, and Nero was quite an enemy to Christians. He was the first emperor to severely persecute Christians. When Nero called for a persecution of Christians after a great fire, which he himself may have set, most Roman officials and commoners heartily approved at first. Romans differed wildly in their religious beliefs and behaviors, but most agreed that Christians were a problem.

Why were Christians a problem? Well, Romans were told that Christians were a problem because they refused to worship Rome's gods. Christians just didn't "fit in" very well in Roman culture. They wouldn't participate in the most ordinary activities, because those activities were associated with idolatry. For example, Christians wouldn't take part in festivals, rituals, or even visit a sick friend at a "hospital" based in a temple. So the masses were all too ready to suspect Christians of sorcery and evil deeds.

The more sophisticated Romans weren't any more friendly to the Christians. Well-educated Romans had grown cynical towards the traditional Roman deities, and many turned to Greek philosophies that seemed to explain life in various comforting ways. In particular, Stoicism (a lifestyle that sought to reduce dependence on the physical world) and Epicureanism (a lifestyle that reveled in the pleasures of the physical world), were eagerly embraced by many thoughtful Romans. But the Christian belief in a crucified Savior and a life of dependence on an unseen God appeared offensive to Roman ideals of strength and manliness, and the claim that He was resurrected seemed foolish.

Generally, then, Christians were deemed atheists! They did not believe in more gods than their one, "pitiful" Savior. This, many Romans felt, was bound to anger the other gods that they believed existed and bring trouble to the Empire!

Romans tolerated any and all pagan gods, but Christianity was different. Christians didn't want to add one more god to the Roman pantheon; they wanted to throw out all the other "gods" and replace them with Christ. After the Roman emperors were declared to be divine, it became every Roman citizen's duty to sacrifice to him once a year and declare during the ritual, "Caesar is lord." Christians were unwilling to make one tiny sacrifice to Caesar, because they objected to calling him "Lord." They insisted they had their own King—Jesus—and, from a Roman perspective, that was a threat to the Empire. Christians had to be dealt with—and they were. The problem was that it didn't work.

Israel under Roman Rule

To understand why Christianity was different from all of the other beliefs that

Rome had encountered, we need to go back in the story to the fifteenth year of the reign of Tiberius Caesar (about 30 AD) and zero in on where these Christians came from: the eastern province of Judea, which had been under Roman control for almost a century.

Pontius Pilate was governor of the province of Judea, which included Jerusalem. Herod Antipas was tetrarch of Galilee and Perea. Although he was called a "king," he ruled only at the pleasure of Rome. The political situation in Jerusalem and Judea was perpetually unstable. There were factions among the oppressed Jews who hovered constantly on the edge of armed rebellion. In fact, the turmoil in Jerusalem was so unstable in Jesus' time that the Jewish leaders decided it was better for one man to die than that the whole nation be destroyed by Rome in retribution for rebellious acts.

Why were there factions? Why didn't Jews band together against the common threat of Rome? It was because the Jews were divided on the subject of Roman rule. Different political factions took different positions on the subject.

There were Herodians, Sadducees, Pharisees, and Zealots, all of whom had strong opinions—plus plenty of common people who just wanted to be left alone. The Sadducees apparently wanted peace at any price. The Zealots wanted a violent revolution as soon as possible. The Pharisees followed traditions initiated by Ezra, sticking closely to Mosaic Laws and promoting cultural isolationism from Roman tyrants. Jesus' own disciples reflect the range of opinion: there were, for instance, Matthew, who had been a tax collector for Rome, and Simon the Zealot.

In Luke 3:12-14, Jewish tax collectors and Roman soldiers came to John the Baptist to be baptized. He told the tax collectors, "Collect no more than you are authorized to do." He told the soldiers, "Do not extort money from anyone by threats or by false accusation, and be content with your wages."

Jesus told His followers how to respond when the Romans didn't follow John's instructions. Under Roman law, soldiers could require inhabitants of occupied territories to carry burdens for a distance of one mile post to the next, but prohibited them from forcing anybody to go further than that. Jesus turned the Roman law on its head—in Matthew 5:41, He said, "If anyone forces you to go one mile, go with him two miles."

The Arrest and Death of Jesus

In fact, Jesus turned just about everything upside down. He was more than the High Priests could handle—more than Herod could handle—more than Pontius Pilate could handle. This overview is too brief to begin to tell the story of His virgin birth, His sinless life, His atoning death, and His bodily resurrection. All we are attempting to do here is to put the greatest story ever told into historical context.

The arrest and trial of Jesus are a strange mixture of Roman and Jewish legal procedures. You need to know that Herod and Pilate had overlapping jurisdictions to some degree. The Jews had no *authority* to put a man to death, but the Romans had no particular *desire* to kill Jesus. Pilate's wife sent word to him, saying, "Have nothing to do with that righteous man, for I have suffered much because of him today in a dream" (Matthew 27:19). Even the most sophisticated Romans took dreams and omens very seriously. It took the shouts of the mob to overcome Pilate's hesitation, but the threat of civil unrest won out. From an eternal perspective, the Scripture had to be fulfilled, and Jesus had to die. The death He died was horrible and a uniquely Roman invention designed to impose Rome's authority on conquered non-Romans.

Crucifixion

Nowadays, we execute criminals out of public view, if we administer the death penalty at all. Not so in the Roman Empire—especially when it came to crucifixion. Crucifixion was a very visible means of torture, pure and simple. Roman citizens couldn't be crucified—which was why Paul (a Roman citizen) was probably beheaded, while Peter was crucified (upside down, by his own request, as legend has it). Crucifixion was intended to be the most public, painful, shameful death a man could experience. Jesus took that death upon Himself—for us. For those who accepted Jesus' sacrifice and His offer of eternal life to all who would trust in Him for salvation instead of their own righteousness, everyday life would never be quite the same.

Roman Daily Life—Education

As we wrap up this topic, we turn our attention briefly to some aspects of daily life in the Empire, from Augustus to Nero. Roman civilization had a great impact on education, so let's take a look at how Roman children were taught.

In Rome, during the elementary years (typically ages 7-10), students learned to read Latin and use basic mathematics. In the *grammaticus* (ages 11 to 15 or so), boys learned in-depth about Latin literature and heritage. In the final phase (which not all students undertook) students studied rhetoric—the art of public speaking. When this was completed, Roman men could write and give speeches, and even defend simple cases at court.

Girls learned to read and write (as did boys), and even attended the elementary schools with them. They weren't expected to make public speeches, though, so as soon as they could read and write tolerably well, they were brought home and educated to the degree their father saw fit. Fathers would often have daughters tutored in Greek and Roman literature, needlework, musical instruments, and dance. They also learned household management from their mothers—a formidable task for wealthy women, since the average household often involved hundreds of slaves.

Roman Society—Slaves

The Roman Empire depended increasingly on slave labor as it grew in wealth and power. At the height of the Empire, there were five slaves for every three freemen in Rome. A poor family might have only three slaves. Wealthy homes regularly used 400.

Not all slaves were treated the same way. Owners found that slaves who were well-treated worked better, and many were allowed to work to earn their freedom. Those who were born slaves in large houses and thus grew up in Italy spoke the Latin language and accepted Roman customs. These often wound up as middle-class freemen.

Many Roman slaves welcomed the new message of Christianity. Surprisingly, so did many upper-class Romans! The Apostles preached a gospel that brought dignity to the meanest slave and humility to the most powerful patrician. As the Roman Empire's culture decayed, Christianity supplied meaning and comfort for many.

Conclusion

Throughout the rest of this year we will study all the way through the story of humanity, but this week we covered the pivot on which everything else turns. At the cross, everything changed—for God so loved the world that He gave His only Son, that whoever believes in Him should not perish but have eternal life (John 3:16). The fundamental question for humankind, from this point on, became, "What do you think about Jesus?" That's a question that rocked the Roman Empire, as we will see in the weeks to come!

Mini-Unit 4, Topic 3
The Zenith of Imperial Rome: Backdrop to the Early Church

Introduction

There's a lot of material to learn about this week. We've got two Roman dynasties, five good emperors, and the growth of the early Church. We also have a tale of two cities—Jerusalem and Pompeii—that got wiped out in spectacular ways.

Diaspora and Church

Many Jews left Israel over the centuries. This scattering, known as the Diaspora, is dated from the era when the Babylonians conquered the Southern Kingdom of Israel. The Apostle Paul was one of these scattered sons of Abraham—he was from the city of Tarsus, in modern Turkey. The dispersed Jews tended to congregate in their own neighborhoods in the larger cities, where they supported one another in living according to the Laws of Moses.

The center of Jewish life in the Diaspora was the synagogue, since they were far from the Temple in Jerusalem. Rabbis replaced the Levitical priesthood, and religious life centered on learning and living out the Law, not on animal sacrifices in the Temple.

Judaism attracted many followers, but few converts. The majestic monotheism of the Jews contrasted sharply with the superstitious and sensual polytheism around them. It attracted many Romans, Greeks, and barbarians, who considered themselves "God-fearers," but who balked at being circumcised so they could become fully Jewish.

When Paul and other missionaries preached in each new city, they generally went first to the Jews in the synagogues. There, Jews usually rejected their message. The God-fearers, however, were perfectly poised to accept the gospel. These often left the synagogues and formed the nucleus of the new churches. From these centers, the gospel spread and became established across the Roman Empire.

The Destruction of Jerusalem

In Luke 23:28, as Jesus was being led off to be crucified, many women followed him, mourning for him. But He said to them, "Daughters of Jerusalem, do not weep for me, but weep for yourselves and for your children."

A little over thirty years later, the Jews openly revolted against Rome in 66 AD. The Roman procurator had confiscated money from the Temple, which led to violence and then open revolt against Rome. Many moderate and aristocratic Jews refused to join the rebellion, so the city was divided.

Roman legions under General Vespasian marched to Jerusalem in 69 AD, but his battle plans were interrupted by Nero's death. Vespasian returned to a civil war at home. Romans called 69 AD the "Year of Four Emperors," because Galba, Otho, and Vitellius each sat on the throne before Vespasian took it and kept it.

Vespasian's son Titus stayed behind to besiege Jerusalem after his father left. In 70 AD, he broke through the walls. The great stone walls of the Temple were toppled, as Jesus had predicted that they would be in Matthew 24. According to the Jewish historian Josephus, the intense flames of the temple fire melted the gold and silver of the temple so that they ran between the cracks of the rocks. Roman soldiers then totally dismantled the temple, stone by stone, to extract the gold.

Titus stripped the Temple of its marble, loaded the loot and Jewish captives onto boats as slaves, and took it all back to Rome. There, he caused those same captives to participate in covering the new Colosseum with the marble. Many of these Jews were then executed there.

According to the Church historian Eusebius, most Christians fled Jerusalem in time. They remembered what Jesus had said would happen (Luke 21:20). The leadership of the Church was scattered. There was no longer a single center of the new

MINI-UNIT 4: CHRIST AND THE CHURCH

Church, so leaders in Antioch, Alexandria, and other cities each became chief pastors.

The destruction of Jerusalem changed Jewish life forever. Temple worship ended, along with animal sacrifices, because God had long ago forbidden that sacrifices and worship to Him be performed in any other place than at His temple. The priests and the Sadducees lost all influence, so the Pharisees, whose religious life centered on the teaching of the Law in the synagogues of the dispersion, filled the vacuum.

Emperors of the Flavian Dynasty

Last week we studied the first five emperors, the direct heirs of Julius Caesar. When Nero killed himself, Rome went through a civil war in the "Year of the Four Emperors," and then Vespasian (whose full name was Titus Flavius Vespasianius) founded the Flavian Dynasty.

The Flavian dynasty consisted of three emperors: Vespasian and his two sons, Titus and Domitian. When Vespasian died, Titus, the destroyer of Jerusalem, took over the Roman Empire. That year, the volcano of Mount Vesuvius blew up and wiped out a vast and populated area on the coast of Italy. Christians and Jews alike called it God's judgment on Rome.

The eruption of Vesuvius was horrific, but it was not the last of Titus' troubles. A major fire broke out soon after in Rome, and then a plague struck the city. Rebellion broke out, too. Titus died of a fever after only two years in office, and his brother Domitian took over.

Domitian was a terrible emperor. The economy took a nose-dive, so he devalued the money and raised taxes. Despite this, he still spent huge amounts of public money building 50 new public buildings around Rome. Domitian had a passion for arts and sports. He began the Capitoline Games, in imitation of the Greek Olympics. He loved gladiatorial combat and came up with novelties such as dwarf gladiators and battles between women.

Domitian was hard on Christians and Jews, persecuting them during his reign. He was also paranoid. He hated the aristocracy, executed many noblemen, and took much power away from the Senate. In the end, several Senators conspired against him, had him killed, and tried to blot out his memory forever. Thus ended the Flavian dynasty!

Vesuvius and Pompeii

Modern archaeologists know a lot about the eruption of Vesuvius because it completely buried two whole cities, Pompeii and Herculaneum, but under ash, not molten lava. The gentle-but-deadly ashes became insulators, so all the fine details of Roman life in the first century have been preserved, frozen in time on August 24, in 79 AD. At that time, the resort area of Pompeii probably had at least 20,000 inhabitants.

We have an eyewitness account of the eruption from Pliny the Younger, whose uncle, Pliny the Elder, died while trying to save people from the eruption. The younger Pliny writes:

> Ashes were already falling, not as yet very thickly. I looked round: a dense black cloud was coming up behind us, spreading over the earth like a flood… We had scarcely sat down to rest when darkness fell, not the dark of a moonless or cloudy night, but as if the lamp had been put out in a closed room.
>
> You could hear the shrieks of women, the wailing of infants, and the shouting of men; some were calling their parents, others their children or their wives, trying to recognize them by their voices. People bewailed their own fate or that of their relatives, and there were some who prayed for death in their terror of dying. Many besought the aid of the gods, but still more imagined there were no gods left, and that the universe was plunged into eternal darkness for evermore.
>
> [Ashes fell on us.] We rose from time to time and shook them off, otherwise we should have been buried and crushed beneath their weight. I could boast that not a groan or cry of fear escaped me in these perils, but I admit that I derived some poor consolation in my mortal lot from the belief that the whole world was dying with me and I with it.[1]

The Five Good Emperors

The Senate appointed a new man to succeed Domitan. This man was Nerva, the first of the so-called Five Good Emperors. These five good emperors were:

- ❑ Nerva
- ❑ Trajan
- ❑ Hadrian
- ❑ Antoninus Pius
- ❑ Marcus Aurelius

---

1 Pliny the Younger, *Letters*, 6.16 and 6.20. From the Penguin translation by Betty Radice. Accessed 10 February 2014. Retrieved from <http://www.u.arizona.edu/~afutrell/404b/web%20rdgs/pliny%20on%20vesuvius.htm>.

Roman historians saw these five men as just and able rulers and noble men. "Good" is a relative term, of course. All of them were "good," as compared with the insane Caligula, the depraved Nero, or the paranoid Domitian. None of them were Christians, and all used violence, to some degree or another, in the course of their reigns. As with all real men, each had his own strengths and weaknesses. But for this relatively brief period, Rome hit the "sweet spot." There was peace and prosperity throughout the Empire. The nightmare of the civil wars had passed. Rome ruled the world—and, even more impressively—it ruled itself.

One reason for this streak is that the first of these five emperors changed the way new emperors were chosen. During his reign, Nerva selected a junior emperor, called a "Caesar," who was to succeed him. He made a point of picking a capable man who was *not* his own child. The next three emperors followed this pattern. You can think of it, in a way, like a President picking a capable Vice President instead of a King siring a son to succeed him.

These five emperors really were remarkably successful. Under Hadrian, the third of the five, the Empire reached its greatest territorial extent. Hadrian added Mesopotamia to the Empire, so that Rome reached from the North Sea to the Persian Gulf. But even during his reign, the Empire began to grow smaller again.

Marcus Aurelius, the last of the five, broke the pattern of picking a non-relative as a successor—with disastrous results. It's really too bad, because Marcus Aurelius was otherwise one of the best rulers of all time—he is one of the few "philosopher-kings" in the history of the world. He was a strong emperor, full of personal virtues and skilled in governing.

But Marcus Aurelius was the last of the five good emperors, and it was his own fault. He gave his son, Commodus, the best possible education, as well as the throne, but it did no good—Commodus was a wicked man and a frightful emperor. (We've seen this before: Solomon was a "philosopher-king," too, but his son Rehoboam split Israel in half because of his wickedness.)

After Commodus died, chaos and violence broke out. Over the next fifty years, sixty men were proclaimed emperor, usually by the armies they led. The *Pax Romana* that had begun 200 years earlier with Caesar Augustus was over, never to return.

Conclusion

By the time the *Pax Romana* ended, however, the Roman Empire had fulfilled many of God's purposes for it. Out of fear of Roman retaliation, Jewish political leaders crucified the promised Messiah. Roman roads and Roman rule enabled the gospel to spread quickly from city to city. Even the imperial persecutions had their purpose: God used the death of the martyrs. Two hundred years after Christ, Tertullian wrote in his *Apologeticus* that "the blood of the martyrs is the seed of the Church."

MINI-UNIT 4: CHRIST AND THE CHURCH

TAPESTRY OF GRACE PRIMER GUIDEBOOK

Mini-Unit 5: The Broken Road

We will learn how the order and stability of the Roman Empire crumbled and a new way of life built around the Church by popes and princes emerged. Note how our seven main "characters" fit in.

 The Author	Roman emperors struggled to hold and maintain power as waves of barbarians attacked. Strong princes arose to establish authority by the sword and of loyalty in a system of feudalism. Meanwhile, the Church was separated into East and West. Popes and princes vied for authority. The Magna Carta showed that even the power of the king was limited.
 People	People in Europe turned to faith and the hope of eternal salvation as the peace and security of Rome failed. Charlemagne took on the mantle of leadership as Emperor of the Holy Roman Empire. Other strong leaders rose up to defend their people or conquer others. New hierarchical bonds based on fealty and mutual responsibility were forged to create security. The Crusades sought to push back growing Muslim expansion.
 Good	In a chaotic world, many sought to do what was good, as they were taught. Knights kept their oaths of fealty and the code of chivalry. The gospel advanced, saving barbarian tribes. Monks lived lives of service, preserving knowledge. People sought to win their salvation by works and Crusades.
 Evil	Rome rotted from the inside as it became increasingly decadent. Hordes of barbarians looted the toppling Roman empire. Viking raiders looted and conquered parts of France and most of England. Learning was almost lost and ignorance was widespread. Life was nasty, cold, brutish, and short. The Church waged bloody religious wars (the Crusades) across the known world.
 The Word	Church councils and doctrines sought to define orthodox theology, examining the implications of God's Word on all aspects of life. Christendom sought to establish the first theocracy in centuries. Knowledge was deep, but it was limited to a few scholars and clergy.
 God's Creation	Without protection, travel became difficult and dangerous. Viking raiders sailed up rivers and along coastlines in flat-bottomed warships. People became isolated, and authority was exercised locally. Later, as order was re-established, the early Crusades began to reconnect West and East.
 Man's Creation	People invented ways to communicate and pass along knowledge, including the use of the town crier and the dramatic play. Europe settled into a defensive stance, with the stone castle and the heavily armored mounted knight controlling the dominant military force.

Mini-Unit 5 Overview
The Broken Road

Introduction

So far, we've covered the beginning of life on Earth, the beginning of civilization, and the beginnings of government, culture, and science. We saw the beginning of the Church, which will continue long after God re-creates the heavens and the earth. We have seen God at work as the Author of Creation, making people to fill and steward it. We have seen people choose their own way instead of the good work God prepared for them. We have seen people exercise their creative abilities to build wonders of the world, and also to oppress and enslave others.

The next two mini-units mark a shift in focus and an emphasis on changes. We will see the modern world we live in largely take shape over the course of the next six topics.

Our emphasis on studying daily life with our students will continue. In this mini-unit, we will learn how people found new ways to live as Rome's central authority crumbled and collapsed. As Roman government ceased, those who had been under Roman rule and protection faced changing threats and changing loyalties. We will see how the English, French, and German cultures emerged in Western Europe. Individual characters loom large in this study. Enjoy introducing your student to the world of the Middle Ages and the people who shaped it!

Collapse into Chaos

We begin this mini-unit with another major milestone on the highway of history: the fall of Rome. Roman rule wasn't perfect, but it had brought order to most of Europe for centuries. Rome's fall wasn't sudden: it was a long, slow slide into ever-increasing political disorder and moral degeneracy. When Rome fell altogether, political and social chaos reclaimed the Western world. Then, like the roads that Rome had built throughout her empire, the *Pax Romana* was abandoned to brokenness and decay.

Roman law and order helped the spread of the gospel, providing a comparatively safe system of roads, courts of appeals, and other advantages that apostles and evangelists used.

By the time Rome started aggressively persecuting Christians under Nero (around 64 AD), the Empire was past its prime. Cultural values such as hard work, personal integrity, and self-sufficiency that had fueled the young republic were long gone. Roman citizen-farmers no longer worked their own land, voted, and defended their homeland. Bloated with wealth and slaves, full of landless citizens and the self-oriented politicians who tried to buy their favor, Rome became propelled by the mob's demands for bread and circuses.

When Nero died, the empire's order was disrupted. As we learned in our last mini-unit, Rome fell back into civil war, putting four emperors on the throne in a single year. In the 200s AD, the Empire descended into anarchy. Over the space of fifty years, sixty different men claimed the title of Emperor, and only three of them died a natural death. The crisis ended when Emperor Diocletian took the throne. He divided the empire into two parts, restored order, increased taxes, and blamed Christians for Rome's troubles. Diocletian began the last great persecution of the Church in 303 AD.

His successor, Constantine the Great, may have been the first Christian emperor of Rome. It's never been completely clear whether Constantine was really a disciple of Jesus Christ. However, he not only legalized Christianity (in 313 AD) but also established it as the preferred religion of Rome (by about 324 AD). Christianity didn't ruin the Empire—but it didn't save it, either.

In Topic 1, we provide you with some background on early Church history that may be new to you. We will look at what happened after the Roman government embraced Christianity, and at the development of the Eastern and Western churches.

Even as Christianity was adopted by a Roman emperor, Roman power continued to weaken. Like mixed iron and clay under stress, Rome began to collapse under her own weight, and the sharks were circling. Unlike the Babylonians, Persians, and Greeks, there was no unified new empire waiting to take control as Rome weakened.

Instead, waves of barbarians—Visigoths, Huns, Vandals, and Ostrogoths—invaded her domains. They were intent on plunder, not power. In their wake, they left chaos. Amidst the wreckage of Rome, the Church and monasteries emerged as lifeboats of learning. These communities of care would survive and help form a new way of life in Western Europe.

The Making of Medieval Europe: Charlemagne

When we say "Middle Ages" or "medieval," we mean the period from the division of the Roman Empire, in 395 AD, to the beginning of the Renaissance in the early 1300s AD. This later date is the era when Petrarch and other scholars began to discover and translate lost works of the Greeks and Romans. That's almost a thousand years between the end of the Ancient World and the beginning of the early modern world.

It's important to remember that the people who lived through all these years didn't think of themselves as being "between" things. Historians are always looking back on what came before to figure out how to live in the present. The people in the Middle Ages were passionate historians, who generally saw the past as far more glorious than the present—and no wonder! For many people, and for several centuries after the Fall of Rome, life in the present was a harsh struggle.

We focus our study of medieval history this week on Charlemagne, who built a strong kingdom in Gaul. At least, that is what Julius Caesar called it; nowadays we call it France. Charlemagne relied on a new kind of government that would eventually make it possible for one man to rule a vast kingdom through layer after layer of lesser lords.

This new form of government came to be called feudalism. Feudalism grew out of Germanic tribal customs. Warriors were arranged in a hierarchy of military and personal relationships that both defined society and protected western civilization from the Vikings (fierce Scandinavian peoples who often raided the coasts of France in their ships) and other marauders that threatened society.

Charlemagne was a mighty warrior and a capable leader. Under his reign, Western Europe enjoyed a brief return to law and order. The effects of his life were profound. His love for the Church, his orderly government, his love of justice and law, his establishment of monasteries, and the brief glow of culture and learning that attended his reign gave western Europeans vision, hope, and a renewed longing to reestablish the best features of the Roman Empire in a Christian context. The moment that captures this lasting desire of Europeans is best seen when Charlemagne was crowned with the title Holy Roman Emperor by the Pope in Rome in 800 AD.

Even under the rule of wise leaders, life after the fall of Rome was very bad for most people, and the rigid, hierarchical feudal relationships that developed were a sensible response to the dangers of the day. Heavily armed knights defended their lands against attack and supported their liege lords in battle when called.

We will learn about some of those who led these secular feudal hierarchies, forming the Great Houses of Europe, such as William the Conqueror of England, the Capet family of France, and the Holy Roman Emperors of Germany.

As we study daily life in medieval times, we'll learn a bit about chivalry and the making of knights. If your student enjoys acting as a brave knight or a beautiful damsel, he or she should be able to let his or her imagination soar throughout this unit!

Popes and Princes

Charlemagne showed how one man could effectively govern a vast area, even under extremely difficult conditions and with limited communications. Other rulers adopted his innovations and built on them to develop the feudal system, in which lords granted control over "fiefs" (lands) to "vassals" (lesser nobles) at lower and lower levels in return for the vassal's homage and loyalty. Feudalism and manorialism, an economic system that bound peasants to the land, together formed the framework of medieval society. These systems were paralleled in the Catholic Church, with a hierarchical ecclesiastical structure led by the Pope.

Popes and princes of the great houses of Europe wielded incredible authority during the medieval period. At times, the "Lords Spiritual" and the "Lords Temporal" clashed over the question of who had ultimate authority. On other occasions, they worked together, as the kings and knights of Europe fought religious Crusades with the blessing of the popes. This entanglement between spiritual and political authority set the stage for both the Protestant Reformation, which ended the Catholic monopoly on spiritual authority over the western Church, and the end of feudalism as the dominant system of government.

Conclusion

As Rome crumbled, it's hard to really imagine what was lost for the people who lived through it. Rome was the leader of Europe for nearly a thousand years, but crumble it did. Life became a struggle for survival for many.

Under that pressure, we want to see where people turned for strength. For many, it was their Christian faith that sustained them. Although some could not read the Word of God for themselves, many of the great rulers of the Middle Ages appear to have loved God, defended the Church, and administered justice. Even in the collapse and breakdown of Roman administration, we can see that God was still at work. In Micah 6:8, we read,

> He has told you, O man, what is good; and what does the LORD require of you but to do justice, and to love kindness, and to walk humbly with your God?

While some men certainly abused their power over others, others feared God and sought to do what was right. This attitude is reflected in the monastic codes of the Benedictine and Franciscan monks, and by codes of chivalry and knightly virtue that were the ideal then and are still admired by many today.

Mini-Unit 5, Topic 1
Collapse into Chaos

Introduction

The rule of Constantine the Great, the first "Christian" emperor of Rome, marks a turning point in history. Up till 313 AD, Rome was an enemy to the Christian faith. Roman soldiers killed Jesus; Nero killed Peter; later emperors killed countless Christians. This week, we read that the Roman Empire stopped killing Christians.

Constantine's turn towards the Christian Church introduced a new thread into the tapestry of Western history—the relationship of Church and state. All the kingdoms of this world have been unable to prevail against the Kingdom of God by force—but we will see that a whole new pattern of advantages and problems arose as the government started supporting the Church.

Diocletian

Before we learn about Constantine and his embrace of Christianity, we need to meet Diocletian, the Roman emperor who launched the last great physical attack on Christians, and who also ended the period of military anarchy that formed the crisis of the third century. He did this by seizing and holding power. Let's take a closer look at some other changes he brought about.

Diocletian divided the Roman Empire into halves: east and west. Each half of the empire had two rulers. There was a senior emperor and a junior emperor in each half, called the "Augustus" and the "Caesar" respectively. This system of having four rulers was called the "tetrarchy," from the Greek words *tetra*, meaning four, and *arche*, meaning rule.

Having four rulers had some advantages. But in no time, Rome was efficiently (and heavily) taxed, with a growing bureaucracy. Diocletian's decrees tied people to their lands and caused stagnation in both physical and professional mobility. Under Diocletian, farmers were not permitted to move and sons were required to follow their fathers' professions whether or not they had any desire or talent for the work. This policy became the expectation for most people in Europe for centuries, long after Rome fell.

When Diocletian retired, he made his co-emperor retire at the same time. The government of the empire was supposed to pass to the two junior emperors, the Caesars, but it didn't work out that way. Instead, the Caesars and their supporters fought each other for sole dominion.

Constantine

One of these two Caesars was Constantius, father of Constantine the Great. He fought the savage Picts in Scotland with his son Constantine at his side. When Constantius died, his troops immediately hailed Constantine as the new emperor. It took a few years, but Constantine eventually became sole Augustus of Rome. He allegedly proclaimed himself a Christian on the same day—although he put off baptism until just before he died, 31 years later.

Constantine rejected Diocletian's plan of multiple emperors, but he kept a major part of Diocletian's division of the Empire. Constantine moved his capital to Byzantium, a city in Turkey, and renamed it after himself. Constantinople became the new center of the empire.

Integration of Church and State

Though his personal conversion is a bit questionable, Constantine did extend legal protection to Christians. This was good news, in many ways. The empire started paying for pastors' salaries and some church buildings. Open preaching, teaching, and discussion of the gospel message were encouraged. Because being a Christian became socially acceptable, positive social pressures made church growth a whole lot easier!

State sponsorship of Christianity had its difficulties, too. As long as Christians were persecuted, worldliness wasn't a big problem, and the genuineness of conversion was constantly being proven. Things were very different in the newly-fashionable Church. Some appeared to join the Church for personal expediency rather than conviction. As the world moved into the Church, some believers became hermits and went to the deserts to pursue a life set apart.

With the increase of the Church's influence in political matters came increased worldly power for Church officials. Many power struggles and ugly situations within the Church arose from selfish ambition and vain conceit among church leaders. Another problem arose: Church leaders could increasingly be controlled by political agents since the Empire often paid their salaries.

The Council of Nicaea

One new problem with the new state sponsorship of Christianity was an issue of control. As the saying goes, "The one who pays the piper calls the tune." Constantine started the practice of calling "ecumenical councils" of the church. The first great gathering of church leaders from around the empire took place at Nicea, in modern-day Turkey. The Council of Nicea met in 325 AD for two and a half months. There were 318 bishops were there, plus Emperor Constantine himself.

The council was called to settle a doctrinal dispute in the Church of Alexandria over the nature of Jesus. Arius, an elder of Alexandria, argued that Jesus was not of the same substance as the Father. Arius took the position held by some today, which was that the Son was the first creation of the Father, not co-eternal with Him. In other words, Arius taught that Jesus was not fully God.

That is why the Nicene Creed, which was written by this council, emphasizes a belief in "One Lord Jesus Christ, the Son of God, begotten of the Father, Light of Light, very God of very God, begotten, not made, being of one substance with the Father."

The Council of Nicea officially opposed the teachings of Arius. The original Nicene Creed ended with an anathema against the Arians. It said:

> Those who say: 'There was a time when he was not'; and 'He was not before he was made'; and 'He was made out of nothing,' or 'He is of another substance' or 'essence,' or 'The Son of God is created,' or 'changeable,' or 'alterable'— they are condemned by the holy catholic and apostolic Church.

East and West

At this point, it was perfectly appropriate to refer to one "holy catholic and apostolic church." "Catholic" is a Greek term that means, "according to the whole" or "universal." ("Catholic," capitalized, has come to differentiate between Catholic and Protestant; "catholic," uncapitalized, refers to the universal Church.) Apostolic means the Church the apostles founded. Even though the Church was spread out across the known world, it was all one communion of saints. Before Diocletian, there was one Empire and one Church.

Diocletian divided the Roman Empire, and Constantine made Christianity the official religion of the Empire. This combination of events eventually pushed Christ's one Church into two separate organizations: Roman Catholicism and Eastern Orthodoxy.

Even though both halves of the Roman Empire are long gone, the Church still shows their influence. Roman Catholicism developed a theology and worship service that centered on the Eucharist (the sacrament of communion) as a pardon for sin in the face of damnation, with emphasis given to the law of God, His justice, and the atoning work of Christ.

As time passed, the Roman church focused more and more on Christ crucified. The Greek or Eastern Church focused on Christ resurrected and the restoration of mankind to a glory that God always intended that we should have.

Their differing theologies were reflected clearly in their church buildings. Roman Catholics erected cross-shaped cathedrals. Eastern Orthodox church architecture centered on a dome (the symbol of Heaven) filled with representations of the risen Christ.

The crucifix (the cross with Jesus on it) became the central symbol of Roman Catholic Christians, while icons (symbolic picture-representations of eternal realities) were the central symbols in Eastern Orthodox Churches.

Church government differed in East and West. For centuries, the bishop of Rome had been at the center of the known world. He was believed to occupy the place of Saint Peter, who died feeding Christ's flock according to His command. It was natural for the Roman church to adopt the best features of the Empire, from an administrative standpoint.

The Eastern Church, by contrast, had no single center. Jerusalem had been wiped out by the Romans, so each major city had its own leadership. No one church controlled any other. When it was necessary to hold a Holy Synod (conference) to discuss church matters, the bishops of each region were equals, with the bishop of Rome serving as "first among equals" (like the moderator of a board discussion) until 1054 AD. In that year, the Roman Catholic and Eastern Orthodox churches officially split.

The equality of bishops in the Eastern Church turned out to be a good thing when Muslim armies conquered Africa and the Middle East a few centuries later. When the great churches of Antioch and Alexandria were overrun, others in the East were able to go on functioning.

Julian the Apostate

Earlier, we discussed how Constantine made Christianity the official religion of the Empire. When Constantine died in the year 337 AD, his son Constantius II seized power and started killing off most of the rest of his family. After some time and further turmoil, Constantius II made his half-cousin Julian (their fathers were half-brothers) the Caesar of the West, while he focused on the East.

However, Constantius II insisted that Julian become an Arian Christian, as Constantius himself was. That, and his attempts to keep Julian as a tame subordinate in Gaul, didn't work—in the end, civil war was avoided only because Constantius II died, leaving Julian his successor. Julian then renounced his so-called Christian faith. He has been known ever since as "Julian the Apostate."

Your child isn't studying Julian in depth, but his life is worth noting. In his life, we see both the effectiveness of the Christian witness and God's active role in history.

Julian wanted to make Rome great by getting Christianity out of the government. He didn't try to kill off the Christians, but he revoked the privileged position of Christianity in the empire. Lands that had been given to the Church were taken back, bishops lost their traveling expense accounts, etc. Julian also prohibited Christian teachers from using pagan sources like the *Iliad*. "If they want to learn literature," he argued, "they have Luke and Mark: Let them go back to their churches and expound on them."[1]

Of course, in some ways this was a blessing for the young church: Christian teachers were forced to rely only on Scripture. But in other ways it was a loss, for now it would be more difficult for teachers to compare and contrast the teachings of the Bible with the literature of the day. Schools had been an important part of Christianity's growing influence in Rome, and at one stroke, Julian's edict eliminated that influence and put a lot of Christian scholars out of work.

Julian tried to beat the Christians at their own game, especially in acts of mercy and charity. He tried to get the pagan temples to provide the same kinds of services the Christian churches did. He said:

---
1 Brown, Peter. *The World of Late Antiquity*: Julian's School Edict. New York, NY: W. W. Norton, 1971, p. 93.

> These impious Galileans not only feed their own poor, but ours also; welcoming them into their *agapae* [literally "unconditional love," though here referring to "love-feasts" or meaning "taken in fellowship"], they attract them, as children are attracted, with cakes.
>
> Whilst the pagan priests neglect the poor, the hated Galileans devote themselves to works of charity, and by a display of false compassion have established and given effect to their pernicious errors. See their love-feasts, and their tables spread for the indigent. Such practice is common among them, and causes a contempt for our gods.[1]

In an intentional effort to irritate the Christians, Julian tried to rebuild the Jewish Temple in Jerusalem. According to contemporary historians, that project was a disaster. There seemed to be supernatural obstacles to its completion. Julian went on to launch a war against Persia, and was struck down by an arrow in battle. According to both pagan and Christian sources, he cried out at his death, "You have conquered, O Galilean!" From this account, we see that God was still at work, shaping the events of history.

Barbarians

After Julian, the Empire turned back to Christianity. But it didn't have a lot of time left. The Empire was now on its final death throes.

Up to now, history had been moving forward. Each empire was bigger than the last, each culture generally grew more sophisticated than its predecessor. But that all ends here. At the fall of Rome, ancient civilized culture was lost as wave after wave of rude, relatively primitive barbarian warriors broke over the Western Empire until it finally collapsed.

Visigoths

The first people to overrun Rome were the west Goths, or Visigoths. In fleeing the fierce Asian Huns, they pushed west, consistently either begging the Empire for protection or threatening to cause trouble on the borders. The Eastern emperors came up with a plan. They decided it was to their advantage to recruit these Gothic tribesmen for their armies. It would ease the burden on the native Romans, and it reduced the risk that some successful general would take over the Empire. What Roman would want to swear allegiance to some barbarian? That's how the mighty Gothic king,

---
1 "Julian the Apostate." New World Encyclopedia. Accessed 10 February 2014. Retrieved from <https://www.newworldencyclopedia.org/entry/Julian_the_Apostate>.

Alaric, wound up fighting for the Eastern emperor Theodosius I—and that's how he learned how weak the Empire really was.

Alaric eventually broke with the Empire. He ravaged Greece and invaded Italy three times. In the year 410 AD, he breached the gates of Rome. That city, which had kept out all foreign enemies for almost 800 years, now lay helpless before the barbarians. The looting was bad, but it could have been worse—churches were spared, and the masses who fled there for sanctuary survived. Alaric took what he wanted and left the city to put itself back together.

The Huns

The Huns were horsemen from the steppes in the middle of Asia. They may have originated in Mongolia. Attila the Hun was the greatest Hun ruler, and he was famous for his cruelty. His empire stretched from Mongolia to the Netherlands, from the Black Sea to the Baltic. He was the enemy of both the Eastern and Western halves of the Roman Empire. Attila besieged Constantinople, marched through France, and devastated Italy. The city of Venice was founded as a result of his attacks—the locals fled to make new homes on the marshy islands in the lagoon and never came back to the mainland.

As Attila marched towards Rome in the year 453 AD, he was met by an embassy that included Pope Leo I, unarmed. After talking with the Pope, for some mysterious reason, Attila turned away, leaving Rome untouched. He died the next year, and the Huns dispersed.

Without Attila's leadership, his empire broke into pieces. But the waves of humanity the Huns had stirred up were still in motion. There were displaced people everywhere—many Angles and Saxons fled the Continent to the relative safety of Britain, for example.

Vandals

The next barbarians to sack Rome were the Vandals. As far as we can tell, they were trying to get away from the Huns, too. The Vandals took the scenic route to Rome—in 406 AD, they devastated France, and in 409 AD, they crossed into Spain. That kept them busy for twenty years, but then they built a fleet and sailed to Africa. The Vandals took Carthage without a fight and then hopped over to Sicily and other Mediterranean islands. From there, Vandal fleets could raid the Eastern and Western empires easily—until Attila the Hun died.

His death freed up what was left of the Roman forces to deal with these pesky pirates. Unfortunately, it didn't turn out quite the way Rome had hoped—the Vandals took Rome in 455 AD and plundered it for two weeks straight. Pope Leo tried to keep them from burning down the city—with some success, apparently. The Vandals did a lot of damage, but, as with the Visigoths, it could have been a lot worse.

Odoacer

A few years later, the West ceased to be an empire. Odoacer, a Germanic soldier who had fought for the empire, led a revolt against Romulus Augustulus, the last emperor—a fifteen-year-old boy. After the revolt, both the Roman and tribal soldiers proclaimed Odoacer "king of Italy." The next year, he captured the boy emperor and compelled him to give up his crown. Odoacer could have claimed it, but that might have created a conflict with the emperor of the East in Constantinople, so he renounced the now meaningless title. He sent a purple robe to Zeno, the Eastern emperor, with a message that said, in effect, "One emperor is enough. I will rule Italy in your name."

Ostrogoths

Constantinople didn't object—immediately—but Odoacer didn't rule in Zeno's name for long. The Ostrogoths were on the move. "Ostrogoth" means "east Goth." They had been subject to the Huns until Attila died, but once he was out of the way, they could flex their muscles. King Theodoric of the Ostrogoths invaded northern Italy a few years after Odoacer took over, in 493 AD.

Theodoric was raised and educated in Constantinople, where he had been a diplomatic hostage. The Eastern Empire supported his attack on Italy, and he killed Odoacer with his own hand. But Theodoric soon grew too strong for Constantinople's comfort. The Eastern Empire didn't want a new rival—so it began pitting one tribe against another, derailing any possibility of restoring the greatness of the West.

A Whimper, Not a Bang

So, when all was said and done, "the end" happened very quietly. It's hard to tell exactly when Rome fell. The year 476 AD was "the end" of the Western Empire because nobody even wanted the title of Western Emperor any more. Roman citizens outside of Italy would not have known that Rome had "fallen" in any sudden or catastrophic way. Roman Britain wasn't overrun—but it saw a steady drain on the soldiers who guarded it and a corresponding increase in barbarian raids upon its borders. Civilization eroded more slowly than you might imagine.

But it did erode—and every loss was permanent. Where cities were prosperous, greedy barbarians came searching for loot. Trade ceased and people either scattered or banded together behind walls. Civilization dwindled into pockets and books were lost; there was little time for art or education. The lights of learning were slowly dimmed all over Europe.

Candles of Learning

Those lights did not quite go out, however. During the fall of Rome, people still sought to find how they should live, and monasticism became attractive for many seeking to escape the violence and chaos for a life of order and discipline. Books were treasured, preserved, copied, and studied in these places. The most famous of these monks included St. Benedict, who founded the Benedictine Order, and one of his monks, who became Pope St. Gregory I.

In Italy, which had once been the center of learning and the hub of peace and administrative order for the empire, Rome's fall seemed like the end of the world. Some people went mad or committed suicide. Some Christians put down their tools and waited for the Lord to return.

Some Romans blamed Christians for the disaster. After Alaric sacked Rome in 410 AD, the famed St. Augustine wrote his great book *The City of God* to refute these claims that the Christians were at fault for Rome's collapse. He reminded his contemporaries how many things had gone wrong with Rome while they were still worshipping idols. He argued that Rome was at her best when she was a self-governing Republic, when virtuous men put the good of the commonwealth ahead of their own pockets or power. Rome may have reached her pinnacle of power under the emperors, but Augustine argued that her best days were over long before Jesus was born. He pointed out that once men began to put their own interests ahead of their nation's, the end was inevitable.

Conclusion

As the Roman government split and barbarians were massing on the increasingly-undefended borders, many people suffered because it was a chaotic and fearful time. Rome had been strong, and seemed to be invincible, but there came a day when it was no more.

Is our nation's longevity any more certain? Many Americans wonder today! Fortunately, our hope is in something stronger than Rome. We end this section with an apt word from Daniel 2:44:

> And in the days of those kings the God of heaven will set up a kingdom that shall never be destroyed, nor shall the kingdom be left to another people. It shall break in pieces all these kingdoms and bring them to an end, and it shall stand forever.

Mini-Unit 5, Topic 2
The Making of Medieval Europe: Charlemagne

Introduction

This week is devoted to understanding how the people of Western Europe slowly began to build a new way of life during the centuries after the Roman Empire fell. The central figure for this week's study is the extraordinary king of the Franks, Charles the Great, who is best known by his Latin title, Charlemagne.

Charlemagne's Background

Charlemagne is one of the best-known kings of the Middle Ages. During his long reign, he ruled the lands that now make up Belgium, France, Luxembourg, the Netherlands, Switzerland, and part of western Germany. Charlemagne was also a Christian emperor. He had a close relationship with the Pope, whom he defended from the Lombards (an Italian tribe).

We know a lot about Charlemagne because of two biographies that were written about him during and after his lifetime. One biographer describes him as more than 6 feet tall, with piercing eyes, fair hair, a thick neck, and a potbelly. He was strong, fond of exercise, and had an alert mind and a forceful personality.

Charlemagne was a "larger-than-life" character with a deep love for learning and

Christianity. His example and administration encouraged a brief renaissance in art and literacy that strengthened the clergy and, after his death, caused many monasteries to be established. As with Constantine, Charlemagne's close relationship with the Christian church set up expectations between emerging kingdoms and the Roman Church, leading to tensions that we will note for the rest of our study of the Middle Ages.

Protecting France and the Christian faith was nothing new in Charlemagne's family. His grandfather, Charles "the Hammer" (Martel), stopped the Muslims from conquering what is now France.[1]

Charles Martel was not a titled king—he was technically just the "mayor of the palace," who exercised authority on behalf of the actual king. The kings at that time were descended from Clovis, the first king of the Franks, who had lived around 500 AD. The heirs of Clovis were known as the Merovingian kings, and they had ruled the Franks for more than 200 years. By the time of Charles Martel, however, the real power behind the throne was the administrative head of the kingdom: the "mayor of the palace."

Charlemagne's father, Pepin the Short, was not content with being merely mayor, however powerful the role might be. He posed a question to Pope Zachary, asking: "Who is the 'king'—the man who holds the title or the person who makes the actual decisions?" Zachary sided with Pepin—which was not all that surprising, since he was heavily dependent on Pepin's forces to protect him from the Lombard tribes that had invaded Italy. With Pope Zachary's backing, Pepin was chosen as king of the Franks, deposing the last Merovingian king, Childeric III.

Church and State

The Pope crowned Pepin King of the Franks, thus beginning a new relationship between the spiritual authority of the Church and the secular power of the State.

Around this time, in the 700s AD, a document surfaced in Rome that claimed to be an imperial decree from Constantine I (who had lived about 400 years previous). This document said that Constantine gave most of his property, rights, and honors as emperor of the West to Pope Sylvester and his successors. The so-called "Donation of Constantine" became the basis of the Church's medieval claims to secular authority.

---

[1] We don't spend much time explaining who the Muslims were, where they came from, or what they believed. There is material in the books we recommend that describes this. In the full *Tapestry of Grace* program, we look at the rise of Islam in much greater detail. Here, we will simply note that the Muslims arose around 600 AD and conquered most of the Middle East and Northern Africa, and were pushing into Europe through Spain. They were stopped decisively by Charles Martel and the Frankish army.

The Roman Catholic Church no longer relies on it, however—it has been generally recognized as a forgery for centuries.

The Donation of Pepin, by contrast, was probably legitimate. Pepin took territory from the Lombards, who owned lots of land at the top of the "boot" of Italy, and gave it to Pope Zachary, turning him from a surrogate ruler of Rome into a prince in his own right, with the attendant responsibilities of land ownership and the necessity to administer and defend them. Ownership of these territories, which were thereafter called "Papal States," also gave wealth and influence to the popes. These lands were located north and east of Rome, effectively dividing the peninsula of Italy in half. They were controlled directly by the popes, retarding political union of the peninsula until Italy was finally united in the 1800s.

People now had a new question to wrestle through. Was this land gift to the Pope a good thing, or not? Furthermore, what was the right relationship between the Church and the secular government?

After centuries of experience with struggles between competing authorities, most Christian theologians now teach that God has created separate spheres of authority. These spheres include the state, the Church, and the family. When one authority tries to control matters that properly belong to another sphere, it usually causes trouble—whether it is a case of Church controlling government, government controlling Church, or either of them trying to take over family matters. But, it took a long time for this viewpoint to become commonly accepted.

Charlemagne's Reign

The relationship between Church and state got even more involved under Pepin's son, Charlemagne. Charlemagne was a successful warrior. He spent months of each year at war. He quickly defeated the Lombards, who had been harassing Italy and threatening the Pope, and became their king. For thirty years, he warred against the Saxons (who controlled territory that today falls into much of western Germany) and finally subdued them. He forced their conversion to Christianity in this process. Charlemagne also conquered Bavaria in southern Germany and took land and treasure from the Avars in Eastern Europe.

By 800 AD, Charlemagne's realm extended across Europe. He waged war in Spain, too, without as much success. In 778 AD, as he returned from an expedition there, the mountain tribes known as Basques ambushed his forces and wiped out his rear guard. The attack was immortalized in an epic poem, *The Song of Roland*. It is cited by many as the first major work of French literature: a "song of heroic deeds."

Coronation

Like his father, Charlemagne always acted to protect and support the Church. Pope Leo III rewarded him by crowning him Holy Roman Emperor in Rome on Christmas Day, 800 AD. It was an immensely symbolic moment with lasting effects. The resurgence of Western Europe signaled the end of any unity between Eastern and Western Roman Empires. The Pope's decision to crown a new emperor without consulting with Constantinople drove a further wedge between East and West. The coronation of an Emperor by a pope created new rivalries between the secular and spiritual authorities of Europe, foreshadowing centuries of tension between Church and state.

Administration of an Empire

It was one thing to be crowned Emperor. It was another thing to rule an empire effectively. The mighty Alps, which were difficult to cross, divided Charlemagne's realm. Also, there was no way Charlemagne could exert his personal influence over the entirety of such a vast territory, especially in a time when the fastest overland travel was still provided by horses and parchment letters were still the only method of long-distance communication.

There were hardly any towns left in Europe, and there was even less in the way of trade or industry. People were subsistence farmers who typically never traveled more than ten miles from the place where they were born. Remember, since the time of Diocletian back in the 200s AD (before Constantine), men in the West had been tied to their lands, and sons were expected to follow their fathers' profession. Local rulers who swore allegiance to Charlemagne still had a great deal of power over the lives of the people who lived on their lands.

To deal with his administrative challenges, Charlemagne appointed vassals. He granted large, landed estates to loyal nobles, who provided military and political services in return. Such nobles were responsible for building fortifications and providing soldiers when Charlemagne needed them. Vassals were also responsible for maintaining roads and bridges on their lands.

Charlemagne kick-started trade by making silver coins and helping to establish markets. He also constantly changed the location of his court so he could check in on his vassals. He was committed to good government and the administration of justice. Charlemagne ordered all courts to be open regularly and insisted that judges base their decisions on recognized law.

Promotion of Learning within His Empire

Charlemagne valued education. He could both read and speak Latin, even though he never mastered handwriting or spelling. He promoted schools and libraries throughout his realm. He set an example by attracting scholars and learned men to his own court to teach at his school there. He had his own sons *and* daughters learn to read and write in a time when almost no women were given education.

Monasteries and the Preservation of Books

Charlemagne's love for learning made a difference to the history of Europe, because education was in bad shape when he rose to power. His support for monasteries helped to salvage learning in Europe. Under his rule, scholars were able to preserve what knowledge was left and begin to build something new out of it: a new culture.

It was like this: suppose that you have been shipwrecked on a desert island with a few hundred other people, and the only books you managed to get to shore were the Bible, a geometry textbook, and *The Adventures of Winnie the Pooh*. If you were to build up a whole society based on only these books, what would it be like? Would future island-dwelling generations who grew up reading *Winnie the Pooh* believe that there are talking animals in the country from which their ancestors came? Would they ever discover algebra or astronomy? Might they write stories in which Christopher Robin is associated with God and Pooh represents mankind?

After the fall of Rome, Western Europe was like that shipwrecked group of refugees who had only a few books out of which to build a new civilization. During those hundreds of years of destruction and anarchy, many books were destroyed or simply not re-copied. The East had the great library at Alexandria, but with the fall of Rome the West lost most works by Plato (philosophy), Aristotle (philosophy and science), Euclid (geometry), Ptolemy (astronomy), and Hippocrates and Galen (medicine), as well as the great Greek plays and some important works by Cicero (a Roman statesman who also wrote on education).

As C.S. Lewis once remarked, "The Middle Ages depended predominantly on books" (*Discarded Image* 5). Medieval men had many fewer books than we do, but their books were probably more important to them than ours are to us! Times were cruel, and few people (besides priests and clerks) had the ability to read or write at all, but men treasured the few precious volumes that survived: copies of the Bible, writings from the early Church fathers, and a few works by Roman authors were typical.

Book-loving men used these to build a whole culture for medieval Christendom.

Charlemagne, with his love of learning, support for monasteries, and restoration of order in Western Europe, helped to make that possible.

Charlemagne's Legacy

Though Charlemagne was a great individual, many of his achievements did not outlast him. The most obvious failure was the political fragmentation of his empire. His son and successor, Louis the Pious, was a good man but not much of a king. His feeble attempts to govern were hampered by frequent Viking invasions, and he died about 25 years after his father had.

Three years after Louis' death, Charlemagne's grandsons split his empire into three parts, then fell to fighting for it and grabbing parts of it from each other. The Treaty of Verdun, agreed on in 843 AD, finally settled the boundaries of their three kingdoms. Looking at these, we can begin to see the outline of modern European states.

Charles the Bald received most of what is now France. Louis the German took almost all of the land east of the Rhine, which became modern Germany. Lothair kept the title of Emperor and a strip of land between his brothers, running from what is now the Netherlands down into Italy. That strip became a battleground of Europe for the next thousand years.

Unfortunately, the sons and grandsons of Charlemagne's grandsons were weak and quarrelsome. Before long, Charlemagne's divided empire was attacked from all sides. Magyars advanced from the east, Muslims from the south, and Vikings from the north. By the late 800s, the Carolingian ("of Charles") Empire no longer existed.

The British Isles

The only part of Western Europe that Charlemagne did not directly influence was the British Isles. During his reign, Britain was divided up into a number of small kingdoms. Germanic tribes of Angles and Saxons had crossed the North Sea into Britain, driving the native Britons into Wales.

Between Rome's fall in 476 AD and Charlemagne's death in 814 AD is the time when there may have been a brave British warrior whose life story grew into the legend of King Arthur. Some say he was descended from the British Romans, or even from Roman rulers. He was perhaps a successful war leader, or perhaps a king, and his name has several variations. One or two of the most reliable historical texts we have (the earliest in 828 AD) do mention a man who may be the historical reality behind Camelot and the Round Table!

After Arthur faded into legend, the most important of the small British kingdoms was the kingdom of the West Saxons, called Wessex. Egbert the Saxon built Wessex into a powerful kingdom, and took Charlemagne's sister (or, possibly, sister-in-law) as his wife.

Wessex wasn't the only kingdom in Britain at this time. There were lots of others, especially the powerful midland kingdom of Mercia. After Egbert took the West Saxon throne, however, he conquered Cornwall, Kent, Surrey, and Sussex, making Wessex supreme. The remaining kingdoms of Mercia, East Anglia, and Northumbria recognized his rule. Egbert's rule in Wessex made it possible to imagine that a single king could rule over all of England.

Meanwhile, there were other northern peoples in and around Britain: the Picts were in Scotland, and Vikings and Danes harassed the British coasts. The Picts were so fierce that even the Romans hadn't wanted to fight them for their patch of frozen highlands. Long ago in the glory days of Rome, under Emperor Hadrian, the Romans build Hadrian's Wall to separate "civilized" Roman Britain from Scotland. The Romans eventually went home, but the Picts remained.

Meanwhile, the Vikings and Danes were seafaring Germanic tribes who lived all over the northern European seas, raiding even as far as Constantinople in their longships! These Vikings were the pirates of their day. Their shallow-hulled boats, equipped with both oars and sails, could slip up a river to raid a village in a single night, and they were a constant terror to anybody who lived near a coastline. Thanks to them, Britain and coastal France were not especially safe places to live in these days.

The Capetians and the Founding of France

Let's look briefly at the foundations of France. Charlemagne's grandsons split up his empire, and before two centuries were out, the nobles of the realm chose another line of kings. They elected Hugh Capet as king, and many historians date the founding of France to the coronation of this first Capetian king.

For a long time, the Capets controlled only a small area of land between Paris and the city of Orleans. Other great noblemen ruled their own domains with little regard for the king. That isn't surprising considering the origins of some of them. The first Duke of Normandy was a converted Christian Viking named Rollo. When told he had to kiss the Capetian king's foot as part of the oath of fealty, Rollo raised the king's foot to his own lips rather than kneel, knocking the king off his feet in the process. The dukes of Normandy were the most powerful of the French lords. Although they were technically vassals of the king of France, one of Rollo's heirs, William the Conqueror, became the ruler of all of England, too.

But the family of Capet grew stronger over time. Every king had a son to succeed him on the throne, and they kept adding territory to their personal lands. Though still powerful in their domains, the French nobles slowly lost the power to choose the next king. When the Crusades began in 1100 AD, many nobles left France to fight the Muslims for the Holy Land, never to return. This increased the slowly-growing power of the French kings.

William the Conqueror's Line

In England, William the Conqueror forcibly united the patchwork of factions in Britain. He was a Norman ("Northman"), descended from the Norsemen (or Vikings) who settled in Normandy (northern France) in the 900s AD. William led a band of Norman knights across the English Channel and defeated the Saxon king in a single battle at Hastings in 1066 AD.

William the Conqueror then established a strong central government, based in London (originally a Roman town called Londinium), where he built a castle called the Tower of London. As king, William claimed all the land of England and then parceled it out as fiefs to his vassals, the great Norman lords. These, in turn, subdivided their vast tracts of land into smaller fiefs awarded to lesser vassals, all the way down to the lowest nobles: the knights. The Angles and the Saxons who had ruled England became serfs, bound to work the land they lived on.

There were struggles between medieval kings and the great lords who served them all over Europe. England was different from most other places in that the kings won all these struggles at first. Next week we'll study a notable exception to that rule that occurred a few generations after William the Conqueror, in the era of Robin Hood. That's when wily King John (brother and heir of Richard the Lionheart) was forced to negotiate a deal with his rebellious barons and wound up signing the Magna Carta (also spelled Magna Charta). For now, it's enough to note that Norman England started off with a central government that was relatively strong.

Conclusion

Even though the government and schools Charlemagne built did not long outlive him, the effects of his life were profound. His love for the Church, his orderly government, his support for justice and law, his establishment of monasteries, and the brief glow of culture and learning that attended his reign gave western Europeans vision, hope, and a renewed longing to reestablish the Roman Empire in a Christian context that they called Christendom.

Charlemagne's innovations in government were copied over the next century and both applied and further developed in what we now know as France and England. Next week, we'll learn more about this system of feudalism and witness the growing struggle between popes and princes.

Mini-Unit 5, Topic 3
Popes and Princes

Introduction

After Charlemagne, we reach the height of the Middle Ages. Much of our emphasis will be on understanding daily life, but we'll also take a look at some of the early Crusades.

We've mentioned that things were bad after the fall of Rome. It is important to realize that when we say this, we mean that they were *really* bad. According to *World Book Encyclopedia*,

> At least half of the land [in Europe] could not be farmed because of thick forests or swamps. War, disease, famine, and a low birth rate kept the population small. People lived an average of only 30 years. There was little travel or communication, and fewer than 20 percent of the people went farther than 10 miles from their birthplace.[1]

Things were so bad that men and women gladly gave up their freedom for protection. That's how feudalism developed: it was a system that brought families some safety and a chance to flourish in exchange for commitment to support and obey their defender. Within the system, individual men wielded enormous power.

As the threats from barbarians subsided, the increasingly powerful Church in Europe turned its attention to the rising power of the Turks and the Ottoman Empire.

---
[1] From a *World Book* article entitled *Feudalism*. Contributor: Joel T. Rosenthal, Professor of History, State University of New York, Stony Brook.

These threatened to disrupt access of Christian European pilgrims to the sites of the Holy Land. Popes responded by launching crusade after crusade.

During this time there was comparative safety and government stability, as well as more food, in Europe. Feudalism, the new relationship between Church and state, and the manorial system, worked—at least, well enough. The fierce Viking raids ended, largely because the Vikings became Christians! Petty squabbles had been largely resolved over time because of the consolidation of many European lands in France and England under a few strong leaders.

Towns and trade began to spring up once again in the shadows of the great castles of Europe. Kings and popes had their quarrels, as did local lords and the heads of local churches or monasteries. Such disputes often resulted in suffering for everybody. Nevertheless, at least now there was order in society.

It was a system that allowed crops to flourish without fear of raiders or embattlement and the establishment of courts to which appeals could be brought. There was more leisure for quiet reflection, and more energy to put towards new innovations. There was more travel, trade, and circulation of ideas. Under these circumstances, culture began to flourish again.

The Crusades had a long-range effect on history. They brought copies of lost Greek and Roman works, together with new ideas by Muslim and Hebrew scholars, back into the West. The return of such works sparked the Renaissance, a revival of learning that led to renewed interest in God's Word. The Crusades propelled large groups of Europeans to travel far from home, which stirred up the culture of western Christendom in all kinds of new ways. Popes and princes were able to set aside their political differences to conduct crusades.

Although the Crusades were morally questionable, bloody, and ultimately ineffective in their stated goal of recovering the Holy Land, we do see that God used these struggles for His purposes. With that as background, let's take a look at feudalism in Western Europe and events leading up to the early Crusades.

Feudalism

The form of government in all these lands from sometime in the 700s AD until sometime in the 1100s or 1200s AD was feudalism. We've seen that one major strand of feudalism first appeared under Charlemagne back in 800 AD. His system of vassals who managed lands and supplied arms made it possible for high kings or emperors to govern large territories effectively. Though Charlemagne's central government dissolved after his death, his idea of government on the basis of delegated ownership of land lived on.

A lord was a nobleman who owned land. Great land owners divided their estates and created vassals. The parcel granted to a vassal was called a fief (from which we get the term "feudalism"). The vassal gave military service (which included equipage such as armor, weapons, and horses) and a regular tithe of money or goods to his lord, in addition to his sworn oath that he would defend the lord, fight his enemies, and embrace his friends. The saying was, "No land without a lord; no lord without a land."

There was a ceremony that made a man a vassal, which included two specific actions. First, the vassal rendered homage, a French word for "man." This made the vassal the lord's loyal man, promising to fight on the lord's behalf. Second, the vassal took an oath of fealty, which means faithfulness. Disloyalty to one's lord was one of the worst crimes possible in medieval Europe.

As the Vikings menaced Europe, strong warriors emerged as overlords who portioned out their lands to lesser lords, who subdivided that among their own vassals (usually fighting men who came to be called "knights"), and then those likewise distributed land among their own lesser knights, who assigned their plots to their peasants to be farmed.

The peasants did not actually own the land they worked and did not fight for their lords, except in dire emergencies when the home manor was under attack. They were more like family dependents or household servants, or even, sadly, like slaves.

Feudalism was a "multi-level" system because a single man could be both a vassal of one and a lord of another. Once a vassal acquired a fief, he could entrust it to some lesser lord as his vassal, and so on down the line. This made for a whole chain of feudal relationships. In theory, the emperor was lord of kings, who were the lords of the peers (high nobles) of the realm, who were lords of the lesser nobility, who were lords of the knights.

Feudalism wasn't just a secular system. The Church had already developed a similar hierarchical pattern, with the Pope at the top and laymen at the bottom. In addition, after centuries of donations by landowners, churches and monasteries held vast tracts of land, which they could distribute as fiefs to bishops and abbots—or to barons and knights. This meant that church leaders became lords in their own right, with troops at their command.

Manorialism

The peasants were a different class than either nobility or clergy. Every lord, whether noble or clergy, was the master of the peasants on his fief. The peasants served under a system called manorialism (a fief was also often called a manor).

In manorialism, peasants (also called serfs) lived on the land of their lord and received his protection. In return, they tended the land, gave a large share of the produce from the land to the lord, and also offered their service as laborers, skilled workers, servants, etc. Peasants were legally subject to the lord of the manor, and to his court. They were bound to the land and whoever controlled it. (Remember that this practice was first established by Diocletian during the waning days of the Roman Empire.)

Distinguishing Between Feudalism and Manorialism

Unlike the nobles and clergy, peasants didn't rule anything. For all practical purposes, they were a part of the property that the nobles or clergy controlled. Because the peasants weren't governed by the feudal oaths like fealty and homage, it wouldn't be accurate to call them a part of the feudal system.

Manorialism was an economic relationship between the lord of a manor and his peasant tenants. Feudalism, by contrast, was a political and military system, not an economic system. It's like the difference between capitalism and democracy: one is an economic system, the other is a political system. Manorialism and feudalism went together like capitalism and democracy.

Popes

During the High Middle Ages, the popes reached the height of their power. They generally prevailed in their clashes with secular rulers because they claimed divine authority. Monarchs simply could not deny their authority, as much as they hated losing power. We see this power struggle most clearly in the history of what is now Germany.

German States and the Holy Roman Empire

In France and England, secular authorities managed to centralize their control. In France, this happened gradually as the Capets gained power. In England, this happened overnight as William the Conqueror defeated the Saxons at the Battle of Hastings.

In Germany, things went in a different direction. The Germanic population originated in a series of independent, semi-nomadic tribes. These had their own traditions of fierce loyalties to chiefs. Then, Otto the Great bit off more than he could chew. Otto's father was Henry I, king of Germany. In 951 AD, Otto crossed the Alps and declared himself king of Italy. As with Charlemagne, his problem now became the Alps.

It wasn't easy for Otto to maintain control over his Germanic lands—in his absence, the other German princes began revolting against his rule. The Slavs of Poland rebelled at the same time, and a fierce people known as the Magyars invaded Germany from the east. Otto fought back, crushing the Magyars, subduing the Poles, and replacing the German princes with members of his own family. Ten years after he crossed the Alps the first time, he crossed them again to squash an uprising in Rome. In gratitude, Pope John XII crowned Otto emperor of what later came to be called the Holy Roman Empire.

This so-called Empire (best summed up by the observation [1] that it was neither holy, nor Roman, nor an empire) never developed into a unified nation-state during medieval times. Instead, it was the setting for one of the most famous conflicts between Church and state in the Middle Ages. A few generations after Otto, an exceptionally able and energetic monk named Hildebrand became Pope Gregory VII.

Pope Gregory made a number of important reforms to the Church. One of them was that he prohibited secular rulers from appointing men of their choice to church offices. This practice, called "investiture," had been an important source of revenue for some time, since high officials in the church received tithe money from their offices, and there were men who were willing to pay a secular ruler a lot to be appointed to wealthy Church positions.

When Pope Gregory decreed that secular rulers must stop choosing Church leaders, Otto's descendant, the German King Henry IV, objected. He did more than object—he called a council at the German city of Worms in 1076 AD and declared the Pope deposed. Henry's father, Henry III, had gotten several popes elected and/or deposed, so the son thought he was well within his rights. Pope Gregory excommunicated Henry for this and released all his vassals from their vows to obey him. Thus, both pope and king attempted to depose the other.

Because of the feudal system, Henry depended on the support of his vassals, and many of these German princes sided with the Pope. Eventually, Henry had to yield. The Pope had retreated to a stronghold in the mountains of Italy, and legend says that he made Henry stand barefoot in the snow for three days before he could kneel at the Pope's feet and be pardoned.

---
1 Voltaire, in *Essai sur l'histoire générale et sur les mœurs et l'esprit des nations*, Chapter 70 (1756).

That wasn't the end of the story, though. When Henry went back to Germany, civil war broke out again. Gregory excommunicated and deposed Henry a second time, and Henry captured Rome and put in a pope of his own choice. The new pope crowned Henry as the Holy Roman Emperor. Gregory died in exile, but his successors took up the struggle and Henry was excommunicated one more time. When one of Henry's sons rebelled against him, Henry was forced to abdicate. He died while preparing to fight to regain power.

Seljuk Turks

Though popes and monarchs struggled for power in Europe, they also joined hands to fight a common enemy: the Turks, relatives of the Huns who had plagued Europe five centuries earlier. The Turks were fierce warriors from the East who took lands from both the Arab Muslims and the Byzantine Empire. They became Muslim, but unlike the Arabs, who had generally respected Christians, the Turks were brutal to the western pilgrims who traveled to the Holy Land.

Turkish hostility changed the course of history because, when they threatened Constantinople in the early 1090s, the Byzantine emperor appealed for help to the western Pope. This was a big deal, because the eastern and western churches had excommunicated each other a few decades earlier, in 1054 AD. Pope Urban II called for Christian knights to sail for Palestine to save it from these unbelievers. In the years that followed, Europe launched nine major Crusades against the Turks.

Pilgrimages and the Cause of the Crusades

Since the days of Emperor Constantine in the 300s AD, before Rome fell, Christians had been taking trips to Palestine to retrace the steps of Christ and see the places where He lived, ministered, and died. Constantine's mother, Helena, was one of the earliest of such travelers, who were called "pilgrims" and went on these "pilgrimages" to the "Holy Land." Over the centuries, even though travel was difficult and dangerous, many western Europeans followed in her footsteps.

When the Muslim forces captured Jerusalem in 1187 AD and began to limit access of Christian pilgrims to the Holy Land, many felt that their salvation was threatened. To understand this, we need to understand the basics of the Catholic doctrine of Purgatory. This was their reason to go to war!

As time went on, pilgrims began to expect to receive a special blessing from the sacred places that they visited and touched in the Holy Land. Christians also began to try to use these trips as a spiritual bargaining chip, vowing that they would go on pilgrimage if God (or one of the saints to whom they prayed) would forgive them for a sin committed, or give them something they wanted (e.g., health for a dying family member). When Christians became unable to safely travel to the Holy Land, this bargaining chip was lost.

Purgatory

The topic of Purgatory may lead to some interesting discussions in your home. This is an area where Catholics and Protestants genuinely disagree. Roman Catholics believe that when Christians die, they go to an in-between place that is neither Earth, nor Hell, nor Heaven. This place is uncomfortable: it involves fire and pain. However, it is not a bad place, since it is where the saints are finally purified of all their earthly sins so that they may join Christ in Heaven. (Note that Roman Catholics would not say that Christians are saved through Purgatory; they believe that Christians are saved through Christ's death, but that Purgatory is necessary to remove the final stains, as it were, of our earthly sinful lives, so that we are ready to be presented to Christ.)

This doctrine of Purgatory is based on a text (Maccabees 12:45) that Martin Luther and other Protestant reformers did not accept as part of the Bible, though the Roman Catholic Church had always accepted it. There are other texts that are also used to support the concept of Purgatory (1 Peter 1:6-7, 1 Corinthians 3:13-15, and Matthew 12:31-32), but these are not nearly as clear as the Maccabees passage. Since proponents of the two viewpoints do not agree on the legitimacy of the book of Maccabees, it is easy for them to disagree!

Indulgences

Indulgences were an invention of the popes that, ironically, played a part in undermining both feudalism and the unity of the Catholic Church itself! An indulgence was an official document that was supposed to act like a "get out free" card for a certain number of years that a person would otherwise spend being purified of his sins in Purgatory. The idea was that an impressively good deed—risking your life to save Jerusalem, for example—would make up for some of your sins.

The popes offered indulgences to anyone who risked their lives to save the Holy Land, which motivated many, but not enough. Pope Innocent III upped the ante—he offered an indulgence for those who paid the way for someone else to go.

This changed the basic equation of feudalism, because up to this point land had been the only means of exchange for military services. Money had seemed too mercenary a reason to fight. Suddenly, because of the Crusades, money changed hands instead of land. The feudal system of land, loyalty, and personal relationships began to be supplemented by a new (and more efficient) system.

Richard the Lionheart

Richard the Lionheart was the great-grandson of William the Conqueror, the fourth-generation Norman ruler of still mostly-Saxon England. Richard took the throne in 1189 AD and left on the Third Crusade the next year. His brother, Prince John, ruled as his regent (substitute king). Richard took with him much of England's money and many of her best men. He was a successful Crusader, but was forced to leave the Holy Land because he realized that Prince John was plotting with the king of France against him. He negotiated a truce with the Muslim leader, Saladin, and headed home.

On the long march back through Europe, Richard was taken prisoner by Leopold of Austria. Henry VI, the Holy Roman Emperor, demanded a king's ransom. Prince John offered to pay him money to not set Richard free. Despite that, English nobles raised and paid the ransom, and Richard was set free. The king of France is reported to have warned Prince John, "Look to yourself, the devil is loose."

King John

Richard was a lionhearted man. When he returned from the Crusades and his captivity, he forgave his brother and named John his heir. In just a few years, Richard died of a crossbow wound and John took over England. John's path wasn't easy—the nobles who paid to get Richard back didn't want John as their king.

Things got worse when John butted heads with the Pope. The Archbishop of Canterbury had died and John wanted one of his supporters to take the post. The monks of Canterbury chose another man, however. When both sides appealed to Pope Innocent III, he surprised all parties by rejecting both nominees in favor of his own man.

This seemed outrageous to these feudal men. The Archbishop of Canterbury was a vassal of the king, and people thought a lord had the right to choose his own vassals. King John retaliated by expelling the monks of Canterbury who had caused the problem in the first place. The Pope struck back by suspending all worship and sacraments in England. John responded by seizing Church property for breaching feudal obligations.

The dispute raged on. Two years later, John was excommunicated with no result. Pope Innocent threatened worse unless he submitted. When John finally gave in, he made the most of the situation—he offered to surrender all of England to God and Saints Peter and Paul.

This was brilliant, in a way—but to understand why, you have to know the rest of John's troubles. Not only was John butting heads with the Pope, he also had troubles with his own barons. They were willing to put up with a lot as long as a king was victorious, but John had lost his battles with the Pope and also lost lands in France, across the English Channel. The barons rebelled against him and demanded concessions. They met John at a meadow near London called Runnymeade and forced him to sign the Great Charter (called *Magna Carta* in Latin).

Here's where King John's concessions to the church paid off. After he signed the document under pressure from his own vassals, he appealed to the Pope to be released from his vows. Pope Innocent ruled that he wasn't obligated by such a vow. The barons were outraged and invited the French to invade England. Nobody knows how long the war might have continued if John had not gotten sick and died. When John's nine-year old son took the throne, the barons relented, preferring to be ruled by a young English prince rather than a mature French king.

Nation States?

Now, although we've been talking about England, France, and Germany, those nations did not yet exist as such. The land was there, of course, but much of Europe was still fragmented into tiny kingdoms and princedoms (called "principalities") that warred almost constantly with one another. People thought of themselves as Angles or Saxons or Normans, not citizens of England. Men were much more defined by their feudal or tribal relationships than by any national loyalty. This changed over time, however. In the next mini-unit, we'll see how that happened.

Castles and Cathedrals

Fortresses of protection had been part of the European landscape since the days of Rome, and new ones were built in the days of Charlemagne. But during the High Middle Ages there was a great increase in the number and complexity of castles. Many, particularly in the Holy Land and southern Italy, Spain, and France, were built as fortifications against the Muslims. Some in the north were built against any would-be attackers (which might include a neighboring lord), or simply as a symbol of the local lord's wealth and power to protect his lands. As the Crusades progressed and new ways of building castles were devised, castles both in the Middle East and in Europe became more elaborate, with multiple towers and concentric rings of walls.

But kings were not the only people who made great stone buildings during the High Middle Ages. It was during this time that large, elaborate churches called cathedrals also began to appear, from which bishops of large regions ruled as lords. These cathedrals were a sign of the growing wealth, power, and organization of the Roman Catholic Church, and particularly of its monastic orders. A cathedral might take as long as a century to build, and like castles, they became more elaborate over time, growing taller and incorporating huge stained-glass windows, many side-chapels, etc.

Castles and cathedrals were symbols wrought in stone of the growing power of both secular and sacred rulers.

Conclusion

Our study of these medieval lords and their people during the feudal era displays a picture of a dynamic society that was changing over time. The ebb and flow of history eventually created the boundary lines of modern Europe. We can learn about the world we live in now by studying these conflicts between kings and barons or popes and emperors.

MINI-UNIT 5: THE BROKEN ROAD

TAPESTRY OF GRACE PRIMER GUIDEBOOK

Mini-Unit 6: Recovery and Discovery

We will watch the Crusaders recover knowledge, explorers discover new worlds, and emerging European nations seek to adapt to new discoveries. Note how our seven main "characters" fit in.

 The Author	Authority began to be redefined. Political authority began to shift from kings to nations. Military power shifted from mounted knight to masses of archers. The authority of the Church was splintered, even as the authority of God's Word was re-established. The printing press and its power were inaugurated. Spanish monarchs claimed new worlds. In England, rulers claimed both secular and religious authority.
 People	The 100 Years' War established a national identity for England and France, represented by Henry V and Joan of Arc. Marco Polo and other early explorers (including Columbus) expanded people's horizons. The ideas of the Reformation challenged the traditions of the Church. Seeking an heir, Henry VIII led England to break away from the Catholic Church.
 Good	The Reformation sought to redefine what was right and wrong based on God's Word, not man's traditions, saying that men were directly accountable to God. Henry VIII thought anything he did was good.
 Evil	Religious differences spilled over into inquisitions, religious wars, oppression of the Jews, and brutality. Henry VIII's selfishness led him to divorce, mistreat, and execute his wives. Conquering Europeans would mistreat indigenous peoples and contribute to the spread of new diseases.
 The Word	Crusaders brought back ancient texts that had to be reconciled. Scholars translated God's Word into the vernacular. The printing press made it possible for the Bible and reformation pamphlets to be widely distributed.
 God's Creation	Marco Polo traveled the Silk Road from Italy to China, sharing his experiences with others through his journals, but over time the Turks closed this access to others. Explorers sought new routes to the East. They pushed out the boundaries of human knowledge, accidentally discovering new worlds.
 Man's Creation	At Crecy and Agincourt, the English longbow shifted the balance of power to massed archers instead of armored knights. Towns became centers of learning, discovery, and trade. The Renaissance renewed culture and invention. Advances in navigation made it possible for Europeans to push beyond the horizon. The printing press spread the new knowledge far and wide. Shakespeare wielded his pen in Elizabethan England.

Mini-Unit 6 Overview
Recovery and Discovery

Introduction

We've seen Rome fall, and we've learned about daily life in feudal Europe. The kings and knights of Europe fended off barbarian attacks and restored a form of order to society. As civilization recovered its footing and authority was increasingly consolidated, we saw the beginnings of a massive struggle between the popes and the princes for the rule of Christendom, that vision of a Christian kingdom ruled by a righteous, God-fearing king that Europeans had treasured since the days of Charlemagne.

For centuries, Western Europe tried to return to this vision of a secular kingdom united under a Christian monarch. Kings and popes would both claim that place of highest authority in the name of God, as their peasants were often trampled under the hooves of their knights.

In our last mini-unit, we saw that during the time between Charlemagne and the Reformation, the Holy Land had been overrun by the Muslims. In both a bid for power and in real distress, the popes repeatedly called on the knights of Europe to go and wage Holy Wars. And Europeans responded. From all ranks of society, people went to the wars.

Recovering Trade, Lands, and Knowledge

Along with stories and scars, the returning Crusaders brought luxury products to trade. Since the Europeans needed to re-open the trade routes across the Mediterranean Sea in order to fight the Crusades (which continued over about two centuries, from 1096 to 1285), goods now flowed freely between West and East.

Wherever the new goods flowed back and forth, cities sprang up as centers of trade and of learning. In addition to importing silks and spices, the Crusaders brought back forgotten texts and ancient philosophies from the Greek world, as well as new innovations from Muslim and Hebrew scholars. European scholars—and the faculty of new universities (which sprang up in those growing European cities that had cathedrals at their hearts)—sought to reconcile the recovered documents and ideas of the ancients with the doctrines of Christianity, as they had consistently done throughout the Middle Ages.

Following the end of the last major Crusade, the monarchs of England and France turned their belligerence on each other. A dispute over the control of the French throne sparked what we now call the Hundred Years' War (1337 to 1453). England began well, conquering vast regions of France, but the French rallied and recovered all lands by the end of the war, throwing off virtually English rule from the continent.

Over its long course, this conflict changed Europeans dramatically, if somewhat invisibly to the people of the day. Looking back, we can see that long fighting established a new sense of nationalism in hearts of the people of both England and France. Another factor was the Black Death (bubonic plague) that swept through Europe, disrupting and destroying the complicated network of feudal relationships. As people recovered, they found new bonds to unit them.

National heroes, such as Henry V "Harry" of England and Joan of Arc of France, captured the hearts and minds of their countrymen and made those who fought think of themselves as "English" or "French."

In both of these emerging nations, people came to identify with their own language and clung fiercely to their rights to be united as English-speaking or French-speaking peoples. Ultimately, the French drove out the English under the banner of Joan of Arc and reclaimed their right of self-government as a united, albeit impoverished, nation.

The conflict also contributed to the downfall of armored knights. Before this conflict, the only warriors were noblemen, because only they could afford expensive equipment and training through their income from the land. During the 100 Years'

War, the rise of disciplined yeoman as the dominant military forces replaced these knights.

The Hundred Years' War reshaped society in other ways. In England, yeoman began to form a new middle class, even as the ongoing conflict led to the frequent taxation of England's middle class (to pay for the services and equipment of increasingly unnecessary knights). The wars also resulted in the effective destruction of French peasantry (since most of the battles were fought on French fields), and since their feudal lords stripped their lands to pay their own ransoms when they were captured instead of improving their holdings.

Explorers, Inventors, and Reformers

Political conflicts and mercantile pursuits were in action on the Iberian Peninsula in Spain, and in Portugal as well. In Spain, the young rulers Ferdinand and Isabella united their kingdoms into one through their marriage, and then expelled the last of the Muslim Moors. Their kingdoms were united in name, but not yet in spirit, however. Meanwhile, Spain's neighbor, Prince Henry the Navigator of Portugal, had financed voyages of discovery to find new trade routes to the East. In 1490, Bartholomeu Dias rounded the horn of Africa.

About the same time, an Italian merchant, Columbus, arrived at the court of Ferdinand and Isabella with a plan to reach the East by sailing West. Feeling the lack a common enemy, Ferdinand and Isabella sought to unite their people behind this new quest. After his voyage of discovery in 1492, Columbus returned without having found a new route to the East, but with stories of a discovery of an entirely new world! This ignited a passionate contest among European monarchs. They eagerly financed expeditions and raced for new lands to explore, claim, and conquer.

Meanwhile, in the universities, new explorations and discoveries were being made as well. In 1382, John Wycliffe completed the project of translating the Bible from Latin (the *Vulgate*) into everyday English; before this, it had only been available in Latin.

In 1455, Johannes Gutenberg printed 180 copies of the Gutenberg Bible (in Latin) using his movable type and the printing press. This invention would utterly transform how ideas spread and usher in wide-scale literacy and the age of information.

In addition, a Roman Catholic scholar named Erasmus printed a Greek-Latin version of the New Testament in several editions, beginning in 1516. In 1517, a monk named Martin Luther published his 95 Theses in German and distributed printed copies far and wide, fueling the Protestant Reformation. Luther would go on to use Erasmus' work to translate the New Testament from Greek to German, and in the process spark the Reformation and further the unification of the German states.

Roses and Reformation

In England, major changes opened the way for the colonization of Columbus' new world. After the Hundred Years' War, England's conflicts turned to an internal struggle for supremacy between rival branches of the royal House of Plantagenet: York (whose heraldic symbol was a white rose) and Lancaster (whose emblem was a red rose).

The trouble began when Henry V (of York) died in 1422, leaving as heir the infant Henry VI. The men of the house of Lancaster revived an old claim to the throne at this point, launching England into a prolonged internal feud that was only settled with the victory of Henry Tudor and his marriage to Elizabeth of York. Crowned Henry VII, he was succeeded by Henry VIII, who was acutely aware of the necessity of producing a legitimate male heir for the peaceful rule of England.

Henry VIII was so desperate for a male heir that he sought the Pope for an annulment of his marriage to Catharine of Aragon (who had been unable to bear a son). When the Pope didn't see it his way, Henry used the growing Protestant Reformation as an excuse to establish the Church of England (Anglican Church). He declared himself the head of this new English church and, thus freed of the Pope's restraint, he divorced his Spanish wife (angering the Spanish royalty) and married his mistress, Anne Boleyn. Catherine and Anne gave Henry his daughters Mary and Elizabeth, respectively, but both women failed to produce male heirs. Impatient again, Henry executed Anne on a charge of infidelity, and then he went on to marry four other women in succession. He probably had syphilis, a blood disease that (after his wives contracted it from him) harmed unborn children, producing several stillbirths. Ultimately, Henry fathered one sickly son, Edward, who died while still a teenager.

Henry's actions failed to stave off internal struggle for the throne of England, and they added a religious overtone to the conflict. After Henry's death, the question became whether England would return to the Catholic Church or remain Protestant. Mary ruled briefly after Henry died, and tried unsuccessfully to return England to Catholicism. Elizabeth followed Mary to the throne, and the issue was decided in favor of Protestantism—if England could remain free.

Conclusion

In the next three topics, we will move our focus to England and events that occurred there. As the medieval period ends, the struggles for power will shift from clashes between popes and princes to heightened tensions between princes and their people. As history unfolds, we will see the justification for authority shift from "the Divine Right of Kings" to "the Consent of the Governed." England, which already had a legacy of limited monarchs, will be among the first to experience this development, both at home and in her colonies.

Our mini-unit ends as the Virgin Queen, as Elizabeth was known, used her political savvy, personal charm, and her country's natural resources to fend off Spain's last attempts to gain control of England. When Sir Francis Drake's English fleet defeated the dreaded Spanish Armada in 1588, English autonomy was secured, and her culture flourished. On the seas, the English navy became a force to be reckoned with in the Atlantic, on the other side of which lay the New World. Religious dissidents and fortune-seekers in England could now look across the Atlantic to find hope for freedom.

Mini-Unit 6, Topic 1
Recovering Trade, Lands, and Knowledge

Introduction

Recovering trade and the growth of towns began to erode the systems of feudalism and manorialism. Feudalism (the form of government based on personal relationships and oaths) had been a response to the threat of barbarians, and required both the fear of peasants and the strength of the knights. Manorialism (the economic system of peasants being bound to their land) only made sense when there was literally nowhere else to go. The relative stability of Europe and the recovery of trade routes to far-off places allowed the growth of mercantile economies. These created opportunities for common men and thus weakened feudalism.

The events of the Hundred Years' War resulted in huge tracts of land in France changing hands, the end of the military dominance of mounted knights, and the rise of nationalism. In this topic, we'll meet a new type of character on the stage of history—the national hero. In England, it was Henry V. In France, it was a young maiden named Joan of Arc.

Some of the famous people of this era transcended national boundaries, though. In the new towns and universities of Italy and France, scholars were seeking to make sense of all of the ancient texts and new ideas that were flowing back from the Crusades. Premier among these scholars was Thomas Aquinas. While we won't study him in detail, it's important for teachers to know his name and have a basic understanding of what he accomplished.

Trade and Towns

Why should the growth of towns weaken feudalism? It had to do with land. The old saying had been, "No land without a lord; no lord without land." The new phrase became, "Town air is free!" In the manorial economy, peasants tilled the land, and their lords protected them from danger. In the towns and cities, a new class of workers, craftsmen, and traders was growing up. These weren't peasants who were bound to the land—they were freemen. They didn't depend solely on a powerful lord and his knights to keep them safe; the city walls protected them from most dangers.

Those walls limited the amount of available real estate, though—buildings in the city were built close together and as high up as they could go, sometimes five or six stories. Towns had no sewers, and cobblestone pavements didn't become popular until the 1200s, so many streets were narrow, dark, and nasty.

Despite the smell and crowds, the towns attracted many people. Life in the country was very limited. If you weren't a noble or a churchman, you were a peasant, bound to the land you tilled. In the towns, people had the freedom to do other things: craftsmen moved there to make their wares, and merchants moved there (or passed through) to buy and sell them. Little by little, as the town grew, the basis of exchange was shifting from land to money. And with this shift came a shift in power as well.

The businessmen in the towns were in competition with each other, of course, but they were also in competition, in a different way, with every other sector of society. The nobles and the clergy had their own interests and demands that were bad for business. Every town had its lord, who enforced the laws the people had to follow and decided the taxes they would have to pay. As individuals, the craftsmen had no way to protect themselves from arbitrary demands, but if they banded together, they could persuade the lord to tax somebody else. The goldsmiths could make more money by banding together in a goldsmiths' guild than they could by underselling their competition while the lord taxed all their profits.

The guilds became an important part of the governing systems of towns. They learned how to pressure the lords into granting them charters that gave them the right to govern themselves, which created a whole new model of bottom-up leadership in the towns. Guild members began to run the new town governments.

The towns changed the dynamics of the countryside. A shrewd peasant could sneak off in the middle of the night to the town, where he could start a whole new life. Some towns had a law that said if a peasant lived there for a year and a day, he would be free. So the brightest (if not the best) peasants ran away from their lords, and the towns grew.

While the growth of towns undermined the power of the land-owning barons, they increased the overall prosperity of kingdoms. Slowly but surely, this tilted the balance of power in the feudal system. There were ways for kings to profit from the new economy, but the landowners were dependent on a purely agricultural system. Guild leaders were far happier to support distant kings with taxes in exchange for protection than they were to support local lords, who might protect but also tended to interfere.

As the guilds gained power and reshaped the laws, the economy grew apace. Trade between towns became more important, which revived the importance of money. Money doesn't matter much in a subsistence agrarian economy—you can't eat gold. But it's crucial to a trade economy. One gold coin might be worth a wagonload of firewood, and was lot easier to carry from town to town!

The Silk Road

If trade was good from town to town, why not trade from kingdom to kingdom? Products from far away were exotic and expensive, but people now had money to spend. Merchants took bigger risks for bigger profits. The most exotic goods came the farthest distances—and nothing was further from medieval Europe than the Far East. Merchants began traveling the Great Silk Road from the Middle East to China.

The Great Silk Road wasn't really just one road. It was a group of ancient trade routes that had been used since 100 BC. The trails led from Constantinople through 5,000 miles of mountains, deserts, and dangers to eastern China. The Chinese had learned the secret of making silk before Christ was born (and kept it), and they thus maintained a monopoly on making silk until the West learned how around 500 AD.

Merchants of the Silk Road transported silk and other Eastern goods on camels. After the Roman Empire collapsed, the Great Silk Road was less traveled. In the 800s AD, traders used ships to carry goods by sea from the East to the Muslim world, but not many came to Europe. In the 1200s, though, the Great Silk Road became busy again. One city made the most of the commercial revival—Venice—which, you may remember, was built in the middle of a lagoon on the northeast coast of the Italian peninsula by people fleeing from Attila the Hun.

Venice was a proudly independent republic that had ruled the waves of the

Mediterranean since the 800s AD. It straddled a divide between East and West, since it was located a few days by land from Rome and a few days by sea from Constantinople. Venetian traders typically picked up Chinese goods in Byzantium and sailed with them all over the Mediterranean, unloading silks in France and Spain. They even sailed out into the Atlantic and around the coast to the Low Countries that are now the Netherlands and Belgium.

Marco Polo

Marco Polo was a merchant who wrote the book on China. He was born in Venice in 1254 (which was two and a half centuries before Columbus discovered new lands) while his father and uncle were away on business. The boy was fourteen years old before his dad came back! The elder Polos had been to Asia and met the Mongol ruler, Kublai Khan. The Khan had invited them to come back to China, so they returned to Venice to prepare for the new expedition. When they left, they took seventeen year-old Marco with them.

The Polos set sail from Venice for a port in Palestine first. From there they traveled the Silk Road paths by camel all the way to the court of Kublai Khan. The Great Khan valued the knowledge that his foreign guests brought. He sent them on official tours of his kingdom, and Marco Polo became a government official for three years.

They might have stayed there forever if the Khan had had his way, but the Polos wanted to go home. They managed to get the Khan to send them on a mission back to Persia. Fourteen Chinese junks sailed from a port in southern China to Singapore, around the southern tip of India, and through the Arabian Sea to Persia. The Polos headed home from there—traveling by land to the Turkish port of Trebizond and on to Constantinople and Venice. All in all, they had been gone for fourteen years!

When they got home, they were rich. Kublai Khan had given them ivory, jade, jewels, porcelain, silk, and other treasures. That might have been the end of the adventure, but Venice was at war with its long-time rival, Genoa, when the Polos arrived. Marco Polo was soon captured by Genoese soldiers and thrown into prison. There, he decided to while away the hours by writing about his travels. His *Description of the World* became a medieval best-seller and fired the imagination of would-be world travelers for centuries to come—including a young Genoese sailor named Christopher Columbus, who we will meet again in the next topic.

The Seeds of Nationalism

In our last mini-unit, we saw that people came into the Middle Ages defining themselves based on their family and tribal relationships, and then subsequently by feudal ones. We mentioned in the Introduction how the Hundred Years' War changed this dynamic. But now we want to focus our attention on the details of just how—and why—people changed their allegiance from tribes to nation-states. We want to ask, "Why did people stop thinking of themselves as Saxons, Picts, or Normans, and start thinking of themselves as Englishmen?"

We can see this development most easily in England. English people were one of the earliest European cultures to develop a national identity. There were several reasons for this. Being an island was an advantage—you might never quite know where France ends and Germany begins, but it's easy to tell where England's borders are: they stop at the sea. But this wasn't the only factor at work in England.

When William the Conqueror won the Battle of Hastings in 1066, he gained an unchallenged claim to all the land his army conquered. Every one of his vassals started off on the same footing in relation to this one leader. In France, by contrast, some lords had as much power and prestige as the kings to whom they swore fealty. In Germany and Italy, the so-called emperors never really did unify their so-called subjects into one nation. The Alps were too much of a barrier, and the Popes were too eager to interfere with the gradual process of nation-building.

Now, England was well-positioned to develop a national identity, but there was an issue: William the Conqueror and the rest of the Normans spoke French, not English. After a Saxon uprising, William the Conqueror dealt fairly harshly with his new subjects. This practice was continued by his heirs. So, it wasn't until the Hundred Years' War that England really began to unify. This long-lived conflict began when the English king, who still held lands in France, claimed the French throne.

England, France, and the Hundred Years' War

France didn't want an English king. France and England had been squabbling for years over trade, fishing rights, and the like. When England fought with Scotland, France took Scotland's side. Then the French king announced that France was taking over Guyenne, England's vassal state in southwest France.

The English king, Edward III, said he had more right to France than the French king did—Edward's mother was the sister of three French kings and the daughter of King Philip the Fair. Edward was the nearest living male relative of the last great

French king.

War broke out in 1337. The war (a whole series of wars, really) lasted 116 years, but it's called the Hundred Years' War. It went on through the reigns of five French and five English kings. The English consistently won the battles, but the French won the war. A century of fighting changed both countries forever.

Crecy

Because the battles of this war were always fought on French soil, the English often faced overwhelming odds. Some of England's most glorious moments occurred during this conflict, however. The Battle of Crecy, in 1346, was the greatest English victory of the war. King Edward III led an English army of 8,000-10,000 men against a French army almost five times as large. Heavily armored French knights had to charge uphill through mud into a hail of arrows. English longbow arrows (a somewhat new technology at the time) could pierce French armor. The knights were cut down or dismounted, and they wallowed in the mud as the relentless arrows continued to rain down on them. The French nobility was decimated that day, cut down by English yeoman peasants. It was an event that became symbolic of the shift in the balance of military (and thus, social) power from mounted knights to massed archers.

Black Death

The Hundred Years' War wasn't over with that battle, though. The next year, it was interrupted by a different kind of calamity. England, France, and the rest of Europe lost 25-30% of their populations to plague in five short years, from 1347-1352. We call this traumatic event of European history the Black Death.

The cause of death was a well-known disease caused by one specific bacterium that lives in rats. It is usually spread to humans by the fleas that ride the rats, drink their blood, and then bite humans, thus transferring the germs. The disease is called bubonic plague when the bacteria infect the lymph nodes and causes them to swell into "buboes." Without proper treatment, plague will kill a patient in about five days. Christendom had no treatment to offer, so millions died.

The Black Death came to Europe by ship. The Mongols were besieging a city on the shores of the Black Sea, and catapulted plague-infected corpses over the city wall. Italian traders from Genoa brought plague-infected rats to Sicily. The disease spread across all of Europe from there.

The Black Death affected Europe surprisingly little, in some ways, and surprisingly much in others. It didn't alter the course of the Hundred Years' War, for example. Both sides lost population, but neither side gained an advantage as a result. The depopulation accelerated deeper, less visible trends that were already under way.

For instance, the peasants who were winning battles overseas in France came to be in higher demand back home in England, as fields lay empty for lack of men to work them because of the plague. And, while killing off a quarter of the population would be disastrous anywhere, it was especially disastrous in a society that depended on personal relationships the way feudal medieval Europe did. The oaths a vassal took to his lord were personal: to the man, not his office. When one out of four people died, the fabric of feudal society started to unravel.

Agincourt

As we said, the Black Death slowed down the course of the war. After the population recovered, England renewed the conflict, but her king went about it differently. Instead of relying solely on his vassals to fill the field with noble knights, the kings raised taxes to pay for commoners to go to war.

In 1415, King Henry V led a badly outnumbered army through the heart of France. Henry had started life as a wild young English gentleman, but he became a great king and hero. He is featured as such in one of William Shakespeare's plays, the climax of which is the Battle of Agincourt. Shakespeare has Henry's cousin and vassal, the Duke of Westmoreland, lament how small the English army is.

Only 7,000 weary English soldiers faced 35,000 French warriors. The French were led by armor-plated knights, while many of Henry's men were mere peasants armed with longbows. In Shakespeare's version, Henry makes the pitiful quantity and the quality of his men an inspiration for victory. He says:

> We few, we happy few, we band of brothers;
> For he to-day that sheds his blood with me
> Shall be my brother; be he ne'er so vile,
> This day shall gentle [1] his condition.

Henry's "happy few" defeated France that day. Once again the English longbows cut down the flower of French chivalry. It was a defeat for feudalism as well as for France. The peasants who became King Henry's brothers undermined the whole idea of aristocracy. The king who appealed to them that day represented a whole new kind of king who based his power on the common people, not on landed lords.

---

1 To "gentle" here means to become a "gentleman," or nobleman.

Joan of Arc

There's one more chapter we must tell of the long story of the Hundred Years' War, and it is about one of the most famous women of France: Joan of Arc. She was a peasant maid, just three years old when Henry won all of France at Agincourt. She was ten years old when Henry V died, leaving nine-month old Henry VI king of England and France. By thirteen, she was hearing voices that persuaded her that God was calling her to rouse the French. At seventeen, she went to see Charles VII, the uncrowned king of France. Charles was forewarned of her coming and put her to the test. She had never seen him, so he disguised himself in the crowd and put a courtier on his throne. But when she came in, she unerringly picked him out of the crowd. She also told him what he had asked of God when he had been praying all alone. Persuaded, Charles gave her armor and a banner to lead his troops.

The English forces then held Paris and the city of Reims, where French kings were crowned, and were besieging the city of Orleans. Joan marched troops to Orleans and raised the siege in ten short days. She pressed Charles to go to Reims to be crowned, even though it still lay in enemy territory. Her troops fought their way through the English lines, and Joan entered Reims in triumph, where Charles was crowned in 1429.

Joan was wounded in the fight for Paris, though, and six months later, she was captured by Frenchmen who supported England. They handed her over to the enemy. The English tried her for witchcraft and heresy. She was burned at the stake, and her ashes were thrown into the river Seine.

Although Joan died at an English stake, her story didn't. She quickly became a national symbol for the people of France. As the peasant girl who led the French troops to repel English invaders and become one of the first to kneel before the newly crowned French king, she fired the imagination of the French people. Joan belonged to *all* French people, and that was how they thought of themselves in relation to her: as French!

Henry VI

These events weren't the end of the Hundred Years' War, but they were the beginning of the end. Charles VII was now king of France, while a little boy sat on the throne of England. That boy, Henry VI, finally lost the Hundred Years' War and triggered another that was fought completely on English soil—the Wars of the Roses. (We will learn more details about the this conflict later.)

Christianity and the Classics—Aquinas

We've seen the recovery of trade routes and the recovery of lands, and now we need to look at the recovery of knowledge. This was the era when Christians of Western Europe acknowledged one spiritual head—the Pope—and one catholic (universal) faith. But there was a threat on the horizon: increased contact with the Muslim world reopened Europe to pagan classics—scrolls by thinkers like Plato and Aristotle. This new knowledge threatened the medieval mindset and faith.

Western Europe had long known, through Latin works by Roman authors, *about* Plato and Aristotle and other important Greek thinkers (including physicians and mathematicians). Now, however, copies of works written by these Greek thinkers (as well as some recovered Latin works by Cicero and others) were coming back into the West!

The works of antiquity had been copied by Muslims, and some had been stored in Constantinople as well. The returning Crusaders brought Greco-Roman classics back, but there were also works by Muslim and Hebrew scholars from the East, who had many ideas to share. New debates and new combinations of ideas began to spring up.

Recoveries of old knowledge led to discoveries of new ways to apply it. As they had always done throughout the Middle Ages, scholars (and the faculty of new universities in the cathedral cities of Europe) sought to reconcile the wisdom of the ancients with the doctrines of Christianity, then apply both together to their understanding of reality.

The writings of the ancient philosophers rocked their worldview. The arguments of Plato and Aristotle dazzled the scholars of the Middle Ages, yet they routinely contradicted Scripture. How could these ideas ever be melded into the great, complex, yet orderly worldview of the Middle Ages, which so far had seemed capable of including secular ideas as harmonious handmaidens of Scriptural truth?

One man uniquely deserves much credit for reconciling Christianity and the classical world—Thomas Aquinas. His great work, the *Summa Theologica* ("The Highest Theology") written between 1265 and 1274, attempted to systematically explain Christian theology in light of the new or newly recovered ideas from Muslim, Jewish, Greek, and Roman sources.

Perhaps most significantly, Aquinas welded Christian doctrine together with the teachings of the greatest ancient Greek philosopher, Aristotle. Aristotle was the master of reason, while Christianity was a matter of faith. Aquinas argued that there is no conflict between faith and reason. Faith and reason both come from God; faith and reason both lead to truth. Any discrepancy between what faith believes and reason thinks must come from an error in one or the other.

Aquinas' work was brilliant, but it also became a problem. Though Aquinas himself never thought of human philosophers as having authority comparable to Scripture's, his *Summa* made it hard to separate human speculations from the level of authority of God's revealed Word. Aquinas tried to synthesize the truth of Scripture with truths that he believed could be found in classical philosophy. He was unwilling to accept teachings that directly contradicted Scripture, such as Aristotle's claim that matter had always existed. But he accepted those teachings that he thought could be reconciled with God's Word (either because he could find a way to explain them so that they harmonized with it, or because they addressed topics that Scripture did not mention, such as what patterns are made by planets in the heavens).

Unfortunately, the result was that Aquinas included many inaccurate beliefs about reality in the *Summa*, which Scripture neither contradicted nor affirmed. (Scripture does not tell us everything about how Creation works!) Thus, when new scientific discoveries came along a few centuries later, which proved Aristotle wrong about how planets and other created things work, both Christian doctrine and Scripture itself were called into question because they had been so tightly tied to Aristotle's fallible ideas.

Conclusion

The Middle Ages were coming to an end. The political and economic structures of feudalism and manorialism were being replaced with mercantilism in the new towns. England and France were established as distinct peoples, each united by common languages. Scholars like Aquinas represented the pinnacle of medieval thinking. Aquinas' brilliant *Summa Theologica* unified the Bible and the ancients, but he made the mistake of adding to Scripture, and later discoveries would show him to be inaccurate. Because the Church embraced his work, it, too, would be discredited. As the Middle Ages ended, something new was waiting just over the horizon.

Mini-Unit 6, Topic 2
Explorers, Inventors, and Reformers

Introduction

This week, you will study the Age of Exploration. We will focus on the late 1400s, when Columbus initiated the great race for land in the New World. We cover the Age of Exploration as one part of one topic in *Tapestry Primer*. In *Tapestry of Grace*, we spend more time studying Columbus and his discoveries of the New World.

Remember, as Europeans returned from the Crusades, they brought back products from the Far East. From studying Marco Polo's story, we know that most of these products came to Europe via a long overland route called the Silk Road. Merchants journeyed from China and India, via Constantinople, and then goods were taken by ship to all the rest of Europe. The Europeans called these eastern lands "the Orient" (meaning the East).

When Constantinople fell to the Muslims in 1453, all that changed. Being physically closer, the Italian traders of Florence, Venice, and Genoa developed exclusive trading relationships with the new Muslim rulers. That was a problem for all the other merchants in lands farther away, like Spain and Portugal. They wanted to import the riches of the Orient, too, but they now found themselves shut out. In this topic, we'll find out how they worked to solve this problem.

In another era, that might have been just too bad for the Spaniards, but this was a new age. Instead of giving up, they looked for a new way to get to the East. Overall, Europe had new energy and enthusiasm. The struggles that had dragged on for so long in France and England and Spain were resolved. The Hundred Years' War was over, the Moors had been driven out of Spain, and the crowned heads of Western Europe had money and vision enough to sponsor voyages of discovery. All these events brought socio-economic changes, as we've noted.

In this topic, we meet John Wycliffe (also spelled Wyclif) and Martin Luther. Wycliffe wanted to translate the Bible out of Latin into the language of the common people. Gutenberg's new printing press made it possible to mass-produce such books. All of a sudden, ordinary men and women could find out for themselves what God was saying. Today, we know these men helped start the Reformation.

Ferdinand and Isabella

Let's pick up the story with Spain. We focused a lot on England and France during the Middle Ages, because it so easy to see how those lands changed from a patchwork of tribes into unified nation-states. We've paid attention to Germany, too, but we haven't spent that much time on Spain. The country we call Spain didn't exist before 1469, when King Ferdinand II of Aragon married Queen Isabella I of Castile. The union of these two smaller kingdoms made it possible to drive the last of the Muslims out of Spain—more than 700 years after they had taken over that part of Europe.

The Inquisition & the Spanish Jews

After Ferdinand and Isabella finished driving the Muslims out of Spain, they tried to figure out what to do with the other unbelievers. More than 200,000 Jews had been living in the Muslim-controlled areas. The King and Queen ordered them to convert to Christianity or leave Spain. Some Jews chose to be baptized under duress, but continued to practice their own religion in secret. Ferdinand and Isabella then instituted the Spanish Inquisition, whose mission was to hunt down unconverted Jews and other Christian heretics and, by means of force, torture, or exile, compel them to conform.

Many Spanish Jews fled to other countries, which their skills and resources helped enrich. Spain lost an enormous amount of human capital because of its choice to drive out the Jews. That didn't appear to matter much over the next century, because so much gold flowed into Spain from the Americas. But when the treasure galleons stopped coming from the New World, Spain had very little to show for it. From 1600 to the present day, Spain's socio-political influence has hardly been felt in Europe. All the gold in the world couldn't replace the value of the ideas and contributions of the people that Spain had driven away.

Great Explorers

Columbus

The Muslims were conquered and the Jews were expelled from Spain by 1492—which turned out to be a momentous year all round. As everybody knows, "in 1492, Columbus sailed the ocean blue." That date is no coincidence. The Spanish victory over the Muslims in January of 1492 made it possible for Columbus to get permission to sail in April. He then planted the Spanish flag on the shores of a Caribbean island on October 12, 1492.

That first landing came nine years after Columbus first tried to sell his idea of a westward voyage to the Indies to a king. He didn't start with King Ferdinand of Spain, though—he started with King John II of Portugal.

Before Columbus' day, the Portuguese had led the world in voyages of discovery. They had invented a whole new kind of ship called a caravel, which used a combination of European square sails and the triangular sails that Muslims favored to enable them to sail closer to the wind. The old square-riggers had to wait until the winds were behind them to go anywhere, but a caravel could tack its way upwind. Before Columbus came to Portugal, the Portuguese had used these sturdy little ships to sail all the way around the southern tip of Africa. They were trying to forge new trade routes to Asia, even if they had to sail all the way to the South Pole to get there.

Columbus thought there was an easier way. According to his calculations, one could sail west from Portugal and reach China. The king's council rejected this plan. It wasn't because they thought the world was flat—they didn't. The most educated people of Europe all agreed that the world was round. The council thought Columbus' math was wrong. They felt sure that the voyage was much longer than Columbus thought it was.

Columbus took his plan to the court of Spain, Portugal's arch-enemy. In 1485, when he got there, the Spanish monarchs were busy fighting Muslims. It took seven years before they were willing to sponsor the voyage. When they won their final victory in January of 1492, things changed. Just three months later, Columbus had the approval—and the ships and supplies—that he needed to sail. They left Spain on August 3 and reached the New World seventy days later.

For centuries, Americans viewed Columbus as a hero and celebrated Columbus Day. In recent years, it has become popular to treat Columbus as an evil imperialist who destroyed the innocent native peoples. But, like most of us, Columbus is more complex than either of these pictures—we probably can't just view him as either an angel or a demon. He was a real man whose own journal reveals a mixture of motives. There is no question that he was brave and persistent and left an enormous mark on history. He was also dead wrong on his math—all the experts kept insisting that the globe was a whole lot bigger than he thought, and they were right. Columbus thought he had reached an island off the shores of China when he landed in the Caribbean. He wasn't even halfway there!

His math wasn't his only error, though. In fact, he wasn't that far off in his math. Columbus only thought the earth was about 25% smaller than it actually is. His larger navigational error, perhaps, was in assuming that the planet was mostly land. He simply couldn't imagine the vast expanse of the Pacific—nearly half the globe is covered by that one giant blue ocean. But, the biggest downside to Columbus' story shows up after his voyage: Columbus proved to be greedy, self-centered, and unkind to the native peoples that he encountered (to put it mildly). Though he saw his name as a significant element of his life's destiny (Christopher means "Christ bearer"), his actions and written words display a man who thirsted for his own glory at least as much as for Christ's.

Vasco de Gama

When all the shouting of victory was over in Spain, the Portuguese still didn't believe that Columbus had found a shortcut to China. Columbus hadn't brought back any spices—and wasn't that the whole point of sailing west? They decided to keep sailing east, around Africa, to see if they could find their own water-borne trade route. In 1497, King Manuel of Portugal commissioned Vasco de Gama to try to sail all the way to Asia. He reached Calicut (modern-day Kozhikode), on the southern coast of India, and brought back spices to prove he had made it. Four years later, the Portuguese sent a larger fleet of ships that bombarded Calicut with a new weapon—cannons mounted on ships and fired by gunpowder. They captured the city and set up a Portuguese outpost.

Renaissance

Cannons and caravels gave Portugal the advantage over the Indians in Calcutta. The Age of Exploration was on—and we'll see how other Europeans interacted with the native peoples they encountered. But we mustn't forget that the Renaissance was still in full swing in Europe!

Leonardo da Vinci

If you look at the time line, you'll see that Columbus, Leonardo da Vinci, Ferdinand and Isabella, and Michelangelo were all contemporaries. This was all happening at the same time! It was an absolutely amazing period of history.

In later years, older students study Leonardo da Vinci in *Tapestry of Grace*. We don't have any clear evidence of what Leonardo da Vinci thought about Columbus. Perhaps he agreed with the Portuguese that Columbus was no big deal. Maybe he was amazed at the reports of the voyage. Or perhaps he was more interested in the crisis in Florence than in some sailor from the rival republic of Genoa.

1492 was a big year for the Republic of Florence. For some years, the Medici family had ruled the town. Their leader was Lorenzo the Magnificent, son of Cosimo, who continued his family's lavish patronage of Renaissance artists and ruled Florence in fact, but not with any formal title. He spent so much money on artworks to impress his neighbors that when he died in 1492, the rest of the family discovered they were out of money. The family bank had to close and the Medicis were suddenly out of power.

Just a few years later, Florence was invaded by King Charles of France. Then the city was taken over by the reforming monk Savanarola, who urged the people to burn all their worldly amusements in the city square. They held a "bonfire of the vanities"— burning playing cards, mirrors, cosmetics, pagan books, sculptures, gaming tables, women's hats, works by immoral poets, and more. It all went up in flames. Three years later, the people of Florence burned Savanarola at the stake in the same square.

Leonardo was not in Florence when Savanarola took over. He was painting *The Last Supper* in Milan, 150 miles away. If his *Mona Lisa* is the most famous painting in the world, *The Last Supper* is easily the most famous religious painting. Leonardo was an absolute master as a painter—but he was interested in almost everything else, too. In your student's assigned readings, you'll learn a little more about some of his inventions.

Johannes Gutenberg

Johannes Gutenberg was another inventor. He wanted to get rich. Gutenberg's secret plan was to cast individual letters out of metal and then put them together on a printing press. This was not as easy as it sounds. The letters had to be identical, spaced right, and there had to be a lot of them. It took him years of trial and error to perfect the type.

Getting the type right wasn't the only problem. He had to come up with ink that would stick to metal long enough to coat the type and then transfer successfully over to paper. After years of experimentation, he found that Flemish painters had an oil-based paint that worked.

These were just two of his challenges! There were any number of disappointments and delays. Gutenberg persevered, though. He was a meticulous craftsman who wouldn't give up. He was also suspicious, secretive, and greedy. This combination of character traits meant that he succeeded at his task but wound up neither rich nor famous in his lifetime.

His press was similar to what farmers used for squeezing oil from olives, with a big beam that turned a screw that pressed the paper on the type. Finally, he got the printing process to function right. We aren't quite sure what things he started printing—this was long before the days of copyrights and title pages. Historians think he printed indulgences for the Roman Catholic Church, among other things. But the big money-making scheme he wanted to pursue was printing the Bible.

This was a huge project. Gutenberg borrowed money from a partner, Johann Fust. In 1455, the relationship soured: Fust sued Gutenberg, accusing him of embezzling his money. The court ruled against Gutenberg, and Fust was awarded full control over the Bible printing workshop and half of all the printed Bibles. Gutenberg died in obscure poverty in 1468, but the press proliferated—and so did Bibles.

John Wycliffe

John Wycliffe was born in England around 1328. He became a professor of Philosophy at Oxford University. It was a challenging time for philosophy professors. How could one explain why God would allow a horror like the Black Death? Why would God permit the Hundred Years' War or the Great Schism in the Church that wound up with three men all claiming to be Pope? To the common folk of England, Church and state seemed equally corrupt.

Wycliffe tried to answer these questions in his lectures and tracts. He argued that "dominion is founded in grace." By this he meant that unjust rulers could not insist that it was God's will for people to obey them. Wycliffe applied this principle to the Church just as much as the state, which got him into trouble. He was tried several times in the Church courts and would have been punished, but the royal family saved him each time.

Wycliffe believed that popes and bishops had claimed more power than they were owed. He zeroed in on the doctrine of transubstantiation. The Church taught that when a duly ordained priest said the right words over the bread and wine during the communion rite, the elements were turned into the real body and blood of Christ, and He was crucified again for the sins of the partaker, bringing absolution. Wycliffe thought that if only priests could turn the bread and wine into the body and blood of Christ, without which no man had any life within him, then they had power indeed. The danger of Wycliffe's rebuttal from the Church's perspective was that without the doctrine of transubstantiation, one would not need a priest to come to God.

Over time, Wycliffe came to see the Bible as the only source of authority for Christian beliefs. He said, "Even though there were a hundred popes and though every mendicant monk were a cardinal, they would be entitled to confidence only in so far as they accorded with the Bible." With help, he translated the Bible into English, and his followers revised and improved his translation in 1388. His followers, called Lollards, spread out across England to take the Word to the common people. The Lollards taught that one did not need the Roman Catholic Church to be saved. They denied the supremacy of the Pope. The nobles were not happy with this development—they thought the Lollards made the poor people dissatisfied. When Henry IV became king in 1399, he cracked down on the Lollards. But despite great persecution, Lollards continued to preach in England for almost twenty years.

The Reformation and Martin Luther

When most people think of the Reformation or Reformed churches, they think of Martin Luther. Brash, bold, and fearless, Martin Luther's actions launched the efforts of many lesser-known reformers into the public eye.

Indulgences

When Pope Urban II launched the First Crusade in 1095, he offered an indulgence for every man who risked his life for the Holy Land. Unlike previous indulgences, which spared a repentant sinner one specific act of penance, Pope Urban offered a "plenary indulgence," a complete pardon from any act of penance ever. That meant that all Crusaders would skip right over Purgatory. Their sacrificial acts of faith and bravery was deemed sufficient to spare them any further penance in this life or the next.

By the Fourth Crusade, in 1198, the Popes started granting plenary indulgences to people who paid for someone else to go crusading. For the first time, one could effectively buy one's way out of Purgatory. By 1500, the Crusades were just a distant memory, but indulgences were big business.

The Reformation officially started with a debate about indulgences (those pre-purchased "get out of Purgatory early" documents that we described earlier). Johann Tetzel was a German monk who had been authorized by the Pope to raise money by selling indulgences. Tetzel was an effective salesman—his catchy slogan was, "When the coin in the coffer rings, another soul from Purgatory springs!" Something about the commercialization of these sweeping plenary indulgences didn't seem right to Luther.

Martin Luther objected to the way Tetzel sold indulgences. This wasn't because he didn't believe in indulgences or the broader concept of penance. On the contrary, Luther initially objected because he believed that penance was a sacrament, which Jesus specifically instituted for His Church. The practice of penance had arisen during Church history to deal with sinners who recognized their sins and confessed them to a priest. The Church taught that Christ's blood was completely sufficient to atone for these sins, but there could still be earthly consequences for bad choices. Among other things, it was all too easy to slip back into the same sins. Priests therefore began to assign specific acts of penance to help sinners change their behavior in the future.

Not everybody confessed his sins, of course, and penance didn't always lead to changed behavior. It is easy to understand how the Roman Catholic doctrine of Purgatory began to supplement the limited penance that was possible here on earth. With Purgatory waiting after death, a prudent person would confess his sins here and now, where penance was relatively mild, rather than wait until the afterlife to be purified.

95 Theses

Luther objected to Tetzel's brazen sale of indulgences. He had questions, but no answers. How, for instance, could one person's money sanctify some other soul? The Pope could excuse a man from the penances he himself imposed, but how could he have power to impose penalties after death? According to tradition, on October 31, 1517, Luther wrote down 95 specific propositions for debate on a piece of paper and nailed it to the door of the castle church at Wittenberg.

The debate that Luther asked for never happened. Instead, some enterprising printer copied Luther's propositions off his paper and started circulating them. It was like throwing a match into gasoline. Within two weeks, Luther's theses were all over

Germany. Within two months, they had crisscrossed Europe. In other words, they "went viral."

Diet of Worms

The Roman Catholic Church was not quick to respond to Luther's criticism. Pope Leo X delegated the matter to Catholic theologians and envoys. In 1518, he is said to have called Luther a "drunken German" who would change his mind as soon as he got sober. But Luther wasn't drunk and didn't change his mind—instead, he began writing book after book articulating his beliefs.

Eventually, the church authorities tried to silence Luther the way they silenced Jan Hus, John Wycliffe, and other earlier critics. The Pope excommunicated him in 1521, and the secular authorities ordered him to appear for trial at a council in the German city of Worms.

If you tell your student about Luther and the "Diet of Worms," he may giggle at the thought. But it is not what it sounds like! A "diet" meant a day of legal proceedings (from the Latin word *dies*, meaning "day"). Luther was called before this council in the German city of Worms (pronounced Vurms, in German). It was dangerous. He refused to come unless he was granted safe conduct—and even that was risky. After all, the Czech reformer Jan Hus had been executed even though he was given such a promise a century before.

At Worms, church officials asked Luther to renounce his teaching, and he asked for time to consider. The next day, he came in and pointed to his collected works which they had asked him to recant. He divided them into three groups. The first category consisted of works which even his enemies accepted. He couldn't reject these, since everyone seemed to agree they were correct. The second category attacked specific abuses and lies in the Church. Luther argued that he could not reject these without encouraging these abuses to continue. The last group consisted of attacks on individuals, which Luther admitted were harsh. But though they were harsh, he thought they were true. His famous summation of his view has rung down the annuls of history as courageous and godly. He said:

> I cannot and will not recant anything, for to go against conscience is neither right nor safe. Here I stand, I can do no other, so help me God. Amen.

Authority

Luther refused to recant because he had come to see Scripture as the only valid source of religious authority. This seems obvious to most Protestants today, but it was a major break with medieval thinking. The accepted medieval view was that authority was equally present in four different sources, which were expected to all say the same thing. The four sources of authority were Scripture, Church tradition, reason, and the Pope.

Luther came to believe that reason was fallible, traditions were inconsistent, and Popes contradicted one another. He thought the Bible was the only thing that never changed, and he refused to back down once he was convinced of his position from Scripture.

Conclusion

Exploration, Renaissance, and Reformation, all during the same time frame! It really did seem like everything was happening at once. Painters and builders and poets and popes and kings and conquerors and explorers and inventors were all at work. We've been following many different threads through the long ages of history, and in this topic so many of them seem to come together at once. We're turning the corner from the Middle Ages to the modern world, and it shows!

Mini-Unit 6, Topic 3
Roses and Reformation

Introduction

Things were changing fast. Students will learn a bit about the Wars of the Roses—a complex tangle of treachery and civil war that effectively finished off feudalism in England and set the stage for the beginning of English colonialism. We want to give you enough background here that you feel you can answer your student's questions well.

Following the Wars of the Roses, we'll learn that Henry VIII wanted an heir so badly that he broke with the Catholic Church, embracing the Protestant beliefs for which followers of John Wycliffe had been persecuted years before. Englishmen were at odds with one another over this issue, and many died for what they believed. When Henry's daughter Elizabeth came to the throne, she finally managed to win the peace *and* maintain Protestantism in England.

The Wars of the Roses and the End of Feudalism

When Gutenberg died, King Edward IV was sitting on the throne of England. How he got there is quite a story. The Hundred Years' War had lasted through five English kings—Edward III, Richard II, and Henrys IV, V, and VI.

Henry VI was a sweet and pious man who suffered from mental illness. He lost the war in France and almost all the foreign territory that England ever fought for. He really wasn't fit to be a king. When a king loses big, like Henry did, his people start to wonder if this is really the best they can do.

There was reason for them to wonder. Henry's grandfather, Henry IV, essentially usurped the throne when his cousin, Richard II, was deposed. By rights, the crown should have gone to another man named Roger Mortimer. Henry IV was such a strong and effective king, though, that he got away with it, and his son who won the great victory of Agincourt easily kept his crown. But the disastrous reign of Henry VI made people think again.

Richard II was of the house of York, and the Henrys who replaced him were of the house of Lancaster. When Henry VI proved incompetent, an heir of the house of York challenged Henry's right to rule. In later years, after the fighting was over, the house of York came to be symbolized by a white rose, while the red rose was Lancaster's symbol. That's where the name "the Wars of the Roses" comes from—and that's the only simple thing about it. The Wars of the Roses consisted of an almost impossibly complex series of usurpations and betrayals.

The kings who reigned through this royal riot were, in order:

- ❑ Henry VI
- ❑ Edward IV
- ❑ Henry VI (again)
- ❑ Edward IV (again)
- ❑ Edward V (a child)
- ❑ Richard III
- ❑ Henry VII

King Richard III, the next to last of this list, really seems to have been a monster. In Shakespeare's play about him, he gets his brother George, the Duke of Clarence, executed for treason and then has Richard's two small nephews smothered in their beds in the Tower of London. One of those boys was Richard's ward and king—Edward V.

Richard was a tyrant and usurper—and he died at the Battle of Bosworth Field, where a man named Henry Tudor led the House of Lancaster to victory. Henry Tudor became Henry VII and finally healed the breach between the houses by marrying Princess Elizabeth, the sister of the smothered boys and daughter of Edward IV.

Western Europe went through many troubles in the 1300s and 1400s. We've looked at some of the big ones—the Hundred Years' War, the Black Death, and the Wars of the Roses. Things finally settled down, however. Henry VII took the throne of England in 1485, ending the civil wars there. Ferdinand and Isabella united the kingdoms of Aragon and Castile and drove the Muslims out of Spain. By 1492, western Europe entered into a new era of peace and prosperity that didn't depend on the military might of feudal barons. Strong kings were no longer dependent on a multi-level system of government that parceled out power to vassals. The form of government we call the nation-state was taking hold.

The Reformation in England

England turned Protestant. How? As with several other European nations, the break with Rome resulted from a clash between king and Pope. Henry VIII of England wanted a new wife. His queen, Catherine of Aragon, was the daughter of Ferdinand and Isabella of Spain. She had been betrothed to Arthur, Prince of Wales, when she was only four, two years before her parents sent Columbus to discover America. She was only fifteen when she married Arthur, who was fifteen months younger than she was. Just a few months later, Catherine and her new husband both got very sick—and Arthur died.

When a crown prince of England dies, the next son becomes the Prince of Wales—unless there is already an heir. Even though Arthur was dead, there was a chance that his young wife was already pregnant. Catherine told the authorities it could not be: she said that she and fourteen-year-old Arthur had never consummated their marriage. Arthur's younger brother Henry took his place as Prince of Wales, and then, by a special dispensation from the Pope, as the husband of Catherine.

Henry's marriage to Catherine was certainly consummated: she gave birth six times. Her first child was stillborn—a daughter. Prince Henry only lived 52 days. Another girl was stillborn, and another son died soon after birth. The next child was a girl who lived—Princess Mary—and she was followed by another stillbirth.

By this time, Henry was getting worried. Catherine was aging fast, and there was no male heir to the throne. The last time a woman had inherited the English throne, two generations after William the Conqueror, it resulted in a bitter civil war. That was long ago, but all of England still remembered the disastrous Wars of the Roses, which had only ended when Henry's father took the throne. A male heir seemed essential!

Henry decided that God must be judging him for marrying his brother's wife. Catherine said she and Arthur had not consummated, but she could be lying. Why else would God curse their union? John the Baptist had rebuked King Herod for taking his brother's wife in the Bible, so why should the King of England be different?

Henry petitioned the Pope for an annulment on the grounds that he was not lawfully married to Catherine. Catherine objected! Unfortunately for Henry, Catherine's nephew had recently captured the city of Rome, where the Pope was a virtual prisoner. The Pope, caught in a conflict between two of Europe's most powerful monarchs, stalled for the next seven years.

In 1531, Henry separated from Catherine, who was now 45 years old. In 1533, Henry married Anne Boleyn, the second of what would be his six wives. In 1534, Parliament passed the Act of Supremacy that separated the Church of England from the Church of Rome.

The Reformation had come to England—sort of. Henry was no Protestant, and when he died, his only male heir only lived a few years. Edward VI was a sickly boy whose Protestant advisors knew he might not live. They tried to set aside King Henry's will to make sure the next person in line to the throne was a solid Protestant, rather than Princess Mary, daughter of Catherine (and Catherine was from Spain and as Roman Catholic as they came). When the young king died at the age of fifteen, his Protestant cousin, Lady Jane Grey, took the throne for nine short days—and then was driven out by Mary, who spent five bloody years trying to bring England back under Catholic control. "Bloody Mary" (as Protestant Englishmen called her) died after just five years on the throne, and suddenly her 25-year-old half-sister, the Protestant princess Elizabeth, was crowned queen and ruled for 45 years!

The Elizabethan Age

Henry VIII was afraid the land would suffer if he could not produce a healthy male heir, and he was right. But God provided a capable leader in Queen Elizabeth I, Henry's daughter by his second wife, Anne Boleyn. Elizabeth had personal strengths and weaknesses, but as a ruler, she presided over (and came to symbolize) a "golden age" of English stability, peace, growth, and culture. She was so successful that her reign is known as the Elizabethan Age.

Elizabeth

Elizabeth was never supposed to be queen. While Mary spent the five years trying to crush English Protestantism, Elizabeth tried to stay out of trouble. As a Protestant who was next in line to the throne, that proved impossible. At one point, after religious rebels tried to overthrow Mary, Elizabeth was imprisoned by her sister, even though there was no evidence that she was connected to the plot in any way. After Mary died, Elizabeth found herself queen.

Religious Settlement

Elizabeth settled the most pressing issue of her reign early on. Since her father's break with the Roman Catholic Church, the English population had been sharply divided between Protestants and Roman Catholics. The men who ruled on behalf of Edward VI for six years had strengthened Protestants by encouraging them. Bloody Mary's five-year reign also unintentionally strengthened Protestantism: she sickened Protestants and moderate Roman Catholics alike by burning 300 Protestants at the stake. Elizabeth hoped to satisfy most of her subjects by establishing a church that was primarily Protestant in doctrine. She therefore signed several laws that are collectively called the Religious Settlement of 1559.

The main law, the Act of Supremacy, reestablished the Church of England, which her father had set up and Mary had tried to abolish. This church was independent of the Roman Catholic Church but had similar attributes. It was dubbed the *via media* (Latin for the "middle way") because of the way it upheld both Roman Catholic forms of worship and substantially Protestant doctrines.

The Act of Uniformity approved a new prayer book and enforced its use, and the Thirty-Nine Articles spelled out the doctrine of the Church of England (also called the Anglican Church). The Articles condemned several important Roman Catholic beliefs and practices, including purgatory, transubstantiation, reverence for saints and relics, indulgences, and the power of the pope. The Articles affirmed the doctrine of predestination and rejected the doctrine of free will.

Despite these clear doctrinal differences with Catholicism, the Church of England retained much of the "look and feel" of Rome. The Anglican liturgy (order of worship) and polity (Church government) are very similar to that of the Roman Catholic Church.

Peace Dividend

Elizabeth was a frugal queen—some even said stingy. She didn't spend a lot of England's money, and she avoided wars of conquest. This freed up funds to build up England's infrastructure, which boomed as a result. The arts also flourished during her long and peaceful reign.

William Shakespeare wrote plays and poetry that both entertained and unified the English people. Shakespeare's works helped solidify the London dialect as the proper way to speak the English language. Speaking one common language—English—continued to be an important trait that unified the diverse people of Great Britain.

Spain

Though Elizabeth was always prudent and conservative, she was no coward. There was a great deal of tension between England and Spain during Elizabeth's reign, which was one reason she never married. She consciously used her status as Europe's most eligible female to keep Spain from attacking England.

That didn't keep her from making Spain angry. She gave aid to the rebellious Protestant Dutch Republic in their fight against their Roman Catholic Spanish overlords. Under her leadership, Sir Francis Drake harried Spanish ships mercilessly—in 1587, he destroyed thirty Spanish ships in port at Cadiz. She even undermined Spain's precious monopoly of the New World by presiding over England's first attempts at colonization.

All of this resulted in the greatest crisis of her reign—the menace of Philip II's Spanish invasion via an armada (fleet of ships) carrying soldiers, who should have overrun England. Because of a series of miscommunications, weather troubles, and brilliant defensive maneuvers by the English, the mighty Spanish Armada was defeated in 1588. This was a turning point. Because England became increasingly secure from foreign aggression, English culture flourished until Elizabeth's death in 1603.

Conclusion

When Elizabeth took the throne in 1558, Spain claimed the entire New World. When Elizabeth died in 1603, Spain's hour had passed. Feudalism was ending. The impact of individual monarchs on history was fading. Events in England resulted in a shrewd, but somewhat unsatisfactory, compromise. As we enter the next mini-unit, England was poised to establish English-speaking colonies across the ocean. Adventurers, merchants, and common, everyday people who disagreed with Elizabeth's moderate middle path would lead the way.

MINI-UNIT 6: RECOVERY AND DISCOVERY

Mini-Unit 7: A New World

We will join adventurers, traders, and pilgrims in their search for treasure, profit, and freedom. Note how our seven main "characters" fit in.

The Author	As they sailed into new worlds far from established authority, the colonists experimented with new forms of shared authority. They began to form the foundation of self-government under God. Meanwhile, absolute monarchs in England and France tried to reign as if they were God, sparking civil wars and driving colonists to the New World as authority changed hands.
People	Waves of colonists settled the New World as people sought a new life to escape unrest in Europe. The English-speaking colonies in Virginia, New England, the mid-Atlantic, and the deep South were very different. As the colonies grew, relationships with the Native Americans changed.
Good	There were acts of great kindness, especially in the stories of Pocahontas and Squanto. People sought to find good in the New World as they defined it. Some sought commercial gain. Some people sought to define a new society. Hard work was admired, and people worked best when they worked to improve their own property.
Evil	Ironically, we see oppression and religious intolerance, even among people who were pursuing religious freedom. The relationships with Native Americans that began with mutual kindness and respect soured into bloody border skirmishes, as distant European powers fought proxy wars in the New World with the aid of their allies. We also see the first signs of slavery in the colonies, which would be an ongoing evil.
The Word	Some colonists sought to establish model societies based on God's Word. Puritans saw themselves as a city set on a hill. Others sought to bring God's word to the Native Americans, working to translate the Bible.
God's Creation	The New World is the stage on which this drama was enacted. The thirteen colonies were initially separated and dependent on their home countries for survival. Each one was very different and was shaped by both the people who settled there and the places in which they settled.
Man's Creation	The colonists learned to adapt to new ways of life in the New World. They depended on a few, simple tools for defense and the development of their colonies. As labor and finished materials were scarce and expensive, people sought new, innovative ways to survive and prosper.

Mini-Unit 7 Overview
A New World

Introduction

We've covered a lot of world history in the last two mini-units—more than a millennium has passed since the fall of Rome. We'll be covering only 150 years (from around 1600 to 1750) in the next two mini-units, with a focus on developments in the New World. Children will learn many fascinating details about the settlement and growth of the British colonies in America.

This period of American history is called the "colonial" period because during this time, the settlements in America were considered colonies of various European countries. The New World was different from the Old World in significant ways, but colonists did not initially think of themselves as Americans. In these colonies, there were Englishmen, Scotsmen, Dutchmen, Frenchmen, Swedes, and Germans who all brought their traditions, their cultural and religious beliefs, and their expectations with them to the New World.

Colonists were driven (or sent) out, or left voluntarily, from Europe in wave after wave and had to contend with the realities of the New World upon arrival. Because of the difficulties of travel and communication, this really was a one-way trip for most. Colonists needed to learn new rules and build new relationships in order to survive. As we'll learn, although there was much grace, sin was just as present in the New World as it had been in the world they left behind.

Early New World Colonies

While Jamestown in Virginia was the first permanent English settlement in the New World, we will focus more attention on the Pilgrims and Puritans who sought religious freedom in Plymouth, Massachusetts. We'll learn about the pressures that drove them to seek a new home and the difficulties they faced in the New World. Both Jamestown and Plymouth might not have survived without establishing new forms of government and gaining the early support of friendly Native Americans, such as Pocahontas and Squanto, who provided protection and assistance.

In Jamestown, Captain John Smith led a mixed group of lazy and privileged gentleman adventurers and their servants. At one point he told them, "You must obey this now for a law, that he that will not work shall not eat … the labors of thirty or forty honest and industrious men shall not … maintain a hundred and fifty idle loiterers." [1]

In Plymouth, Governor William Bradford changed from the initial communal gardening model to one based on private benefit from use of the plantation's property.

> This had very good success, for it made all hands very industrious, so as much more corn was planted than otherwise would have been by any means the Governor or any other could use, and saved him a great deal of trouble, and gave far better content. The women now went willingly into the field, and took their little ones with them to set corn; which before would allege weakness and inability; whom to have compelled would have been thought great tyranny and oppression.[2]

Partly because of the wilderness setting in which they were founded, the early American colonies were established on a foundation of hard work and individual benefit from that hard work. These character qualities helped drive the growth of the colonies.

Though the Pilgrims were the first to arrive in New England, they were soon joined by other Puritans who also sought religious freedom. The Puritans who came to establish Massachusetts Bay Colony north of Plymouth came to dominate the region. They sought religious freedom when leaving Europe, but they then imposed their own strict beliefs on all they governed. Some colonists disagreed sharply enough with those who governed them that they left Massachusetts and established other New

---

[1] *Colonial Williamsburg Journal* Vol. 16, No. 3 (Spring 1994) p. 14. Accessed 10 February 2014. Retrieved from <http://www.history.org/foundation/journal/smith.cfm>.
[2] *The Founders' Constitution* Volume 1, Chapter 16, Document 1. New York, NY: Modern Library, 1967. Accessed 10 February 2014. Retrieved from <http://press-pubs.uchicago.edu/founders/documents/v1ch16s1.html>.

England colonies nearby. Providence, in Rhode Island, came into being in this way.

Waves of Colonists

Not only were there waves of colonists, but there were also waves of governing overseers. Sweden planted a colony in what is now New Jersey, but the Dutch took it over—then England took it from them. While French and Spanish possessions in the New World grew slowly, England's colonies thrived—in part because of political troubles back home. Many modern Americans are unaware of how tumultuous the seventeenth century was for England. Englishmen overthrew their government three times in less than fifty years (between 1640 and 1688). Each change in England sent new waves of refugees to the colonies. Interestingly, America has had one revolution and one civil war in her entire history.

While this was a tumultuous period for Europe, it resulted in the rapid establishment of a number of English-speaking colonies on the East Coast of North America. Over time, these colonies would see the advantages of banding together as relationships deteriorated with the Native Americans and foreign powers from Europe threatened their security.

Colonists and Native Americans

The relationship of the colonists and the Native Americans has always been one mixed with good and evil on both sides. We see incredible forbearance and forgiveness in the stories of Pocahontas and Squanto. The British colonies might not have been established without their aid! Colonial leaders like Roger Williams and William Penn treated Native Americans with great dignity and respect. But as a group, over time the colonists became threats to the Native Americans because the two cultures did not easily coexist. Warlike Native Americans attracted the attention of European powers. Both the English and the French formed alliances with them and stirred up their allies to fight proxy wars.

We cannot ignore Europe's troubles as we study the New World. France, England, and Spain competed for control of Europe, fighting war after war on that continent. Each European war had its colonial counterpart, where settlers and their Indian allies killed each other in the forests in the name of some faraway king. To make matters worse, distant European diplomats (who treated overseas colonies like minor bargaining chips in their peace negotiations with other European powers), often erased the hard-won gains of these American battles.

While our focus with our young children in this mini-unit will be New World developments, we teachers should remember that, in Europe, Louis XIV of France claimed and exercised an absolute right to rule as he saw fit into the late 1650s, without any checks or balances on his powers as the Sun King. Other monarchs (in England and elsewhere) tried to mimic this absolutism, with varying degrees of success. As Europe's kings sought to establish their powers, Europe's colonies became pawns on an increasingly global chessboard. As some kings asserted their absolutist rights, their citizens pushed back, setting the stage for revolutions and experiments in government without a king.

Conclusion

The political and religious storms in England sent wave after wave of immigrants to America, and the thirteen colonies that resulted bore the marks of England's strife. Two and a half centuries after the American Revolution, it might seem inevitable that these colonies would have united to assert their common interests against an empire across the sea, but the more you know about the American colonies, the more surprising the existence of the United States becomes.

Your child will spend this unit getting to know what life was like for these colonists. For students, we focus less on the political upheavals of Europe and more on the adventures of building a new life in a New World. For teachers, we provide more details about the process by which these separate states unified so that you can better appreciate God's amazing grace in that union.

Mini-Unit 7, Topic 1
Early New World Colonies

Introduction

This week, we will look at the early British colonies of Jamestown, Plymouth, the Massachusetts Bay colony (which included what is now Maine), Rhode Island, New Hampshire, and Connecticut. These colonies were settled for very different reasons, as we'll soon see.

Jamestown

Capitalism

Jamestown was founded by "gentleman[1] adventurers" (and their servants) who were looking for a way to make money. The Spanish had discovered vast amounts of gold in the New World—why shouldn't the English? Many Europeans believed that America was littered with the stuff. Of course, it was a dangerous enterprise. Ships could sink on the long voyage, and there might be hostile natives to deal with once they reached the foreign shores.

As far back as the Middle Ages, merchants had learned how to form joint stock companies to pool their resources and limit their risks. Membership in a joint stock company entitled investors to a share of the profits of the company, but limited their

---

1 Note that, at this time, the term "gentleman" referred to an economic class of men and was a class-status term. It did not have anything to do with the men's behavior.

share of any losses to the amount they invested in the stock. A group of merchants and other investors formed the Virginia Company of London, like any other business venture, and sent a ship to Jamestown.

Gentlemen Adventurers

The problem is, colonizing a new world isn't just a business venture. It's more like being in a war, where working hard and working together makes the difference between life and death. The 105 men who landed in Virginia in the spring of 1607 were radically unprepared for the challenge before them.

It's not that they weren't clear on their mission. They came to look for gold and silver, and, if possible, convert the Indians to Christianity. The problem was that they had the wrong mission and the wrong men. What they ended up needing was food, not gold—and it's not so clear that the adventurers themselves had really been converted to Christianity. Also, many of them were sons of rich men, hence called "gentlemen adventurers," who considered it beneath them to work, follow orders, or keep their hands off the food supplies.

Troubles in Jamestown

Getting the mission and the men wrong was bad, but these settlers' next big mistake was their choice of location for the new colony. The ground around Jamestown was swampy and there was no good source of fresh water. Since they were looking for gold and silver, not a lasting supply of food, they lived off their dried English food supplies instead of choosing land suitable for planting crops and getting to work.

Poor nutrition weakened them just when they needed all the strength they could get. The natives were anything but friendly, but Indians weren't their deadliest enemy. Mosquitoes and microorganisms were worse—the first carried malaria, and the second gave them dysentery. Both were common in swamps. Then, when it got cold, pneumonia set in. Two-thirds of the adventurers died after the first couple of years.

John Smith

The colonists of Jamestown might have all died if it had not been for Captain John Smith, a soldier who had fought some of England's wars in Holland and Eastern Europe. When the Turks captured him there and sold him into slavery, he escaped and made his way back to England by way of Russia. Smith's father was a farmer, and he himself was merely a tough former soldier. Like all of us, Smith had a mix of personal strengths and weaknesses. Men tended to either love him or hate him. He believed in action, not tact. He forced the adventurers to give up the quest for gold in order to find food. He was both brave and quarrelsome—a little too ready for a fight. Still, after the first dreadful year of dying, the survivors elected him their president. He whipped them into shape in no time, with a simple motto: "Work or starve!"

Smith bought corn from the Indians—a risky business, since thirty tribes had united under the leadership of one chief, Powhatan. On one trip to the Indian camp, Indians captured Smith, and Powhatan prepared to crush his skull. His young daughter, Pocahontas, cradled Smith's head in her arms and pled for his life.

She became Smith's friend and later warned him of at least one Indian attack. That didn't keep Smith from treating the natives harshly, though. He used force and fear to keep his enemies at bay. That worked reasonably well while he was in command, but an accident in 1609 sent him back to England.

The Starving Time

More bad days for Jamestown came after Smith went back to England. The colonists suffered from fire, drought, disease, attacks, and another winter of starvation. They were helpless without a strong leader. The colony dropped from 500 men to 60, during what later colonists called "the starving time."

Fresh ships alone saved Jamestown from abandonment. These brought new settlers, supplies, and Jamestown's first royal governor, Lord De La Warr. The colonists welcomed him—by this time, they were glad of any help they could get.

Pocahontas

After John Smith went back to England, the colonists didn't see Pocahontas for a few years. In 1613, she was lured on board an English ship and held captive. There, she met another Englishman named John Rolfe. Pocahontas became a Christian and was baptized and given the name Rebecca. She married John Rolfe, and the two of them went to England in 1616, where she was welcomed as an Indian princess.

Sadly, Pocahontas contracted smallpox while she was getting ready to sail home to America from England. She died before her ship left harbor. Her little son, Thomas Rolfe, got sick, too. He stayed in England for some years before returning to Virginia, where he became a prominent citizen. Many Virginia families still trace their heritage back to Pocahontas.

Puritan Pilgrims in Massachussetts

Background to the Puritans and Pilgrims

During Elizabeth's reign, the Protestant faith made significant inroads into England, although not in the form that some would have preferred. Elizabeth spent her first years on the throne establishing a religious compromise that was politically strong but theologically weak. The compromise minimized the amount of persecution on religious grounds, and gave the moderate Church of England a chance to develop popular support, although a more radical movement grew up alongside it. This was the Puritan movement—so called because it sought to purify the Church of England from within.

After Elizabeth I's death in 1603, her distant cousin James VI of Scotland took the throne as James I of England. James was intent on ruling as an "absolute" monarch. He claimed the authority to do this on biblical grounds by invoking the divine right of kings—the idea that Scripture commanded subjects to obey their rulers absolutely. James believed that his right to rule was established by God, and, as a result, he was not subject to any other earthly authority, including limitations imposed by the Magna Carta or the Pope.

It was obvious to James that the Puritan ideas were egalitarian (believing that rulers, like their subjects, were equally under the law), autonomous (they wished to interpret the Bible for themselves and choose their own ministers), and individualistic (each man should be able to follow his own conscience and interpretation of the Bible on matters of faith and practice). James made it clear that he would never favor such views, and thus yield his power as head over both Church and state.

The Puritans had strong views on what should be the proper method of Church government. They thought that each church should be led by a local council of elders. Some Puritans liked John Calvin's plan for broader Church government, in which local elders would gather in regional groups called presbyteries. Other Puritans preferred a congregational style of government, in which each congregation was a complete church in itself, chose its own leaders, and retained total control over its own affairs.

Puritans sought to purify what they saw as errors arising from theological inaccuracies in worship and Church government (whether Presbyterian or Congregationalist). They also were earnest in their pursuit of personal holiness, and thought everyone should be so as well. It is important to note that while the Puritans were very sincere in their beliefs, they were not very open to the fact that others might believe differently than they did, especially in what Paul refers to in Romans 14:1 as "disputable matters."

Scrooby to the Mayflower

Some of the Puritans began to suspect the Church of England could never be changed. They decided it was time to break off and form their own church, where they could worship God as they believed the Bible taught. This led to severe persecutions. Today's Americans know them as the "Pilgrims," named thus for their years of wandering.

These Separatists were often persecuted. When James became king, things got worse for these dissenters. Separatists like the Pilgrims fled to Holland, a region of the Netherlands, to find a place that would accept them.

It all began in 1606 in a little town called Scrooby, in northern England. Pastor William Brewster helped a group of believers separate from the Church of England. It was against the law to meet as a separate congregation in England, however, so they tried to flee to the Netherlands. They were caught and charged with breaking English law by "stealing" the king's subjects—themselves! Some of them kept trying to leave England, though, and most of them managed to escape to the Dutch city of Amsterdam.

The Netherlands was a bustling place at this time; most of her wealth and power came from having become a center for commerce in Europe. The Netherlands was taking over the world, but the Pilgrims weren't taking over the Netherlands. Amsterdam was worldly and expensive. Without a command of the language or social standing and connections, the Pilgrims had trouble finding any work, so they relocated to the city of Leiden. They could not get jobs as skilled laborers, so everything was difficult. After a number of years, as they watched their children become more Dutch than English and more worldly than spiritual, the Pilgrims began to consider another move. The colony of Jamestown had been planted in Virginia in 1607, and though it had faced great difficulties, its mere existence proved that the New World was an option.

The New World wasn't an inviting alternative to Europe at this time. The Pilgrims would have heard that America was a hard place to survive, where food was scarce and savage Indians killed the colonists. But the alternative in the Netherlands seemed worse.

Despite the dangers, the Pilgrims decided to move to America. There was a new joint-stock company of merchants in London that was willing to pay for their trip. Forty-one Pilgrims and sixty-one other Englishmen who hoped to better their lives by moving to America (many of whom were "gentleman adventurers" of the type we talked about earlier) got on board two ships, the *Speedwell* and the *Mayflower*. The *Speedwell* was old and leaky, and the group had to return to England twice. In September of 1620 one ship—the *Mayflower*—finally set sail for America.

The Mayflower Compact

The *Mayflower*'s voyage was not easy. They were blown off course, far north of the territory designated by their original charter. A sovereign God is in charge of every event, however. This new location meant they were independent of the colony in Virginia and free to develop according to their convictions. Still, it was disconcerting to be out on their own, without any clear authority from the king. This unanticipated situation led them to write a remarkable document: the Mayflower Compact, which created a whole new government by agreement between the colonists—a "social compact," for an unanticipated situation. The colonists wrote and signed this document while on board their ship because they realized they were not within the borders of the territory they were supposed to settle.

Plymouth

The Pilgrims reached the tip of Cape Cod on November 21, 1620, and then found a more protected harbor at Plymouth a month later, on December 21. The site they chose was good. The Pilgrims found a stream with clear water, some cleared land, and a high hill that could be fortified. This site had once been a Patuxet Indian village, but smallpox wiped them out in 1617. While the site was good and harbored no enemies, it was still winter in New England and the colonists were weak from poor food and months of travel. Out of 102 persons, 47 survived the first three months in America, and years of struggle followed. Many more might have followed them but for God's amazing providence.

Squanto

One Patuxet brave had survived the epidemic that wiped out his village. Squanto had been captured and taken to England as a slave before the sickness came. There, he learned to speak English and was trained as an interpreter! After many adventures, he returned to his home a year before the Pilgrims arrived, only to find his village gone.

Squanto was a godsend to the Pilgrims, in the truest sense. He taught them how to grow food using Native American ways. The Pilgrims raised enough crops to celebrate the original Thanksgiving with the friendly natives that lived nearby at harvest time in 1621. Squanto acted as a diplomat between the Pilgrims and Massasoit, the chief of the Wampanoag tribe, who controlled much of southeastern Massachusetts. Relations between the Pilgrims and the Wampanoag were good for fifty years.

William Bradford

Another evidence of God's provision was a wise and godly leader, William Bradford. He was the second governor of the colony, and led it capably for twenty years. He was fair to Native American neighbors and an able leader among his own people. He could have claimed all the land for himself—ten years after they landed, a new charter gave him all the land in southeast Massachusetts. But, instead of keeping it for himself, Bradford shared it with the other settlers.

Common Purse

According to the original joint-stock agreement for Plymouth colony, all profits were supposed to go into a common fund, which would be split up into shares at the end of seven years. Until then, the colony was basically structured as a commune. Unfortunately, it has never been easy to get people to work hard for everybody else's benefit—even Puritans. After three years of working with a common purse, even the shareholders back in London realized it wasn't going to work out. They allowed the colonists to distinguish and farm their own plots, and things got better quickly. The London shareholders sold their interest in the company to the Pilgrims at the end of the seven years.

More Puritans at Massachusetts Bay

The success of the colony at Plymouth led other Puritans to consider the New World. In 1628, Puritans established another joint-stock company, the New England Company. John Endecott led a group of colonists to a settlement he called Salem. The next year, King Charles I granted a new charter that changed the name of the company to the Massachusetts Bay Company. Four hundred more settlers arrived in 1629, and over a thousand had settled the area around Boston by 1630.

The Massachusetts Bay colony had many advantages over Plymouth. They were better situated and better funded. Soon there were thousands of Puritans in

Massachusetts, but the little colony at Plymouth didn't grow much bigger. It limped along with a relative handful of people. Eventually, Plymouth joined with the larger colony into what became the state of Massachusetts.

New Colonies in New England

Having studied Virginia on the mid-Atlantic coastline and Massachusetts in the north, let's look at the other New England colonies near Massachusetts, which were established for a range of reasons. Three new colonies were settled largely by people who moved out of Massachusetts. Rhode Island became a place for people to escape from Puritan orthodoxy. New Hampshire lay north of the Massachusetts Bay Colony boundaries. Originally founded as a planned colony of England in order to harvest the rich fishing grounds of the North Atlantic, it was prime real estate and people soon migrated there. New Haven, which is now in Connecticut, was established as a Puritan theocracy. It eventually joined with three other settlements nearby to form Connecticut.

Religious Freedom and the Founding of Rhode Island

Rhode Island was largely founded by people who were banished by the Puritans. One of these dissenters was a strong-minded pastor, Roger Williams. He thought the Anglican Church was apostate, and believed the Puritans didn't go far enough in their calls for reform. Williams refused to call King James a Christian. These and other outspoken opinions got him into trouble with the Massachusetts authorities, who exiled him. They were going to send him back to England on a ship to face the consequences of such talk, but he snuck out of Salem in the middle of the night and hiked through the woods to reside with his Native American friends. In 1636, he founded a new settlement at Providence on land he bought from the Narragansett tribe. He welcomed people of any religion there, and in time Rhode Island became a haven for Baptists.

One of the more famous people who came to Providence was Anne Hutchinson, who was banished in 1638 for leading a Bible study that included men, for criticizing the Puritan leaders, and for claiming that God spoke directly to her soul. She helped found Portsmouth in what is now known as Rhode Island. In 1647, that settlement united with Providence and two other towns to form "Rhode Island and Providence Plantations."

Rhode Island was unique in allowing anybody to worship as they chose. There is evidence of a Jewish community in Newport as early as 1658, long before any other European community had any thought of treating Jews as fellow citizens.

New Hampshire, Maine, and Vermont

New Hampshire's motto is "Live Free or Die," and its independent spirit goes all the way back to its beginnings. It was founded by free-wheeling settlers who were looking to make money or escape from Puritan control. Massachusetts insisted it controlled the territory, but many New Hampshire settlers objected. They agreed to submit to Massachusetts in 1641, split from Massachusetts in 1679, reunited in 1686, and divided again in 1691. New Hampshire was back under Massachusetts rule in 1698 and separated for the last time in 1741.

Maine, further north, didn't escape the rule of Massachusetts until after the American Revolution. That's why it isn't one of the thirteen original colonies, even though it is one of the six New England states. Neither is Vermont—New York and New Hampshire both claimed that territory for years. Vermont was the first new state to join the Union, after a brief stint as the independent "Republic of Vermont."

Connecticut

The Dutch had a small fort at what is now Hartford, Connecticut, but the first permanent European settlement there was made by Puritans from the Massachusetts Bay Colony. New England doesn't have many major rivers—the Connecticut River is the one real exception. Settlers from Massachusetts established a number of towns along the river.

Without any clear charter to govern them, three of these new towns united in 1636 to form what was called the River Colony, or the Connecticut Colony. Other Massachusetts Puritans founded New Haven as another independent colony, which was to be run as a pure theocracy. Soon other towns joined the New Haven colony. The independent New Haven and Connecticut colonies were eventually merged into one colony under direct control of King Charles II in 1662.

Conclusion

As we learn about these early colonies, note the diversity of faith among the settlers. Jamestown was founded by loyal Englishmen who were members of the Anglican Church, so Virginia was Anglican. The Pilgrims who landed at Plymouth Rock had very different beliefs and established churches that often shared core beliefs, but were Congregational in governance. Settlers in Connecticut sought to establish a pure theocracy. Rhode Island allowed all to worship as they chose. Other settlers from England and the Netherlands sought to harvest the riches of the New World.

Aided by God's providence and the friendship of Native Americans, the faith and sacrifice of the first settlers in both places made it possible for a trickle, then a stream, and then a flood of people to migrate to the New World. There's a saying: "Only those who see the invisible can do the impossible." The Pilgrims, who were looking for a city whose builder and maker is God, had their eyes firmly fixed on the invisible.

Mini-Unit 7, Topic 2
Waves of Colonists

Introduction

As we mentioned earlier, events in Europe directly affected the formative years of the American colonies, so we will spend some time reviewing the highlights of these complex events with you, the teacher. It is up to you how much you want to share with your student. Your student should understand that the colonists gave up everything to start a new life in the New World, but that they left home for many different reasons.

Maryland, Delaware, New Sweden, and New Amsterdam

Roman Catholics joined Puritans in criticizing the Church of England, but for the opposite reason. To the Catholics there was rather too much Protestantism than Catholic ritual in the Anglican Church! During the time before the English Civil War (more on that in a moment), Roman Catholics (who were increasingly in the minority in England) found some comfort in the fact that King Charles I appeared to be sympathetic to them. He granted Lord Baltimore, an Irish Catholic, the colony of Maryland as a haven for Catholics, among other actions. Lord Baltimore named his new colony "Maryland" after Henrietta Maria, the princess of France who had become Charles' Roman Catholic wife.

Maryland was a diverse colony, established around the same time the New England colonies were being settled. The Maryland Religious Toleration Act of 1649 was the first document of its kind stating that settlers had the right to worship freely. Unlike Rhode Island, though, Maryland limited its toleration to Trinitarian Christians.

England wasn't the only country settling the eastern seaboard—Sweden planted the first settlements in what are now New Jersey and Delaware. Lord Baltimore's land grant included some land already settled by Sweden. They had built a trading post at what is now Wilmington, Delaware, and called their New World holdings "New Sweden."

New Sweden didn't last long—all of its colonies were taken over by the Dutch Republic. It was the golden age of that nation—the Netherlands was the world's greatest sea power, with half of Europe's ships. Dutch explorers had ranged from Australia to Siberia. The Dutch East India Company had driven the British and Portuguese out of what is now India and governed there. They took over Sri Lanka and the southern tip of Africa. The Dutch even sent an Englishman, Henry Hudson, to look for a "northwest passage" over the top of America to China for trading purposes. Though he didn't find the route they sought, his explorations allowed the Netherlands to lay claim to what is now Delaware, New Jersey, New York, and parts of Connecticut.

Dutch merchants set up trading posts with the Indians around the Hudson River. By 1625, the Dutch founded New Amsterdam on the island of Manhattan.

English Civil War

As we said, James I tried to rule as an absolute monarch. His son, Charles I, followed in his footsteps. His attempts to rule with absolute power led to the English Civil War. After years of working around and outside of Parliament, which had a Puritan majority, the Puritans took up arms against their king. By 1642, a full-blown civil war had broken out.

Parliament raised its own army, then captured, tried, and beheaded King Charles I. Such a thing had never been seen—only a few decades before, Mary Queen of Scots (James I's mother) had refused to be tried by a court because, as a queen, she considered herself divinely appointed by God and not answerable to a court. Now, English subjects had not only tried but also *actually executed their king*! Europe was appalled.

While Charles I was in power, Puritans fled to the colonies. Now, it was the king's supporters who fled to the colonies, many to Virginia. For nearly twenty years, England was a Puritan Commonwealth—not a kingdom—ruled by a Puritan named Cromwell. But the Puritan experiment in government failed. The rule of the Puritans didn't turn England into a holy nation that shone as the light of the world, as many

Puritans had hoped it would. The Puritan parliament passed strict rules that sought to control public morality. After twenty years of Puritan rule, the English people kicked the Puritans out and restored the monarchy in the political chaos that followed the death of the Puritan leader, Oliver Cromwell. The years from 1660 to 1688 are thus known as the Restoration Period in English history. Fed up with the Puritan's moralistic military rule, most people in England welcomed Charles II back as king. Now the Puritans were on the run, and new waves of refugees fled from England to friendly colonies in New England.

Over the course of these tumultuous years in England (from 1642 to 1688), Puritans and Royalists in England went back and forth from being persecuted to becoming the persecutors, and as a result different areas of America became concentrated with people of widely varying beliefs. New England was settled by thousands of Puritans. Royalists mostly populated Virginia. The English-speaking colonies swelled. Charles II also used his power take over Dutch colonies in what is now New York, New Jersey (originally New Sweden), and Delaware.

New World Colonies under Charles II

King Charles II left quite a mark on the New World. He had no love for the people of Massachusetts, for a number of reasons. They would not help his officials find his father's "murderers." They resisted his Navigation Acts (laws that restricted colonial trade with other European powers), coined their own money, would not make officials swear allegiance to the throne of England, and refused to allow the Church of England to be established in their colony. Charles took away their original charter rights in retaliation. Massachusetts was turned into a crown colony and placed under a royal governor.

At times, Charles II granted ownership of American lands that he did not yet rule! For instance, in 1663, his brother James, then the Duke of York, purchased a lapsed land title to a part of the American coastline. The Dutch had settled the area around the mouth of the Hudson River, and there were several Swedish settlements in what are now New Jersey and Delaware. This same territory had been conferred on the Earl of Sterling by Charles I. When he took the throne, Charles II gave his brother the right to colonize and rule the region between New England and Maryland.

In 1664, James sent an expedition to New Amsterdam. This was a shrewd move—the Dutch West India Company had foolishly chosen not to place any garrison there. James' naval forces took control of New Amsterdam without firing a shot.

As a result, New Amsterdam became the personal property of James—a proprietary colony, not a royal one. James, Duke of York, promptly named it New York after himself. James then granted the land between the Hudson River and the Delaware River (which eventually became New Jersey) to two loyal royalists: Sir George Carteret and Lord Berkeley of Stratton. Along with New Amsterdam, the English now controlled the former New Sweden in what is now Delaware.

The Carolinas

Charles II granted the territories that became North Carolina and South Carolina to eight of his main supporters. These men had been loyal to him during his hard times. These Proprietors (as they were called) attempted to set up a grand new feudal system in their new lands, but their colonies failed. Because North Carolina had very few natural resources to support growth, it grew very little. South Carolina, with its busy Charles Town harbor, grew rapidly.

There was initially more freedom of worship in the Carolinas than in many other European settlements. People of many different faiths came to these new colonies. Huguenots from France, English Quakers, religious refugees from Germany and Ireland, and Jacobites from Scotland all found homes in the Carolinas.

Penn's Woods and Delaware

William Penn founded a haven for dissenters as well. Penn's father had been a prominent supporter of King Charles II during the difficult days of the English Commonwealth. In 1681, Charles II took land that had been under the control of his brother, the Duke of York, and granted it to Penn, insisting that it be named "Penn's woods"—Pennsylvania. Penn applied his Quaker principles to the new colony. For example, even though the woods were full of Indians, Penn governed as he preached: Quakers were confirmed pacifists. Therefore, Pennsylvania had no armed militia for generations.

As governor, Penn wrote and brought with him the colony's first constitution, called the Frame of Government. From the beginning, Penn treated the Native Americans with utmost respect and fair dealings. He made his colonists buy their land from the Indians, although English law did not require them to do so. As a result, no other colony had a better relationship with their native neighbors.

Pennsylvania's history involves the neighboring territory of Delaware. King Charles II gave land to William Penn that did not include any access to the sea. The land between Pennsylvania and the ocean was all held by James, the Duke of York. James leased the territory at the mouth of the Delaware River to Penn. The territory we now call Delaware was known as the "Three Lower Counties," because it was downriver from Pennsylvania.

At first, Pennsylvania and Delaware had an equal number of representatives in their local colonial legislature, but Pennsylvania kept growing. By 1701, the Delaware delegates refused to meet with the Pennsylvania legislature. They asked William Penn to give them their own legislature, which he did. The Delaware legislature began meeting in its own right in 1704, but had the same governor as Pennsylvania. The two colonies were not formally separated until the time of the American Revolutionary War.

Glorious Revolution

Back in England, Charles II tried to rule England as an absolute monarch. So did his younger brother James II, who took the throne after Charles died without an heir. Charles II had flirted with the Roman Catholic faith (which was still the state religion in France, where he had been raised in exile). He supported his cousin (French King Louis XIV) in war, and even (it was said) entered a secret agreement to convert to Roman Catholicism. When he died, James II went even further towards Roman Catholicism than had his brother. England wasn't eager to return to Roman Catholicism, but since the only immediate heirs to the throne were Protestant (James' two adult daughters, Mary and Anne), it seemed like all the nation had to do was wait for James to die in order to get a Protestant ruler.

But dark clouds appeared—James took a young, Italian, Roman Catholic bride. When she gave birth to a healthy baby boy in 1688, James made no secret that the little prince would be raised Roman Catholic. That's why Parliament invited a Dutch prince, William of Orange, to invade England and drive out their king. William was James' son-in-law: he was husband of Princess Mary, the nearest Protestant heir to the crown. King James II threw the Great Seal of England into the river (the sign of abdication) and tried to flee the country. Parliament declared he had abdicated and gave the crown to William and Mary, in what was called the Glorious Revolution of 1688. (It was considered glorious because it was bloodless, and because the majority of Englishmen wanted a Protestant monarch.) As you might guess, another round of political refugees fled from England to America.

House of Hanover

You'd think, by now, that England would be finished overthrowing kings for religious reasons, but there was one last change of hands before the final English colony in America was planted. William and Mary had no children, so the throne went to Mary's younger sister Anne. When Anne died without an heir, it looked like the crown would go to her half-brother—that little baby boy whose birth had brought in William and Mary. By an act of Parliament, however, the crown passed to a German lord named George—a man who could not even speak English! He was Protestant and had royal blood, so he would have to do. The last English colony, Georgia, was named for him.

Georgia

Georgia, planted late and far to the south, was a bold experiment in charity, partly funded by the British government. It was supposed to be a refuge for the deserving poor, a place where hard liquor was outlawed, slavery was prohibited, and each settler had a small plot of his own land to farm. The proprietors of the colony tried to run it all as a planned economy. Georgia was also supposed to be a buffer against the hostile Spanish forces in Florida. Georgia succeeded in fending off Spain, but failed at all its other goals. After twenty years, the colony was taken over by the crown, which allowed big landholders to run their huge plantations.

Conclusion

The rise and fall of the English Puritans affected who moved off to America. Each new wave of immigrants brought people with special talents and viewpoints to America and contributed much to the rich and varied culture, opinions, and growth of this great nation. Each of the original American colonies had its own history and culture. The Puritans who settled New England shared the same ideals as the Puritans who cut off the head of King Charles I, but had very little in common with the royalists who settled Virginia, or with those who moved to the Carolinas—colonies named after King Charles II.. Given the civil war between their families back in Britain, who could have imagined that one day Massachusetts men would stand shoulder to shoulder with men from South Carolina?

Mini-Unit 7, Topic 3
Colonists and Native Americans

Introduction

In our survey of American history so far, we have been studying the founding of each colony in historical sequence. This week, we're going to focus more thematically on the original inhabitants of the land. We'll start with how the Native Americans lived before the Europeans arrived, and then take a look at their conflicts with their new neighbors in what are often called the Indian wars.

Throughout, we must remember that the Spanish and French had not been passively standing by as English colonies were established. While their American holdings were driven by trade rather than settlement, the French controlled vast amounts of territory throughout the Great Lakes and down the Mississippi River. The French were very adept at making friends with the Native Americans, and their trappers and traders often learned to speak native languages and blended right in with the tribes. As relationships between France and England deteriorated in the 1700s in the Old World, both European powers would use their relationships to stir up hostility in the New World.

We end this topic with a brief look at the forces that fostered the institution of slavery, especially in the southern colonies. Slaves had been used on Caribbean plantations since the 1500s, but the growing economic dependence on slavery in the southern colonies ensured that this would be a dark thread that running through American history.

Native Americans

Let's take a different look at North America, examining the native peoples who were there before the white men came. The New World was a big place, and there were many native tribes, which were very different from one another. One way that scholars divide the North American tribes up is by geography, because different regions had unique resources and challenges, and the North American tribes adapted to them. The Indians of the Northeast lived one way; the Plains Indians lived another. The people in the Southwest built pueblos and the Northwest natives carved totem-poles. So, geography shaped the lifestyle of each tribe. We'll focus first on the tribes the English settlers first encountered, in the Northeast and Southeast.

Northeast

The Northeast tribes lived in one vast forest that stretched from the Canadian tundra to the Great Plains. Many of the Northeast tribes spoke some dialect of the Iroquois language. The Cayuga, Mohawk, Oneida, Onondaga, and Seneca were major tribes, and they formed a league known as the "Five Nations." This Iroquois Confederacy included most territories of New England, upstate New York, and parts of Pennsylvania. It also covered parts of Ontario and Quebec. The Hurons were the only major Iroquois-speaking tribe that refused to join the league.

In most Northeastern tribes, the men hunted and fished while the women gathered nuts and berries and grew corn, beans, and squash. They dressed in deerskins, which they made soft by chewing on them. God's common grace was revealed in these people and their ability to live off the land.

Southeast

The great American forests stretched to the south as well, but the Indian tribes' cultures changed as the climate grew warmer. Without the birch trees of the cold north woods, the southern tribes dug (or burned) out canoes from heavy tree trunks. In warmer places, some Indians wore little more than tattoos. That doesn't mean they were more backwards than their neighbors to the north. The Natchez Indians, one of these Southeastern tribes, had the most sophisticated governmental structure north of Mexico. The Natchez had a complex social order complete with temples and palaces.

In later years, several of these southern tribes became known as the "Five Civilized Tribes." These were the Cherokee, Chickasaw, Choctaw, Creek, and Seminole nations.

Conflict

The first English settlers to live side-by-side with the Native Americans were in the Southeast, in Virginia. Some of their interactions were friendly. We've learned how Pocahontas saved the life of Captain John Smith, for instance, and that Smith bought corn from her tribe. But in general, the tribes under Chief Powhatan were strong and hostile, and the settlers at Jamestown weren't exactly rich in people skills. Captain John Smith was a capable soldier who kept the natives at bay, but after he had to leave Virginia, Jamestown was almost annihilated by attacks from the thirty tribes that Powhatan led.

Plymouth Plantation

The Indians to the north started off with better relations with the settlers. We have already seen how Squanto saved the Pilgrims from starvation in their first year at Plymouth. That settlement enjoyed peaceful relations with a neighboring Wampanoag tribe for more than fifty years, but it came under increasing pressure over time.

Massachusetts Bay Colony and the Pequot War

The Puritans who settled Massachusetts Bay to the north of Plymouth had more trouble. Conflicts over land erupted between the Puritans and the powerful Pequot tribe in the 1630s, which resulted in the Pequot war in 1637. The Puritans allied themselves with the Pequot's traditional enemies, the Narragansett tribe, to achieve victory.

King Philip's War

Years later, relations between the Plymouth Colony and its native neighbors broke down completely when Plymouth authorities executed three Wampanoag men for murdering an Indian who had become a Christian.

Fighting began in 1675 and spread across New England. Metacom, the son of old chief Massasoit, had been agitating for the complete extermination of the English settlers, who called him King Philip. He formed an alliance with the Narragansett tribe, who fought against the English this time. The natives battled colonists across New England in what was known as King Philip's War—which, given the small English population at the time and the number of English deaths, was one of the most devastating wars in America's history.

Tuscarora Uprising

In the North Carolina territories, Native Americans were led by Tuscarora chiefs to attack European settlers. The colonists were taken completely by surprise and massacred in significant numbers. With help from South Carolina and Virginia settlers and friendly Indians, the North Carolina colonists fought back. The Tuscarora retreated to New York and joined the Iroquois Confederacy (making it the League of Six Nations) in 1720.

French Influence

While they did not plant as many colonies, the French influence in the New World penetrated as deeply as the England's. Via the St. Lawrence River, French traders and trappers gained access to the Great Lakes and then to the Mississippi River. Jesuit priests sought to convert the Native Americans to Roman Catholicism, while merchants built trading posts. New France, as it was called, was less thickly or permanently settled than New England, but its influence was not friendly to English settlers and provided a base of operations from which the deadly French and Indian Wars would spring.

Critiquing the Conflict

It has become popular to blame these conflicts between Europeans and Native Americans on the evil white man, who came across the sea to drive the innocent natives from their sacred lands. That may be popular, but it isn't biblical. If we're going to blame Europeans, let's look at their behavior in light of Scripture, not multiculturalism. How do the colonists measure up in light of the Bible?

Most of the European settlers were professing Christians. Jesus commanded us to preach the gospel to all the nations. That could be hard—many Indians were genuinely hostile—but Jesus told us to love our enemies. We have many records of European colonists preaching Christ to their Native American neighbors with sincere hearts, and also treating them fairly. Clearly, though, Christians are still able to sin, and we are not claiming that all were blameless.

Many European settlers were also probably not Christians at heart, so it is not surprising that these men acted with unrestrained and unregenerate human hearts, which is as much to say, wickedly. Most of the authors your students will read this week will be quick to point this out. Part of the mistake made by Europeans was to judge the primitive peoples that they encountered worldwide as "lesser" than themselves on the basis of both cultural advancements and cultural Christianity.

It goes without saying that the Native Americans were also unregenerate. In some ways, the settlers had good reason for calling them "savages." They were brutal to their enemies (whether European or Native American) and despised the members of other tribes or cultures. It was normal for members of a tribe to consider themselves "the People" and everyone else something less. For example, the Catawbas of South Carolina called other Indians "dogs" or "snakes" and they called the white colonists "Nothings."

Good Treatment

Unregenerate people of all races are savage in their own ways. In light of that, the big surprise is in how many years there were of peaceful coexistence between the Native Americans and the settlers, with much mutual aid between the two peoples. The cultural impact wasn't all bad. Many Native American families were enriched by trading opportunities offered by Europeans. The Indians' habitats, tools, farming techniques, and ability to hunt improved from contact with their white neighbors. Some, like Pocahontas, accepted the gospel and received the eternal gift of salvation. While modern secular scholars won't see this for the treasure it is, it's nonetheless true that many Native Americans would have died in their sins if Europeans had never come to their shores.

Unintended Harms

Unfortunately, some of the cultural advances introduced by European colonization were more harmful. The advanced weapons that made it easier for natives to hunt game made it easier to settle old feuds, too. European technologies made wars between tribes much more lethal.

The Europeans also brought diseases—like smallpox—that caused entire villages to be wiped out. This, too, was unintentional—at first. It was part of broken people living in a fallen world. Tragically, in time, some Europeans gave smallpox-infected blankets to the Indians on purpose.

European trade disrupted the traditional Indian economies, bringing them to become ever more dependent on manufactured goods. In this way, survival skills and tribal traditions were lost or modified, and dependence of natives on Europeans was built. One of the greatest dangers to the Native American people was alcohol—which has been destroying Indian lives from the time it was first introduced to the present.

Missionaries

Ephesians 5:18 says, "Do not get drunk with wine, for that is debauchery, but be filled with the Spirit." Again, the most important gift the Europeans brought the natives was the gospel, which was often well-received. Christian missionaries made sincere—even heroic—attempts to bring the gospel to the Native Americans. John Eliot and Experience Mayhew gave their lives to bring the gospel to natives in their own language.

John Eliot led the missionary effort to the Massachusetts Indians for nearly sixty years (1631 to 1690). After learning their language, he created an alphabet for Algonquian and translated the Bible. Eliot's Algonquian Bible was the first Bible printed in America. Eliot led an effort to give "Praying Indian" converts their own self-governing towns. His model settlement was Natick. There, Native Americans dressed, worshipped, and farmed as Englishmen and women did in nearby settlements in New England.

Eliot's mission to the Indians suffered a disastrous setback during King Philip's War. The Colonists were understandably distrustful of all Native Americans, even Praying Indians. Eliot asked the General Court of New England for help. The Court sequestered the Praying Indians on Deer Island as winter approached. They were suddenly and forcibly evacuated there without ample food, clothing, or housing supplies. As the winter dragged on, many died. Some were even enslaved. After the war, many Praying Indians were dead, many had lost their faith in Christ, and a few returned to their ruined settlements and attempted to rebuild.

Slavery in the South

The use of slave labor in the colonies was a long-established, albeit tragic, part of colonial life, especially in southern colonies. Plantation owners in the Carolinas and Virginia made use of slave labor to raise cash crops. For a time, it seemed as though Georgia might be different from its southern neighbors. Originally, Georgia was settled as a charitable experiment. Unlike the colonies further up the coast, Georgia did not permit slavery. Another big difference from the other colonies was Georgia's limit on land-ownership. Nobody was allowed to hold more than 500 acres, and laws about the transfer of land prevented the development of a plantation system like the one in

South Carolina. This may have been the real reason that Georgia prohibited slavery—not because the proprietors objected to slavery as such but because they opposed big landowners. Every settler was guaranteed at least fifty acres for his own farm, but he wasn't allowed to decide what he wanted to raise. That was decided by the colonial government.

Georgia did not live up to the charitable dreams of its founder, James Oglethorpe. The colonists did manage to keep Spain from encroaching on British possessions in King George's War in 1742, but they also resented the limits on hard liquor, land ownership, and slaves because they wanted plantations and the prosperity that went with them. They wanted some say in running the colony. In 1752, the original proprietors of the colony surrendered their charter to the King, who appointed a royal governor. Before long, thousands of African slaves were at work on great plantations along the coast of Georgia.

Why did slavery flourish in the southern colonies? In the early 1700s, England was beginning to enter the Industrial Revolution. Inventions revolutionized the production of textiles, enabling English factories to produce cheap cotton cloth. Prior to this, weaving textiles was a manual, time-consuming process that produced expensive products. Demand for the raw cotton was low. The Industrial Revolution changed that. Suddenly, factories couldn't get enough cotton.

This demand created a need for lots of dedicated human labor. Raising cotton was a difficult, painful job, and it was not easy to find volunteers. In a time when slave ownership was not as widely questioned, slavery provided a quick solution to wealthy plantation owners' need for labor.

Conclusion

Roger Williams, who helped found Rhode Island, wrote:

> Boast not proud English of thy birth and blood,
> Thy brother Indian is by birth as good.
> Of one blood God made him, and thee, and all,
> As wise, as fair, as strong, as personal

As we have learned so far in our study of world history, no human society is without sin or perfect in all its ways. Yet, all have strengths and weaknesses because all have been ordained by God for a time and a purpose. Help your child keep an eternal perspective on what he reads this week. We should grieve when men act wickedly, but we should also rejoice because a good God was working all things together for His purposes, which are always perfect.

With the establishment of Georgia, we have studied the foundation of all thirteen original British colonies. They began as little pockets of very different people, but the eastern seaboard of America grew up fast. As they grew, relationships with England began to change as well.

MINI-UNIT 7: A NEW WORLD

Mini-Unit 8: One Nation

We will follow the struggles of the established colonies to unify as one nation, under God, with liberty and justice for all. Note how our seven main "characters" fit in.

 The Author	Citing a long string of abuses and taxes, the colonies declared their independence, establishing one nation, under God, and launching an experiment in self-government. The Founding Fathers deliberated long and hard whether they had the authority to declare independence.
 People	George Washington bridged the proxy-war conflicts of the French and Indian War and led the colonists against one of the premier military powers of the day, aided by assistance from abroad. Patriots fought for liberty in Boston, while others helped lay the foundation of a new nation.
 Good	Some people saw God as distant, setting up rules for the world, but leaving them to be followed without intervention. This attitude was called Deism. Thrift, industriousness, and independence were seen as good. At the same time, issues of social justice and conscience began to be more broadly considered. In England, slavery was abolished, thanks to John Newton and William Wilberforce.
 Evil	Not isolated to the colonies, the reality of generational slavery was present, especially in the southern colonies. As in every society, greed, exploitation, dishonesty, and hatred were present. The French and Indian Wars and aspects of the Revolutionary War were dark chapters.
 The Word	God's Word was not silent or powerless. The First Great Awakening made itself known in England and then in America, resulting in the rise of people freshly committed to live according to God's Word.
 God's Creation	From the Applachian Mountains to the shores of Yorktown and further south, the Revolutionary War helped to connect and co-mingle colonists up and down the Eastern seaboard. Distance also affected the ability to communicate and coordinate the war efforts. Key patriots were sent overseas to act as ambassadors in order to win support for the fight.
 Man's Creation	Inventors like Benjamin Franklin performed experiments as part of the ongoing Scientific Revolution. Innovations and industrialization made raising cash crops like cotton more profitable. Continuing to adapt, the colonists abandoned European military precision and fought "Indian Style," making use of their skill with the far-ranged, accurate rifles.

Mini-Unit 8 Overview
One Nation

Introduction

Our focus in this mini-unit is the American Revolutionary War that united the diverse colonies against what they saw as English abuses. Although most of what we will cover with our students occurred in the New World, it's important for teachers to understand how much events in the Old World influenced the development of the American colonies.

Things were still happening worldwide as the colonies grew strong. Scientific discoveries and journeys of exploration were made. As part of a scientific voyage to help determine the earth's distance from the sun, Captain James Cook explored the South Pacific and discovered Australia, which he claimed for Great Britain. In France, chemistry was turned upside down when Antoine Lavoisier discovered oxygen. In Britain, James Watt invented the steam engine. In America, Benjamin Franklin developed practical inventions (like the Franklin Stove, bifocals, and public libraries) and performed experiments showing that lightning was really electricity in clouds. Such discoveries paved the way for the Industrial Revolution that would dominate the following century.

The world was changing, and as it did, tensions built up between the English colonies and their mother country. As you read, remember that many of the colonists still thought of themselves as Englishmen. Most would have considered themselves "loyal subjects of the king." There may have been a sense of betrayal when they realized that the King and country for whom they were toiling in the wilderness did not care about them or their interests. When the breach came, it came after many years of disappointment. The Declaration of Independence, written in 1776, gives us great insight into their grievances:

> We hold these truths to be self-evident, that all men are created equal, that they are endowed by their Creator with certain unalienable Rights, that among these are Life, Liberty and the pursuit of Happiness.--That to secure these rights, Governments are instituted among Men, deriving their just powers from the consent of the governed, --
>
> That whenever any Form of Government becomes destructive of these ends, it is the Right of the People to alter or to abolish it, and to institute new Government, laying its foundation on such principles and organizing its powers in such form, as to them shall seem most likely to effect their Safety and Happiness.
>
> Prudence, indeed, will dictate that Governments long established should not be changed for light and transient causes; and accordingly all experience hath shewn, that mankind are more disposed to suffer, while evils are sufferable, than to right themselves by abolishing the forms to which they are accustomed.
>
> But when a long train of abuses and usurpations, pursuing invariably the same Object evinces a design to reduce them under absolute Despotism, it is their right, it is their duty, to throw off such Government, and to provide new Guards for their future security.
>
> Such has been the patient sufferance of these Colonies; and such is now the necessity which constrains them to alter their former Systems of Government. The history of the present King of Great Britain is a history of repeated injuries and usurpations, all having in direct object the establishment of an absolute Tyranny over these States.

What were these repeated injuries and usurpations? Let's learn a bit more about them.

French and Indian War

Part of the tension between England and her American colonies was due to the French and Indian War, which changed how the colonies viewed themselves in relation to Great Britain and how George III of England regarded his colonies. This conflict was fought on American soil between English colonists and French colonists (who had strong Indian allies). Yet it was rooted in a war between the major powers of Europe, including England and France.

Teachers should note that the French and Indian War was part of a global conflict, with battlefields in Europe, North America, Central America, the West African coast, India, and the Philippines. It would not be inappropriate to think of this as a colonial version of the World Wars that would come in the twentieth century. The conflict ended with an expensive English victory that broke the back of France in the New World, but also moved England toward losing her American colonists. In our study, we will emphasize the impact on colonists and their core relationships with England.

Gathering Clouds

The French and Indian War (also known as the Seven Years' War in Europe) gave Britain a new, global empire, but it increased the British national debt by a million percent. King George needed money, and Parliament—not the colonial legislatures—decided to make the American colonists start paying taxes. This decision violated some fundamental assumptions about the relationship between English kings, Parliament, and their subjects.

Remember that King George was of German stock, that the American colonies were far away, and that wars are expensive. It may have been expedient for George to demand that they pay for protection and thus to have Parliament (which did *not* include colonial representatives) raise taxes. England's insistence on levying taxes and the colonists' refusal to pay them put them on a course that was bound to end in war.

Give Me Liberty!

Blood was spilled in April, 1775 when Redcoats and Minutemen started shooting one another at a bridge in Lexington, Massachusetts. That exchange escalated into war when the American colonies assembled their representatives at a Continental Congress and there agreed that it was time to take up arms in self-defense. Skirmishes turned to battles, and battles to campaigns as each side waged war.

Conclusion

The American colonists would win their independence from Great Britain over the course of the Revolutionary War. As we'll see in later weeks, even though they were politically united into one new nation in name, it would take many years and many trials to unite them in spirit. At this point in American history, it was more proper to refer to our country as *these* United States than *this* United States of America. The states were at first more different than similar, and the initial Federal government was not what you'd call effective. Only later would the emphasis in the country's name shift to the *United* States of America.

MINI-UNIT 8: ONE NATION

Mini-Unit 8, Topic 1
French and Indian War

Introduction

This topic, we set the stage for the American Revolution by studying the four French and Indian Wars, so named because the British colonists in America fought the French and their Indian allies. The American colonists called the first three of these "King William's War," "Queen Anne's War," and "King George's War." You can see from these names that the colonists didn't think of the wars as their own. These first three wars made little lasting change on the balance of power or territory. The fourth and last of these is what we usually think of as *the* French and Indian War, lasting from 1753 to 1763. It was part of a much larger conflict: the Seven Years' War in Europe.

Together, these wars have been collectively termed the Great War for Empire. Winston Churchill called it "the first world war," because the European countries that fought were striving to develop colonies and trading posts around the globe. The people in these colonies took up the conflict between their parent countries in every corner of the globe. As always, we want to help our students understand what it meant for colonists to live in these dangerous times.

This "first world war" changed the shape and destiny of America. In the last mini-unit, we learned how very different the individual colonies were from one another. In the 1750s, the colonists were anything but united. Benjamin Franklin tried to get them to join together in the face of French and Indian hostility, but got nowhere. Outright war changes things, though. The colonists began to appreciate each other over almost ten years of conflict. Soldiers from various regions traveled to other colonies during the years of battle, learning about one another and receiving help from one another in the process. As a result, the colonists began to unify despite differences in backgrounds, customs, and religions.

Also during this time, the colonists' view of England began to shift. The British army was then one of the best and most respected armies in Europe, where the tactics they employed were virtually irresistible. When they fought in America, however, it was a different story. In the wilds of America, parading their bright red coats in close-packed formation through the woods turned the well-drilled British soldiers into sitting ducks for the French or Indian sharpshooters who took cover in the trees. The colonists had a more effective approach to warfare in America: they dressed in browns and greens and fought Indian style—hiding behind fences or trees to pick off their opponents. Thus, the colonists learned that the British ways of doing things were not always best, nor were England's armies as invincible as was commonly thought overseas!

The end of the French and Indian War (and its European counterpart conflict) brought more changes in attitude. The French lost their territory to the east of the Mississippi by agreement of the Treaty of Paris of 1763. The Proclamation Line of 1763 established a tall mountain border between the British colonists and the Indians. As a result, the colonists felt less of a need for British protection than they ever had before. Thirteen years later, we'll see those colonists express this new sense of independence in writing!

Washington and Fort Duquesne

The first shot of the French and Indian War was fired under orders from a young colonial officer named George Washington, in a then-wilderness region of the Ohio Valley. In 1753, Governor Robert Dinwiddie of Virginia had decided to demand that the French to withdraw all troops from the Ohio Valley region. He appointed young major Washington to take a message to the French military commander. Washington delivered his message to a French outpost near Lake Erie, but the French rejected Dinwiddie's demand. Their orders, they said, were to take and hold the Ohio Valley.

Washington brought the bad news back to the governor and urged him to build a fort where the Monongahela and Allegheny Rivers join to form the Ohio, the site of present-day Pittsburgh. Before the month was out, Dinwiddie sent frontiersmen to build it. Washington, at the age of 22, was promoted to lieutenant colonel. He was ordered to recruit soldiers to man that fort—a task made harder by the discriminatory policies of the British army: English troops and officers were paid more than their American counterparts, even though their dangers and hardships were the same.

By April, 1754, Washington set out for the new fort with a force of 160 raw recruits, only to learn that the French had already captured and renamed it Fort Duquesne (after one of their own military leaders). Washington pressed on anyway. His troops surprised a group of French soldiers, whom Washington attacked. It was his first experience of battle, and these were the first shots of a war that would last for nine years—the first war ever to circle the globe. Washington's force lost one man, but killed 10, wounded 1, and captured 21.

While he waited for reinforcements, energetic George Washington built a new fort sixty miles south of Fort Duquesne and named it Fort Necessity. He was promoted to the rank of colonel. In June, 180 more Virginians arrived—but brought no food. Two weeks later, 100 British Redcoats joined them with vitally needed supplies. Then the French attacked. Many of Washington's men were sick, and all were hungry. Thirty were killed and seventy wounded that day as a rainstorm turned the battlefield to mud and soaked what little gunpowder he had left. By nightfall, Washington's position was hopeless. He surrendered the fort to save his men.

The colonists didn't blame Washington for the lost fort. Washington's military career seemed secure, until new orders from Britain arrived, prohibiting any colonial from holding a post higher than captain. Washington refused to be demoted and resigned from the army.

Albany Congress

Conflict escalated as the French urged their Indian allies to attack British settlements. Concerned colonists gathered at Albany, New York, where they met with representatives of the Iroquois Confederacy. Benjamin Franklin proposed that the colonies unite. The delegates liked the plan, but neither Britain nor the colonial legislatures took it seriously. Even in the face of a very real and present enemy, the colonists could not overcome mutual suspicion and disagreement.

Braddock and Fort Duquesne

The following year, the British tried to retake Fort Duquesne. They sent out a general and a large force of British regulars (professional soldiers). General Braddock intended to start with Fort Duquesne and then move on to pick off every other fort of French Quebec in one short campaign. Washington went along as an unpaid aide to Braddock, but the general had no interest in what he or any other colonial soldiers might know about the situation in the Ohio Valley.

Braddock's troops made slow progress through the wilderness. As they neared the fort, the narrow roadway made Braddock string his men out in one long line. Suddenly, French and Indian soldiers ambushed the Redcoats, fighting "Indian style" by shooting from behind bushes or trees. In Europe, men faced each other at predictable times in open fields, stood courageously when fired upon, and then returned fire and advanced. Braddock either could not or would not adapt. He insisted on playing by the rules (as he saw them) and commanded his men to "stand and fight." Braddock was mortally wounded and his men were routed. Washington was unhorsed twice during the battle, but lived to lead the survivors back to Philadelphia.

The French Advantage

Indian tribes were drawn into the war by both sides, but the French had an advantage in winning Indians to their side. As we learned last mini-unit, the French mostly set up trading outposts, not permanent French settlements.

Without settlements of their own, French trappers tended to mingle with the Indians and adapt to their way of life. The French learned enough of their languages to trade. French Jesuit missionaries were also fairly successful in bringing Indians into the Roman Catholic Church. Thus, France rarely disrupted or displaced the native people.

By contrast, English-speaking settlers came to settle down. They cleared lands, built farms, and fenced in fields. When the English moved in, the Indians moved out. Compared to the French, English colonists posed a much greater threat to the Indian way of life.

Treaty of Paris 1763

The French and Indian War and the Seven Years' War ended when Britain and France signed the Treaty of Paris in 1763. It changed little in Europe, but radically rearranged North America. France lost everything east of the Mississippi that it had claimed on the American mainland. Spain ceded Florida to Britain. The French settlers in Canada were allowed to follow their religion freely "as far as the laws of Great Britain permit." (This would not have been very freely!) That made a difference in the eventual religious make-up of America—Roman Catholics remained a minority because the people who crossed the Appalachian Mountains from the Eastern Seaboard to settle America's interior took a Protestant faith to the frontier.

Britain after the Seven Years' War

Britain had gained a new king named George III, who took the throne in 1760. His reign began and ended badly, since it was he who presided over the American Revolutionary War that lost him his American colonies. He spent the last ten years of his life in seclusion in Windsor Castle, hopelessly insane. In the years in between, George's reign was marked with troubles. Though capably served by William Pitt the Elder, one of England's most remarkable statesmen, George wanted peace at any price and made bad decisions in his attempts to get it.

Indian Troubles

After making peace with France, George tried to pacify the Indians. Pontiac, chief of the Ottawa tribe, launched a major uprising in 1763 to drive all soldiers and settlers out of the Great Lakes Region. Pontiac's warriors destroyed eight forts and killed or captured hundreds of colonists. The British Army responded with force, but also with diplomacy. King George issued the Royal Proclamation of 1763, which placed a boundary on the westward expansion of the American colonies. By keeping settlers east of the line (near the Atlantic Ocean), he hoped to avoid sending soldiers west.

Conclusion

The French and Indian War taught the colonists some lessons about the country from which they were soon to seek independence. Although British soldiers were feared in Europe, European warfare didn't work as well in America. Americans soon learned that England's army was not an invincible machine. It could be defeated in North America using new methods of warfare that were better-suited to colonial resources.

The Americans learned a lot about British military leadership, too. The British officers did not seek the advice of the colonists who knew the territory. They would not give them equal pay or rank with British soldiers. They failed to recognize the usefulness of Indian allies and the strength of Indian enemies. The colonists lost respect for these arrogant British generals. Colonial leaders counted on these traits when they came to fight British officers during the American Revolutionary War.

As colonial confidence in British military leadership dwindled, their confidence in themselves grew. Colonial soldiers like George Washington had gained valuable experience in both warfare and army management. Americans had learned that they could protect their homes and families as well as the British could—or better. Seeds were thus planted that would blossom as colonists sought to "institute new Government, laying its foundation on such principles and organizing its powers in such form, as to them shall seem most likely to effect their Safety and Happiness."[1]

---

[1] Declaration of Independence, by Thomas Jefferson.

Mini-Unit 8, Topic 2
Gathering Clouds

Introduction

This week, we are going to study a period of American history that we might call the "calm before the storm." Over the space of twelve years (1763 to 1775), about three million British subjects went from taking pride in being a part of the most powerful empire on earth to waging a war for independence from that empire. This week, we study the events and trends that led to their change of heart.

Great Britain had been fighting wars with European adversaries on and off for 75 years. After the decisive French and Indian War (and Seven Years' War) concluded in 1763, King George III and his British Parliament had peace in Europe *and* huge war debts to pay. They felt that their prosperous colonies had been well defended by British soldiers and money. They decided to govern these hard-won colonies much more strictly and extract more revenues from them in the future.

That made sense to the British—but the American colonists had their own perspective. For their part, the colonists had just finished fighting shoulder to shoulder with the British against the French and the Indians. They had seen first-hand the weaknesses of the Redcoats and endured their snubs. They had also experienced a heady feeling of success from the courage of their own troops. There was thus a growing feeling in the colonies that they didn't really need the help of their mother country anymore, and that they had actually been more effective than the English troops in protecting themselves.

Mounting Debts and Tensions

After George III issued the Royal Proclamation of 1763, which bounded westward expansion of the colonies, his advisers urged him to maintain a standing army of 10,000 troops in America to protect the colonies. Lord Grenville, the Secretary of the Treasury, estimated this would cost Britain 200,000 pounds (almost $60 million in current American dollars!). That was a problem—Britain's national debt had risen by one million percent over the last ten years: from 75,000 pounds before the Seven Years' War to 800 million pounds in 1764. It's easy to see why King George needed money for war debts, and also why an army in America was a major expense. King George grudgingly agreed to send English troops to America, but wanted the colonists to pay for it—or, at least, part of it.

Trade, Slaves, and Taxes

To that end, Britain began to enact a series of revenue-raising acts. The Sugar Act of 1764 put a three-penny tariff on every gallon of molasses brought to New England from a foreign port. Britain had islands in the Caribbean, like Jamaica, that produced molasses, but their prices were nowhere near as high as those of the French or Spanish territories. New England merchants were hit hard by this tax because they depended on cheap Caribbean molasses to make strong New England rum.

The ships carrying molasses and rum sailed two sides of a triangle that had its three corners in the Caribbean, New England, and Africa. The ships on the third leg of the triangle carried slaves. Molasses flowed from the Caribbean to New England, rum flowed from New England to Africa, and slaves kidnapped in Africa were shipped back to the Caribbean.

John Newton was an infamous slave trader who sailed this route. After his conversion to Christianity, he became a pastor and an advocate for abolition of the slave trade in England. He had a profound influence on William Wilberforce, who would ultimately triumph in abolishing the slave trade throughout the British Empire. John Newton wrote hymns, and his most famous one, "Amazing Grace," tells of the change that salvation by grace wrought in his life.

The Sugar Act hit American merchants hard. Britain cut the tariff from three pennies to one after a couple of years, but kept looking for other ways to raise revenues and cut expenses. In 1765, Parliament passed the Stamp Act and the Quartering Act. The Stamp Act required colonists to pay a tax on newspapers, playing cards, and legal documents. The Quartering Act forced them to provide British soldiers with living quarters, firewood, candles, and beer, and to house them in public buildings, inns, and even on private property.

American colonists were irritated by the Sugar Act—especially New Englanders, who used imported molasses to make rum. They dragged their feet in complying with the Quartering Act, giving British soldiers less than their due. But they were outraged by the Stamp Act, which seemed to violate a settled principle of British law—no taxation without representation.

Taxation without Representation

Most American know the phrase, "no taxation without representation," but not all know how well it expressed the traditional relationship between the English people and the crown. Under the unwritten British Constitution,[1] English kings had no right to impose taxes on the people. Taxes were supposed to be a gift from the people to their king, and could only be levied by the people's representatives in Parliament assembled.

That worked fine as long as everybody who got taxed had some kind of representative in Parliament, but the colonies didn't have such representatives. They considered themselves loyal subjects of King George III, but not of Parliament. The colonists had their own colonial legislatures. These could have lawfully imposed taxes on the colonies—if they had wanted to. The colonial legislatures might have voluntarily raised taxes if King George had asked them to—but he didn't. It was a matter of control, pure and simple. Neither King nor Parliament was willing to concede the point that the colonists insisted on: their right to representation.

The colonists refused to obey the Stamp Act. Britain tried to enforce it from an ocean away using tactics that violated even more fundamental principles of English liberty. Nine colonies sent delegates to a gathering in New York City in 1765 called the "Stamp Act Congress," which drew up a series of resolutions. The Congress spelled out American objections to the Stamp Act and the methods used to enforce it.

The Townshend Acts

These clumsy and controversial efforts to squeeze money out of American colonists outraged William Pitt, the architect of Britain's victories in the Seven Years' War. He was no longer part of George III's administration. In 1766, Pitt made an

---

[1] "Unwritten" only in the sense that there was no single document for it: the British Constitution was a set of functional principles and boundaries for government based on a long series of historical court decisions called "precedents."

impassioned speech against the Stamp Act on behalf of the colonists:

> Gentlemen, Sir, I have been charged with giving birth to sedition in America. They have spoken their sentiments with freedom against this unhappy act, and that freedom has become their crime. Sorry I am to hear the liberty of speech in this house, imputed as a crime.[1]

Pitt argued that the Stamp Act was both unconstitutional and impractical. Parliament repealed the unpopular Act a few months later, but replaced it immediately with a new act proposed by an English politician named Charles Townshend. The Townshend Act placed tariffs on items that had never been subject to taxes before—lead, paint, paper, china, and tea. Again, Americans saw it as an unconstitutional tax and responded with boycotts. British merchants were caught in the middle of this struggle between crown and colonies. They risked their capital to send valuable cargoes across the Atlantic, only to have them shipped back for lack of customers. The merchants complained to King and Parliament, and by 1770, most—but not all—of the Townshend Acts had been repealed.

The Tea Trick

Britain left one tariff in place—a tax on tea. Once again, Parliament insisted on this to prove that they had a right to tax the colonies without the colonists' consent. Tea was more popular in the colonies than in England. In one of history's little quirks, England preferred coffee at that time and America's English population preferred tea. British leaders kept the duty on tea but then lowered the price of tea itself. The East India Company cut prices so low they even undercut smuggled tea. They were willing to lose money to get the colonists to concede the constitutional point.

If the colonists paid the taxes on this tea, England would have won the essential argument. But the colonists saw through the tea trick. They remained firm, even though it meant spending more money or drinking coffee instead of tea. No major American port would allow the East India Company to unload or sell its tea.

Boston Massacre of 1770

Britain grew increasingly impatient with her increasingly contrary colonies. Boston was particularly stubborn. British soldiers fired on an unruly Boston mob in 1770, killing five citizens in what was called the Boston Massacre. The soldiers who fired the

---

1 "William Pitt's speech on the Stamp Act January 14 1776." Accessed 10 February 2014. Retrieved from <http://www.let.rug.nl/usa/documents/1751-1775/william-pitts-speech-on-the-stamp-act-january-14-1766.php>.

shots were put on trial, where Massachusetts attorney John Adams (a future American president) defended them. Adams was a leader of the Patriot cause, but he was also a firm believer in the rule of law and the right to a fair trial. With Adams' help, six of the soldiers were acquitted, and the rest got off with a manslaughter charge instead of being convicted of murder.

Boston Tea Party of 1773

Boston never really settled down after that. Things came to a head in December of 1773, when the British officials threatened to force port authorities to unload three ships' worth of tea. Massachusetts citizens petitioned the royal governor to intervene, but he went into hiding instead. So, the citizens took matters into their own hands. A group that called themselves the "Sons of Liberty" disguised themselves as Indians and snuck onto the ships. There they destroyed the entire shipment of tea, ripping open the chests and dumping them into the harbor. The event was named the "Boston Tea Party"!

Intolerable Acts of 1774

King George was furious when he heard about the Boston Tea Party and ordered Boston harbor closed until its residents paid for all the ruined tea. He ordered the immediate alteration of the government of Massachusetts and its courts. He sent four new regiments of soldiers to Massachusetts, commanding them to be quartered in colonists' homes. These punitive acts were intended to crush Boston's resistance and were collectively referred to as the Intolerable Acts of 1774. King George, quoting Julius Ceasar, said, "The die is now cast, the colonies must either submit or triumph." Bostonians faced a stark choice: financial ruin or capitulation to the King.

Conclusion

Last week, we saw that the colonies were divided and dependent. They had ignored Benjamin Franklin's Plan of Union that he offered back at the start of the French and Indian War at the Albany Congress. Colonial victories in that war and the oppressive British policies that followed it changed the equation. In just twelve years, new emotions and events were producing enough feelings of unity and strength of resolve to propel the colonies into the Revolutionary War.

Mini-Unit 8, Topic 3
Give Me Liberty!

Introduction

This topic starts off with a bang—the shot heard round the world. Our time frame is from April of 1775 to 1783, the years of the American Revolutionary War. The tensions that had been building for ten long years boiled over into armed confrontation. People on both sides of the conflict paid the ultimate price for what they believed.

From April 1775 until July 4, 1776, Britain focused on one trouble spot—Massachusetts. King George's ministers could hardly imagine that the other colonies would take Boston's side against the British Empire. Imagine their surprise when all thirteen colonies joined in a unanimous Declaration of Independence!

First Continental Congress in 1774

In our last topic, we learned about the Intolerable Acts, which Britain enacted to crush the resistance in Massachusetts. Massachusetts had no reason to hope the other colonies would come to her aid, but representatives of twelve of the colonies met in Philadelphia to give a surprisingly united response to the Intolerable Acts. Why were so many colonists so upset? They viewed themselves as British subjects, loyal to the crown, but not without their rights under the common law. Centuries of English precedents, they felt, had drawn lines that not even a king could cross.

King George III didn't see it that way. He saw the colonists as stingy, stubborn, and rebellious. Britain had huge debts to pay, but the colonists balked at the tiniest taxes. George underestimated how zealous and vigilant the colonists were for their liberties. In February of 1775, Parliament declared that Massachusetts was in open rebellion. This made it lawful for British troops to shoot troublemakers on sight. That sent shock waves through the rest of the colonies.

Give Me Liberty

In Virginia, on March 23, 1775, a young lawyer named Patrick Henry rose to address the House of Burgesses. He passionately urged Virginia to take up arms against the gathering British forces. We quote key passages from his famous speech here:

> This is no time for ceremony. The question before the House is one of awful moment to this country. For my own part, I consider it as nothing less than a question of freedom or slavery… Should I keep back my opinions at such a time, through fear of giving offense, I should consider myself as guilty of treason towards my country, and of an act of disloyalty toward the Majesty of Heaven, which I revere above all earthly kings.
>
> Sir, we have done everything that could be done to avert the storm which is now coming on. We have petitioned; we have remonstrated; we have supplicated; we have prostrated ourselves before the throne, and have implored its interposition to arrest the tyrannical hands of the ministry and Parliament. Our petitions have been slighted; our remonstrances have produced additional violence and insult; our supplications have been disregarded; and we have been spurned, with contempt, from the foot of the throne! In vain, after these things, may we indulge the fond hope of peace and reconciliation. …If we wish to be free—if we mean to preserve inviolate those inestimable privileges for which we have been so long contending… we must fight!
>
> Is life so dear, or peace so sweet, as to be purchased at the price of chains and slavery? Forbid it, Almighty God! I know not what course others may take; but as for me, give me liberty or give me death!

Paul Revere

The British government ordered General Gage to attack the Massachusetts militia and arrest colony leaders like Samuel Adams and John Hancock for treason, but these patriots got the orders before Gage did. Adams and Hancock fled the city.

Gage decided to go after the arms and ammunition that colonists had stored in the little town of Concord, northwest of Boston. Paul Revere was one of three men who rode through the night to warn town militias throughout the colony that the British were coming in arms. Henry Wadsworth Longfellow later wrote a famous poem that immortalized that ride:

> Listen my children and you shall hear
> Of the midnight ride of Paul Revere
> On the eighteenth of April, in Seventy-Five;
> Hardly a man is now alive
> Who remembers that famous day and year.

Lexington and Concord

About seventy Minutemen (colonists who were young, mobile, enthusiastic, well-trained, and thus able to show up for fighting "at a minute's notice") met the Redcoats on their way to Concord at the little town of Lexington. Eight Minutemen were killed and ten were wounded. Only one British soldier was hit. Nobody knows which side fired the first shot—but it has been called the "shot heard round the world." It marked the beginning of a new era in world history.

The British pressed on to Concord, where more Minutemen met them at North Bridge. Three Redcoats were killed there, as were two more Minutemen. The British turned back, heading for Boston. On the way back, the colonists shot at them "Indian style" from behind trees and stone fences. The Redcoats, in their tight-packed European formations, were easy targets. By the end of the day, 250 Redcoats were dead or wounded, compared to 90 colonial casualties.

Second Continental Congress

The Second Continental Congress came together in Philadelphia to debate how the colonies should respond to these hostilities from England. On July 6, 1775, they passed the Declaration of the Causes and Necessity of Taking Up Arms, which described their reasons for taking up arms to defend their liberties against the Intolerable Acts of Parliament. This declaration stopped short of declaring independence from British sovereignty. That would come later.

They also created the Continental Army (made up of colonial soldiers from the North American sub-continent)—but they needed someone to lead it. As we learned, George Washington had risen to the rank of colonel in the French and Indian War before Britain changed its policies to prohibit any colonist from rising above the rank of captain. Washington had angrily renounced his commission rather than be demoted, although he went on to serve as an unpaid volunteer. Now he was promoted to General of the Continental Army.

Although they believed it was necessary to take up arms, most colonists didn't want war. The Continental Congress sent one last petition to King George in July, 1775. In this "Olive Branch Petition," they declared their loyalty to the king and asked him to address their complaints.

Battle of Bunker Hill

Meanwhile, the British were busy. They wanted to put artillery around Boston, but the colonists had already started digging in at Breed's Hill, just north of the city. They originally planned to fortify Bunker Hill, but Breed's Hill was closer. On June 17, General Howe led British troops against their position there. The colonists had so little ammunition that their commander told them not to fire until the enemy was so close you could see the whites of their eyes. The patriots drove back one British charge, and then another—and then they ran out of ammunition. The next British wave crashed over Breed's Hill, and the Americans had to flee. The battle, usually known as the Battle of Bunker Hill, was the bloodiest single battle of the entire war.

When General Washington heard what a courageous stand the colonists had made, he said, "Then the liberties of our country are safe!" The British took Breed's Hill at the cost of 1,000 casualties, while only 400 Americans were killed or wounded. More colonists were coming to join the fight every day, while the rest of the British army was an ocean away.

Washington at Boston

On July 3, Washington rode to Boston to take command of the Continental forces. They needed it. The militia was poorly trained and completely undisciplined. They had few weapons and other supplies. Their camps were disorganized and filthy. Washington set to work. He issued a flood of orders and fired the officers who couldn't (or wouldn't) carry them out. Soldiers learned the meaning of discipline!

Washington knew he needed artillery to really take on the British forces. Fortunately, the colonists had some guns. Colonels Ethan Allen and Benedict Arnold led Vermont's "Green Mountain Boys" to take Fort Ticonderoga without a shot from a sleepy British garrison on Lake Champlain in upstate New York. The British soldiers didn't know the war had started.

There were cannons there, along with a huge stockpile of gunpowder. Washington's chief of artillery suggested they move the guns by sled across Vermont's snow-covered mountains. By late January, Washington had guns. By early March, those guns were mounted on Dorchester Heights, south of Boston.

The British were in trouble. General Howe knew his forces could not hold Boston against artillery. He decided to evacuate. On March 17, 1776, Howe's troops retreated to Canada.

Northern Campaign

The Continental Congress was afraid that British forces might attack the colonies from the north, so they ordered an invasion of Canada. Benedict Arnold led one force against Quebec, while Richard Montgomery successfully took Montreal, then moved on to help Arnold with Quebec. Their combined forces attacked the city during a blizzard on the last day of 1775. The attack failed: Montgomery was killed and Arnold wounded. The American survivors limped back to New York.

Southern Battles

New England wasn't the only place where there was fighting, however. To the south, American forces won several battles before the Declaration of Independence was signed.

In November, 1775, Virginia's royal governor, Lord Dunmore, offered to free any slaves who would fight for Britain. More than 1,000 rose to join him. The white colonists fought against this mixed force of black and British soldiers. They managed to drive Dunmore out of Virginia by December.

North Carolina's governor urged all the royalists in his colony to join him on the side of Britain. More than 1,500 colonists joined Governor Martin in a march to the coast to meet up with new British troops arriving by sea from Boston. They were met by American revolutionaries at Moore's Creek Bridge, near Wilmington, North Carolina. The royalists lost that battle on February 27, 1776.

British warships moved on to Charleston, South Carolina, where they opened fire on a fort outside the city. American forces returned fire, damaging the ships, which pulled back.

Declaration of Independence

With shots being fired from Quebec to Charleston, the last chance for peace with Britain had passed. On June 7, 1776, Richard Henry Lee of Virginia introduced a resolution to the Second Continental Congress. It stated that "these United Colonies are, and of right ought to be, free and independent States." After days of debate, Congress appointed a committee to come up with a declaration of independence. King George had violated a distinctly English agreement that had been a part of the British constitution since the Magna Charta. But one could hardly cite those precedents as reasons to break with England altogether.

A declaration of independence from Britain needed a whole different foundation. The committee put Thomas Jefferson in charge of drafting the Declaration. He turned to natural law to make the case for independence. He wrote:

> When in the course of human events it becomes necessary for one people to dissolve the political bands which have connected them with another and to assume among the powers of the earth, the separate and equal station to which the laws of Nature and of Nature's God entitle them, a decent respect to the opinions of mankind requires that they should declare the causes which impel them to the separation.

The Declaration was written less to England and more to the other European powers as an announcement and justification. The colonists hardly thought that England would change her course, but they might gain aid from England's rivals if their cause was just. The Declaration reflected the changing ideas of the times concerning where power came from. Rather than acknowledging "the Divine Right of Kings," as Louis XIV, James II, and other absolutist monarchs had done, the colonists appealed to the idea that all people are created equal by God and that the consent of the people under government was the foundation of its authority. By declaring this, they were declaring the beginning of a great experiment in self-government without a king.

On July 2, 1776, Congress adopted Lee's resolution, and then began to debate the Declaration. They made a number of changes to Jefferson's draft. On July 4, they voted to accept it. As president of the Congress, John Hancock signed his name to it there and then—in a hand large enough, he is reputed to have said, for the King of England to read it without his spectacles. Then he told Benjamin Franklin, "Now we must all hang together!" By this, he meant that now they would surely all be hanged for treason.

"Yes," replied Franklin, "We must all hang together or we shall most assuredly all hang separately." Franklin meant that, united, they had a stronger chance of surviving.

Battle of Long Island

The American colonies were committed now, but so was Britain. By July, 45,000 British soldiers landed on Long Island, where they faced 20,000 raw American recruits. On August 27, Redcoats crushed the Continental Army at Long Island, but General Howe was a slow mover, and Washington escaped with most of his men. General Howe took New York City in November.

Washington Crosses the Delaware

Things looked bad for Washington. His discouraged forces retreated to New Jersey, then fled before British forces to Pennsylvania. Less than 5,000 men were fit to fight, and two thirds of those were short-term recruits who would leave at the end of the year. Congress abandoned Philadelphia as the British advanced.

On December 25, however, Washington regrouped. In a surprise move, he led 2,400 men across the Delaware River in a fleet of small boats by night. The next morning, they struck the unprepared German mercenaries (men serving in the English army even though they were not English, for the sake of getting paid) at Trenton and took 900 prisoners. A week later, America won a major victory at Princeton, New Jersey. As winter set in, Washington moved his men to Morristown, New Jersey. The Continental Army had survived its first battles with Britain. Now they had to make it through the winter.

Weapons

"Continental Army" sounds impressive—but it was a small, ragtag force of volunteers. Soldiers usually provided their own weapons. Your child doesn't study this in detail, but you may want to discuss how weapons affected tactics in this war.

The flintlock musket was the main gun used by European armies at the time. It was very effective for large masses of soldiers in open fields, since it could be loaded relatively quickly (three rounds per minute) and fired a big lead ball. It wasn't very accurate, though. Troops had to advance very close to one another before their muskets were of much use. A typical musket was effective within 75-100 meters (about the length of a football field). Also, soldiers could usually only get a couple of rounds off before they closed ranks (came into contact with the enemy), when they switched to bayonets (short stabbing blades attached to the front of the gun) and fought hand-to-hand. Few American soldiers had bayonets at first, though, so the British were much better equipped for close combat. This was a huge advantage.

While the musket was a soldier's weapon, many of the frontiersmen were skilled hunters who depended upon their skill with their long rifles. The rifle might have seemed a strange weapon to commanders of the day. As we said, muskets allowed rate of fire of about three rounds per minute. Muzzle-loading rifles took roughly six times longer to load (about 1.5 minutes between shots). However, those muskets were only accurate up to 100 yards, at the most. Rifles were accurate at over twice the distance (200–500 yards). Grooves in the rifle's barrel caused their bullets to spiral through the air like a well-thrown football, resulting in greater accuracy. While the grooves made rifles harder to load and use effectively in battle for raw recruits, the speed and skill of frontiersman was a real plus, especially when they fought "Indian style" from behind trees or fences where they did not have to worry about a charging enemy.

The heavy weapons of the warfare in this era were cannons. They could be used at long range for bombardment or at close range against advancing troops. The British had the edge, here—they had far more cannons than the Continental Army.

Financing the War

The Articles of Confederation gave the Continental Congress no power to raise taxes, but they were allowed to print money. In 1775, they started printing paper currency called "Continental dollars." That seemed to work at first, but there was nothing to back it up. As they kept on printing, these "Continentals" became nearly worthless. For real money, America depended on countless loans from patriotic citizens who hoped the nation would somehow survive and pay them back.

Foreign Aid

The French had suffered a humiliating defeat in the Seven Years' War. They envied England's success but were not ready to risk her wrath—so they began to aid Americans in secret. From 1776 to 1778, France sent loans, gifts, and weapons. As Americans proved themselves in battle, France grew bolder. They signed a treaty of alliance in 1778 and began sending troops and ships. Britain's other European rivals also joined in support of the American revolutionaries: Spain joined the war in 1779, and the Netherlands in 1780.

France wanted to block England's control in the West Indies and India and weaken England's supremacy on the seas. King Louis XVI hoped that friendship with

Americans would profit his kingdom in the future. Some of his subjects had other reasons for supporting the revolution—they had their own hopes for liberty.

This foreign aid made victory possible for America, but it still didn't come easily. The men who fought were volunteers with little to no support from their own colonial governments. They were desperately short of food, clothing, and shelter. Soldiers alternately froze, baked, or went soaking wet for days on end. In the winter, they built their own unheated huts. Many walked barefoot through the winter. Rations were always short or non-existent. Disease and starvation killed many unsung American heroes of the Continental Army.

Major Campaigns

So how did these shivering, starving volunteers defeat the well-trained, well-supplied Redcoats and German mercenaries? The American officers started off with less training, but they learned from their mistakes, while many British officers lacked the daring to make full use of the advantages they had. Also, America lost its share of battles—and armies—but they didn't give up the fight. As foreign nations joined the fight, it was to be Britain who lost the will to win the war.

The Revolutionary War can be divided into two major theaters (north and south) and two minor ones (east at sea and west). Britain lost the battle for the north early on, but was more successful in the south. Americans did well in the west and better than expected on the sea. Let's pick up the thread of the war with the northern campaign.

The Fight for Philadelphia

In the north, as you may recall from where we left the story earlier, British forces had taken New York City and were threatening Philadelphia. Washington struck back at Trenton and Princeton, then camped out for the winter at Morristown, New Jersey.

Washington's overall strategy for the war was clever but cautious. He knew that his troops would not easily defeat Britain head-to-head, and he knew a big defeat would demoralize America and undermine any hope of foreign aid. His army therefore avoided large, pitched battles in open country. He would hold positions as long as it seemed expedient, but did not hesitate to run away so as to fight another day. He relied on a network of spies to figure out his enemy's positions and broadcasted "disinformation" to keep his opponents off guard. Washington mastered the art of spreading rumors, leaking fake battle plans, or issuing false memos to mislead the British.

In the spring of 1777, General Howe sailed his troops from New York City around into the Chesapeake Bay, advancing on Philadelphia from the south. Washington had received new weapons from France and stationed his revitalized Continental Army between Howe and Philadelphia, where the Continental Congress sat. The armies met on September 11, 1777, at Brandywine Creek. Howe encircled the American forces, who had to retreat. Howe took Philadelphia two weeks later. The Continental Congress fled to York, Pennsylvania, which briefly served as the capital of the United States.

Washington struck back in early October, but his battle plan was too complicated for his troops. Fog descended, and patriots began shooting each other. The Americans had to retreat a second time.

Victory at Saratoga

Things looked bleak in Pennsylvania, but Americans did better in upstate New York. The British hoped to divide the American colonies in half by gaining the Hudson River Valley. They already held New York City, at the mouth of the river. British Lieutenant General John Burgoyne moved an army south from Canada and took Fort Ticonderoga back from the Americans without a fight on July 6, 1777. However, Burgoyne found progress through the wilderness slow going. Patriots blew up bridges and cut down trees to block the roads. Snipers fired into the Redcoat ranks from the woods. Burgoyne's army crawled south while running short of food and supplies.

The Continental Congress appointed popular Major General Horatio Gates to command the northern forces while Washington was in Pennsylvania, and many New Englanders volunteered to join his army. Burgoyne's slow progress gave the Americans time to build fortifications in the wilderness north of Albany. On September 19, 1777, Burgoyne's men unsuccessfully attacked a fort in what is known as the First Battle of Freeman's Farm. Only nightfall and German mercenaries saved the British from destruction.

By this time, the American forces outnumbered the British, but Burgoyne refused to retreat. He attacked again on October 7. Against him, Benedict Arnold led the colonial troops to victory. Now Burgoyne decided to pull back, but it was too late. The Americans encircled him at Saratoga. On October 17, Burgoyne surrendered 6,000 men and their weapons. It was a turning point in the war, largely because it showed France that America was a bet worth taking.

Valley Forge

As winter set in again, Washington's army huddled together at Valley Forge, outside of Philadelphia. There were 10,000 men at the start of the winter, but a quarter of them died before spring. Diseases like smallpox and typhoid killed many, while cold and hunger ate into others. The army shrank even more as some soldiers deserted.

In February, a Prussian aristocrat arrived at Valley Forge. Baron Freidrich von Steuben offered to teach the American army how to fight European style. He showed the men how to march, charge, and use bayonets in close quarters. The Marquis de Lafayette arrived from France, full of enthusiasm for the revolution. Lafayette served Washington as a major general without pay.

Stalemate in the North (1778)

The new year brought new hope to the Continental Army. British General Clinton left Philadelphia in June, 1778, marching back towards New York City. Washington stalked him. On June 28, Washington attacked the British near Monmouth Court House in New Jersey. The British rallied, but this time the Americans didn't fall back. The battle ended in a draw—and it was the British who retreated this time. The Battle of Monmouth was the last major confrontation in the North.

Washington tried to combine his forces with French fleets to drive the British out of New York City, but he was disappointed. Meanwhile, Indians and royalists were causing problems on the frontier. Washington had to send some forces to deal with Iroquois uprisings in western Pennsylvania and upstate New York.

West and Sea

The United States did better than expected out west and at sea, as we mentioned before. British outposts on the western frontier fell to George Rogers Clark. At sea, Captain John Paul Jones raided the coast of England in 1778. The next year, Jones' ship was crippled by the British warship *Serapis* and eventually sank. The British demanded his surrender, but Jones famously replied, "I have not yet begun to fight!" He went on to capture the *Serapis* in that battle. These victories were bright spots in the face of grave American losses in the south.

Southern Strategy

Once France had formally joined the fight for America in February of 1778, Britain changed tactics. They stopped their drive in the North and began making their presence felt in the South, where they hoped for more support from colonists who had traditionally been royalists. They found less colonial help than they expected, but still won a series of battles. Britain took Savannah, Georgia in 1778. From there, the Recoats moved into South Carolina. Almost all of the American army in the South was forced to surrender when the British took Charleston in 1780.

Almost all—but not quite. Francis Marion and other patriots kept up a guerilla war. The "Swamp Fox," as Marion was known, kept the British off balance. With his small band of men and a swamp for his Sherwood Forest, he became America's version of Robin Hood.

Meanwhile, the Continental Congress attempted to raise a new southern army. American General Gates gathered militiamen near Camden, South Carolina, but an unexpected encounter with trained British troops caused them to panic, and Gates suffered heavy losses.

It was then, at America's lowest ebb, that Benedict Arnold changed sides. Arnold had been the hero of more than one American fight, but he had been passed over for promotion and he objected to joining forces with France. Rejected, he turned bitter. He made plans to hand the important fort at West Point over to the British, but the plot was discovered before he could carry them out. While he survived the war, his name has been a synonym for treason in America ever since.

Virginia

In October, 1780, Congress put a new general in charge of the southern army. General Gates had lost one too many battles. Nathanael Greene took charge. Greene used his troops far more effectively than Gates had. He split them up and moved them around, harassing the British forces. English General Cornwallis tried to trap them, but wound up trapped, himself, in the battle of the Cowpens in South Carolina. By 1781, the small rebel army was running circles around the larger but slower-moving British force.

Cornwallis moved the British army to Virginia—a sign of weakness, because it showed that in his view the Carolinas were far from secure. He took a defensive position near the coast at Yorktown. French and American forces pinned him down there. By September, 1781, Cornwallis knew he was trapped on the peninsula. He surrendered his army of more than 8,000 men on October 19, 1781, while his band played "The World Turned Upside Down."

Treaty of Paris 1783

The British started peace negotiations in Paris the next year. Benjamin Franklin, John Adams, and John Jay negotiated for the United States. Congress gave them clear instructions to consult with France before agreeing to anything, but these three went ahead and signed a preliminary treaty of peace with Britain on November 30, 1782. Congress decided to approve the treaty anyway. It was signed on September 3, 1783.

The treaty recognized the United States as a sovereign and independent nation and established its borders. Britain gave up all lands east of the Mississippi and south of Canada. Spain got Florida; the United States got the rest.

Conclusion

America was united in its opposition to Britain, as proved by the brutal war that tested that unity. The British expected they would easily and quickly crush these American upstarts. But, as pamphleteer Thomas Paine wrote, "These are the times that try men's souls," and through that trying, Americans proved their commitment to hang together.

At the beginning of the war, the world wondered how a band of ragtag colonists could ever hope to defeat the global empire of King George. By the end of the war, however, the tables had turned. How could Britain possibly prevail against a continent full of patriots backed up by the weapons and warriors of France, Spain, and the Netherlands?

Many factors contributed to America's victory. The skill, innovation, and courage of frontier riflemen contributed. The unpaid volunteers who marched barefoot through the snows of Valley Forge contributed. George Washington's character and courage contributed. Patriotic citizens who pledged their lives, their fortunes, and their sacred honor contributed to the victory. These heroes loved liberty more than life itself. Americans will always be in their debt.

Mini-Unit 9: Growing Pains

We will watch the young nation struggle to find a place in the world, grow westward, and begin to become industrialized. Note how our seven main "characters" fit in.

The Author	Having won independence, many Americans believed that God had given them the authority to pursue their "Manifest Destiny" to stretch from "sea to shining sea." Around the world, other nations began to develop their empires, spreading into and taking over lands that they discovered.
People	Thomas Jefferson bought the Louisiana Purchase from Napoleon, doubling the size of the United States. Lewis and Clark explored, looking for a passage to the West Coast and ultimately opening the Oregon Trail. Inventors developed machines that would revolutionize work and travel.
Good	When people thought about what was good, they valued growth and expansion. Independence and self-reliance were valued, especially as American pioneers ventured further and further westward. Inventors and scientists were held in great respect, and technological and scientific progress seemed nothing short of miraculous. Abolitionists sought to bring an end to slavery, and conditions in factories raised concerns.
Evil	Initially, the founders hoped that slavery would become economically infeasible. But, as industrialization demanded raw materials, forced slave and child labor increasingly supplied it. With expansion came the "resettlement" of Native Americans, often involuntarily. Progress provided an excuse for broken promises, oppression, and materialism.
The Word	There were those who read God's Word and saw slavery as an evil to be abolished. The Second Great Awakening led to the rise of Methodism in the United States and in England. Other sects formed as people sought to live according to God's Word as they understood it. Meanwhile, textual criticism was leading others to question the trustworthiness of the Bible.
God's Creation	As the West was settled, the United States began to adopt increasingly regional identities, with clear differences in the way of life in the West, North, and South. The geography, climate, and resources of each section of the country contributed to the rise of an attitude of Sectionalism.
Man's Creation	Harnessing steam and electricity, the inventors of this time ushered in the Industrial Revolution. Textiles and the ability to create inexpensive cloth was the first major application of the new technologies. Eli Whitney's cotton gin, Robert Fulton's steamships, Morse's electric telegraph, and others helped people to work, travel, and communicate faster.

Mini-Unit 9 Overview
Growing Pains

Introduction

These United States of America had won their war for independence, but the young colonies would have to grow, change, and struggle before they could win the lasting peace of unity. Even after the Revolutionary War, the colonies were not permanently unified. The Articles of Confederation that provided the initial frame of government were woefully inadequate to meet the needs of the growing nation. After a new Constitution was drafted, there was serious doubt as to whether it would be ratified by the states. No one knew whether this experimental government of the people, by the people, and for the people would actually work. In this mini-unit, we'll follow the story as the young nation grows westward and, ultimately, grows apart.

Jefferson and the Louisiana Purchase

In 1803, Thomas Jefferson bought the Louisiana Purchase from Napoleon in the greatest bargain of American land sale since the Dutch bought Manhattan for $24. Needing money to finance his expensive European wars, and not interested in the complexities of transatlantic empire building, Napoleon sold a vast territory to the new United States. The land that changed hands now makes up almost a third of the United States, including Nebraska, Kansas, South Dakota, Oklahoma, Iowa, Missouri, and Arkansas, as well as large parts of Colorado, Wyoming, Montana, North Dakota,

Louisiana, and Minnesota. It was a *big deal*!

We'll read about the early explorers Lewis and Clark as they surveyed the new national holdings. Finding ways to settle this territory would be a major goal of the United States throughout the 1800s. Eventually, "Manifest Destiny" became the name given to the developing belief that the United States was meant to stretch "from sea to shining sea." The trail that Lewis and Clark explored would be followed and improved by thousands of American pioneers who would travel the Oregon Trail as these United States expanded westward.

The Oregon Trail

A girl born in 1765 would have seen the size of her country double by the time she was 38, with the Louisiana Purchase. If she lived to be 80, she would see her country expand even further with the yielding of Florida by Spain in 1819 and the annexation of the Republic of Texas in 1845. If she lived ten more years, she would see the contiguous United States reach its current size with the acquisition of the Oregon Territory in 1846, the acquisition of California in 1848, and the purchase of New Mexico in 1853. That is a remarkable amount of change in one lifetime.

The settlers who moved into these new lands in the West were pioneers and immigrants, either from Europe or from the Eastern United States. They were not looking back. Travel was very difficult at this time, and most of them knew that their journey was a one-way trip. They made the difficult overland passage slowly across prairies, deserts, and mountains via the Oregon Trail. Such brave travelers were looking ahead to a new life that they would create when they arrived.

Industrial Revolution

We'll learn about the early years of the Industrial Revolution (from the 1780s to the 1820s) and meet some of the inventors who ignited it. This was a time of amazing technological change. For example, in the beginning of the 1800s, the only forms of transportation were by foot or animal on land, or by wind or oar power by water. On land, people traveled no faster than they had in Abraham's day. In 1804, it would take Meriwether Louis and William Clark a year and a half to lead their Corps of Discovery on a journey from St. Louis to the Pacific. Eventually, this time would be shortened to about six months for other pioneers traveling by similar means. By 1869, when the Transcontinental Railroad was completed, the trip to the Pacific would be cut down to only one week.

Travel wasn't the only change in this revolution, either. Textile manufacturing, communications, roads, waterways, and homes were all affected by the fast-paced development of new inventions and technologies in this century. Inventors didn't just change the way people traveled or worked. They changed the way they lived, played, and related to each other.

Historians call this sweeping transformation the Industrial Revolution because the most dramatic changes happened first in the realm of industry—that is, manufacturing. The changes were grand enough, certainly, to merit the title of "revolution," but we need to remember that the Industrial Revolution unfolded over many years and the changes may not have been as dramatic as the name suggests to those who experienced them. We've experienced some of this kind of revolution ourselves—our kids may not be able to remember a world without home videos, and they can barely imagine a life without cell phones or the Internet.

In America, industrialization took hold quickly, especially in the northern colonies. Steam engines (often powered by fast-moving streams) allowed colonists in this region to make better use of their abundant natural resources. Because of the relatively poor farming conditions, the North had always been more oriented towards manufacturing of various kinds. Thus, the innovations of the age were better suited to this region than to the agriculturally-oriented South.

Men like Benjamin Franklin were praised for their inventive genius as they designed better spectacles and stoves and experimented with electricity. Cities quickly sprang up around centers of industry, especially in the North. In the South, the mass production of the raw materials of the Industrial Revolution (such as cotton) brought prosperity to the plantation owners even as it tightened the chains of the slaves who were imported to work the fields.

With the changes came differences and growing tensions between the increasingly industrialized North and the more agricultural South. Eventually, these would have to be worked out on the battlefields of Antietam and Gettysburg, between the factory boys of the North and the farm boys of the South.

North, South, and West developed into three distinct regions in these United States. As they did so, citizens came to focus more on their differences than on their similarities. Sectionalism—being more interested in the needs and goals of your section of the country than in the United States as a whole—was one of the factors that eventually led to the outbreak of the Civil War as the South attempted to secede altogether from the Union.

Conclusion

As the nation grew, it grew apart. The colonies had unified against the tyranny of Great Britain and became the first states. Once the danger from Europe diminished, states sought to pursue their own regional interests. Many thought of the country as *these* United States (where the emphasis was on individual states who were linked by mutual goals, not on the unified whole). The conflict that we know as the Civil War would determine whether the name of the country would be *these* United States of America or *the United* States of America.

Mini-Unit 9, Topic 1
Jefferson and the Louisiana Purchase

Introduction

In the early years of the United States, the power of government was primarily in the hands of the state legislatures. Under the Articles of Confederation (which preceded the Constitution), the Federal (national) government had no power at all over individual citizens—only over state governments (if they chose to obey). The Constitution gave more power to the Federal government, but many still felt that these centralized powers should be few and limited.

This week, we'll study Thomas Jefferson again and look at events that occurred during his first term in office as the President of these United States. After two terms as our first President, George Washington announced that he would not seek re-election. Thomas Jefferson ran against John Adams and was elected President in 1800. He had a vision of a small federal government with limited powers and no standing army, but his actions while in office ended up expanding its powers.

The Louisiana Purchase

Jefferson did several important things during his first term as president. One was to purchase a huge amount of land called the Louisiana Territory from Napoleon in

France. At the time, Spain owned the Mississippi River, which formed the western boundary of the new American nation, but France was in position to take it over. Jefferson realized that America's ability to trade or even travel on the river could be impeded, so he sent ministers to France to negotiate with Napoleon for rights to travel on the river.

Napoleon had been obsessed with the idea of an American empire, but after suffering a devastating defeat in Haiti, he began to have second thoughts. Realizing that war with Britain would begin soon, Napoleon decided to cut his losses and offer the entire Louisiana Territory to America. They ended up selling it for about $15 million. Jefferson agreed to this, and borrowed enough money for the purchase, which doubled the size of what was then the United States.

The Lewis and Clark Expedition

Ever since he took office in 1801, Jefferson had been planning to sponsor an expedition to chart a route through the Louisiana Territory and the Oregon region. He wanted to find a water passage to the Pacific Ocean. With the purchase of the Louisiana Territory, the time had come. Jefferson sent two men named Meriwether Lewis and William Clark to explore the new territory. Under Jefferson's orders, Lewis and Clark gathered together fifty men into the Corps of Discovery for the expedition. These were mostly soldiers who were also skilled woodsmen and hunters. They were used to hard labor and tight discipline.

In May of 1804, the party set out from St. Louis. They paddled up the Missouri River to North Dakota, where they spent the first winter. They had several encounters with the Indians, but all were relatively peaceful. While they were camping, a French-Canadian trader named Charboneau and his wife, Sacagawea, joined them.

Sacagawea was a Shoshone Indian who became the expedition's primary interpreter. She had been captured as a child by another tribe, who sold her to Charboneau, who married her. She had just had a baby who also went with them on the expedition. Although it was odd to take a nursing mother on the expedition, it helped avoid trouble—the Indian tribes they met didn't think Lewis and Clark would bring a woman on a war party!

The group traveled all through 1804, always westward. In the spring of 1805, about thirty of the men (plus Charboneau, Sacagewea, and the baby) continued on. The rest went back to St. Louis with specimens and reports for Jefferson. Lewis and Clark continued to follow the shrinking Missouri river with difficulty, carrying their boats and supplies for miles around falls and rapids. They met a band of Shoshone

Indians whose chief was Sacagawea's brother. They were able to trade with him and obtained a guide through the Rocky Mountains.

Coming out of the Rocky Mountains, Lewis and Clark met the Nez-Pierce Indians and again got new supplies. They continued to follow rivers until they reached the Pacific Coast in December of 1805. There they built a fort where they could spend the winter before returning home. They made it back to St. Louis by September of 1806.

The expedition enabled the U.S. to lay claim to the Oregon region, which was not a part of the Louisiana Territory. Lewis and Clark never found a waterway to the Pacific, but they learned an enormous amount about the continent of North America and the wildlife and Indians who lived there. In 1846, when Britain finally gave up its claims to the Oregon territory, the United States would stretch from sea to shining sea.

This amazing project might not have happened without Thomas Jefferson, but then Jefferson was an amazing man. Besides serving as President, purchasing a huge amount of land for his country, and sending men to explore it, he was also a farmer, scientist, architect, and lawyer, and he spoke five languages, founded a college, drafted our Declaration of Independence, and helped to hammer out the American Constitution. Although we focus on the Lewis and Clark expedition with our students this week, it's important to realize that the energy and vision of Thomas Jefferson had a profound impact on our country. In later years, students will learn much more about this man.

Conclusion

We will end this section with a story that reveals how much Jefferson is still admired. One day in the 1960s, American President John F. Kennedy was welcoming a group of 49 Nobel Prize winners to the White House. During his speech, he declared to them that they composed "the most extraordinary collection of talent, of human knowledge, that has ever been gathered at the White House—with the possible exception of when Thomas Jefferson dined alone."

Mini-Unit 9, Topic 2
The Oregon Trail

Introduction

In the last topic, we learned about the Lewis and Clark expedition and read a little bit about how that trip gave Americans the ability to claim the Oregon Territory for themselves when England gave it up in 1846. This territory is in the upper left corner of the American map, and it is big! What was once labeled "Oregon Territory" now makes up the states of Washington, Oregon, and Idaho—not to mention parts of Wyoming and Montana! But of course, before it could be turned into states, the Oregon Territory needed to be settled by American citizens. That's where the Oregon Trail comes in. Its long, snaky route crossed most of a continent, and at its end, American pioneers expected to find a new Promised Land, or at least some really good farmland.

What was it like to be a pioneer on the Oregon Trail? How fast did people go? How far was it to the West, anyway? What kinds of things did they see as they traveled? Was it expensive to move west? What were the dangers and hardships of the trail? What did pioneers do for fun? These are the kinds of questions we are going to answer in this topic as we look at the everyday lives of the individuals who literally put feet to the doctrine of Manifest Destiny (the idea that it was clearly God's intention that Americans settle the North American lands between the Atlantic and Pacific Oceans) as they headed west.

Geography

The Oregon Trail started in Independence, Missouri, and ran as far as Oregon City, Oregon. The trail wound over 2,000 miles of prairies, deserts, and mountains. After crossing the vast grassland of the Great Plains, the pioneers had to climb the Rocky Mountains. Beyond the mountains was a stretch of near-desert called the Great Basin. Then, finally, Oregon! From the mid-1830s to the late 1860s, roughly 400,000 pioneers made the difficult journey west.

Settlers

Why did so many people head west? There were lots of reasons. Farm families back East were often large, with many children. As the population grew in the East, many felt inclined to move where there was more space, more land, and more opportunity. The potential of this new life seemed limitless.

For similar reasons, many of the foreign-born immigrants who arrived on the East Coast chose to settle in the West, also seeking a better life than they could easily find in the already-populated East. These included German-Russians, Scandinavians, Italians, Portuguese, and Irish people from Europe.

Others who moved to the West included the Native Americans, Mexican-Americans, and former African slaves. Altogether, non-white or foreign-born immigrants made up a third of all the settlers between 1846 and 1880.

The Journey

The pioneers generally set out from Independence (some after traveling a long way by boat to get *there*) with one wagon. Most family members walked. Mules, oxen, or horses usually pulled the wagon, and family members would take turns riding or driving these. A trip from Independence, Missouri to Oregon or California usually lasted four to six months. They would start in the spring and try to make it over the Rockies before snow blocked the passes.

Conestoga Wagons and Prairie Schooners

At first, the settlers used covered wagons to go west. The Conestoga was the most common—a wide, heavy wagon that could carry eight tons of goods. It was hauled by four or more mules or oxen. Unfortunately, the Conestoga wagons proved to be too heavy for the hard trail west—they had a bad habit of killing off the oxen that hauled them, leaving the pioneers stuck in the middle of nowhere.

Because of this problem, Americans invented a new kind of wagon called the Prairie Schooner. It was a tiny house on wheels, only half the size of the Conestoga. The wagon beds were nine or ten feet long and four feet wide. Most of them had a false floor 12 to 15 inches off the bottom so there was room for reserve supplies. That kept the floor free for little children, sick men, or pregnant women. These wagons were covered with canvas that had been waterproofed with paint or linseed oil, then stretched over five or six bows of bent hickory wood. A man could barely stand up straight in the middle of the average wagon.

A Day on the Trail

A typical day on the trail involved a 10- to 20-mile walk. The pioneer family got up before dawn, stopped for a rest near noon, and rounded up the wagons in a protective circle at night. A good day was an uneventful one, where there were no heights or rivers to cross. Long, flat stretches allowed the wagon train to go further in a day than did ones involving obstacles. Sometimes the men went hunting for game, or Indians approached the wagon train wanting to trade.

Collecting the dry dung of the wild buffalo that lived on the plains became a chore for most children on the trail. This burned well and was used in place of hard-to-find firewood on the treeless plains. Sometimes the children used the dung in their games, as well!

Evenings were probably the most entertaining and memorable time for pioneers. After a dinner of dry bread and bacon, or perhaps some fresh game from a recent hunt, the travelers often enjoyed the music of a fiddle or banjo, or perhaps a story told around the fire.

Challenges

Life was hard on the trail; many of the pioneers died before they reached their destination. Sicknesses like cholera, typhoid, and malaria were common and devastating causes of death. Accidental gunshots killed many people. Some died from falling under the wagon wheels or being trampled by oxen. Others were killed after being bitten by rattlesnakes. Sometimes people drowned when their wagon rolled off a ferry at a river crossing. Many pioneer women made the trip while pregnant, and some did not survive childbirth on the harsh trail. Let's learn a bit more about some of the types of people who made this difficult journey.

Travelers

Missionaries: Whitmans

A few of the folks who headed west did so for the noblest of reasons—they wanted to preach the gospel to those who had never heard it before. Marcus and Narcissa Whitman were two such Christians. They barely knew each other when they got married in upstate New York in 1836, but they shared a single vision—evangelization of the Indians in the Oregon Country.

Two months later, the Whitmans took the road westward with another young Presbyterian couple, Henry and Eliza Spaulding. The four set out to start a mission to the Indians near what is now Walla Walla, Washington. Narcissa and Eliza were two of the first white women ever to travel over the Rocky Mountains on their way to the Northwest!

In 1837, the two couples started building the Whitman Mission, which became a stopping point that ministered to thousands of travelers on their way along the Oregon Trail. Sadly, though the Whitmans went to the Oregon Country to evangelize the Indians who lived there, the Indians resented them and the steady arrival of white people on Indian lands.

In 1847, an epidemic of measles ravaged the mission, probably spread from those on the wagon trains. It was hard on the white settlers, but deadly for Indians who had never been exposed to the disease before. Although Dr. Whitman tried to help the tribe, the Indians could tell that many of them were dying from measles while most of the whites were not. Tensions mounted until the Indians attacked the mission. Marcus and Narcissa and twelve others were murdered during this sudden Indian raid.

Immigrants: Potato Famine

The Whitmans were old New England stock who moved west, but there were many newly arrived immigrants who took the places they left behind back East. Many of these newcomers to the east coast of America were Irish.

Ireland was part of Britain's United Kingdom, but was not happy about it. England had enacted laws that prohibited Roman Catholics from owning land in Ireland, and the majority of Irish were Catholic. As a result, most Irish farmers had to rent their land from Scottish or English landlords. The laws the lords made were hard on poor farmers, which meant that many Irishmen were on a one-way trip from poverty to desperation. The English said it was because the Irish were lazy and unruly. It was a classic case of blaming the victim. Most Englishmen simply despised the Irish.

Despite the hardship, the population of Ireland kept growing. As the amount of available land per person went down, the price of land went up. By the 1840s, most farmers had to sell any grain they produced to pay the rent. They used the rest of their land to grow potatoes because these were cheap and plentiful. In this era, it is estimated that one third of the Irish lived on nothing else. The problem with growing so much of any one crop, however, is that it raises the risk of plant diseases jumping from field to field. Starting in 1845, a series of potato blights—diseases of the plants themselves—destroyed potato crops. The bottom third of the Irish population began to starve. A million died, and millions more emigrated.

The trip to America was hard—starving peasants had no money for passage overseas. Some landlords paid to ship their tenants to America on what were known as "coffin ships." If the Irish survived the journey, they faced hostility and obvious discrimination as old prejudices awaiting them across the Atlantic. Many Americans advertising jobs added a line that said, "No Irish need apply."

Mormons

Other people, like the Mormons, headed west for religious reasons. They often experienced persecution in the east because of their unorthodox beliefs and practices.

The Church of Jesus Christ of Latter Day Saints was established in the state of New York in 1830. Joseph Smith and his followers moved first to Ohio and then to Missouri, but were driven out in 1838 after the Governor of Missouri signed an executive order calling for the extermination or expulsion of all Mormons. They moved across the border to Nauvoo, Illinois, where they built a city that grew bigger than Chicago was at that time (15,000 people).

In many Americans' minds, the Mormons had become a threat to both Christianity and the economy of the United States. They were forced out of several states before they moved west. In 1844, their leader, Joseph Smith, was murdered by an armed mob, and two years later, in 1846, Illinois ordered them out of the state. They headed west to Utah, eventually settling by the Great Salt Lake.

Things were hard in their first year in the Great Salt Valley. A plague of black crickets attacked the Mormons' crops, and there was nothing they could do to save their harvest. Then, one day, seagulls from the islands in the Great Salt Lake began to arrive. For days they flew in by the hundreds and gorged themselves on the crickets.

There was then enough of the harvest remaining to sustain the Mormons through the winter. To this day, the seagull is the state bird of Utah.

Despite adversity, the Mormons held on. Their persistence in the face of hardship enabled them to build a new community by the shores of the Great Salt Lake. In working to help other Mormon travelers to Utah, the Mormons greatly improved sections of the Oregon Trail, and thus made a great contribution to the expansion of America.

Conclusion

There were lots of different people on the westward trail who went for lots of different reasons. Wherever they started, the people who made it out to Oregon or California were changed forever by the experience—and so was the nation, as new settlements along the West Coast added a whole new aspect to America.

Mini-Unit 9, Topic 3
Early Industrial Revolution

Introduction

What do we mean by "Industrial Revolution"? Historians use the term to refer to a period of time that lasted from about the 1750s through the end of the 1800s, when there was a significant acceleration of developments and changes in technology, manufacturing, agriculture, communication, and transportation. Of course, technology did not stop developing in the year 1900; it has only continued to accelerate since then. However, the period of the Industrial Revolution was an era in which many of the major innovations in technology took place that were further developed and refined in the 1900s.

This revolution overlapped both the American Revolution and the Westward Expansion that we've been learning about. However, we study it on its own because the Industrial Revolution was a key force that displayed stark differences between the industrialized North and the cotton-producing, agrarian South. These differences went deep enough to bring the nation into a bloody Civil War, as we'll see in our next mini-unit.

The Industrial Revolution began in Great Britain in the 1750s and spread to the United States in the early 1800s. Let's follow the story from Britain to the United States. Throughout, notice how much geography and the availability of natural and human resources shaped the development the industrialized culture. Factories were built around available sources of power or raw materials. Cities grew up as laborers filled the factories. Factories and cities were built for maximum production, not primarily for safety (although standard precautions were put in place where they made sense). They could be difficult, dirty, and dangerous places to work.

You'll want to talk with your student about what it would have been like to live in a time of so much change, or possibly to work in a factory like the ones described.

The Industrial Revolution began with one important commodity—cloth. Spinning thread and weaving it into cloth on a loom takes a lot of time, which is why clothing has historically been such a major expense. Few modern children instinctively understand why Jesus asked, "Why do you worry about clothes?" in the Sermon on the Mount, but the children in His audience would have. Clothes cost a lot of money—so much that in ancient times we read that people have sued each other for their clothes, or used their cloak as collateral for a loan. They even gambled at the foot of Jesus' cross to see who would take His cloak!

The Industrial Revolution in Britain

Textiles

British inventors worked hard to solve this problem. As a result, the Industrial Revolution sped up the process of making cloth. Among the first inventions of this period were John Kay's "flying shuttle" in 1733 and James Hargreave's "spinning jenny" in 1770, both of which made the production of cotton cloth much quicker and easier, assuming you had a source of power to run them. These new technologies tapped into water power: engines were often powered by mill wheels, which needed lots of water (such as might be found in a river or a fast-flowing stream) to work. This led to the practice of locating factories near water supplies.

Steam Power

Then came the steam engine! Back in 1712, Thomas Newcomen had invented a primitive engine that could be powered by the force of steam pressure. In 1769, James Watt turned that engine into a workhorse that changed the world. Steam engines could power trains, textile looms, and all manner of machines. Also, steam-based factories needed water, but not flowing water. Thus, factories could be built anywhere, not just by rivers. Factory owners chose to build near existing cities, where the labor force lived.

Coal and Iron

In order to make and power new machines like steam engines (and, later, locomotives), coal and iron became increasingly necessary. One reason why Great Britain was the first nation to undergo an industrial revolution was that there were plenty of coal and iron in England.

Iron and coal are heavy. How do you get iron from one end of Britain, and coal from the other, to the factory in the middle where the people are? Improve methods of transportation! With the amount and pace of new goods being produced and traded, transportation also underwent great changes in Great Britain.

Transportation

James Watt's steam engine was first harnessed to an iron carriage on rails by Richard Trevithick in 1804. Soon, railroad tracks were being laid down all over England—then all over Europe. Steam-powered locomotives would transport raw materials, goods, and even people at increasingly high speeds, transforming not only industry but also social life, as people could now move more comfortably and quickly than ever before in human history!

The Industrial Revolution in America

During the early part of the Industrial Revolution, the American colonies depended upon European manufactured goods, providing raw materials in trade. After the American Revolution, Europeans were still willing to trade with the American colonies. But, as the French Revolution and the rise of Napoleon caused political tensions in Europe to worsen, naval blockades and embargoes going on among European powers during the Napoleonic Wars (late 1700s until about 1815) made it hard for manufactured goods to get to America from Europe. This pressure forced Americans to industrialize more quickly in order to make up for the lack of fine clocks, furniture, cloth, etc., that they had previously purchased from Europe. Let's look at how American industry developed.

Textiles

Britain had the means to manufacture cotton-based textiles quickly and cheaply and sell the finished goods to her global colonies at a price that was cheaper than what it would cost them to spin by hand, but much more than what it cost to manufacture them in Britain. Here was a great economic windfall! However, Britain did not have the raw material—cotton—to make the cloth. That had to be imported from her colonies, including the southern colonies in America, where it would be grown and harvested, often by slaves.

The British innovators knew that if the secret of the wonderful textile machines ever made it to the colonies, there would be no need for them to buy expensive British products. They could make them themselves. Therefore, laws were passed in Britain in 1774 forbidding textile workers to travel to America and prohibiting the transportation of textile machinery or manufacturing plans outside of the country.

America was quick to catch up with England in textile production, although someone cheated in order to make it happen. Even though Britain had made it illegal to export mill or manufacturing plans, Samuel Slater memorized the plans before he traveled from Great Britain to Rhode Island. There, he set up Slater Mill and started spinning thread.

Cotton

The mills made thread and fabric faster, but cotton production still took a lot of manual labor. Cotton pickers had to remove the seeds from the cotton by hand. They produced an average of only one pound per day. In 1793, Eli Whitney's cotton gin changed all that. A man using a cotton gin could produce fifty pounds of clean cotton in a day. The revolution was on, but at a cost! The capacity to grow and export cotton meant that plantation owners became recommitted to racial slavery in the South. Without the gin, slavery might have died out there of "natural causes." But, with the cotton gin, slave labor became essential to Southern profitability. We'll note this in even more detail further on.

Steamboat

As America industrialized and sought to move the raw materials needed to feed its growing industrial capacity, it faced its own challenges in transportation. The British locomotive (1769) was followed by Robert Fulton's American steamboat in 1807. Nations used these boats—which never needed to rely on the wind for power—to chug up rivers. They also dug new canals to connect bodies of water for greater ease of water transportation. They widened streams and constructed new lighthouses, roads, and bridges as well.

Telegraph

There are so many different inventions to learn about, but because of its sweeping impact and its ability to connect the widening nation, we suggest that you take note of Samuel Morse and his electric telegraph that ushered in a new era in 1837. With the telegraph, messages could be sent almost immediately across vast distances. News that would have taken days or weeks to make its way across the colonies could now be sent in across the country minutes or hours. Talk with your student about ways that this would make a big difference in people's everyday lives.

Human Impact

In fact, we need to talk about how all forms of rapid industrialization affected people. This is a theme throughout *Tapestry Primer*. For instance, we have already studied the effects of the printing press on human society.

New technologies tend to change lives in both good and bad ways. While industrialization led to great advances overall, it also led to serious suffering for societies whose way of life was changed by it. In a fallen world, even a step forward usually has its costs.

Slavery

Take technology's impact on slavery, for example. At the time of the Constitutional Convention, in 1787, many Americans hoped that slavery would slowly wither away in the United States. For most jobs, free laborers proved to be more efficient than slaves, and the number of slaves being imported into the South was dwindling in those days.

Unfortunately, picking cotton wasn't one of the jobs that favored free laborers. In addition, there was no industrial revolution in the cotton fields—cotton picking was hot, hard, manual labor, the same as it had always been. Because the cotton gin suddenly made cotton so much more profitable once it was picked, southerners bought up land and slaves and started clearing new plantations in the Deep South. Slavery entered a new and even harsher phase because of a deadly combination of industrialization and human greed.

Factories and Cities

Industrialization also affected entire cities. Before the Industrial Revolution, only ten percent of people in Europe lived in cities. As we learned when we studied the Reformation and explorers, European cities were mostly built around centers of trade, learning, or craftsmanship. In America, where cities were few and small, almost everyone lived in the country and farmed until this time. However, because of increasing populations and the rise of factories, cities began to boom.

Cities had to be built near sources of power or transportation. Often, their development was not planned around the people living in them. People crowded in. Entire families squeezed into one room; whole buildings had a single toilet, or a single water pump. The water was polluted and disease was common. Coal-fed steam power from nearby factories resulted in so much smoke and soot filling the air that the average city dweller experienced air pollution on a scale most twenty-first-century American children can't even imagine.

Child Labor

Because the jobs at factories required little skill, men, women, and children alike could do them. Factory owners gave their jobs to the cheapest laborers, no matter who they were. If a man wanted a job, he had to take the going rate, whether or not it would keep his family alive. So everybody in the family had to help earn enough to eat—which is why women and children started working in the mines and factories, too. Many factory and mill owners were quick to accept child workers because their fingers were nimble and they could handle machinery even better than adults.

Though children often worked 10- to 14-hour days in deplorable conditions in the mines, factories, and mills, and though they were made to exert the same strength as adults, they were paid far less than grownups. Many of these children were injured or killed at work, while the ones who survived grew up without an education or any special skills that would give them hope of a higher income in the future. Their growth was often stunted or their bodies permanently harmed by the harsh conditions. They were doomed to a lifetime of running someone else's machinery for the lowest possible wage.

The Middle Class

A new class of working poor was growing in the cities, but it wasn't the only social group that was changing. The middle class British economic theorists wanted to keep business free of government control. This sort of unregulated capitalism turned out to be a perfect fit for industrial development. Since neither the greed of the upper classes nor—sadly—concern for the working conditions of the poor was allowed to influence the laws affecting when, where, and how manufacturers operated their factories, they were able to do as they wished. And what they wished was to build larger and more profitable financial empires.

The laws of supply and demand were all it took to change the power structures of Great Britain. The old aristocracy, whose wealth was based on land rather than manufacture or trade, was largely left out of the transformations that were taking place in England. A new middle class of hard-working men whose wealth came from business and industrialization became more and more powerful in society and government. Many of them had risen from poverty and now owned factories, ran railroads and mines, and helped operate banks. They gradually gained enough influence to challenge the power of traditional upper-class aristocrats.

Materialism

All this new wealth and increased production created new opportunities for an old sin. Greed has been a human tendency from the beginning. However, the modern world has added a new dimension to man's relationship to things.

Historically, Europeans felt that a person's social and political status had more to do with the circumstances of birth than with individual talents or accomplishments. For centuries in Europe, people believed that since God places individuals in certain spheres of responsibility and influence through birth, it would be undesirable and even wrong of them to break into other spheres. Both high and low were agreed on this: a duchess was expected to be gracious, but if she tried to make best friends of the kitchen servants, she would only offend them. The servant saw a dignity in fulfilling her role and enjoying its unique privileges (privacy, for one), and would not thank the duchess for her intrusion into a sphere into which she had not been born.

So, a duke outranked an earl, no matter which one had more money, because a duke was born to higher privileges and greater responsibilities than an earl. Jewish bankers in the Middle Ages usually had more money than kings and noble lords, but even the poorest peasants often looked down on the richest Jews. That seems bizarre to the modern mind, but it is because we have changed the way we view people and possessions.

Of course, there had long been a middle class in England that straddled this line between aristocrats and peasants. Never before, however, had that class possessed as much money or power as the upper classes. Gradually, material wealth was becoming not only *a* factor but *the* factor in determining who mattered and who did not.

The Industrial Revolution gave rise to new ideas about what matters most. Some people began to believe that men could achieve peace on earth by redistributing material goods. "Materialism" is such a common term today that it is hard to know what it means. We'll see it often as we study the next two centuries, but here's a sneak peek: we might describe materialism as "salvation by stuff."

Conclusion

The Industrial Revolution changed Western civilization—for the better in some ways, and for the worse in others. Poor country folk in Britain left their huts in the fields for crowded apartments in filthy cities. Factory owners would eventually replace dukes and earls as the leading men in England. Machines transformed nations. But through it all, human hearts didn't change much. New challenges revealed existing weaknesses and strengths in new ways, but the need of fallen people for a Savior has never changed since Eve first ate the forbidden fruit!

MINI-UNIT 9: GROWING PAINS

Mini-Unit 10: A House Divided

We will see the country deal with internal division and fight the Civil War to determine the future of the United States of America. Note how our seven main "characters" fit in.

 The Author	With external enemies at bay and differences internally, states struggled with whether they had the authority to force other states to stay in the Union. In this conflict, both sides claimed that God was on their side and that they had the authority to act as they pleased.
 People	Abraham Lincoln is a central figure in our study, as we watch his rise to the Presidency and look at the choices he made while in office. We learn about brave men on both sides of the battlefield who fought for their cause, including Robert E. Lee, "Stonewall" Jackson, and Ulysses S. Grant.
 Good	Abolitionists ran the Underground Railroad to help escaping slaves reach freedom. Especially as the war went on, the question of the morality of slavery became increasingly central. President Lincoln eventually issued the Emancipation Proclamation, freeing the slaves of the seceded states. In the South, defended the morality of their cause for war.
 Evil	War is always terrible, but the Civil War pitted brother against brother in an especially terrible way. The use of "modern" weapons without the benefit of "modern" tactics resulted in devastating casualties. War was waged against civilians in an attempt to break the spirit of the South. After the war, "carpetbaggers" swept into the South, plundering the remains.
 The Word	God's Word is not as central in this mini-unit, with churches embracing both sides of the cause of war. While this was occurring, the seeds were being sown for the American Red Cross organization and the spread of world-wide missions, explored more fully in *Tapestry of Grace*.
 God's Creation	The Civil War saw the development of trench warfare and the strategic, tactical use of the battleground. Many famous battles featured key landmarks, such as Burnside's Bridge at Antietam, Little Round Top, or the Copse of Trees that was the aim of Pickett's Charge during the Battle of Gettysburg.
 Man's Creation	Industrialization and inventions were put to work in the war. Railroads carried troops quickly across the country. The telegraph enabled quick communications. Rifled muskets increased the accuracy and deadliness of bullets. Ironclads fought in the waters. Images of people and battles were captured in living detail as photography came into play.

Mini-Unit 10 Overview
A House Divided

Introduction

Our focus this mini-unit is the tragic story of the American Civil War, which raged across five Aprils, from 1861 to 1865. Our approach to the topics that cover the course of the Civil War is open-ended, because this is a topic that our many families will wish to approach differently.

Some families are already well acquainted with this fascinating era and will want to study the Civil War in detail. For other families, the topic may be relatively new and they will want to learn the overall story without diving into the details. Our study divides the war into three parts (the first 18 months in Topic 1, July of 1862 to July of 1863 in Topic 2, and the close of the war in Topic 3).

In the South, as the war unfolded, it turned into total war. Sherman fought to defeat the will of the South to fight. This resulted in hardship and loss for many families. The devastation is powerfully captured in the story of *Gone With The Wind*, by Margaret Mitchell. You may remember the classic movie based on this story. We do not assign this resource for reading or watching with small children.

Alternately, you could study the role of inventions and the development of military tactics during the Civil War. The Civil War is described as the first "modern" war. The development of accurate and inexpensive rifles, revolvers, early machine guns, hot air balloons for aerial reconnaissance, mortars and artillery, as well as the telegraph for communications, railroads for troop and supply movement, and even photography all changed the face of war. Sadly, military strategy did not keep pace, and the resulting cost in lives was appalling. Trench warfare was spontaneously invented as rifled muskets tripled the lethal range of the soldier's basic weapon.

Here's yet another approach: maybe you want to zoom in on a couple of key figures and study their legacies. President Abraham Lincoln, General Robert E. Lee, General Ulysses S. Grant, General "Stonewall" Jackson, Colonel Joshua Chamberlain, and other fascinating heroes loom large on the scene of history during this mini-unit. What lessons can we learn from their lives?

We know of one man in our family history who served as a spy during this war and had fascinating escapades. Does your family have a Civil War connection? Which side of the conflict would your ancestors have taken, most likely? Do you agree or disagree with their stance? If so, study their stories as well as those of more famous Civil War figures.

Even today, people adopt different views about the morality of the Civil War. Many will feel passionate about the cause that North or South pursued at the cost of blood and tears. One thing is clear: the Civil War dramatically shaped the direction in which the United States of America would develop.

Lincoln and the Start of the Civil War

In a time full of memorable men, Abraham Lincoln, the self-educated "rail splitter" from Illinois, has come to be one of the best known figures of the Civil War era. The war began as his election drove seven states to secession. Thinking that reconciliation of sectional disagreements (particularly over slavery) was impossible, key states in the south sought to leave the Union. In our first topic, we'll learn about the growing tensions between the different regions through the eyes of Honest Abe as he overcame hardship to win election to the presidency in 1860. A few short months after his inauguration in 1861, the first guns of the Civil War began to fire on Fort Sumter. This topic takes us through the end of the first year of the conflict.

Decisive Years of the Civil War

The story of the Civil War is punctuated with battles that have engraved the names of formerly sleepy little towns in the minds of students of American history. Bull Run, Antietam, Fredericksburg, Chancellorsville, Gettysburg, and Vicksburg marked the turning points of the war in the blood of thousands. The Confederacy, led by one of America's most outstanding generals, Robert E. Lee, fought to prove to potential allies that it could win. The Union, plagued with poor leadership, went through general after general trying to find a path to victory. During the decisive years of the Civil War, in 1862 and 1863, the Union would come to define its cause in order to answer the question of what it was fighting for, on behalf of both soldiers and citizens. The Emancipation Proclamation placed the issue of slavery near the heart of the conflict. For Lincoln, though, even more central was the preservation of the Union. In the Gettysburg Address, Lincoln defined the conflict as one that would ensure "that government of the people, by the people, for the people, shall not perish from the earth."

Closing Years of the Civil War

While the overall course of the war was largely decided by 1863, it would take several more long, bloody years to bring the conflict to a conclusion in 1865. As the war dragged on, the Union advantages of men, materials, and industrialization increasingly tilted the conflict in its favor, even as the Union forces coalesced under the capable, though unrelenting, command of General Ulysses S. Grant and incrementally won more and more victories. These allowed the Union Army to campaign deep in Southern territory, striking at the Confederacy's desire and ability to make war. General Sherman's march through Georgia helped end the open war, but sowed seeds that would grow deep roots of bitterness. After General Robert E. Lee was finally forced to surrender at Appomattox, there was hope that the nation could begin to heal. These hopes were dashed as an assassin's bullet took Lincoln's life, disrupting plans for reunification.

Conclusion

As we work our way through history, every unit brings us closer to our own era. The pace of life was getting faster as history unfolded. There was real technological progress in this era as human innovations become more and more advanced. But human beings themselves really haven't changed that much. The problems of good and evil remain, and there is only one real answer to that problem: our Savior. Without Him, people will continually find ways to define good and evil based on what they think is right rather than on God's definition. After the Civil War, slavery was illegal, but racism continued to oppress black people. As with the rest of history, new empires rose even as the old ones fell.

New technology made it possible for people to move and communicate faster—but these enabled them to kill people faster, too. As in every era of human history, we see both God's grace and man's sin at work. In this era, for instance, there was much common grace in the gift of raw materials and intelligence with which to make technological advances; conversely, there was sin in the uses men made of their intelligence to abuse other human beings.

Mini-Unit 10, Topic 1
The Civil War (Part 1): Lincoln and the Start of the Civil War

Introduction

In this topic, we begin our three-part study of the Civil War. This topic will cover the first battles of the war and the first part of Abraham Lincoln's presidency. Lincoln had been in office for a little over one month when the first shots of the war were fired, as the Confederates attacked Union forces at Fort Sumter on April 12, 1861. We'll begin by studying Lincoln's character as he led the Union forces with courage, humility, and patience in these opening days of the war.

Lincoln

Abraham Lincoln was born near in a log cabin in the slave state (where slavery was legal) of Kentucky. The Lincolns moved to the free state (where slavery was not legal) of Indiana a few years later—in part because his father, Thomas Lincoln, didn't believe in slavery. Life was hard there: they had to clear the land before they could plant anything. Hard work and poverty shaped Abe's character: he started swinging an axe by the age of eight, and later campaigned as the "Rail Splitter."

Lincoln's rise to the highest office in the land was anything but smooth. Here's an incomplete list that sums up his career path:

- ❏ Lost job, 1832
- ❏ Defeated for legislature, 1832
- ❏ Failed in business, 1833
- ❏ Elected to legislature, 1834
- ❏ Sweetheart (Ann Rutledge) died, 1835
- ❏ Had nervous breakdown, 1836
- ❏ Defeated for Speaker of the House in Illinois, 1838
- ❏ Defeated for nomination for Congress, 1843
- ❏ Elected to Congress, 1846
- ❏ Lost renomination, 1848
- ❏ Rejected for Land Officer, 1849
- ❏ Defeated for Senate, 1854
- ❏ Defeated for nomination for Vice-President, 1856
- ❏ Again defeated for Senate, 1858
- ❏ Elected President, 1860

All these setbacks taught Lincoln how to deal with disappointment and how to persevere in difficult circumstances—two traits that stood him in good stead during the first hard years of the Civil War. That well-known list that we've just named highlights Lincoln's perseverance, but understates his successes. He served four terms in the state legislature, where he rose to a position of leadership. His law practice prospered and he married a woman he loved, Mary Todd, though there was friction enough to make the marriage a challenge at times.

Long before he thought of running for president, Lincoln was a success by any reasonable standard. Although he lost his position as Congressman after one term, his political activity was not over. He campaigned for Zachary Taylor, who won the presidency. President Taylor offered Lincoln a post as governor of the Oregon Territory (first explored by the Lewis and Clark Expedition). Lincoln turned that down and settled down to practice law in what was now his hometown of Springfield, Illinois. He was one of the leading lawyers in Illinois in the 1850s.

Lincoln's Rise

It was Lincoln's character that propelled him into politics—in particular, his opposition to slavery. When Congress overturned the Missouri Compromise to let Kansas and Nebraska decide for themselves whether or not to permit slavery, Lincoln was not an abolitionist—he did not have a commitment to "an immediate end to slavery, gradually achieved." But he did think slavery was evil and that it should wither and die, in time. To him, the Kansas-Nebraska Act seemed to offer slavery a new lease on life.

So the next six years were filled with politics as Lincoln stood up against slavery at every opportunity. In 1854, he ran for Senate, but lost. In 1856, he joined the new Republican Party and campaigned for John C. Fremont. His slogan said it all: "Free Speech, Free Press, Free Soil, Free Men, Fremont, and Victory!" Fremont lost to James Buchanan, but Lincoln's efforts on Fremont's behalf got him noticed in the Republican Party.

In 1858, Lincoln was nominated to run for Senate. In his acceptance speech, he said these memorable words:

> A house divided against itself cannot stand. I believe this government cannot endure, permanently half slave and half free. I do not expect the Union to be dissolved—I do not expect the house to fall—but I do expect it will cease to be divided. It will become all one thing, or all the other. Either the opponents of slavery will arrest the further spread of it, and place it where the public mind shall rest in the belief that it is in the course of ultimate extinction; or its advocates will push it forward till it shall become alike lawful in all the States—old as well as new, North as well as South.

Lincoln's Senate campaign against Stephen A. Douglas featured debates across Illinois. Newspapers wrote down the arguments that the candidates made over whether or not slavery should be extended into free territory. Lincoln lost that Senate race but gained more national recognition.

In 1860, Lincoln went to the Republican nominating convention with a reputation as a moderate politician with little experience but no serious enemies. There were more prominent men in the running, but after three ballots, the delegates to the convention united around Lincoln. He ran against three other candidates in the general election—the Democrats had split into northern and southern parties by this time, and there was a candidate for the short-lived Constitutional Union Party, too. All the free states voted Republican, giving Lincoln a clear majority in the electoral college, even though he only got 40% of the popular vote.

Secession

When the votes were counted, people in the South knew that the writing was on the wall. Seven states declared their decision to leave the Union (secede) before Lincoln was even inaugurated. The Deep South went first: South Carolina, followed by Mississippi, Florida, Alabama, Georgia, Louisiana, and Texas.

War Begins at Fort Sumter

Soon after Lincoln was sworn in, war broke out in earnest, despite his attempts to avoid it. Lincoln took no direct steps against the seceding states, but he insisted that all federal property—especially forts and arsenals—must remain the property of the United States. Things came to a head at Fort Sumter, in the harbor at Charleston, South Carolina, where a small Union garrison had been holding out since December. Lincoln announced his intention to supply them with food, and South Carolina considered that an act of war.

On April 12, 1861, Southern General Pierre G. T. Beauregard launched a bombardment of Fort Sumter. The Union troops surrendered the next day. Lincoln ordered the Union Army to retake Fort Sumter. The entire United States army had consisted of 16,000 men before states began to secede, and many of them were from the South. Lincoln called for 75,000 men to volunteer for the army.

The Union At Risk

That call triggered another wave of secessions: Arkansas, Virginia, Tennessee, and North Carolina left the Union over the next two months. The slave-holding states of Missouri, Kentucky, Maryland, and Delaware might have seceded, too, if Lincoln had threatened to free the slaves. He did not—his stated goal was to preserve the Union, not to end slavery. The Constitution protected the right to slavery, and he thought he should do so, too.

That doesn't mean that Lincoln was a constitutional purist—he was anything but. No other American president has ever defied so many constitutional provisions so openly. Lincoln arrested Southern sympathizers and suspended their right to seek a court review of their imprisonment, even though the Constitution specifically prohibited that. He spent money Congress never authorized and expanded the army beyond the size that Congress set. But Lincoln did believe that he was acting according to the Constitution: he argued that his office as Commander in Chief gave him the constitutional authority to do whatever it took to save the Union in a time of war, regardless of anything else the Constitution might say.

War Begins

First Battle of Bull Run/Manassas

The war didn't start out well for the North. The first major battle after Fort Sumter was disastrous. The First Battle of Bull Run (which the South called the Battle of Manassas, because of the nearby town) occurred on July 21, 1861. Manassas was an easy carriage ride from Washington, DC, so Union spectators came out to watch what they thought would be their army crushing the rebel upstarts. Unfortunately for the Congressmen and wealthy Washingtonians who spread out their picnic blankets near the battlefield, the untested Union troops suffered a crushing and humiliating rout at the hands of equally green Southerners!

Generals

The South started off with some brilliant military leaders: Robert E. Lee and Stonewall Jackson were astounding warriors as well as men of remarkable personal integrity. Lincoln had to go through a number of generals before he got to basic competence. George McClellan was his first pick—a great organizer and trainer who lacked the courage and initiative to actually win battles.

Ironclads

The Union blockaded Southern ports and rivers. This type of warfare provided the perfect opportunity to develop a whole new style of ship. The South raised a sunken federal ship called the *Merrimack* and covered its wooden exterior with iron plates, using steam technology developed during the Industrial Revolution to power it. They named it the *Virginia*. On March 8, 1862, it attacked the Union ships that were blockading Hampton roads. This first ironclad attack sunk two ships and grounded three more. The *Virginia* came back the next day for more, but this time it found an armored opponent waiting—the Union's *Monitor*. This ship had been designed from the keel up for armored warfare on rivers or in protected harbors. Both ships survived that day's battle, but from now on, armored ships would dominate naval warfare.

Western Successes

As we said earlier, it was hard for Lincoln to find generals who would fight and could win battles. McClellan was good at raising an army, but disappointing at actually using one. The man who would eventually command the Union forces, Ulysses S. Grant, started way out in the western theater of the war early on.

On April 6, 1862, after nearly one full year of warfare, the Union commander Grant had his first major success. At the Battle of Shiloh (or Pittsburgh Landing), in southwestern Tennessee, Grant turned a surprise attack by Southern forces into a major Union victory. It was the bloodiest battle of the war so far, but it laid Mississippi bare before the federal troops.

That same month, Union Admiral David Farragut sailed a fleet of boats and rafts into the teeth of artillery fire at New Orleans. The Southern troops mutinied and forced a Confederate surrender, opening up the mouth of the Mississippi River to Union forces as well.

Conclusion

That just gets us up to the end of the first year of the actual fighting. The Civil War lasted four whole years, and we will spend two more topics on it. Next week we'll learn about the decisive battles that turned the tide of war to Union victory—but that was only the beginning of the end of this long, bloody, and bitter conflict.

Mini-Unit 10, Topic 2
The Civil War (Part 2): Decisive Years of the Civil War

Introduction

This topic covers twelve months—from July 1862 to July 4, 1863—and includes some of the bloodiest battles of the Civil War. Men of both the North and the South reached the point where they realized that there were only two options: victory or death. America entered a new level of warfare, one that began to affect civilians as well as soldiers. Emotionally, physically, and mentally, the war was draining all the people it touched. No one was bringing picnic blankets to watch battles any more.

Abraham Lincoln had a hard job! Though General Ulysses S. Grant made significant progress in the West, Lincoln tried four different men as commanders of his largest army—the Army of the Potomac—before he could get a significant victory in the East. Until then, this army suffered horrific losses in battle and terrible suffering during the winter, both of which ate away at their morale. Lincoln was always aware of critics in Congress, the press, and the people living in the North, who were all ready to blame him when things went badly—or, worse, give up the war effort altogether!

During this time, Jefferson Davis, the President of the Confederate States of

America (the government that seceding states had created for themselves), also faced massive disappointments. By July 4, 1863, he lost his hold on the Mississippi River Valley, which had been a means of vital supplies from Mexico. Southern ports remained effectively blockaded by Union navy ships, and no European country would send him badly needed aid. The European powers didn't want to back a loser, nor did their people support slavery. By the end of this one-year period, Davis knew that the South's only hope was to fight a defensive war on their home soil and prove to possible European allies that they were winning the war—or, failing that, pray that Northerners would lose their will to continue the fight.

What Are We Fighting For?

Abraham Lincoln had never wanted war, and at first he tried to keep the focus off of slavery to avoid alienating the remaining slave states that hadn't seceded. But his strategy had its downside—many northerners were passionate about abolishing slavery, so keeping slavery off the table didn't inspire them. Also, his strategy made Europeans cynical about the war. After all, if there was no great cause such as the ending of slavery in America, why should Europeans see the war as anything but an internal power struggle within a nation too weak to preserve a union they had won less than a century ago?

Then there was always the fear for Lincoln that Europeans would actually send help to the Confederacy. European citizens didn't like slavery, and European politicians didn't want to back a loser, but the Industrial Revolution in France and England meant that they depended on the South's cotton. Also, European powers didn't much care to have a Great Power in the form of a united America on the other side of the Atlantic. If the Confederacy had a strong chance of winning, Europeans had reasons to support it—so Lincoln needed to make sure they weren't winning!

By the middle of 1862, the war in Virginia was going so badly that the Union cause seemed to be unraveling. Lincoln knew that more slaveholding states (like Delaware and Kentucky) might leave the Union. If slaveholding Maryland seceded, the federal capital of Washington, D.C. would be surrounded by Confederate territory: Maryland to the north and Virginia to the south.

Lincoln came up with a way to rally northern support without losing the border states. He decided to free the slaves—but not all of them. He only freed the slaves in the states that were in active rebellion, while leaving things unchanged in the border states. He knew such a proclamation would be controversial—so he decided to wait for a significant Union victory before he issued it.

Major Battles

Second Battle of Bull Run

Lincoln had to wait a while for that victory, at least in the East. We covered the First Battle of Bull Run, which the North lost, in the last topic. The Second Battle of Bull Run, on August 29, 1862, was just as bad: Southern troops under Robert E. Lee, Stonewall Jackson, and General James Longstreet attacked Union troops stationed at Manassas. Their bold attack succeeded—General McClellan's Army of the Potomac had to retreat to Washington.

Antietam

Lee's army marched onto Union soil a few days later. He sent Stonewall Jackson off with soldiers to capture the federal arsenal at Harpers Ferry while he took the rest of the army to the little town of Sharpsburg, on Antietam Creek in the border state of Maryland.

Lee had issued secret orders to his army, but a Union scout found them wrapped around three cigars at a Confederate campsite. The Union general, McClellan, couldn't believe Lee would be so stupid as to split up his army—he thought it must be a trick, and held his 90,000 men back. That delay was costly—it gave Jackson's men time to join up with Lee. The two armies clashed at Antietam in the bloodiest single day of the Civil War—2,000 Union troops were killed and 2,700 Confederates. Nearly 20,000 men were wounded, of whom another 3,000 eventually died.

It was a costly battle with no decisive winner, but it was a strategic victory for the North since Lee had to retreat back into Virginia. But General McClellan let him go without pursuit! This was too much for Lincoln—he fired McClellan and replaced him with General Ambrose E. Burnside.

Emancipation

Lee's retreat from Maryland gave Lincoln the opportunity he had been waiting for to issue the Emancipation Proclamation. He declared that all slaves in states that had seceded from the Union were forever free, and ordered Union troops and other federal agents to treat them as free men.

Lincoln's proclamation seemed odd—it freed all the slaves in the states he didn't control, and none of the slaves in the states he did. There was a reason for this oddity, however, and it wasn't just that he wanted to win over the abolitionists, who wanted to destroy or "abolish" the practice of slavery without losing the border states. Lincoln was relying solely on the President's war powers as he maneuvered. He believed the Constitution gave the Union whatever powers it needed to preserve itself. As Commander in Chief in a time of war, he believed he had the authority to exercise whatever powers he had. He thought emancipating the slaves in rebel territory was one more weapon in the Commander-in-Chief's arsenal.

Fredericksburg

Lincoln's new general, Burnside, marched down to Fredericksburg, Virginia, to take on Lee. McClellan had been too cautious to win; Burnside proved to be too bold. He tried to storm 73,000 Confederates who had dug into the hills overlooking Fredericksburg, and it cost him 13,000 casualties. Burnside asked Lincoln to relieve him of command—and Lincoln did.

Chancellorsville

Lincoln appointed Joseph Hooker in Burnside's place. By now, the Union Army was much larger than the Confederate Army. On April 27, 1863, it looked like Hooker was poised to outflank Lee—but Hooker hesitated. That gave Stonewall Jackson the opportunity to just about cut the Northern army in two. The battle has been called "Lee's perfect battle" because he defeated a force twice his size—but it cost him dearly. Jackson was accidentally wounded there by his own men. His arm was amputated, and he died two weeks later. Lee said, "Jackson has lost his left arm, but I have lost my right arm."

Battle of Gettysburg

Jackson was sorely missed at the next major engagement—the central battle of the war, fought in the Keystone State of Pennsylvania. This was the South's boldest advance yet. If they could take the war into Union territory—and not just a slave state like Maryland, but the Quaker State of Pennsylvania—they might be able to kill the North's will to fight.

Lee marched across Maryland and pushed seven miles north of the Mason-Dixon Line into Pennsylvania. On July 1, 1863, 75,000 Confederates reached Gettysburg. Lincoln had replaced his top general again—now it was General George Meade whose 90,000 Union troops encountered Lee's forces. The South pushed the Union back on the first day, but Lee no longer had a general with Stonewall Jackson's drive. Lee ordered General Richard Ewell to take Cemetery Hill, an important piece of high ground on the north side of Gettysburg, "if practicable." Ewell let him down—and it cost Lee dearly.

On the second day of the battle, Lee sent his troops down to the south side of town, where Little Round Top was the last outcropping of high ground on which Union troops had placed artillery. Lee was determined to take Little Round Top and then work his way north along the ridge. But 385 soldiers from Maine held that hill against an assault by the Alabama Brigade (composed of several thousand men). Colonel Joshua Chamberlain's Maine men were outnumbered, out of ammunition, and about to be overrun when he ordered a bayonet charge down the hill. It worked—the Alabama troops fell back, and the Union held its ground.

That was the beginning of the end for Lee. His effort to take the ridge from the north end fell short the first day, and his assault on the south end failed the second day. So on the third day, against his better judgment, he ordered a full frontal attack on the Union lines. Major General George Pickett led the charge.

Pickett's charge might have worked twenty years earlier, when armies mostly used inaccurate muskets, but rifled barrels had changed the face of war. Pickett's men marched across an open field that laid them bare to such murderous Union fire that their advance was doomed from the outset. His men were slaughtered, ending Lee's chance of victory at Gettysburg—which in turn ended the South's best shot at winning the war.

Gettysburg Address

Gettysburg is probably the most famous battle of the Civil War. It was certainly the bloodiest. More than 25,000 Confederates were killed or wounded, and there were 23,000 Union casualties. Four months later, President Lincoln traveled to Gettysburg to dedicate a cemetery for the 3,000 who died there.[1]

> Four score and seven years ago our fathers brought forth on this continent, a new nation, conceived in Liberty, and dedicated to the proposition that all men are created equal.

Ironically, Lincoln thought that "The world will little note nor long remember what we say here." He didn't know that the Gettysburg Address would be one of the best-remembered speeches in American history. Lincoln's brief speech focused on

---

1 NOTE: "Casualties" include both injured and wounded. There were 48,000 casualties, and of those, 3,000 were killed in action.

whether or not America's experiment in self-government would succeed. Speaking of the dead, he said:

> It is for us the living rather to be dedicated here to the unfinished work which they who fought here have thus far so nobly advanced. It is rather for us to be here dedicated to the great task remaining before us--that from these honored dead we take increased devotion to that cause for which they gave the last full measure of devotion--that we here highly resolve that these dead shall not have died in vain, that this nation under God shall have a new birth of freedom, and that government of the people, by the people, for the people shall not perish from the earth.[1]

Vicksburg

The day after Lee lost Gettysburg, Ulysses S. Grant won a major victory on the Mississippi. Vicksburg, Mississippi was a Confederate strong point on the river that kept Union shipping from moving north. After months of trying to operate in the muddy marshland, Grant decided to march troops down the other side of the river and ferry them across to the Vicksburg side. He tried to sneak a fleet past Vicksburg's artillery one moonless night. The Confederates spotted the boats and shot at them, but the boats survived the attack and transported Grant's troops across the river. In a series of brilliant strokes, Grant cut Vicksburg off from the rest of Mississippi. He couldn't take the city by direct assault, but a two-month siege ended in the surrender of Vicksburg. Within days, another Union general took the remaining Confederate stronghold on the river, and the Union controlled the Mississippi. The Confederacy was now vertically split in two.

Conclusion

The battles at Gettysburg and Vicksburg turned the tide of the war. Up until July of 1863, it was anyone's war—the North had more men and resources, but had trouble maintaining the will to fight. The South lacked factories, but Britain and France might have been convinced to send all the equipment the South needed—as long as it looked like the South might win. After these two decisive battles, however, the North got its second wind and Europe got cold feet. From here on out, Union victory was well-nigh certain. But the South was not about to abandon its cause just because it was lost—there was still another year and a half of terrible suffering ahead for both sides!

---

1 "The Gettysburg Address." Accessed 10 February 2014. Retrieved from <http://www.abrahamlincolnonline.org/lincoln/speeches/gettysburg.htm>.

Mini-Unit 10, Topic 3
The Civil War (Part 3): Closing Years of the Civil War

Introduction

This is the final topic in our study of the Civil War. We'll look at battles from July of 1863 to April of 1865. Generally speaking, things were worse in the South than in the North during these years. Southerners saw their fields and cities become battlegrounds, whereas Northerners did not. Lincoln urged his generals to use every means at their disposal to force the South to give in. Equally determined, Jefferson Davis vowed never to give in and to fight with every possible resource left to the South. The results were misery and death for soldiers in both armies—as well as for civilians in the South.

Major Battles

Battle of Chickamauga

On September 19, 1863, Union General Rosecrans lost a major battle in southeast Tennessee at Chickamauga. Chattanooga was a prime military target because it was a railway hub on a navigable river, and was thus known as the Gateway to the South. It was also surrounded by mountains that made it easy to defend—and hard to take. The

South held this position, and the Union launched a campaign to seize it. The armies fighting to seize or defend Chattanooga would meet at Chickamauga (loosely translated, "The River of Death").

The armies were well matched—about 60,000 men on each side. A few days before, the Southern troops evacuated Chattanooga for better positions. The Union troops moved into the city, but still had to deal with the Southern army. They met at Chickamauga Creek and fought for two days. It was a Union loss that would have been a disaster but for General George Thomas, whose heroic stand during the battle and orderly retreat earned him the nickname "Rock of Chickamauga" that day. The defeated federal troops retreated into Chattanooga, where they were bombarded by Confederate artillery from the heights around the city. A humiliated Rosecrans relinquished his army.

Battle of Chattanooga

In the aftermath of the Battle of Chickamauga, the besieged Union troops engaged in the Battle of Chattanooga. Three days after Rosecrans relinquished his army, Ulysses S. Grant, the new commander of all Union troops in the west, led the breakout from Chattanooga. Grant ordered William T. Sherman and Joseph Hooker to attack the left and right flanks of the rebel army. Hooker's men fought on the top of Lookout Mountain in what has been called the "Battle Above the Clouds."

Sherman's men made no progress on the right flank, so Grant ordered a dangerous attack at the Confederate center. His men were hungry for revenge for Chickamauga—they drove the Confederates from their fortifications. The Gateway to the South was truly taken.

After receiving the news of victory, President Lincoln declared the first national day of thanksgiving. People in the North began to hope the war might soon be over.

Overland Campaign

In March, 1864, Lincoln called Grant to Washington and made him commander of all the Union armies. Lincoln said, "Grant is my man and I am his the rest of the War." It was an effective choice—with a price. Grant intended to end the war quickly; his goal was to save the Union, no matter what the cost. He was prepared to sacrifice his own men in staggering numbers if that's what it took, and to treat enemy civilians like military targets. Grant was called a butcher, and his subordinate, William T. Sherman, earned the hatred of the whole South.

Grant attacked Robert E. Lee's Army of Virginia, which was still a force to be reckoned with. Neither side could manage a decisive victory in Virginia. The Battle of the Wilderness in May of 1864 was a bloody, three-day draw. The Battle of Spotsylvania lasted almost two weeks without a clear victor. The Battle of Cold Harbor in June saw thousands of Union troops slaughtered in a hopeless attack on Lee's fortified troops, but it served Grant's greater purpose. Lee pulled back to Petersburg, Virginia, a suburb of Richmond, where Grant's army settled in for a ten-month siege.

War Weary

The siege was effective, but not very inspiring for a nation grown weary of war. Journalists told the story of the war to the folks back home. Soldiers' lives were hard—disease, malnutrition, and exposure killed many who were never even wounded. Also, this was a modern war: technology was making armies deadlier. Railroads, telegraphs, and rifled bullets expanded the range of war faster than the generals could adapt. As a result, thousands of men died quickly—shockingly so—in Civil War battles.

Down South, in the summer and fall of 1864, William T. Sherman was slowly advancing on the city of Atlanta in Georgia, driving his adversary, General Joseph Johnston, from one fortified position to the next.

As the war dragged on, President Lincoln faced challenges to his leadership and even his continued role as President. Both he and Confederate President Jefferson Davis had instituted a draft by this time. Lincoln allowed wealthy men to pay poorer men to go and fight in their stead. The United States had never had a draft before, and it was very unpopular.

In the North, violent riots broke out in New York, especially among Irishmen. Sadly, many Northerners also felt that they were being forced to fight for the freedom of blacks, a cause in which many did not believe and for which they were not prepared to die. Tragically, outraged Northern whites lynched innocent blacks.

Reelection Campaign

This unrest on the home front and the losses of men on the battlefield gave hope to the Democrats who thought they might be able to defeat Lincoln in the 1864 election. Over the last two weeks you've learned about General George McClellan, whom Lincoln fired because he was too cautious to win. The Democrats nominated him for President in 1864.

McClellan tried to win votes by steering a middle course on the war. He drafted an open letter inviting peace negotiations and signaled that the abolition of slavery would not be a deal breaker. Lincoln, by contrast, insisted on both union and abolition. From his perspective, there would be no true peace without freedom.

Fall of Atlanta

Things looked bad for Lincoln by late summer, when he had no reason to expect to be reelected. But things can change quickly in politics—and in war. From Chattanooga, General George Sherman marched his troops towards Atlanta, Georgia, the Confederates' second largest city.

As Sherman marched, his men fought several battles against Confederate General Joseph Johnston, all while pushing south. Even after Johnston was replaced by General Hood, the Union army got closer and closer to Atlanta. Sherman originally planned to besiege Atlanta, but decided to cut Hood's supply line first. Hood was forced to evacuate the city, and Sherman's men marched into Atlanta the very next day, September 2, 1864. From that point on, Lincoln's reelection seemed sure.

Total War

During the period that we study this week, the Civil War fighters turned to a "total war" effort, which blurred the lines between civilians and combatants. In total war, every citizen was viewed as part of the conflict. This was very different from how wars had always been fought. Most commanders sought to treat civilians well during war in order to win the peace. Sherman's "scorched earth" approach was the opposite. "Scorched earth" meant he didn't just defeat enemy soldiers who stood in his way—his men took all property they could carry and burned what they couldn't, right down to the crops in the fields. He destroyed railroads and agricultural infrastructure and destroyed private property in order to disrupt the Southern economy. Sherman's men caused an estimated $100 million in property damage on their way to Savannah. Soldiers were no longer the only ones under attack. This effectively destroyed resources that the South could have used to support their fight, but it was also terribly hard on the civilians who lost their homes, furnishings, animals, and crops. Sherman adopted these tactics under the direction of his commanding officer, General Ulysses S. Grant. Indeed, General Grant's commitment to crush the enemy's will to fight earned him the nickname "Unconditional Surrender Grant."

Second Inaugural Address

Lincoln took the oath of office on March 4, 1865. By then, the North's victory was certain—just a matter of time. Lincoln therefore set the stage for the peace with his Second Inaugural Address. He considered the condition of the North and South from God's perspective, saying:

> Both read the same Bible and pray to the same God, and each invokes His aid against the other. It may seem strange that any men should dare to ask a just God's assistance in wringing their bread from the sweat of other men's faces, but let us judge not, that we be not judged. The prayers of both could not be answered. That of neither has been answered fully. The Almighty has His own purposes. 'Woe unto the world because of offenses; for it must needs be that offenses come, but woe to that man by whom the offense cometh.' If we shall suppose that American slavery is one of those offenses which, in the providence of God, must needs come, but which, having continued through His appointed time, He now wills to remove, and that He gives to both North and South this terrible war as the woe due to those by whom the offense came, shall we discern therein any departure from those divine attributes which the believers in a living God always ascribe to Him? Fondly do we hope, fervently do we pray, that this mighty scourge of war may speedily pass away. Yet, if God wills that it continue until all the wealth piled by the bondsman's two hundred and fifty years of unrequited toil shall be sunk, and until every drop of blood drawn with the lash shall be paid by another drawn with the sword, as was said three thousand years ago, so still it must be said 'the judgments of the Lord are true and righteous altogether.'
>
> With malice toward none, with charity for all, with firmness in the right as God gives us to see the right, let us strive on to finish the work we are in, to bind up the nation's wounds, to care for him who shall have borne the battle and for his widow and his orphan, to do all which may achieve and cherish a just and lasting peace among ourselves and with all nations.[1]

Appomattox

As Lincoln spoke these words, Grant was still besieging Lee's starving troops in Virginia. Lee decided to attempt an evacuation of Petersburg and Richmond, but by now his men were so hungry and weak that the Union army was able to block them

---

[1] "Second Inaugural Address of Abraham Lincoln." Accessed 10 February 2014. Retrieved from <http://avalon.law.yale.edu/19th_century/lincoln2.asp>.

at every direction. After many casualties and at the point of sheer exhaustion, Lee was forced to surrender.

On April 9, 1865, at Appomattox Court House in Virginia, Robert E. Lee handed Ulysses S. Grant his sword. Lincoln had insisted his general be relentless in fighting the war, but was equally insistent that they be gracious in winning it. Grant allowed no cheering among the Union troops when Lee surrendered. He fed the starving Confederate troops, let them keep their own horses to ride home on, and allowed Confederate officers to keep their side-arms.

Assassination

Now was the time when Lincoln's call for charity toward all and malice towards none really mattered. Lincoln's grim resolve had crushed the Confederacy—could his mercy rebuild the Union? We will never know.

Five days after Lee surrendered, John Wilkes Booth shot the President in the head while Lincoln attended a play at Ford's Theatre in Washington. Booth shouted "*Sic semper tyrannis!*" (a famous Latin phrase meaning "thus may it ever be to tyrants") which is the motto on Virginia's flag. Lincoln died the next morning—and with him died the Union's best chance of winning the peace.

Conclusion

In a sense, the Civil War was the next act of a drama that began with the Declaration of Independence, when the Founders declared the self-evident truth that "all men are created equal." It took 620,000 American lives to bring about liberty for *all* Americans, black as well as white—more than every other American war combined, from the Revolutionary War to Iraq.

The Civil War was the next act in America's story of liberty and equality, but not the last. The slaves were now equal with their fellow white Americans in that they were free from the legal ownership of another human being. Unfortunately, in many, many ways they were still not treated as equals. Many Southerners continued to believe in the rightness of their cause, even though that cause was lost. As we shall see, that meant that generations of white Southerners inherited both racism and resentment. It would more than a century before the truths of the Declaration of Independence began to seem self-evident down in Dixie.

MINI-UNIT 10: A HOUSE DIVIDED

Mini-Unit 11: Engines of Empires

We will watch inventions change the world, enabling the growth of empires and the outbreak of worldwide conflict. Note how our seven main "characters" fit in.

The Author	Imperialistic ambitions drove the expansion of major world powers. In this time, people began to turn their backs on God as Darwin's theory of evolution was applied to society as well as biology. God's authority as Creator was openly questioned.
People	We'll meet some of the major figures of the Gilded Age, when the promise of wealth, prosperity, and liberty drew the poor, weary, huddled masses of the world to America. Some would become wealthy industrialists, others pioneers, and still others became inventors. We will also see how the world slipped into World War I, contrary to people's hopes and dreams.
Good	While we do not emphasize this with younger students, during this time people continued to define "good" as that which made them stronger. Social Darwinism and the Gospel of Wealth justified acts of selfishness. "Might makes right" was the attitude. People believed that the world would get better and better over time as humanity advanced.
Evil	Released from accountability to their Creator by Social Darwinism, people did what was right in their own eyes. This led to oppression of the poor, broken promises to Native Americans, economic domination by "Robber Barons," and deep-seated racism, especially in the South after failed attempts at post-Civil War Reconstruction.
The Word	Textual criticism bore fruit as seminaries and theologians abandoned the authority of Scripture. In response to this, we saw the rise of Fundamentalism, which sought to restore foundational truths.
God's Creation	Scarcity and famine led to increased immigration. Industrialization continued to increase mobility, the migration of people to cities, and population density. Industrialization also led to the unchecked exploitation of seemingly limitless natural resources. Distances shrank as the Transcontinental Railroad reduced the time needed to cross North America from six months to a week.
Man's Creation	Several major inventions were developed after the Civil War, including the telephone, the airplane, and the automobile. These would transform the way that people lived, worked, traveled, and fought. Many of these inventions were used for the first time during World War I.

Mini-Unit 11 Overview
Engines of Empires

Introduction

In this mini-unit, we look at how forces of industrialization helped drive political imperialism from the late 1860s to the early 1900s. In America, the Civil War ended in 1865 with the South's military surrender and its addition back into the Union, but this left deep wounds and much unfinished business. The war had determined that our country would be *the United* States of America rather than *these* United States of America, and this was important. The war also demonstrated that industrialization had changed the world.

Powerful inventions and innovations—steam engines, railroads, telegraphs, factories, revolvers, machine guns, and many others—demonstrated the ability to overcome geographic barriers and drove forward a new Age of Imperialism around the globe. While it would seem to people of the day that the direction of progress would be driven irrevocably upward by the tools that humans invented, little had changed in human hearts. Indeed, efforts to redefine good and evil using the doctrines of Social Darwinism and the Gospel of Wealth would be used to justify very inhumane treatment in the name of the survival of the fittest. Upward progress was anything but guaranteed. The devastating impact of World War I would demonstrate that the engines used to build empires could also be used to destroy them.

Reconstruction and Expansion

In this mini-unit, we will study the aftermath of the Civil War in America and efforts to reconstruct the Union, even as new lands were beckoning for westward expansion. After the war, the states were again united in name, but definitely not in spirit. Hostility seethed in the South toward both the northern carpetbaggers and the freed slaves. Frustrated by slow progress, violence, and political opposition, the will to reunite the country in spirit as well as in name faded out.

With the election of Rutherford B. Hayes, leaders began to direct energy toward the wide open western spaces. Fueled by a belief in the manifest destiny of the United States to stretch from sea to shining sea, or drawn by the promise of free land to anyone who could live on it and improve it, settlers flocked to the American West. Connected by railroads and telegraph wires, the new nation grew westward.

Industry and Immigration

The United States, eager to fill the continent it had acquired, welcomed immigrants. These immigrants surged westward, building the rails that would connect America. They also worked in the factories that drove the economy of the growing nation. As symbolized by the Statue of Liberty, America opened her doors to the "huddled masses" of Europe. The huge influx of new Americans brought inevitable changes.

Inventors like Thomas Edison tamed sound (phonograph, 1877), distance (telephone, 1878), and darkness (electric light bulb, 1879). As economic prosperity increased, the United States entered a new era, riding high on a global wave of optimism that modern science and technology would propel humankind to ever-increasing heights!

Because inventors were making amazing technological advances, many middle-class Americans enjoyed a better standard of living than any people had since the beginning of the world. Yet those experiencing the blessings of freedom had not yet embraced their responsibility to their brothers and neighbors. New theories, such as biological and social Darwinism, gave the wealthy a plausible excuse to look after their own interests, not the interests of others.

Without the salt and light of the gospel, people were quick to take advantage of their neighbors. Mark Twain called this period of time the "Gilded Age." That is fitting, since the "gold" on America's surface was only painted on. If you scratched beneath the top layer of society in America's cities, you found horrid slums where desperately poor people lived in shamefully dirty, crowded, and dangerous conditions.

Despite all this, America's golden sheen attracted people from all over the world. Students will learn about the millions of people who immigrated to America. Millions of people came through the doors of Ellis Island and other gateways. America was seen as a land of opportunity where hard work and individual responsibility could lead to prosperity. This is an important part of our national identity, and continues to be true to this day.

Airplanes and Automobiles

There was good reason to be optimistic in the late 1800s. Industrialization had made manufactured goods cheaper and more plentiful than ever. Most major political threats from European nations had been overcome, and the United States was free to grow from sea to shining sea. Advances in transportation and communication made overcoming worldwide distances seem simple. Jules Verne published *Around the World in 80 Days* in 1873, which features every form of transportation available in a journey around the globe. Western influence spread around the globe, and it was said that "the sun never sets on the British Empire." The invention of the automobile, with its tireless horsepower, and the airplane, with its metal wings, only fueled this sentiment.

Politically, Europe had experienced a period of relative peace since the defeat of Napoleon in 1815. After almost 100 years without significant conflict between the major powers of Europe, World War I arrived with devastating impact, shattering the complacency and materialism of the modern world. By 1918, the same engines that had powered their empires would be used to leave a generation of their young men shattered, broken, and disillusioned.

By the end of this mini-unit, we enter the twentieth century. This century was breathtakingly good in some ways. But in other ways, it was horribly bad. We've touched on a few of these themes already. While you may not want to cover the darker parts of the twentieth century with your student, it is worthwhile for you as a teacher to understand our moment in history.

Conclusion

This mini-unit is titled "Engines of Empires." At the time we're studying, the British Empire stretched around the world, as you can see when you look at a map of Britain's holdings in 1900. Inventions such as the steam engine, the railroad, the airplane, the telegraph, and the telephone made the administration of such vast empires possible.

But, as we will see, they also made it possible for these empires to be pulled into World War. The power of these engines, combined with a departure from the foundational truths of the Bible and a lack of accountability, propelled humanity into an era where great discoveries would be accompanied by great atrocities.

Christians would continue to seek to remain faithful to the mission to proclaim the good news of salvation, redemption, and new life in Jesus Christ. World missions continued to flourish as the message of hope traveled around the world. New technologies would be employed in continuing to bring God's word to people from every language, tongue, and tribe!

Mini-Unit 11, Topic 1
Reconstruction and Expansion

Introduction

We left off our study of American history with the closing days of the Civil War and the assassination of President Lincoln. As you can imagine, things looked very bleak to most Americans during those days. The Southern states had been the primary battleground for the last two years of the war, and the stiff resistance of its leaders to the North had led to the utter devastation of its farmlands and principal cities. Both civilians and soldiers who survived the war were starving. Bitterness and anger towards both Northerners and blacks were common (but not universal) among whites in the defeated South. Victorious Northerners had little to crow over. They were uncertain as to how to put away the enmity of the past four years and rebuild the nation. Many despaired as to whether it could even be done.

President Lincoln had sketched a plan for the readmission of Southern states, but it left many questions unanswered. Overall, Lincoln wanted reconciliation without retaliation. He insisted on protecting the freed slaves and their friends in the South, but had no desire to punish those who submitted to the Union. Lincoln got part of this agenda started with the Freedmen's Bureau Bill, which created an agency to provide assistance to the freed slaves. This was part of the War Department, which was consistent with the way Lincoln had used his powers as Commander in Chief to emancipate the slaves. The Freedmen's Bureau started 4,000 schools and 100 hospitals for former slaves. After the war, it took the role of a military court for legal issues involving Blacks. The Bureau's efforts to be fair to the freedmen soon aroused the ire of their old masters.

As Congress discussed the weaknesses of Lincoln's plan, some debated whether the President or Congress should take leadership in determining policies for Reconstruction. Lincoln's sudden death silenced that great man forever on the topic of how the nation should be reunited and left lingering questions about the proper leader for the necessary work ahead.

After Lincoln's assassination in April, a Southern man who had been Lincoln's Vice President, Andrew Johnson, became President. Soon thereafter, Congress adjourned without having put any laws into effect regarding the rebuilding of the nation.

The Reconstruction era is confusing because there were so many strong and urgent, yet conflicting, priorities for individuals, leaders, and government. It seems that it would have been impossible for all the strong desires of all participants to be well satisfied. As with all crisis situations, the best and the worst aspects of people were brought to light by the intense heat of events during this era.

Reconstruction Under Johnson

Andrew Johnson was born in North Carolina and raised on the Tennessee frontier. He was a tailor by trade, and his wife helped educate him. He was a serious man with a prickly pride, but he rose to serve in Congress, as Governor, and as a Senator. Like his political hero, Andrew Jackson, Andrew Johnson considered himself the champion of the common man—the common white man, that is. He distrusted the rich and despised the slaves.

Johnson was for the Union and for slavery—which almost got him killed in his home state of Tennessee. While his state had seceded, Johnson was the only Senator from the South who refused to secede with his state. Once the Union armies conquered Tennessee, Lincoln appointed Johnson military governor of that area. Lincoln then chose Johnson as his vice president when he ran for reelection in 1864.

After Lincoln was assassinated, Andrew Johnson took the helm. Johnson hated traitors, as he called the Confederate leaders. He thought the Southern aristocracy had misled the common people of the South. He wanted to punish their generals and politicians but believed in a full restoration of rights for the Southern men who had served in the Confederate Army.

Congress was out of session when Lincoln was shot, so Johnson started implementing his plan for Reconstruction in its absence. Six weeks after the assassination, he granted a general amnesty to Southern soldiers who were willing to sign an oath of loyalty to the Union. He appointed provisional governors and ordered them to start reorganizing the state governments. He left it up to each state to decide whether or not freed slaves would get to vote.

Black Codes

Unfortunately (but not unpredictably) the new Southern state governments formed under Johnson's plan started passing laws called "black codes," which perpetuated the oppression of freed slaves. In various Southern states, the following laws applied:

- A black person under the age of eighteen was forced to work as an apprentice to a white man.
- If a black person left his employer, he could be arrested and fined, or forced to work without wages.
- A black person was not allowed to work as a skilled tradesman without a license.
- A freed slave could not own a weapon.
- It was against the law for a black person to purchase or rent farm land.

Laws like these meant that freedmen found it extremely difficult to meet even the simplest daily needs. The freed slaves were also threatened by violence. The Ku Klux Klan (KKK) and other secret organizations emerged to threaten blacks and their supporters in the South.

Congressional Reaction and Impeachment

None of this sat well with the Republicans, who came back to Congress the winter after Lincoln's assassination. They refused to admit the newly elected Congressmen from the South. The radical Republicans in Congress wanted to punish the whole population of the slave-owning South, not just their political and military leaders. For the next year, Congress passed Reconstruction bills, Johnson vetoed them, and Congress overrode his veto.

Before the mid-term elections of 1866, Johnson campaigned across the Northern states to present his views to the people. It didn't help—the Radical Republicans won a clear majority of seats in Congress. The conflict between Congress and the President escalated into impeachment—the House of Representatives voted 126-47 to impeach Johnson. The eleven articles of impeachment against him accused him of breaking specific laws and of conspiring against Congress and the Constitution. Johnson was barely acquitted by the Senate. It takes two-thirds of the Senate to convict a President—he was acquitted by a single vote.

Carpetbaggers and Scalawags

Meanwhile, back in the South, power shifted from the former slaveholders to their enemies. A coalition of freedmen, Northerners, and southern Republicans took control of the new state governments. Many Union soldiers decided to stay down south, and other Northerners took advantage of the new opportunities there. These outsiders were known as "carpetbaggers" because Southerners claimed they were so poor they could fit everything they owned into the cheap suitcases (made of carpet) that they carried. The southern whites who became Republicans were called "scalawags." Before the Civil War, that term applied to worthless cows—"all of the mean, lean, mangy, hidebound, skinny, worthless cattle" [1] in any drove. But now Southerners used it for the so-called "white trash"—people who sided with blacks and Yankees.

Reconstruction under Grant

Ulysses S. Grant became President after Johnson. He came into office four years after the Reconstruction of the South had begun. From 1864-1874, the Republicans dominated Congress. During this time, Federal troops occupied portions of the South. Many Southerners resisted federal directives to allow blacks equal protection of the laws and the right to vote, while Northerners became preoccupied with their own problems and lost interest in keeping troops to enforce laws in the South.

Reconstruction was hard work, and America has always had trouble maintaining the political willpower to stick with something hard over time. By the end of Grant's first term, Republicans had become disgusted with the widespread corruption in government at both state and federal levels, and were increasingly disheartened by the ongoing violence of the KKK and White Leagues that frightened black voters away from the polls. Simply put, ongoing Southern white resistance to federal forces and laws, along with disillusionment with the corruption of government leaders exposed at many levels, led to a significant loss of support from Northerners in the Reconstruction process. They had won the war, but Republicans slowly gave up on winning the peace. Grant still wanted to carry on with Reconstruction, however. He was reelected

---

1 "Scalawag," *Wikipedia*. Accessed 10 February 2014. Retrieved from <http://en.wikipedia.org/wiki/Scalawag>.

in 1872, even though some discontented Republicans formed a splinter party and ran a candidate against him.

The Democrats, meanwhile, saw an opportunity to reclaim political power. As more and more Southern states rejoined the Union, whites regained control over those representing them in Congress. There was an economic panic in 1873 that led to quick-fix legislation by Congress, which Grant vetoed. Americans didn't like that, and Democrats swept into the majority in Congress during the midterm elections of 1874, rendering Grant more or less a lame duck for his last two years in office.

The Congressional Democrats promptly launched a series of investigations into Grant's administration—which turned up a lot of dirt. Although Grant himself was not corrupt, many of his political appointees had taken personal advantage of their positions of power. Grant's political problems helped end America's commitment to Reconstruction. By the end of his second term, the country was pretty much ready to move on.

The End of Reconstruction

The disputed presidential election of 1876 killed Reconstruction completely—Rutherford B. Hayes was chosen for President in an otherwise deadlocked election because he promised to pull all federal troops out of the South if he got the job. He was elected, and he promptly kept his promise. With federal troops gone, the oppression for freedmen had no opposition. We'll learn more about that as we progress.

That wraps up the South for now—so let's take a look at the American West. We're entering the brief era of the "Wild West," when cowboys and Indians galloped over the vast plains.

Moving West

We already learned how the continental United States had grown to its full size before the Civil War began. The Homestead Act of 1862 was passed in the early years of the Civil War after the South seceded. This allowed any homesteader to get land for free as long as he built a 12-by-14-foot dwelling and grew crops. The Homestead Act was designed to make it attractive for settlers to move to the free states in the west, and it worked. In the years following the passage of the Act, pioneers from the Northeast, the South, and Europe would flock to America's western lands.

Your student can listen to stories from *Little House on the Prairie* and may do projects that help him understand what life was like for homesteaders. Early pioneers made the difficult journey west over the Oregon Trail in prairie schooners, as we've seen, but by 1869, the barriers to the West were coming down, thanks to the engines of the Industrial Revolution.

The great Transcontinental Railroad project was started while America was a divided nation—the Civil War was still raging back East, and East and West had little to nothing in common. Before the railroad was finished, it took the average overland traveler half a year to reach the Pacific coast. When it was finished, one could travel from New York to California in about a week. The process of building the railroad also helped to diversify the nation: the railroad companies imported many Chinese workers for the project. The Chinese were hard and skillful workers who earned the respect of many white Americans.

Broken Promises

Immigrants from all over the world helped build the rails across America, and many stayed to settle. Others, drawn by the promise of free land, headed west. As the West was explored and people realized its potential, leaders continued a disturbing pattern of breaking the promises that they had made to its original inhabitants. Native Americans were pushed out of lands they had been promised in order to make room for the new settlers. Even as we learn about the bravery and diligence of the pioneers who settled the West, we must understand that the lands that seemed so empty came at a price.

When the United States started pushing Native Americans out of their native lands in the 1830s, they promised them the western Indian Country for "as long as the rivers shall run and the grass shall grow." The Indian Country included almost all the land between the Missouri River and the Continental Divide—a vast but arid region. In reality, those treaties lasted only as long as the land seemed worthless to farmers—but when whites discovered gold and silver there, the rush was on to squeeze the Indians onto ever-smaller reservations.

Cowboys

Gold wasn't the only thing that brought settlers west—there was a whole new world of opportunity out there. Take, for example, cattle drives. The new railroads and modern meatpacking plants made it possible to ship western beef back east, which created a whole new kind of cattle rearing. Cows were allowed to roam wild in the West after being marked with the brands of their owners. In the spring, men on horses rounded them up, branded the new calves, sorted them out, and then drove a part of the herd across hundreds of miles of open country to the nearest railhead. Abilene, Wichita, and Dodge City boomed as they became major centers for this new industry. The cowboys who did all this work had hard and dangerous jobs. Their wild and lonely lives tuned them into icons of the American West.

Plains Indians Wars

Movie-makers in the 1930s and 40s churned out countless epics of noble cowboys fighting evil "Injuns." In reality, cowboys didn't usually fight the Native Americans. Not that there wasn't fighting—it's just that it was the U.S. Army that fought the Plains Indians Wars. Most historians date the close of these conflicts at December of 1890, when a massacre at Wounded Knee, South Dakota, crushed any lingering hopes of Native American peoples.

Unlike most of America's other wars, the Plains Indians Wars were a series of disconnected skirmishes and battles. Each Native American tribe is technically a nation of its own, although not a sovereign nation like the United States. The simplest way to learn about these wars may be to learn about some of the individual Indian chiefs who led their people in armed resistance.

Sitting Bull (1876)

Sitting Bull was a Sioux leader and holy man who encouraged his people to defend themselves against the white man. The Sioux people lived in the northern plains from Minnesota to Montana. Sitting Bull's forces defeated cavalry leader George Custer and his men in 1876 at the Battle of the Little Big Horn. Later, after the Sioux were finally defeated by federal troops, Buffalo Bill persuaded Sitting Bull to join his Wild West show as a major attraction.

Chief Joseph (1877)

Chief Joseph was a Nez Perce chief who tried to preserve peace with the white men. The Nez Perce tribe originally lived in Washington, Oregon, and Idaho. (You may recall that Sacagawea, who traveled with the Lewis and Clark expedition, was a Nez Perce Indian.) The U.S. government signed a treaty that gave the Nez Perce a large amount of land in 1855, but they changed the deal seven years later to give the Native Americans a much smaller territory. Some of the Nez Perce agreed to move to the new land in order to get benefits like hospitals and schools, but Chief Joseph and his people refused to leave their homes.

Chief Joseph did everything he could to hold onto his homeland without war, but in 1877, when violence became inevitable, he led many of his people in a desperate flight for the Canadian border after being told that they would be forced onto a small reservation. Joseph led 750 of his people 1,800 miles into the Bear Paw Mountains of Montana. There, just forty miles from the Canadian border, the Army cut off their route of escape. Despite thirteen victorious battles against federal troops, cold weather and exhaustion were killing off the Nez Perce women and children, which finally forced Chief Joseph to surrender. That was the last great battle between the U.S. government and an Indian nation.

Geronimo (1886)

Geronimo was an Apache, and he was the last major Indian leader to surrender to the United States government. The Apache people were scattered from Texas to Arizona. Until Geronimo finally surrendered, he was an elusive raider who successfully dodged the army until they sent Apache scouts to track him down in the Sierra Madre Mountains. They finally captured him in 1886.

Lakota Sioux (1890)

The battles between white men and Indians ended with the Massacre at Wounded Knee, South Dakota, in 1890, when the army surrounded a camp of Lakota Sioux who had been refusing to go off to the reservation. What was supposed to be a peaceful surrender turned chaotic when one brave refused to hand over his gun. More than 300 Indians died there—and that slaughter marked the last major violence of the Plains Indians Wars.

Conclusion

Clearly, the stories about both the course of Reconstruction and the expansion of settlers into the West show how people continued to need God as they advanced technologically.

In Washington, President Johnson and Congress both wanted vengeance against their enemies: Johnson hated "traitors," while the radical Republicans hated every aspect of slavery. Revenge is a dangerous motive that seldom bears good fruit. James 1:20 tells us "the anger of man does not achieve the righteousness of God." As attempts at Reconstruction fizzled out, deep wells of bitterness, hostility, and racism remained.

Free slaves started off with great hopes at the end of the Civil War, but those hopes were dashed when Congress gave up on Reconstruction during Grant's second term. Reconstruction was hard work, and the South didn't want to change. It was expensive. It was slow. But when the majority in Congress gave up the goal of making sure that every American enjoyed the equal protection of the laws, it abandoned generations of blacks to injustice. We'll pick up the thread of race relations in America briefly in the next mini-unit.

In the West, the United States treated Native Americans badly in the nineteenth century. In Psalm 15, King David asked, "Who shall dwell with God? He who walks blamelessly and does what is right and speaks truth in his own heart—the one who swears to his own hurt and does not change." David knew how God treats those who violate solemn oaths. In 2 Samuel 21, while David was king, God sent a famine on all Israel for three years because King Saul broke a covenant that Joshua had made with the Canaanite people of the city of Gibeon almost 400 years earlier. Time after time, America entered into solemn treaties with the "savages" and then turned around and broke their promises as soon as they proved inconvenient. The Native Americans weren't the only ones who suffered from America's broken promises.

Mini-Unit 11, Topic 2
Industry and Immigration

Introduction

This week, your student will read about the millions of people who immigrated to America. We will focus on the process that immigrants went through as they entered America.

Your student will learn about President Grover Cleveland this week. He served his country during the era of immigration, responding to the problems of a nation that wanted its government to cater to the demands of citizens, who included the very newest Americans as well as the descendants of those who had come over on the *Mayflower*. You will also meet Teddy Roosevelt, one of America's "larger than life" characters who had a great impact on America as the nation entered the twentieth century.

Land of Opportunity

The United States in the Gilded Age was seen by outsiders as a type of "promised land." In fact, many Europeans referred to it as the "golden land," brimming with promises of a better life, freedom, equality, and opportunity for individuals. And America *was* better than the alternative for many immigrants.

Some people escaped to the United States from unbearable conditions back home, such as the Irish Potato Famine. Other people left their homelands due to devastation caused by drought. In other places, people left their homes because of the hardships they experienced under their oppressive governments. (For example, many Russian Jews fled the persecution and violence they were experiencing from the government who sought to eliminate them from society.)

Many immigrants left their homes for more positive reasons. They believed the promise of a better life in America, or they wanted to live where land and opportunity was available to people of modest means. They wanted to have a real chance to succeed on the basis of their own hard work.

Growing up, you may have watched *An American Tail*, the animated video that tells the story of a young Jewish mouse who immigrates to America with his family to escape persecution in Russia and encounters some of the struggles that human immigrants might have experienced. If you haven't, it might be a great way to introduce your student to this era. The song that the mice sing as they come to the new world playfully sums up the rosy picture that many immigrants had. They sing, "There are no cats in America, and the streets are paved with cheese!"

Statue of Liberty and Ellis Island

Millions of foreigners, dreaming that America's streets were paved with gold, poured into her busy harbors. Many of them sailed into the New World under Lady Liberty's shadow. The majestic copper statue at the entrance to New York harbor was given to the people of the United States by the people of France in 1884. French citizens donated the money for Auguste Bartholdi's statue, but poetess Emma Lazarus put into words the hopes of humanity that made it such an icon of America:

> Give me your tired, your poor,
> Your huddled masses yearning to breathe free,
> The wretched refuse of your teeming shore.
> Send these, the homeless, tempest-tost to me,
> I lift my lamp beside the golden door.[1]

Over the years, many new Americans started their story of a new life in a new country at Ellis Island in New York harbor. The immigrants had to prove at Ellis Island that they were mentally and physically healthy and ready to become citizens. They were inspected before they were admitted, and these inspections were serious business—about 2% of the immigrants were sent back home because they had contagious illness, had committed past crimes, were in trouble for political reasons, or because the inspectors didn't think they could support themselves in their new country.

---

1 "The New Colossus," by Emma Lazarus.

The inspectors had a big job, trying to process so many people from so many places. Just trying to spell their names could be next to impossible. They did the best they could, but many immigrants came out of Ellis Islands with new names that bore little resemblance to what they had been called back home!

The immigrants who made it through began to pass on tips on how to beat the system when they wrote home. For example, new immigrants had to prove that they could read their own language, so some memorized passages to make it look like they could read. They had to prove that they had $25 of their own money, so they often borrowed the $25 they needed to show the inspectors—then paid the money back before they left. In some cases, immigrants would secretly pass the same $20 bill from one passenger to the next in the inspection line.

Racism and Xenophobia

Most Americans didn't think much about what life was like for the "huddled masses" once they squeezed into the crowded tenements of American cities. They weren't aware of the sufferings of poor, black sharecroppers in the South or the Chinese coolies in the West. Many didn't know because they didn't care. That may seem odd for a nation that had so recently gone to war over slavery, but it was the sad reality of the times.

Lady Liberty may have welcomed the wretched refuse of Europe, but many living Americans did not. It was an era of overt racism and xenophobia. "Xenophobia" comes from two Greek word—*xenos*, meaning foreigner, and *phobos*, meaning fear. Left to themselves, humans tend to despise what is below them, envy what is above them, and fear what they don't understand. In our day, churches and schools work to temper these impulses, but in the late 1800s, science and religion seemed to favor racism.

Herbert Spencer, a British philosopher during the late 1800s, was the first to directly apply the theory of Darwinian evolution to human society. Darwin said the struggle for survival was the basis for our advancement; it was the reason why humans had risen above the apes. If that was true, Spence argued, prosperous people should stop feeling guilty about the way they treated fellow humans. The social Darwinists argued that oppression was good for the species overall. Let the weak starve, if they must—the survival of the fittest (in this case, the wealthy) ensured the improvement of the race!

William Sumner helped popularize this new theory in America. Social Darwinism made perfect sense to affluent Americans who felt themselves to be superior to the wretched refuse of humanity that toiled in their factories. But times have changed society's view of social Darwinism. Darwinism with relation to human (and animal) origins has become America's new orthodoxy, upheld by legislation and court cases, but public schools don't teach its darker social implications. It is no longer considered politically correct to callously allow the weak and oppressed to die off.

Christians have a good reason to care for the poor—In Matthew 25:40, Jesus said, "As you did it to one of the least of these my brothers, you did it to me." Unfortunately, there were Christians in the late nineteenth century who had trouble thinking of Jesus when they looked at people of different skin colors. Many Southern whites still seethed with resentment from the Civil War and comforted themselves with theologies that justified their lost cause. Southern preachers had long taught that Africans were the cursed offspring of Ham, doomed to serve the white race.

In the face of these evils, it took real courage and determination to seize the opportunities that America offered. You can decide to read more with your student about one of the most famous of these men, who rose from being an immigrant to become a captain of industry.

Andrew Carnegie

Some poor immigrants became wealthy and powerful. Students can learn about the life of Andrew Carnegie, whose family left Scotland for a new life in America when he was thirteen years old. When Andrew came to America, he worked in a cotton mill in Pennsylvania. He later got a position as a messenger boy, which gave him a chance to see the big city of Pittsburgh. From an earthly perspective, Carnegie had what it took to succeed. He was diligent, friendly, and humble, yet full of enthusiasm. He always wanted to learn new things.

But there were lots of new Americans who were just as eager, curious, and hardworking. God put opportunity in Carnegie's path. He and his fellow messenger boys attended the theater and formed a debate club, which they called the Webster Literary Society. A very kind, wealthy man allowed the messenger boys to borrow books from his enormous library. Carnegie took full advantage of his generosity. He never forgot how much that one man's kindness meant to his future.

After a year and a half, Carnegie had been promoted from messenger boy to telegraph operator. He made good money and was able to provide for his family. Soon he became his boss' right hand man. By the time he was 24 years old, he had risen to a very important position within the railroad industry.

Railroads were quickly becoming very big business. Carnegie's position gave him access to the opportunity to make some very lucrative investments. As the Civil War unfolded, Carnegie invested in steel-working mills. After the war, Carnegie continued to expand his holdings in iron and steel manufacturing, building up a massive commercial empire and unbelievable personal wealth.

Gospel of Wealth

Carnegie tried to live a moral life, but he was not a Christian. Carnegie was a fervent Social Darwinist, and he wrote an essay in 1889 called "Wealth." In close alignment with the ideas of Social Darwinism, this "Gospel of Wealth," as it was known, held that the vast differences between rich and poor were just as they should be.

Although Carnegie didn't have any objection to the rich getting richer, he had strong ideas about what wealthy men should do with their money. He didn't believe in just giving it away, whether to one's heirs or to the poor. He thought that both the idle rich and the idle poor were all too likely to waste what was handed to them. But, as a poor boy who gained his education by reading books from a rich man's library, Carnegie softened the harshest edges of Social Darwinism.

Carnegie thought the man of wealth should consider how best to help those who will help themselves. He was against any kind of government intervention in the market, and opposed charity as such, but he was all in favor of rich men voluntarily creating resources that would allow poor people to improve themselves. For instance, towards the end of his life, after having enjoyed his riches for years, Carnegie founded over 2800 libraries, where the poor could educate themselves as he himself had.

Backlash against "Robber Barons"

Carnegie was not alone in his success or in his beliefs. Other Captains of Industry, as industrial leaders were called by Thomas Carlyle in his book *Past and Present* in 1843, included people such as J.P. Morgan, Andrew W. Mellon, and John D. Rockefeller.

Despite Carnegie's lofty aspirations, ordinary Americans did not trust these super-rich Social Darwinists. Captains of Industry built the infrastructure that created what came to be known as "big business"—huge empires that controlled entire industries, usually with one "captain" at the helm of each. Big business grew America, but it proved to be hard on employees, consumers, and smaller, competing businesses. Regardless of their intentions, the Captains of Industry at the helms of big businesses would also become known by another term: "Robber Barons."

Big business made high profits by paying low wages, and if workers complained, they lost their jobs, because when businesses gained a monopoly in the market, they could call all the shots. Monopolies hurt employees, and they hurt consumers, too, who had no choices when it came to products that a big business controlled. Monopolies were hard on smaller businesses, too. Railroad companies became notorious for price fixing, kickbacks, rebates, and other unfair practices that tilted the playing field against smaller businesses. All in all, the giant corporations were good for their owners but hard on everybody else.

As concerned citizens, muckrakers (reporters who dug up the muck of society and reported on it) and reformers publicized the miserable conditions in which the urban poor labored and lived, and public opinion turned against the Captains. People started to demand regulation and reform. The Grange was formed by disgruntled Mid-western farmers in protest. Labor organizations like the Knights of Labor were formed, and violent strikes broke out. Congress responded to the public outcry, enacting the Interstate Commerce Act and the Sherman Antitrust Act to give the government a role in regulating big business.

Teddy Roosevelt

This week your student will learn about Presidents in the late 1800s, but one of these stands out larger than life, even today. If Carnegie personified the archetypical Captain of Industry, Teddy Roosevelt personified other important aspects of the fearless, self-made man of this era. His love of the outdoors, his charge up San Juan Hill in 1898 during the Spanish-American War, his "speak softly and carry a big stick" foreign policy, his anti-trust actions, and his efforts to encourage conservation have become an iconic part of American history.

Boyhood and Youth

From his early childhood, Roosevelt was frail and weak, often struggling to breathe. Roosevelt's father told him that "man was not intended to be an oyster" and urged him to exercise—to make his body strong. He did, and though ill health plagued him throughout his life, he became the very model of a vigorous man.

He wasn't just sick as a child—he was fearful. Roosevelt read a book that explained that if you act like you are not afraid, then you will not be afraid. He took it to heart and exemplified courage. Roosevelt saw war as the ultimate test of manhood, patriotism, and strength. From his youth, Roosevelt made up his mind that if war ever came, he would serve as a soldier. Meanwhile, politics beckoned. At age 24, Roosevelt became the youngest member of the New York State Assembly, where he served until 1884.

Although his home was in the state of New York, Roosevelt came to love the openness and vastness of the West through a heartbreaking personal tragedy. When his first wife Alice died two days after giving birth in February 1884, he became depressed, quit politics, and moved to the West. There, he enjoyed outdoor adventures such as hunting and cattle driving. On his Elk Horn ranch, he relished the life of a cowboy.

Public Service and Political Life

Roosevelt was passionate about everything that he did. When he first got involved in politics, Roosevelt disliked simply talking about a problem. He was always itching to do something about it. This is why some gave him the nickname "The Young Reformer." In 1895, Roosevelt was back in New York. He became the U.S. civil service commissioner. In this position, he worked hard to stop corruption in the government. Roosevelt continued his reform efforts in New York City when he became the police commissioner in 1895.

In 1897, President McKinley appointed Roosevelt to be the Assistant Secretary of the Navy. He served in this post until he resigned from it in order to lead the Voluntary Cavalry Regiment (Rough Riders) in the Spanish-American War. Roosevelt's Rough Riders helped win the Battle of San Juan Hill in Cuba, and the subsequent sensational media coverage made him a national hero.

When he came back from Cuba in 1898, Roosevelt served as the governor of New York. President McKinley asked him to be his vice-presidential running mate in his bid for reelection in 1900—which Roosevelt initially saw as a "do-nothing job," and which he took very reluctantly. However, it wasn't a do-nothing job after all! Everything changed when McKinley was assassinated just a few months after taking office. Roosevelt became the youngest man to become president at the age of 42.

In his first term as President, Roosevelt earned a reputation as a "trust buster." He fought against the power of big businesses, including those in the railroad and oil industries. In 1902, Roosevelt instructed his attorney general to sue J.P. Morgan's Northern Securities Company, which had been created to eliminate the competition between rival railroads by creating a monopoly. Morgan's monopoly violated the Sherman Antitrust Act, but federal government had not really dared to use the Act against big business before this time. After two years, the Supreme Court decided that Morgan had acted illegally and ordered the Northern Securities Company to be dissolved. That was the first of many big corporations that Roosevelt took on.

Roosevelt's foreign policy is easy to remember: he is the one who said America should "speak softly and carry a big stick." The soft words represented diplomacy; the big stick was a strong American military. For example, in 1902, Roosevelt began talking to Colombian officials about building a canal across Panama. Colombia refused, but shortly after this exchange, a revolution erupted in Colombia. With American support, Panama declared itself an independent republic. Within two weeks, the United States and the Republic of Panama signed a treaty granting the United States permission to build a canal.

Roosevelt earned another nickname, the "Great Conservationist," because he believed in preserving unspoiled land and wildlife for future generations. He added around 150 million acres to the national forests and set up 5 national parks, plus 25 irrigation or reclamation projects, 18 national monuments, 51 federal bird reserves, and 4 national game preserves. No wonder this larger-than-life figure wound up with his face on one of America's most famous national landmarks—Mount Rushmore.

Conclusion

The last quarter of the nineteenth century certainly glittered in America. There was much worldly wealth and prosperity. For the wealthiest families—those Captains of Industry—life was fantastic, and middle-class families of the era enjoyed a lifestyle that the elites of earlier eras could not have believed possible. But the wealthy and the genteel middle-class Americans enjoyed these "golden" lifestyles in part because others—immigrants, poor factory workers, and farmers—toiled and lived in crushing conditions of discomfort, filth, and poverty.

As Carnegie noted in his essay "Wealth," the new models of commerce inevitably produced enormous differences between rich and poor. Some grew fabulously wealthy and powerful, but the new methods of conducting business had a human cost. Laborers worked long hours in terrible conditions for little pay so that businessmen could profit. Smaller competitors were purposefully undercut when they challenged the prosperity of big business leaders.

Despite these negatives, we don't take the position that these super-wealthy men were evil "Robber Barons" who ultimately hurt America. With all their all-too-human failings, these Captains accomplished much that was positive. They pioneered the modern capitalistic system by which Americans do business today, which has been the most successful economy in history and benefitted the most human beings in this world—so far!

This was an era of larger-than-life characters who deserve some degree of admiration. Teddy Roosevelt was a remarkable man by any human standard. He learned to rely on his own grit and effort in his boyhood, and he accomplished amazing things. Christians can appreciate his energy, enthusiasm, and his demonstrated gift of leadership, yet still wonder—how much more might he have done if he had relied on God instead of Teddy?

Mini-Unit 11, Topic 3
Airplanes and Automobiles

Introduction

The twentieth century starts off with a bang. Most everything that we'll look at—from cars to planes to weapons to the American presidency—will get bigger and faster and more powerful from here to the end of the year. Buckle your seat belts—it's going to be a wild ride!

This new century was breathtakingly good in some ways. But in other ways, the twentieth century was horrifically bad. Between wars, revolutions, purges, plagues, disasters, and abortion-on-demand, it has been estimated that in the twentieth century alone there were at least 1,380,000,000 inflicted deaths. That's more than 80% of the total human population at the start of the century.

These frightful statistics are enough to make a caring parent ask, "Does my child really need to learn about this evil?" *Tapestry of Grace* attempts to lead students through the harsh realities of history in age-appropriate ways. We study the past so that we remember how it happened, and with a hope that we might keep from repeating its mistakes.

But the best reason for Christians to study history is to see the hand of God at work. Even when times are evil or perplexing, God is still there—and is still very much in control. He reveals more and more of Himself as the world progresses, and we also see that—no matter how mankind tries—he cannot succeed in gaining the most important things of life apart from the enabling grace of God. We have seen that in a big way this year during our studies. The twentieth century continues to reveal the depths of human sin and the heights of divine mercy. God's wisdom, mercy, justice, kindness, and grace towards ill-deserving people have been on full display this year, and they will continue to be as we near the end.

Inventors

There's a theological term for God's kindness towards all people in general. It is called "common grace," and the twentieth century is full of it. One aspect of common grace is technological improvement that aids people in living better lives. This was advancing rapidly in the new century. Students are learning about two big developments in this topic: Orville and Wilbur Wright's airplane and Henry Ford's automobile.

As we've noted before, not every technological change made life better. Most became two-edged swords that could cut two ways, depending on the hand that wielded them. Europe had been largely at peace since the end of the Napoleonic Wars in 1815. By the turn of the century, many young men in England, France, and Germany longed for triumphs on the battlefield. What they did not realize was that military technology had "advanced" through all those years of peace: from muskets to rifles to machine guns to mustard gas. Europe had avoided war for so long that young men romanticized its glories while ignoring its horrors.

World War I's Beginnings

We do not study World War I in detail in *Tapestry Primer*, but we do note that it occurred. Here's a short version of how it happened for your overview.

The "powder keg" of Europe had been filled during decades of military posturing and development with no outlet for expression. The fuse that led to this keg was a labyrinth of treaties, developed over years, that bound countries to go to war in support of one another, should their allies be attacked. The spark that detonated all of Europe was struck in Serbia.

The Serbs wanted to control a neighboring territory that was populated by the closely-related ethnic group of Bosnians, but a treaty between Russia and Turkey gave Bosnia to Austria-Hungary instead. Nobody was all that happy with the deal at the time—Austria coveted Serbia, Serbia coveted Bosnia, and Bosnia wanted its independence. A secret Serbian organization called the Black Hand hired and trained three Bosnian activists to assassinate the archduke of Austria on his visit to Serbia and then commit suicide so no one could ever trace the killers.

The plan was only half-successful: the terrorists killed the Archduke but not themselves. Their cyanide pills were duds. When Austria discovered the Black Hand had set up the assassination, they blamed the Serbian government for the killing. They insisted Serbia should accept responsibility and pay damages. When Serbia refused to comply with every last detail, Austria-Hungary finally had the excuse it needed to declare war on Serbia.

Austria-Hungary declared war on Serbia on July 28, 1914. Three days later, Serbia's ally, Russia, began to mobilize its troops, in compliance with mutual assistance treaties that had been drawn up previously. Germany saw this as an aggressive move against its ally, Austria, and declared war on Russia on August 1. Great Britain and France were similarly allied to Russia, so France mobilized troops in support of Russia. The French support of Russia moved Germany to declare war on France on August 3. Germany marched into neutral Belgium and little Luxembourg in order to attack France's undefended Belgian border. Britain had long been pledged to aid neutral Belgium, so Germany's invasion caused Britain to declare war on Germany on August 4. It only took seven days for the dominos to fall all over Europe. They lined up as the Central Powers (Austria-Hungary, Germany, and the Ottoman Empire) against the Allies (mainly Great Britain, France, and Russia).

The Schlieffen Plan

If the problem with Europe was all the interlocking alliances, why did neutral Belgium end up on the front lines? It was all part of Germany's Schlieffen Plan. In 1899, German military theorists had thought through the implications of war in Europe. Alfred von Schlieffen thought France would hit Germany from the west and Russia from the east. Schlieffen thought Russia would need six weeks to mobilize its troops, though, because their railroads were so primitive. That would give Germany time to take out France—except that France had built major fortifications along its border with Germany. Schlieffen's plan was to race west through undefended Belgium, then south to Paris, and force France to surrender in the first few weeks. Germany could then pull its fighting forces back by rail to defend the Eastern Front against Russia.

Unfortunately for Germany, no military plan survives first contact with the enemy. Belgium put up a real resistance to the German advance, and Britain rushed in troops to support them. Russia took everyone by surprise by moving troops into East Prussia (what is now Poland) within days. The German army could not reach Paris and, quickly enough, had to defend the ground they had taken there on the Western Front.

Trench Warfare and Tanks

Europeans on both sides of the conflict had confidently expected to win the war that started in July of 1914 by Christmas of that year, but nobody realized how new weaponry would change the course of war. Machine guns turned battlefields into slaughterhouses. Men who stepped out into the open were torn to shreds. If you wanted to stay alive, you had to take cover—and that meant digging trenches. Soldiers dug down instead of marching forward. Since neither side knew when the enemy might try to break through the lines, they stayed down where they were shielded from most of the enemy fire—except for weapons like mortars that lobbed explosive shells up and dropped them straight down on the heads of the huddled soldiers. Trench warfare was an unending nightmare of boredom punctuated by panic—such as when men were ordered to make the occasional assault across no-man's land, into the teeth of machine guns and artillery, which predictably mowed them down like blades of grass.

Eventually, the technologies found in the automobile would be adapted for the battlefield and the armored tank would help break the stalemate. Unfortunately for millions of soldiers, those developments were a long way from being ready for the battlefield in the early part of the war and took years to become effective.

The Western Front

The battles that were fought in 1915 and 1916 were some of the bloodiest in history. After Germany's original plan to take Paris within weeks fell apart, Germany decided to beat France with a war of attrition, which meant killing so many soldiers the other side couldn't resupply and would have to surrender. German Chief of Staff Falkenhayn picked the French city of Verdun as the target of a new German offensive because he believed France would defend it to the last man. The German artillery started lobbing shells onto Verdun in February, 1915.

The battle of Verdun raged on without a break until mid-July. As Falkenhayn had predicted, France refused to give up the city, even though it cost them nearly a third of a million dead or wounded men. The Germans suffered more than a quarter million casualties. Verdun itself was practically obliterated.

Britain launched a major offensive on the Somme River in 1916, but it, too, was a bloodbath. England lost 60,000 men the first day. Four months and 1.2 million casualties later, the battle lines had only shifted seven miles.

The Eastern Front

On the Eastern front, Austria-Hungary was having a terrible war. They couldn't defeat little Serbia (despite three separate assaults), and they kept losing battles to Russia. Then Italy joined the Allies, and Austria-Hungary had a whole new front to defend.

Russia wasn't doing all that much better. With the Ottoman Empire (modern Turkey) in the war, Russia's already sizeable front got bigger. Russia had already lost many of her best troops in the first few months of the war. The ones who were left were spread too thin, badly supplied, and led by incompetent commanders. The Germans attacked Russia in the north and pushed the Russians back 300 miles, gaining Poland in the process. These enormous losses prompted Tsar Nicholas II to take direct and personal control of the armies, which meant that any future defeats would be his fault.

Submarines and the Lusitania

As armies dug into the ground, navies dove under the waves. Submarines changed the way sea battles were fought. By May 15, 1915, the island of Britain was surrounded by a German submarine blockade. The Germans were ordered to sink any vessel that might be carrying enemy troops or supplies. The *Lusitania* was a British ocean liner renowned as one of the biggest and fastest passenger ships in the world. Although the morning newspapers announced that no ship should enter the "war zone" around Britain, the *Lusitania*'s captain dismissed the caution, thinking the Germans would not dare to attack a passenger ship as famous as the *Lusitania*. When a German U-boat spotted the *Lusitania*, however, it fired a torpedo directly into it. Within eighteen minutes, the *Lusitania* had sunk, killing 1,198 people, including 120 Americans.

The attack on the *Lusitania* caused international outrage, especially in Britain and the United States. President Woodrow Wilson sent the German government strong protests, demanding an immediate end to submarine warfare. Anti-German sentiments became strong in the United States, and people felt that it would not be long before the United States joined the war.

Airplanes

By early 1916, although airplanes were a recent invention, both sides quickly began to use them as weapons. At first the only thing enemy pilots could do was shoot at each other with pistols when they met in the air. Within a short time, however, they were mounting machine guns on the planes. Unfortunately, when pilots pointed their machine guns straight ahead, they tended to shoot off their own propellers. A French pilot put steel deflectors on his propeller blades to bounce the bullets off. Then a Dutch designer named Anthony Fokker improved the German planes by adding a synchronization gear that fired the bullets through the gaps between the rotating propeller blades. His was the first successful fighter plane.

Fokker's plane initially devastated the Allied airforce, but both sides kept building better warplanes. A German fighter pilot named Manfred Baron von Richthofen was known as "the Red Baron" because of his bright red plane. His and other brightly-painted German aircraft were nicknamed the "Flying Circus" by the Allied soldiers. Each country's best fighter pilots were known as "aces." American ace Edward Rickenbacker shot down 26 planes in just a few months. Frenchman Georges Guynemer had 53 kills. None of them equaled the Red Baron, who had 80 kills.

By late 1917, Allied airpower overtook the Germans. Britain's new Sopwith Camel was the best plane in the air. Baron von Richthofen was shot down in 1918, and the Flying Circus was soon destroyed. The Allies finally dominated the sky.

Home Front

The pressures of modern warfare changed more than the front lines. There were changes on the home front, too. As we've mentioned before, nations had to put their domestic economy on a war footing to survive. While some men signed up to fight on the battlefield, others went to work in munitions factories and other war-related industries. In some countries, men had to be called from the front to work in factory positions on the home front. In the emergency of war, women started filling jobs that had only been open to men before.

Women and governments had to take on these new roles if nations were to survive the unique conditions of wartime, but the changes, once made, had a lasting impact. Women went back to more traditional roles after the war was over—but they had proved that they were able to do jobs that had been previously reserved for men, and some women began to demand that they have such jobs permanently.

Telecommunications

We mentioned in the last mini-unit that the 1800s saw the rise of worldwide empires as the major nations of Europe pursued their imperial objectives around the world. Inventions such as the steam engine, the telegraph, and the railroad made this possible initially. Toward the end of the nineteenth century and the beginning of the twentieth century, new technologies made this even easier. On Christmas Day, 1900, the first international telephone call was placed. In 1915, the first transcontinental call would be made between San Francisco and New York City. Ten months later, a trans-Atlantic call would be placed between Arlington, Virginia and Paris, France.

The ability to simultaneously communicate across immense distances made it possible for more people to share news and coordinate activities. It also made it more difficult for people to stay out of trouble. World War I was triggered with the June 28, 1914 assassination of Archduke Franz Ferdinand of Austria. Though a web of interdependent alliances and imperial aims quickly drew the major powers of Europe into the war, the United States sought to keep its distance until it became clear that neutrality was not an option. Interestingly, telecommunications played a direct role in the entrance of the United States to World War I.

In January 1917, the German Foreign Minister sent the Zimmermann Telegram. He invited Mexico to join the war as Germany's ally against the United States. In return, the Germans offered to finance Mexico's war and help Mexico recover the territories of Texas, New Mexico, and Arizona. Britain intercepted the telegraphic message and presented it to the U.S. embassy in Britain. From there it made its way to President Wilson, who released the Zimmerman note to the public, and Americans saw it as a cause for war.

America had pursued a policy of non-intervention before this point, despite German attacks on American shipping. President Wilson mobilized support by the war by describing it as the "War to End All Wars." The irony of this would soon become apparent.

Rapid communication also allowed news of the end of the war to spread quickly. When the Armistice was declared on the 11th hour of the 11th day of the 11th month of 1918, the news quickly rang out around the world. Americans took to the streets, celebrating in Times Square, New York, and all over the country. This was a far cry from the War of 1812, where Andrew Jackson's famous Battle of New Orleans was fought after the war was officially over! Advances in communication also made it possible to know that the last American to die in the war was Private Henry Guther, who died sixty seconds before the declaration of the Armistice.

Winning the War and Losing the Peace

Americans gave vital aid to the desperate European Allies during the crucial battles of 1918. Germany finally reached its limit and asked for an armistice. The shooting stopped, but the war wasn't over till the peace treaty was signed. Unfortunately,

President Wilson's "War to End All Wars" ended with the "Peace to Start Them Up Again"—and it was largely Wilson's fault! The Treaty of Versailles was negotiated over months by the victors, and was a complicated process. Its harsh demands on Germany planted the seeds for an even bigger world war a generation later.

The Treaty of Versailles dismantled the German army and forced them to give up significant territories (which the Germans had controlled as far back as the 1700s and 1800s) to Poland, France, and Denmark. They also gave back all the lands that they had occupied during the war in France, Belgium, and Russia. The "war guilt" clause of the treaty forced the Germans to accept responsibility for starting the war. The Allies also demanded that the Germans pay the Allies war reparations in the amount of over £6,600,000,000 (that's more than $300,000,000,000 in today's currency) since they were blamed for starting the war.

At the Paris peace talks, the leaders of Britain, France, America, and Italy redrew the maps of three continents. The war had toppled empires: Tsar Nicholas II of Russia and Kaiser Wilhem II of Germany both abdicated, the Austro-Hungarian Empire collapsed, and the Ottoman Empire was crumbling. The Treaty of Versailles redistributed Germany's overseas possessions in Africa, and Russia's Baltic territories became independent nations. The European victors redrew the lines of the map in areas of the Middle East that had been under Ottoman rule, too—and the consequences of this are still being felt today.

Redefining Physics

Though your student won't study it, we should note with you that physics was being transformed at a fundamental level in the first few years of the twentieth century. Max Planck's research and experiments led him to originate the quantum theory. Planck's work laid the groundwork for one of Albert Einstein's three big breakthroughs in 1905—Einstein got a Nobel Prize for showing light could be treated as packets of energy which we now call "photons." He also published a paper about relativity that year. Relativity and quantum theory would mushroom into a whole new kind of physics by the middle of the century. The last time breakthroughs like this changed the way people viewed the universe was during the Scientific Revolution that followed the Reformation and Renaissance.

Conclusion

By the end of World War I, many of the utopian dreams that human society would inevitably rise upward as we evolved toward perfection lay crushed in the dust of

European battlefields. The young men who returned broken, shattered, and blinded from the War to End all Wars would be known as the Lost Generation. After the war, the victors plunged into the silliness of the Roaring Twenties while the losers struggled with their defeat and plotted vengeance.

The engines of imperialism in the 1800s and new ways of looking at the world may have made it seem like people had fundamentally changed for the better. But, as we've seen throughout our study of history, our fundamental problem lies in our hearts. As much as people of this time sought to explain the world without its Creator, the story of history has an Author. When society cast off the moorings of the belief that all men are created equal and are accountable to God for their actions, whether good or evil, the doors were opened for the betrayal of Native Americans, the oppression of immigrants, and even the horrors of world war.

Mini-Unit 12: A Smaller World

We will learn how closely we are connected. Note how our seven main "characters" fit in.

The Author

As people sought meaning after World War I, they tried to escape into laughter in the Roaring Twenties, struggled through the Great Depression, found themselves in World War II, worked hard to get to the Moon, rebelled, and sought their own pleasure. Nothing could satisfy like God. People are still seeking a firm foundation on which to build their lives.

People

Various events led up to World War II, and we'll meet some men who led during that conflict. As the Cold War set in, the Civil Rights Movement and the Space Race were important as America sought to move forward. We meet key figures responsible for bringing about the end of the Cold War as well as recent American leaders.

Good

In an increasingly pluralistic society, good is often defined as "tolerance" and "diversity" by secular authorities. God's Word continues to stand unchanged, calling us to love the Lord our God with all our heart, soul, mind, and strength while we love our neighbors as we love ourselves.

Evil

While not something to emphasize with young students, evil is far from absent. The past century has witnessed propaganda, genocide, slavery, racism, abortion, cybercrime, terrorism, and more. We know that God has not abandoned us and that He will ultimately win every victory.

The Word

Following the rise of Fundamentalism, there have been multiple "movements" in which Christians have participated, including the Civil Rights Movement. These movements have often sought to bring about a change or shift in society toward a direction defined by God's Word, with differing degrees of success. There has also been an increasing emphasis upon the importance of sound doctrine and Christian apologetics.

God's Creation

Campaigns of World War II were fought simultaneously around the world. The Space Race led to the exploration of Earth's Moon. Satellite imagery allows us to explore the world in new ways, raising awareness of our responsibilities as God's stewards of His Creation.

Man's Creation

The pace of invention has only increased. We'll learn briefly about the use of radio and television at key moments in the twentieth century. Rockets were invented to take people to the Moon, satellites continuously photograph the world, and the Internet connects computers and phones in real time.

Mini-Unit 12 Overview
A Smaller World

Introduction

This is our final mini-unit. Congratulations! You are about to complete a survey of the history of the western world! We hope that you have enjoyed making connections and deepening your understanding of our moment in history.

Over the next three topics, we'll rapidly bridge the gap from the end of World War I to the start of the twenty-first century. As we continue to make connections with daily life, we want to highlight how certain technologies that we use every day have been influential. We will see how the television was used to keep the war effort going for both Axis and Allies. Television was also used to bring Americans closer together during the Civil Rights Movement. We'll learn about the rockets that took mankind to the Moon and how they were developed during the Space Race as part of the Cold War. Finally, we'll learn about how the Cold War ended, leading to the privatization of technologies like the Internet.

Wired Worlds at War

By the end of World War I, the telegraph and telephone had been on the scene for years and were well-established means of quickly distributing ideas in the form of words—or even voices. After World War I ended, a new medium of communication arose. This was the ability to send moving pictures over distance, and it was called television.

In the United States, broadcast television began in the late 1920s and continued to increase in sophistication throughout the 1930s and 1940s. More importantly, moving pictures or "movies" were fused with recorded sound by the end of the 1920s, creating "talking pictures." These image-dominated means of communication began to change the way that people shared ideas and became a means of escape and entertainment for many during the difficult years of the Great Depression, during the 1930s.

As with World War I, the United States did not at first get involved in World War II. It was generally viewed at first from American shores as "Europe's conflict." (We will look at how the war got started in detail in Topic 1). It took a Sunday morning attack by the Japanese on peaceful Pearl Harbor in Hawaii to involve America.

It is a proverbial truth that "a picture is worth a thousand words." The power of images is undeniable. Hitler used images incredibly effectively, establishing a Department of Film as part of his Nazi Ministry of Propaganda. Television was used on both sides as World War II took hold. Newsreels carried patriotic messages and calls to action to combatants on both sides of the battle lines. Images of the war and appeals for participation were seen around the world, stoking the conflict. World War II was truly an example of total war, where every citizen felt personally involved in the war effort and sought to do his or her part, largely because moving pictures made it seem near and necessary.

In the United States, factories that had been producing domestic products were repurposed for military use. The industrial capacity of the United States of America boomed during these years, lifting it out of a decade of severe economic depression. America first supported the war effort as the "Arsenal of Democracy," providing materials for the war under the Lend-Lease Act, but not entering as a direct combatant. After the attack on Pearl Harbor, and again, due to the prevalence of mass communications, President Franklin Roosevelt was able to crystallize the moment as "a day that will live in infamy" (via the radio), and the United States surged into the war.

Throughout the war, a fascinating thread for adults to follow is the battle for information. Whether the capture of the Enigma Machine (which allowed the Allies to read the most top secret German naval communications), or the desperate struggle to communicate with Resistance forces inside occupied Europe, or the amazing effectiveness of the Navajo Windtalkers, the role of communications in warfare is full of interest. The ability to transmit information more quickly dramatically increased its value as the wired world found itself at war.

One Small Step for Man

As the war ended, industrialized nations found themselves in possession of new technologies and in need of new national projects. Germans had begun experimenting with rocket technology at the end of World War II as a way to overcome the Allies' air dominance. During and after the war, prominent German rocket scientists found their way to the United States and to the Soviet Union.

The Union of Soviet Socialist Republics (USSR) was a growing threat to world peace. Since the end of World War II, Joseph Stalin's USSR had been increasing in size and aggression. A war-tired world did not want to be engulfed in another bloody conflict. As a result, the Cold War would be played out in a series of proxy-struggles and arms races. The Space Race became one such contest.

Things did not begin well for the United States, with the first attempt to launch an unmanned satellite ending in an explosion on the launch pad in front of a live, worldwide television broadcast. Over the 1960s, though, American technology caught up.

As Armstrong was taking small steps on the Moon, America was making dramatic leaps forward toward national unity. Although slavery had been outlawed in America since Abraham Lincoln's Emancipation Proclamation, black and white Americans were far from unified nearly a century later. In fact, in many places laws existed to enforce segregation between people of different skin colors.

The Civil Rights Movement can be linked to the 1954 *Brown v. Board of Education of Topeka Kansas* Supreme Court decision. This decision ruled that "segregation of white and colored children in public schools has a detrimental effect upon the colored children. The impact is greater when it has the sanction of the law; for the policy of separating the races is usually interpreted as denoting the inferiority of the Negro group." This led to the integration of schools—often amid significant opposition from both blacks and whites!

After a long, mostly non-violent, struggle, Civil Rights were recognized in the Civil Rights Act of 1964. The Act barred discrimination based on "race, color, religion, sex, or national origin" in employment practices and public accommodations.

At Our Fingertips and in His Hands

Electronic computers were initially developed in the 1950s and were used to perform the calculations that would guide rockets through space and back, and they were essentially very powerful abacuses until they learned to talk. In 1982, a new language was standardized. The Internet protocol suite [Transmission Control Protocol / Internet Protocol (TCP/IP)] provided a way for computers to talk to one another over a network of telephone lines.

The precursor to the Internet (ARPANET) was a response to the threat of nuclear attack during the Cold War. Centralized communications were susceptible to sudden, devastating attacks. Decentralized communications that could find a way to get the message through, even if there were major disruptions, were needed. After President Ronald Reagan succeeded in out-competing the Soviet Union and effectively ending the Cold War, this communication network was opened to commercial use by private Internet Service Providers (ISPs).

As bandwidth, processing power, and sophistication increased, the Internet grew incredibly. Personal computers that had enabled people to write papers, play games, and run businesses could now share information with other computers around the world. Interconnected databases with simple, powerful user interfaces began to put an unbelievable amount of knowledge at human fingertips. Communication protocols that supported electronic commerce turned the Internet from a library into a marketplace. The Internet experienced the same communication revolution that America experienced—but at a blinding pace, historically speaking! From simple textual messages to printed pages, to images, to spoken words, to full video messages, the Internet now carries a phenomenal amount of the chatter across our closely connected planet.

The creation of an artificial constellation of navigational satellites in the 1970s, combined with the need to observe our adversaries without coming under attack, has led to the photographic mapping of the entire earth. This has yielded machines that can give us (and others) our position on our planet within a few feet. This capability, integrated into many of our devices, makes it possible for people to know where they are physically located. It also allows them to virtually travel almost anywhere in the world instantaneously. Through online mapping tools, we can check out neighborhoods in Argentina from the comfort of our own homes.

This interconnectivity is not without its price. Our increased dependence on our connections to the conveniences of life has also opened the door for human nature to display its darker side. Identity theft, cyber-crime, pornography, bullying, cyber-weapons, slander, hate, theft, espionage, terrorism, and blackmail have all benefitted from the ubiquity of connectivity. As we go forward into a new century, there are many questions about our privacy and safety from enemies, both foreign and domestic.

Conclusion

In the beginning, God created the heavens and the earth. God placed Man in a Garden and gave it to him to work and to enjoy. Male and female, God created us. We were meant to live full, meaningful, complementary lives in unbroken fellowship with each other and with our Maker. Yet, seeking to be wise, we have become fools, and have exchanged the glory of God for shame and for the worship of images of men and animals and reptiles. But God is not finished.

God's plan for the end of history is clearly written. He who began a good work will be faithful to complete it and to redeem His Creation. We rest in God's hands, looking forward to the day when all will be made new. Until then, we seek to be salt and light, holding out the word of truth in the midst of darkness. As those who follow Christ through His story, we know that our confidence does not rest on our power, but on His.

Mini-Unit 12, Topic 1
Wired Worlds at War

Introduction

After World War I, America entered the Roaring Twenties, a period that was replete with flappers, prohibition, and speakeasies. As the Monty Python sketch says of Camelot, "It was a silly place." After the horrors of World War I, many disillusioned people sought to find an escape in the ridiculous. Many also openly rejected the traditional values of their elders in reaction to the War, since these seemed to have failed. In *Tapestry of Grace*, we note many seeds of the bitter spiritual fruit that were sown during this time. However, this period did not last long. After a decade of headlong pursuit of pleasure, Americans were plunged first into what we now know as the Great Depression and then into World War II.

The Great Depression

America's troubles began with a stock market crash. The first day of widespread panic about falling stock market prices occurred on Thursday, October 24, 1929, but it took five more days for the worst to hit. On Black Tuesday, October 29, investors frantically unloaded 16,000,000 shares. Stocks lost more than $26 billion dollars in value in one day. Some brokers and financiers were so devastated by their financial losses that they committed suicide; a few even leaped out the windows of tall buildings on New York's Wall Street. This was scary for observers, and it helped start a domino effect that led to the Great Depression. What began as one bad week on Wall Street turned into a ten-year economic slump.

Here's how it happened. Many middle-class Americans saw the stock markets as a sure-fire way to get rich. When the markets crashed, many middle-class Americans lost their savings. Some lost more than just their savings. With no savings, they could no longer buy discretionary items that they did not absolutely need. Many manufacturers made these non-essential items. When demand for their products fell, they cut back significantly on production, which meant laying off many workers. In turn, these unemployed people did not spend money on unnecessary goods, since they had been laid off, and a cycle was born.

The cycle was constantly repeated on a national scale: as markets shrank further, more people were laid off, etc. As unemployment soared and people were unable to pay their loans, families pulled their money out of banks, which then had no assets with which to make loans or even, in some cases, cover their deposits when troubled families wanted their money. Banks began to fail—or survived by keeping people from accessing their own accounts. This smaller cycle kept people from putting their money back into the national economy as well.

President Hoover responded to this economic crisis to a degree. He asked American businessmen to maintain prices and wages. He proposed a federal tax cut and interest rate cut, and proposed a plan that would aid home owners who could not meet their payments. This was as far as he was willing to go, since Hoover's principles kept him from directly offering federal funds as handouts to individuals. Tax cuts that let people keep more of the money that they already had was one thing. Giving them money that they could not earn was another. He thought that was not the role of the federal government—instead, he thought states and/or private charities should relieve the needs of the unemployed.

The problem was that state governments and private charities were all overwhelmed by the crisis. They could not handle the widespread and deepening emergency; they were unable to meet the great financial needs that their communities were facing. That left Hoover caught in the middle. While some Americans felt that Hoover was stepping beyond his bounds and turning the government into a radical socialism with the measures that he *did* take, most felt that he wasn't doing enough to help.

When 15,000 war veterans decided to march on Washington to request relief, Hoover refused to budge. Without aid, many of the veterans had nowhere else to go, so they set up camp in shantytowns on the Anacostia Flats near Washington. Hoover ordered General Douglas McArthur to clear them out. Hoover never recovered his political footing with Americans after the widely publicized spectacle of soldiers using tear gas and tanks on impoverished veterans.

Hoover paid a price for his principles. Shantytowns (makeshift houses of cardboard or tin cans, warmed by scrap-wood fires in oil drums) formed in vacant lots or along highways as people lost their homes and jobs and had nowhere else to go. These were disease-ridden, cold, and miserable places, eventually dubbed "Hoovervilles" for the "do-nothing President." Broken-down cars, which became homes for people, were hitched to mules for locomotion. These were derisively called "Hoover wagons." People wrapped themselves in discarded, dirty newspapers to try to keep warm. Cold and homeless people called these "Hoover blankets."

One of the few things Hoover did do about the crisis did more harm than good. In 1930, he supported the Smoot-Hawley Tariff, an Act of Congress which was supposed to protect the American economy by imposing extra costs on foreign producers. Unfortunately, Hoover didn't count on all the foreign countries retaliating by passing their own protective tariffs. Between the general depression and all the new tariffs, the value of world trade fell by more than 50% by 1932.

A natural and man-made disaster called the "Dust Bowl" added to the nation's woes. The Roaring Twenties had not been kind to farmers, but things got worse in 1930 when a severe drought exposed the damages wrought by over-farming and over-grazing the arid lands of the Great Plains. An overabundance of cattle had eaten the prairie grasses right down to the roots. When it didn't rain, there was nothing to hold the dusty soil together. People were driven from their homes on farms by the massive dust storms that destroyed their land and made farming impossible. As these families made their way west to California, they increased the number of unemployed people looking for work and only deepened the problems of the Great Depression.

While Herbert Hoover adopted a hands-off approach, the governor of New York, Franklin Delano Roosevelt (5th cousin of Teddy Roosevelt), adopted a hands-on one. Roosevelt led the New York State government in setting up a Temporary Emergency Relief Administration (TERA) to provide jobs for the unemployed, as well as food, clothing, and shelter for those who had none. His approach was rewarded with his election to the Presidency in 1932. People trusted him at this dark hour to help the economy recover. Roosevelt infused new hope into Americans by his promises of immediate action, his good cheer, and his confidence. They believed him when he said that they had "nothing to fear but fear itself" and promised that he would give them a "New Deal."

Roosevelt did not disappoint the people who voted for him once he took office! He delivered on his promises with immediate action. In the first 100 days of his first administration, Roosevelt proposed (and Congress passed) more new legislation than any administration had ever done in the past. And not only were there a lot of new laws, but collectively the laws themselves created a whole new relationship between the American people and their government. Roosevelt was not only committed to aiding suffering individuals in the short term and to helping the overall economy to improve, he also thought that the federal government should pass laws to ensure that a national economic collapse of such epic proportions could never happen again.

As American leaders struggled to restore the economy of the United States, economic forces and propaganda were aiding a World War I corporal's rise to power in war-torn Germany.

World War I and Hitler's Early Career

Adolf Hitler served in the German army in World War I and reached the rank of lance corporal. He was a courier, a runner who carried messages across the battlefield. It was one of the most dangerous jobs on the front, but Hitler seemed to lead a charmed life. He was fearless at the front—most historians agree that he believed he could not die in the trenches. He seemed to have amazing good fortune, especially when instinct told him to move right before shells landed.

Hitler felt devastated when the war ended. He broke down in tears. The war had given him stature, vocation, and a purpose; now he faced the loss of these. Before the war, he had failed at most of the things he'd tried to do. With the war over, he would go back to the life of a vagabond.

As the Treaty of Versailles and horrific financial conditions of Germany unfolded, Hitler blamed the new Weimar Republic for Germany's ills. He decided that those who led the German government were Jews and communists: the back-stabbers of Germany. It was their fault that Germany had given up fighting the war and had accepted the humiliating treaty, with its admission of responsibility for the war and its crushing financial burden of war reparations. Unfortunately, Hitler was anything but alone in such beliefs. As he worked with subversive elements of the German political scene, he became their leader and decided to use them to gain the power he needed to punish "Germany's enemies" and restore her fortunes.

Hitler had natural gifts that propelled him into a leadership role. He had a good mind; he could think clearly and organize effectively, and he had strong, practical ideas. His artistic talent enabled him to design strong symbols and the flag of a new movement. He resurrected the ancient swastika (a religious symbol from India) as a symbol of anti-Semitism and of the purity of the Aryan race. He placed this strong black symbol in a white circle and then on a field of red, and had it made into flags. Hitler also had enough insight into people to write effective propaganda. He recognized that people were gullible and would believe lies that were repeated. In fact, he came to believe that people would swallow really big lies if these were told with conviction and repeated often enough. Hitler was also an effective orator. He could sway crowds through his speeches—as long as the people started out desperate or disgruntled. His power was almost hypnotic, and it was remarkably lasting. Once people were swayed, Hitler commanded great loyalty among his listeners.

In 1923, Hitler tried to take over his home state of Bavaria. He had 15,000 brown-shirted followers armed with rifles or machine guns. At a rally in a beer hall in Munich, the capital of Bavaria, Hitler proclaimed a Nazi revolution. He tried to seize the state government the next day. The police opened fire and killed sixteen of his men. Hitler was arrested, convicted, and sentenced to five years in prison.

He only spent nine months in jail, and he used the time to write a book he called *Mein Kampf*—"My Struggle." There he revealed his core beliefs: anti-Semitism, racism, and the Big Lie are all recorded in *Mein Kampf* in detail. Like Lenin, Hitler preached war and believed that struggle was "the father of all things." "God the Father," Hitler wrote, "intended nations to fight until the stronger won. He who wants to live must fight … and he who does not want to do battle in this world of eternal struggle does not deserve to be alive." Hitler made it clear that once he came to power, he intended to "end democracy, abolish civil liberties, destroy the workers' trade unions, [and] set up a police state."

Hitler also planned to rebuild the German military and take back every inch of territory lost by Germany in World War I. He was intent on both preserving the "purity" of the German race and in expanding its territory for its growing population in Eastern Europe. Hitler thought the Slavs who inhabited the land to the east were worthless: he planned to use them as slaves or to exterminate them as vermin. He claimed Slavic lands like Poland and Russia as *lebensraum*—"room to live." But for Germans to live in the lands to the east, Slavs must die. This would be a positive thing, in Hitler's way of thinking.

No one paid attention to Hitler's book because he was a "nobody" when it was published. The book was also difficult to read, and the first editions were riddled with errors. No scholar of the day took it seriously, and no one in politics did either—until it was much too late.

Hitler Takes Power with Propaganda

The dark clouds of war were gathering. The economic crisis in Germany that resulted from World War I and its harsh treaty helped Hitler take over. Desperate and discontented Germans turned from their traditional leaders to radicals on the left and right. Many Germans were angry that life was so hard, and they blamed either losses in World War I or the current government for their troubles. Hitler's propaganda purposefully capitalized on these feelings and inflamed them.

Hitler used thugs—untrained bullies who loved violence and torment—to intimidate and even murder opponents. One can think of these men as counterparts to American gangsters, except even more brutal. These were called the Brown Shirts. Hitler used radio ads, the press, books, and speeches to promote his "big lies" and also to misinform the German people about any events that challenged his regime. Hitler consistently used whatever power he had to seize more. Thus did he soon make himself the master of Germany.

Hitler's ambitions were furthered by other extremist leaders: Benito Mussolini and Francisco Franco. Benito Mussolini of Italy was a fascist like Hitler. He had a much poorer country, but he had big ambitions. Generalissimo Francisco Franco of Spain wasn't a Fascist, exactly—unlike Hitler and Mussolini, who wanted to create a whole new kind of society in Germany and Italy, Franco wanted to take Spain back to its Catholic roots. Fascist or not, Franco launched a revolution in Spain and spent the next four years fighting a civil war. Hitler used this conflict as a training ground for his troops!

Japan was another country with big ambitions. Unlike the European fascist states, Japan had no single dictator. Instead, a group of military leaders sought the greater glory of Japan by conquest. They did not directly aid Hitler in his rise to power, but they became an important ally of Germany in World War II.

All of these forces and people set the stage for the return of world war. It would be carried out with even greater devastation than the one before. The armed descendants of the Wright Brothers' airplane (bombers and fighters) and the automobile (tanks) would wage war across continents and oceans before the guns of war were silenced by the explosions of the first atomic bombs.

World War II[1]

It started with Poland. In *Mein Kampf*, Adolf Hitler said the German super race of Aryans needed *lebensraum*—room to live—in order to multiply, prosper, and fulfill their destiny. He looked on neighboring Poland as the place to start. In Hitler's opinion, the Slavs and Jews of Eastern Europe were unfit to live; they would become slaves as long as they were useful, and then they would die. On September 1, at Hitler's word, the Germans invaded Poland without warning. Using highly coordinated modern war machines, the Germans conducted a *blitzkrieg*—a German term meaning "lightning war."

Hitler first ordered a squadron of bombers to destroy the Polish air bases, railway stations, military headquarters, and ammunition centers. Once this was accomplished, dive bombers attacked the front line of the Polish troops. Tanks and other vehicles pushed through the weak spots in the Polish line and then attacked the Poles from behind. Lastly, large numbers of foot soldiers handled any further resistance. The *blitzkrieg* against Poland took only a number of days. Although the Polish army was larger than the German army, the Poles had fewer tanks and aircraft and could not withstand the power of the attack.

The Poles in lands further to the east could not help their brothers: seventeen days after Germany's invasion, according to a secret agreement between Hitler and Stalin, Russian troops overran eastern Poland. As soon as they were in control, both conquering armies set about taking political and cultural prisoners and began the systematic extermination of millions of "undesirable" people. Hitler sent in the SS (Nazi special forces) to kill Jews and anyone who might oppose him.

The Western democracies had warned Hitler that they would declare war with Germany if Poland was attacked. They dutifully did so, but there's a difference between declaring war and fighting it. It was too late for the western allies to do nothing to prevent Hitler's and Stalin's overthrow of Poland. After its sudden and complete overthrow, though their countries were at war, Germany and the Allies (primarily England and France) did not exchange hostilities for about eight months. Both sides mobilized troops and laid plans for a clash in Western Europe.

Western Front

When the fighting began, Hitler attacked Norway and Denmark, subduing them

---

[1] Although these introductory notes are unusually long, we want to provide you with a summary of the major turning points of World War II. Since your youngest student will not study this in detail, it's optional for you to take the time to read through these sections.

quickly so as to have control over key air and naval bases there. Again, his *blitzkrieg* was spectacularly successful; Denmark and Norway fell within two weeks as the Western powers failed to stop him.

Hitler then turned to the strong defenses of France. France had spent decades building an impregnable line of defense against Germany on its western borders. Hitler had a simple solution for this Maginot Line: he went around it. He attacked the Low Countries: the Netherlands, Belgium, and little Luxembourg. The Germans pierced the Allied defenses in Belgium and then swept through the Netherlands. Belgium fell in a day and the Netherlands in five days: Hitler's version of the Schlieffen Plan had worked. Then the Battle of France began.

It is arguable that, if the Allies had taken action sooner and chosen the location of the front lines, Hitler would not have had the ability to circumvent the Maginot Line. As a result of earlier diplomatic mistakes concerning Czechoslovakia and then Hitler's success in the Low Countries, British Prime Minister Neville Chamberlain ultimately lost the confidence of his constituents and was forced to resign. King George VI named the head of the war cabinet, Winston Churchill, as the new prime minister.

Dunkirk and Winston Churchill

The speed with which the German armies moved caught a large Allied force off guard. The Allied army was cut off in northern France by a German armored advance to the English Channel coast at Calais, France. Over 330,000 Allied troops were thus caught with Germans advancing from the south and northeast. These hundreds of thousands of men could not be reached by larger troop carriers because the harbor was choked with wrecked ships. They had to stand out to sea. Men could not swim to the ships, and they could not transport their heavy machinery without vessels.

Churchill, who had only been prime minister for a couple of weeks, put out an urgent call, and private citizens from Great Britain, the Netherlands, Belgium, France, and Poland set out in whatever small boats they had to brave the murderous artillery and bombardment from German aircraft and take Allied soldiers off the beaches to safety in England. Over 300,000 men—the bulk of the British Army—were thus transported safely off the beach at Dunkirk and miraculously saved.

This amazing rescue prompted one of Winston Churchill's most famous speeches. The day that the last man was pulled off the beaches of Dunkirk, Churchill stood on the floor of the House of Commons and said:

> We shall go on to the end, we shall fight in France, we shall fight on the seas

and oceans, we shall fight with growing confidence and growing strength in the air, we shall defend our Island, whatever the cost may be, we shall fight on the beaches, we shall fight on the landing grounds, we shall fight on the fields and in the streets, we shall fight in the hills, we shall never surrender…

The event gave much-needed cheer to the British, but it left the French to face Germany alone. France signed an armistice shortly thereafter. Winston Churchill solemnly announced, "The Battle of France is over. I expect the Battle of Britain is about to begin."

Battle of Britain

Churchill was right. With Italy and Germany linked as the Axis powers, France fallen, the Low Countries occupied, Scandinavia occupied or neutralized, and Spain under Franco, Germany's only opposition in Western Europe was Britain. Hitler launched Operation Sea Lion: Germany's attempt to invade Britain

Operation Sea Lion began with the task of achieving air superiority over the English Channel. The commander-in-chief of the German Luftwaffe was Field Marshal Hermann Goering. Goering planned to draw British planes into battle by attacking convoy ships in the Channel. Once the planes came out, the Germans would destroy them and prepare for the invasion. Goering thought he could neutralize the Royal Air Force (RAF) in a matter of days.

Goering underestimated the RAF, however. In the dogfights over the Channel during the summer and autumn of 1940, the RAF destroyed 600 Luftwaffe planes—twice as many as the RAF lost. Goering responded by ordering attacks on British airfields and airplane factories. The RAF struggled for survival.

Then, one day, the Germans bombed London by accident. It was an outrage to attack a civilian target—but it gave Churchill an opportunity to trick Hitler into making a strategic mistake. Churchill sent the RAF to bomb Berlin in retaliation. Churchill hoped Hitler would lose his focus on the strategic goal of taking out the RAF—and it worked. Hitler was furious about the bombing of Berlin and ordered Goering to focus on bombing London. Thus, on September 7, 1940, began the "Blitz" that lasted until May 1941. The Blitz included both daytime and nighttime bombing of London and other cities. If your family has read *The Lion, the Witch and the Wardrobe* by C.S. Lewis (or seen the movie), you will understand why the four children in that book were sent to the Professor's house in the country. Many British parents sent their children out of London during this dangerous time.

Churchill praised the brave young men of the air who held off the Luftwaffe, famously saying, "Never in the field of human conflict was so much owed by so many to so few."[1] The Blitz was a time of terror for Londoners—but it gave Britain the time it desperately needed. Although the Blitz caused a great deal of damage in cities, the RAF had time to repair its airfields and rebuild itself. The Germans' failure to destroy the RAF was the turning point in the Battle of Britain. Hitler was forced to recognize, for the first time in the war, that his will had been thwarted.

Air War over Europe

As the Battle of Britain subsided, bombs began falling on Berlin. Roosevelt later noted in 1944, "Hitler built a fortress around Europe, but he forgot to put a roof on it!"[2] Raids on Hamburg and Dresden set so many houses on fire that it produced a lethal updraft of flame and oxygen called a firestorm. Between 300,000 and 600,000 German civilians were killed by Allied bombs before the war was over.

First, under the Lend-Lease Act that enabled Americans to send help to the Allies in the form of war material, and then later, as America entered the war after Pearl Harbor, American factories churned out long-range heavy bombers. These had some success, but were plagued by the stiff defense of short-range German fighters. The toll taken on bomber crews was devastating, both directly and indirectly. Downed Allied fliers filled the German *stalags* (prisoner of war camps). A better long-range fighter escort was needed to protect the bombers. In a brilliant example of rapid engineering, the North American Aviation group developed and flew a prototype in less than six months. By 1943, this prototype had become the P-51 Mustang, the workhorse long-range escort fighter of World War II.

Eastern Front

After the beginning of the war, with Britain holding out against Germany, Hitler decided to turn on Stalin. In December, 1940, he started making plans to invade Russia. In June of 1941, he launched Operation Barbarossa, which sent 4.5 million soldiers into the Soviet Union. At first, many Russians hailed the Germans as liberators who had come to free them from Stalin's violent rule. Soon, however, the Russians discovered that the Germans viewed them with racial contempt, believing them to be inferior beings marked for destruction.

---

1 History Learning Site. Accessed 10 February 2014. Retrieved from <http://www.historylearningsite.co.uk/never_field_human_conflict.htm>.
2 *Always Out Front*. Accessed 10 February 2014. Retrieved from <http://www.ibiblio.org/hyperwar/AAF/Bradley/Bradley-7.html>.

Hitler ordered a three-pronged attack: one army group went north to Leningrad (originally named and now renamed St. Petersburg), one group went east to Moscow, and one group went south into Ukraine. At first, the German armies cut through Russia like a hot knife through butter. But the *blitzkrieg* tactics that worked so well in small and middle-sized countries broke down in a nation as vast as Russia. Tanks could race hundreds of miles into enemy territory, but they had to be supported by foot soldiers at some point—and it took weeks for them to walk across Russia. The northern and southern German army groups were bogged down.

Hitler ordered the middle army group—the one headed for Moscow—to slow down its advance so that all three would achieve simultaneous victories. When his generals asked for extra supplies for winter fighting, he turned them down. He insisted that the army would triumph in short order and that neither the soldiers' clothing nor their war machinery needed to be prepared for winter.

Both decisions proved to be arrogant—and disastrous. Napoleon had learned how hard Russia can be on invaders. As the Soviet Army stiffened its resistance, Hitler's forces slowed. The Germans were caught far from home by Russia's old ally: winter. The German war machine broke down on the vast plains of Russia and Ukraine.

German General Friedrich von Paulus thought he could take the southern city of Stalingrad in a day, but he was terribly wrong. Stalingrad was a large city with many factories and steel works. It was also a major transport hub and had a large population. The Soviets resisted the German onslaught fiercely; they were stubborn defenders and fought the invaders for each room, floor, and building of the city. Because the city had been bombed, the rubble gave important cover for the Soviets who defended the city. As the Soviets received reinforcements and grew stronger, the German assault faltered.

Instead of being done in one day, the assault on Stalingrad dragged on through the fall. With winter approaching, General von Paulus requested permission from Hitler to leave Stalingrad before his army was destroyed by the cold and the continued advances of the Soviets. Hitler would not let his army retreat. Because the army was ill-prepared for the harsh Russian winter, Paulus' men began to freeze to death. Although he was assured that they would receive supplies, the German planes could not deliver them. They were attacked by Russian fighters and prevented from flying by freezing fog. Those planes that did get through were simply too few to adequately supply the starving, freezing army. Meanwhile, the Soviets grew in strength and numbers and surrounded Stalingrad. Paulus surrendered to the Soviets on January 31, 1943. It was a major turning point of the Russian front. Six months later, at the Battle of Kursk, Soviet forces overcame the German Army and started to drive them back.

The Soviets on Germany's eastern front marched relentlessly westward towards Berlin. On June 22, 1944, three years to the day after the Germans had invaded the USSR, the Soviets launched a huge assault against the German Army Group Centre. The Germans were totally defeated. Throughout late 1944, the Soviets continued to advance toward Germany. (By this time, Americans were fighting and closing in on Berlin from the West, but Eisenhower stopped his men at the Elbe River and allowed the Soviets to take Berlin.) The Battle of Berlin between the Soviet and German armies began on April 16, 1945. By April 24, the city was surrounded by the Soviet army. As the Soviets made their way through the city, they were merciless to the Germans, committing many crimes against the German civilians who remained in the city.

The Soviet push resulted in large amounts of German territory being under Soviet control at the end of the war, foreshadowing a sharply divided Germany that would persist until the end of the Cold War between the USA and the USSR, when the Berlin Wall was toppled in 1989.

Pacific Theater

Let's look at America's entry into the war. Before Japan attacked Pearl Harbor, most Americans felt strongly about staying out of the war in Europe. Although they did not support Hitler's aggression and did aid the Allies, they did not want to participate actively in the war. Americans weren't eager to get into a war with Japan, either, although there were growing concerns.

The Japanese Empire had started on one island chain but now included big chunks of Asia. Japan took Formosa from China in 1895, part of Sakhalin Island from Russia in 1905, Korea from Russia in 1910, Manchuria from China in 1931, Inner Mongolia in 1936, and invaded China directly in 1937. Japan had joined the Axis powers in 1936 with Germany in order to combat communism. America supported China's effort to fight back, but wasn't directly involved in the war. Then, suddenly and without warning, world news got personal. On a Monday morning, Americans heard their President's voice coming over the radio:

> Yesterday, December 7, 1941—a date which will live in infamy—the United States of America was suddenly and deliberately attacked by naval and air forces of the Empire of Japan.

FDR explained that America had been at peace with Japan, and was actively and intentionally deceived by the Japanese, who planned their sneak attack far in advance. He told the shocked Americans of the extent of the damage to U.S. and other forces:

The attack yesterday on the Hawaiian Islands has caused severe damage to American naval and military forces. I regret to tell you that very many American lives have been lost. In addition, American ships have been reported torpedoed on the high seas between San Francisco and Honolulu.

Yesterday the Japanese government also launched an attack against Malaya.

Last night Japanese forces attacked Hong Kong.

Last night Japanese forces attacked Guam.

Last night Japanese forces attacked the Philippine Islands.

Last night Japanese forces attacked Wake Island.

And this morning the Japanese attacked Midway Island.[1]

Congress immediately declared war on Japan. Japan's ally, Germany, declared war on the United States. That was just the first of many wartime radio addresses by FDR, who successfully used them to inspire Americans to rise to the new challenges of this global conflict. Factories started churning out supplies and munitions. The United States mobilized the largest military force in history. The Great Depression ended as the U.S. economy roared into life.

After Pearl Harbor, the Japanese scrambled to expand their empire before the United States could strike back. For six months, their lightning campaign to take over the Asian Pacific was successful. They targeted and occupied the Allies' colonies in the Pacific and Far East, including Hong Kong, Burma (now Myanmar), Malaysia, Borneo, the Philippines, and Singapore. The United States built up its forces fast. When it did, it fought back hard. Americans stopped the Japanese advance across the Pacific in the Battle of the Coral Sea. The American victory at the Battle of Midway was Japan's first major defeat and became the turning point of the war in the Pacific.

Japan had counted on being able to beat the U.S. Navy, but Americans effectively combined naval and air forces in their attacks in the Pacific. Although aircraft carriers had been built during World War I, this conflict was the first time they had been used in combat. During World War II, aircraft carriers became the world's most powerful weapon. Before the aircraft carrier, planes were limited by the range of their engines, and Japan was relatively safe from the devastating air war that Europe experienced. Planes had to take off and land on airstrips. The Pacific Ocean is huge, and the Allies often lacked islands with enough flat surface for a runway at strategically necessary

---

1 Digital History. Accessed 10 February 2014. Retrieved from <http://www.digitalhistory.uh.edu/disp_textbook.cfm?smtID=3&psid=1082>.

positions. Aircraft carriers changed all that, since they were movable airstrips that brought almost any location within the reach of America's bombs and fighters.

After the Japanese advance had been stopped, the Allies began the arduous task of reclaiming territory that had been seized by the Japanese. They did this in a series of assaults on various islands in the Pacific, leapfrogging from one hard-won island to the next. The Japanese controlled large islands like the Philippines and tiny atolls like Okinawa and Iwo Jima. They would not relinquish one inch of these islands without making the Allies pay dearly in blood. The Japanese cultural and military values compelled them never to surrender but to die fighting. And so they did, month after month, as the Allies liberated first one island and then another at the cost of many lives and much heartache.

The Japanese proved themselves fierce warriors who chose death before dishonor. Kamikaze pilots steered their planes into American ships at the cost of their own lives. Japanese soldiers blew themselves up if they could take out one more Allied soldier by doing so. As they drew near to Japan itself, the Allies assumed the Japanese would fight even harder for their home islands if they were invaded. Every prudent calculation said it would take at least half a million Allied casualties to conquer Japan. Most assumed a million.

North Africa and Italy

Let's turn from the war with Japan to the fighting in Europe and Africa. Allied and Axis tanks fought each other in the deserts of North Africa, a harsh but strategic wasteland. Although Allied bombers pounded Europe from above, the war could not be won with air power alone. The Allies needed to take the fight to Hitler on the ground, and that meant finding a way into Europe. Hitler had strongly defended the coastline of "Fortress Europe," but Allied leaders thought that there might be a way in through the Italian underbelly controlled by the less-effective Mussolini. North Africa could serve as a base to invade Italy, and both sides wanted the Suez Canal, which controlled access to the Red Sea.

German Field Marshal Erwin Rommel, nicknamed "the Desert Fox," was one of Hitler's best commanders. He fought brilliantly, but was defeated at the Battle of El Alamein by British General Bernard L. Montgomery. A few months later, Montgomery was joined by three American commanders who would become famous: Dwight D. Eisenhowever, George S. Patton, and Omar Bradley. Together, they coordinated Operation Torch, which combined the U.S. and British invasion of North Africa.

Japan and Germany were totally committed—but Italy was not, and Italy was in trouble. The Allied victory at El Alamein in North Africa in 1942 pushed Axis forces back to Tunisia, just a hundred miles across the Mediterranean from the Italian island of Sicily. In early 1943, when the Allies broke through the last defenses at Tunis, 230,000 German and Italian troops surrendered. Allied troops invaded Sicily and prepared to cross over to the mainland.

Hitler realized he had made a mistake in picking Italy for an ally. That summer, at his orders, Mussolini was deposed and imprisoned. The Italians secretly negotiated with the Allies for surrender, but Hitler sent troops to hold Italy against the Allied forces. After months of bitter fighting, Allied forces liberated Rome.

The Western Front–Again

No amount of bombs could replace "boots on the ground." The Allies knew they had to break through immense German fortifications along the Atlantic Coast. On June 6, 1944, one day after the Allies liberated Rome, they launched their greatest operation of the war: D-Day.

Allied leaders selected five points along the northern coast of France for British, American, and Canadian armies to land. The preparations for the landing were extraordinary—many books have been written about all the special weapons, logistics, and maneuvers that made it all possible. On the night before the invasion, paratroopers dropped behind the enemy line to disrupt German communications. Meanwhile, the trip across the Channel commenced in the dark: 9,000 aircraft covered the fleet of 5,000 ships as they moved across the southern part of the English Channel towards the Normandy coast. At dawn on June 6, 1944, the D-Day landing commenced. By the evening, 150,000 Allied troops had successfully landed in Normandy and established beachheads.

Once they took the beach, the Allies went for Paris. George S. Patton led the breakout from Normandy. It was quick—Allied troops swept through northern France and liberated Paris on August 25, 1944. It seemed like the German troops were melting away.

Hitler ordered one last major offensive against the Allies. On December 16, the Germans attacked the American forces stationed in the Ardennes Forest of Luxembourg and southern Belgium. Hitler hit the weak American lines by surprise and created a massive bulge in the lines. But General Patton led a brilliant counterattack that drove the enemy back. That Battle of the Bulge broke the back of Hitler's western front.

Beginning of the End

As the Allies closed in, Hitler began to wonder whether the Germans were truly worthy of him. He came to believe that everyone around him had failed him. On April 29, 1945, Hitler married his long-time mistress, Eva Braun. The next day, he and Eva committed suicide in a bunker beneath Berlin. Soviet troops were already in Berlin as he died. The Germans immediately offered to surrender. V-E day—Victory in Europe—was declared on May 8, 1945.

At the announcement, Americans were filled with joy—and sorrow. President Franklin D. Roosevelt had led them through the Great Depression and the world's greatest war, but he died two weeks before Hitler killed himself. Vice President Harry S. Truman, a plain-spoken Missouri man, became President. It was Truman who saw "Victory in Europe" day declared—and Truman who made the fateful decisions that ended the war with Japan.

Manhattan Project

Truman was briefed on a number of national security matters after he took office. On April 24 (five days before Hitler's death), Truman was stunned to find out that America had been working on a super-bomb. The "Manhattan Project" was so top secret that the Vice President of the United States didn't even know about it—and now he had to decide whether or not to use it. As we saw in the summary of the Pacific theater, there was a reason why he made the choice he did.

The Japanese had not yielded one inch of territory easily. Truman decided that Japanese civilians, not American soldiers, must pay the price for the stand that the Japanese military leaders had chosen to take. It took two atomic bombs to humble them. The Japanese officials couldn't believe what they heard about the devastation after the first atomic bomb fell on Hiroshima, so Americans showed their determination by dropping a second atomic bomb on Nagasaki, the only Christian city in Japan. More than 210,000 Japanese civilians died in those two blasts. The emperor of Japan capitulated: he announced Japan's surrender on August 15, 1945, which became known as V-J (Victory over Japan) Day.

World War II was finally over.

Conclusion

Hitler and FDR took office within a few months of each other, rising to power during the Great Depression on both sides of the Atlantic. Both made vast and arguably unconstitutional changes to their respective countries. Elites in Berlin and Washington alike believed the free market had failed and called for government intervention—and Hitler and FDR each obliged. But, though there were these eerie similarities between the men, there were vast differences.

Roosevelt enraged Republicans, but he never needed secret police to maintain his power. He was popularly elected and remained popular through his unprecedented four terms in office. Roosevelt offered help to Americans in need. Hitler, by contrast, used thugs and the distress of others to climb to the heights of personal power. His core message was an offer of revenge to Germans who felt humiliated. FDR promised to pay more people. Hitler promised to make people pay!

The 1930s were a time of trouble: economic distress, rising dictators, and military adventures. Hard times put hard men in power. People around the world were in distress, and they cried out for answers. Men like Hitler, Mussolini, and Franco offered answers. "Give me power," they said, "and I will save you." They got the power they asked for—but they did not save. There's a saying: "Power corrupts, and absolute power corrupts absolutely." It doesn't apply to Hitler. Hitler had no power when he languished in a German jail writing *Mein Kampf*, yet he spelled out his principles and his plans in detail. Power didn't corrupt Hitler. Hitler was corrupt already.

Does that seem judgmental? It isn't. Hitler was corrupt—and so are you and I. All humans are. Power does not corrupt, for God has all power, and He is perfect. Power just removes the restraints that keep corrupt people like you and me from showing our true colors.

Ultimately, Hitler was defeated. The biggest war in human history was over—a war in which a million died in a single battle, where cities died with a single bomb, where more than eight million people were killed just for being Jewish. The men and women who struggled those times have been called "The Greatest Generation" for good reason. One reason to study this inglorious era of our history is that we can learn from their example as we lead future generations forward and face forces of wickedness in our own days.

Mini-Unit 12, Topic 2
One Small Step for Man

Introduction

Even as World War II ended, the alliance of convenience between the Soviet Union and the other Allies began to erode. Winston Churchill's "Sinews of Peace" address of March 5, 1946, at Westminster College, used the term "iron curtain" in the context of Soviet-dominated Eastern Europe:

> From Stettin in the Baltic to Trieste in the Adriatic, an "Iron Curtain" has descended across the continent. Behind that line lie all the capitals of the ancient states of Central and Eastern Europe. Warsaw, Berlin, Prague, Vienna, Budapest, Belgrade, Bucharest and Sofia; all these famous cities and the populations around them lie in what I must call the Soviet sphere, and all are subject, in one form or another, not only to Soviet influence but to a very high and in some cases increasing measure of control from Moscow.

The tensions between former Allies eventually centered on the relationships between the United States and the USSR. As the embers of World War II died out, a Cold War began, predicated on the grim reality of the atomic bomb and the threat of mutually assured destruction.

Under this cloud, Americans came home from World War II and tried to settle back into life at home. Soldiers bought houses and started families. Housewives ran their homes using the new appliances that American factories began producing. As Americans from all walks of life came home from fighting for freedom overseas, domestic issues of injustice came to the forefront.

This week, your student will be learning about the ongoing efforts of Martin Luther King, Jr. and the movement to obtain civil rights for black Americans during these years.

There's another new thread that we will follow together through this week: the Space Race. Beginning with the Soviets' surprising launch of Sputnik, the world's first satellite, we will learn how the superpowers fought the Cold War by conducting a race to see which of them could put a man first into orbit around the earth and then send men to walk on the moon.

New technologies will continue to play a major role in the cultural changes that unfold in this topic. We'll encourage your student to go on a scavenger hunt to find different household appliances that were mass-produced after American factories stopped making planes and tanks at the end of World War II. It's a long list, and includes your washing machine, refrigerator, and vacuum cleaner.

During this period, America became better connected by the Interstate Highway System, the original portion of which was under construction from 1956 to 1992 (but it is still being expanded today). Designed as an aid to fast troop movement within America during the Cold War years, it enabled civilian car owners and commercial carriers to travel freely at high speeds throughout the country.

Even more transformational and disruptive was the increased use of television. The 1950s has been called by many the "Golden Age" of television. Half of middle-class families became able to afford a TV sometime during that decade. TV became the dominant feature in most living rooms and the most common evening entertainment. It was a subtle feature of the decade that families turned from reading aloud or talking together to clustering around their TVs together. Evening schedules began to be regulated by the times that shows aired. Social interactions inside and outside the family began to be dictated by TV programming, and the fact that shows were aired from coast to coast helped to unify American culture in new ways.

Civil Rights Movement

As we learned in the last mini-unit, Reconstruction efforts at equalizing the rights of black freedmen after the Civil War were largely abandoned in failure. Southern states were left to determine how they would handle their governments' and societies' relations with the newly freed slaves, and their response was to oppress them wherever they could.

Although black Americans were guaranteed equal rights to vote under Reconstruction-era Constitutional amendments, racial tensions in the South resulted in a system of segregation that perpetuated racism into the 1950s. "Jim Crow" segregation laws had been passed regionally by Southern states. While not what was intended by either the civil rights amendments to the Constitution or those who sought full reconstruction of the Union after the Civil War, segregation was permitted by the Supreme Court in the infamous *Plessy v. Ferguson* case in 1896.

In January, 1953, 21 states operated what were called "separate but equal" public schools for black and white children. Sixteen months later, in 1954, the Supreme Court ruled in *Brown v. Board of Education* that segregated public schools violated the Constitution's guarantee of equal protection under law but did not issue any directions about how the states should change their schools. A year later, the Supreme Court answered the outstanding questions of *Brown v. Board*—it did not order states to let black children into white schools immediately, but instructed states to begin a gradual, court-enforced process of integration "with all deliberate speed." This was a highly explosive issue for all Americans!

The effort to desegregate the public schools hit a major snag in 1957 when Arkansas governor Orval Faubus ordered the Arkansas National Guard to block the access of nine black students to a high school in Little Rock, defying the Supreme Court's 1954 *Brown v. Board* decision. President Eisenhower had tried to avoid the controversy over desegregation, but Governor Faubus' disobedience was a direct challenge that Ike could not ignore. He sent 1,200 U.S. Army paratroopers to Little Rock to escort the black students into the high school. Television showed battle-ready U.S. soldiers being mobilized to defend nine black high school children. Many Americans were shocked.

That was a step forward in the march toward racial equality—but just one small step. There was no lasting change in Little Rock. After those teenagers finished that year at the public high school, Governor Faubus shut down every public high school in Little Rock, and some whites put their children in private schools. Things seemed to be getting worse for blacks in Little Rock, and Governor Faubus became a hero to Southern whites. Civil rights for blacks seemed like a lost cause.

Martin Luther King, Jr.

The *Brown v. Board* decision shocked and angered white southerners, who declared a campaign of "massive resistance" to what they saw as a federal attack on their way of life. But it also stirred a new generation of activists who sought to end

American racism once and for all. The most famous of these was Martin Luther King, Jr.

King was born in Atlanta in 1929, the year the stock market crashed. Young Martin was a bright boy—he skipped 9th and 12th grades and then progressed through college, seminary, and graduate school. He got a Ph.D. in theology from Boston College in 1955, then moved back down south and took a job as a minister. But King quickly discovered his life's work: organizing non-violent protests against racial injustice. King was not perfect, but he was a brave man who changed America. It started when one black woman named Rosa Parks went to jail because she refused to give up her seat to a white rider on a city bus.

King helped lead a boycott of the segregated public bus system in Montgomery, Alabama. One of King's heroes was Mohandas Gandhi, who led India's non-violent bid for independence from Britain. King intentionally followed Gandhi's example of non-violent non-cooperation, but unlike Gandhi, he articulated his vision in explicitly Christian terms. When terrorists bombed his house in January, 1956, King rushed home to find angry black men getting ready to attack the white policemen. He begged them to put their weapons down. King described what happened next in his autobiography. He said:

> If you have weapons, take them home; if you do not have them, please do not seek to get them. We cannot solve this problem through retaliatory violence. We must meet violence with nonviolence. Remember the words of Jesus: 'He who lives by the sword will perish by the sword.'

King urged them to leave peacefully.

> We must love our white brothers no matter what they do to us. We must make them know that we love them. Jesus still cries out in words that echo across the centuries: 'Love your enemies; bless them that curse you; pray for them that despitefully use you.' This is what we must live by. We must meet hate with love.

It took over a year and a Supreme Court case, but the city of Montgomery finally agreed to integrate the buses.

Then, one day in February, 1960, four black college students entered a Woolworth's department store and asked to be served at the "white-only" lunch counter. They were ignored by the serving staff, but they sat there peacefully until closing time. The next day, more students joined the "sit-in." After that event in 1960, sit-ins became a popular form of opposition, and the Civil Rights movement gained fresh momentum. In a sit-in, people would remain seated in a public place until they were either forced out or had their complaints addressed.

Martin Luther King, Jr. saw the potential of the sit-ins early on. It was a non-violent form of protest, like the ones Gandhi had successfully used in India during its battle for independence from British rule. This technique proved effective because it revealed the moral weaknesses of the oppressors, who often relied on brute force to remove the demonstrators. Not only did non-violent demonstrations display the flaws of the legal authorities, they gained sympathy for demonstrators from onlookers. Sit-ins were made-for-TV events: broadcasts of sit-ins played a large part in their effectiveness as wider audiences became aware of local conflicts.

Unlike the bus boycott in Montgomery, Alabama from 1955-1956, the sit-ins broke the law. Blacks were prohibited by law from sitting at the whites-only counters throughout the South, but they peacefully defied these segregation laws in 1960. Their example inspired young adults of the Baby Boom generation. White college students across America began to stream south to join the protests. The white Student Non-Violent Coordinating Committee (SNVCC) volunteers became the "shock troops" of the Civil Rights movement.

Civil Rights advocates sought to bring attention to injustices and to enforce equal treatment for all Americans, regardless of race. In 1963, Martin Luther King, Jr. delivered his famous "I Have A Dream" speech on the steps of the Lincoln Memorial in Washington, DC.

In response, President Kennedy proposed legislation that would become the Civil Rights Act of 1964. Kennedy's assassination on November 22, 1963 interrupted the legislative process. Interestingly, the legislation was initially blocked by Southern legislators. It would not be signed into law until President Lyndon Johnson was able to get the bill through Congress with the support of Northern Senators and Congressmen, despite a 54-day filibuster on the Senate floor. The Act barred discrimination based on "race, color, religion, sex or national origin" in employment practices and public accommodations.

Eventually, President Lyndon B. Johnson signed the Civil Rights Act of 1964, but laws don't change people—enforcement does. Many Southern blacks remained understandably terrified of whites who did not care about the law's authority. The right to vote was still seriously undercut by a number of Southern state regulations, such as the poll tax, limited registration days, difficult forms, "citizen tests," and other requirements that made it virtually impossible for black people to vote. Where racists dominated the state legislatures, black Americans were still in trouble.

Martin Luther King, Jr. and many others continued the struggle for full and equal rights for blacks. King's leadership in Selma, Alabama in 1965 focused the nation's attention on white violence against black protesters. In Selma, black voter suppression had been practiced to such an extent that only 2% of blacks were registered to vote. King led a 5-day, 54-mile march to draw national attention to the situation.

Lyndon B. Johnson was forced to take a stand for or against full voting rights for blacks—and finally announced that he was sending new legislation to Congress. The Voting Rights Act of 1965 outlawed literacy tests, poll taxes, and other tactics southern states had used to keep blacks from voting. On paper, at least, blacks finally had full civil and political rights in America.

The Space Race

Now, let's turn to space. On October 5, 1957, the USSR launched Sputnik into orbit around the earth. Especially because of the background of the Cold War, Americans were shocked and dismayed that the rival superpower should have overtaken them in a highly technical advance. Americans thought of themselves as the global technology leaders and of Russia as underdeveloped in this area. So, America's first reaction was surprise—followed quickly by fear. If the Soviets could send satellites overhead, could they not develop nuclear bombs? Americans stared up into the evening sky and trembled. They could actually see their enemy overhead!

From fear, many Americans quickly passed on to anger. Many said that, if the Soviets had moved ahead in science, then America's schools must have failed! Science education suddenly became a matter of national security, right down to the grade school level. Congress passed the National Defense Education Act less than a year later, which offered funding for scholarships for science students in college and graduate schools.

The Soviets had won the first round of the Space Race by launching the first man-made satellite, Sputnik 1, into the October sky. Early attempts of the United States to duplicate this success met with humiliating failure. The Project Vanguard launch failure in 1957 occurred in front of the first live television broadcast of a rocket countdown in the United States. The rocket launch was a catastrophe, and the rocket exploded a few seconds after launch. America was the laughingstock of the world's newspapers. The satellite appeared in various newspapers under the names Flopnik, Stayputnik, Kaputnik, and Dudnik. In the United Nations, the Russian delegate offered the U.S. representative aid "under the Soviet program of technical assistance to backwards nations.[1]

Embarrassed, the United States went back to the drawing board and successfully launched the Explorer 1 satellite four months after Sputnik 1 took to the skies. The Space Race escalated when the Soviets successfully put the first cosmonaut (Yuri Gagarin) into orbit in 1961. A month after Gagarin's famous flight, President John F. Kennedy declared a national objective of "landing a man on the Moon and returning him safely to the earth" by the end of the decade. On February 20, 1962, America took its first big step in that direction—astronaut John Glenn orbited the earth. Throughout the 1960s, both sides traded successes and failures.

On July 20, 1969, Neil Armstrong accomplished half of President Kennedy's goal as the commander of the Apollo 11 mission by taking "one small step for man, one giant leap for mankind." The rest of the mission was accomplished with the successful return of Apollo 11 on July 24, 1969, splashing down in the Pacific Ocean. Once again, television played a major role, as Neil Armstrong's first steps were witnessed live by 500 million terrestrial TV viewers.

Conclusion

The Greatest Generation came home from winning World War II and faced a new set of challenges, both on the home front and with changing relationships with former allies. The world was changing and shrinking very quickly. Rockets took men to the moon. Television took Americans into the schools and neighborhoods of the segregated South, showing the oppression of racism.

While it is encouraging to see the results of efforts toward racial reconciliation in this era and the success of the Space Race, we must remember that the opposition of political hostility and hatred cannot be easily overcome by new gadgets, court decisions, or even laws. The problem that humans face is fundamentally a problem of evil in our own hearts. As Pogo Possum famously said in the cartoon *Pogo*, "We have met the enemy, and he is us." As ever, we need a Savior to bring lasting peace on a new earth and true goodwill between all people.

---

1 "Space Race," *Wikipedia*. Accessed 10 February 2014. Retrieved from <http://en.wikipedia.org/wiki/Space_race>.

Mini-Unit 12, Topic 3
At Our Fingertips and in His Hands

Introduction

This topic covers the conclusion of the Cold War and introduces you to Ronald Reagan, whose pivotal presidency led to the relaxation of the tensions that had dominated world politics since the end of World War II. Reagan's tenure also saw events that would ignite the rise of terrorism.

We continue our focus on world-changing technologies. After the Berlin Wall fell, resources that had been used for the war effort, such as Global Positioning Software (GPS) and the pre-cursor to the Internet, the Advanced Research Projects Agency Network (ARPANET), were turned to civilian purposes with surprising results.

The things that we study this week likely overlap your own life! One of the activities that we encourage you to do with your student as you finish up *Tapestry Primer* is to make a time line of the past few decades and note major events in your own life. By bringing history home, you can help your child connect everything he has been learning this year with the everyday lives of your own family. To help you review and connect themes that we've studied this year, we will take time to review the ground we've covered at the end of this topic.

Ronald Reagan and the Cold War

Reagan was born the son of an Illinois shoe salesman in 1911. As a young boy, he loved nature and cowboys. While in high school, Reagan acted in school plays and was elected student body president. He was a sophomore in college when the stock market crashed in 1929, and he graduated into the Great Depression. His first job after college was as a sportscaster, broadcasting over the radio. Reagan was paid $10 per football game.

In 1937, Reagan moved to Hollywood, where he took a screen test at a movie studio. He had a wholesome look that landed him a contract with Warner Brothers—where he wound up making more than fifty movies. He didn't fight in World War II, but the movies he made about courageous soldiers reflected his own beliefs about fighting for freedom.

In his younger years, Reagan was a Democrat who loved Franklin Delano Roosevelt and supported the New Deal. He was a member of the Screen Actors' Guild and then became president of that union, serving five consecutive terms.

He hosted a television show, the General Electric Theater, and became a public spokesman for General Electric. In this role, Reagan consistently interacted with "the folks"—blue collar workers of the heartland of America. In this capacity, and being a people person, he listened and learned. He gradually changed his liberal views of government to conservative ones during these years. Reagan began to stress increasingly conservative ideas, such as the importance of free enterprise and the dangers of too much government. Though he was still a registered Democrat, he campaigned for Eisenhower in 1952 and Richard Nixon in 1960.

His changing views finally led him to officially join the Republican Party in 1962. He won national fame with a speech supporting Barry Goldwater, who lost to Lyndon Johnson in 1964. That notoriety propelled him into politics, where he won the election and became Governor of California in 1966. As governor, Reagan reformed the welfare system, balanced the state's budget, cut taxes, and ordered gas attacks on antiwar demonstrators. His governance caught the nation's attention.

Reagan was quite a contrast to Jimmy Carter and Gerald Ford. Neither of those Presidents had been able to inspire the nation, which was limping along enduring "stagflation," high energy prices, and the aftermath of the Nixon scandal. Americans were losing faith in their leaders, and indeed, in the system that upheld them!

Reagan was called the "Great Communicator" because of his ability to convey big thoughts with clarity and conviction. Reagan's election campaign for President against

President Carter (up for re-election after one lackluster term in 1980) included many memorable moments. He told America, "A recession is when your neighbor loses his job. A depression is when you lose yours. And recovery is when Jimmy Carter loses his." Where Carter had scolded America for their "crisis of confidence," Reagan exuded optimism. He insisted that "America's best days are yet to come." That was what the public wanted—and Reagan won 44 states to Carter's 6.

That landslide victory gave him the mandate he needed to get things done. Democrats controlled both the House and the Senate, but Republicans and conservative Democrats united to pass his tax cuts. Reagan believed in supply-side economics, the core idea of which is that, if wealthy people are released from government regulations and heavy taxation, they will use more money to build businesses and create jobs. In a "trickle-down effect," then, both investment and demand will increase, making the entire national economy stronger for all segments of society.

In the Republican primary, one of his rivals labeled that idea "voodoo economics." Opponents labeled his program "tax cuts for the rich" and said it would drive up the deficit. Supporters said it would boost the economy so much that tax revenues would actually go up. It took two years before America saw the results of Reagan's tax cuts, but in the end, the economy did strengthen, and so did tax revenues. However, the national deficit (where our nation spends more than it makes, and borrows to make up the difference) also increased under Reagan, due to increased spending on the military and other matters.

Reagan spent a lot of money on the military. He believed the Soviet Union was a significant threat to the United States and called it a "force of evil." Reagan's stance was similar to earlier Presidents, but it came as a shock after the Carter years. Many were dismayed when Reagan openly called the Soviet Union "the Evil Empire."

Reagan's answer to this evil was to restore America's policy of containment (opposing the spread of Communist governments), by funding what he called "freedom fighters" around the world. In connection with this policy, Reagan provided arms to the *mujahideen*, the "Holy Warriors" in Afghanistan—which included a young militant from Saudi Arabia named Osama bin Laden. Democrats in Congress objected to this use of national funds, and passed an amendment that banned direct funding of the "contras" who were fighting the Communist government of Nicaragua.

The biggest scandal of his presidency occurred when members of Reagan's administration negotiated with Iran to get money for the contras. When the news of secret deals first broke, Reagan loudly insisted that nobody had done anything wrong. Then, as more details emerged, it became clear that his staff had sold arms to Iran in exchange for the release of hostages held by pro-Iranian factions in Lebanon, and then used the Iranian money to supply the Nicaraguans. Although Reagan insisted that he never knew about these secret deals, and took full responsibility for what happened, the scandal left a lasting stain on his credibility.

Iran needed the American weapons. They had been fighting Iraq for six years by the time the Iran-Contra scandal became public—a long, ugly struggle that echoed the worst features of World War I. After quick initial victories by Iraq and significant land gains in the opening days of the war, things became bogged down. Saddam Hussein, Iraq's leader, had assumed that ethnic Arabs inside Iran would rally to his call—but they didn't. As the Iranians regrouped, they launched offensives that left both sides with staggeringly high casualties. It became a trench war, complete with the artillery fire, infantry assaults, and the poison gasses of World War I—even though Iraq had signed the international treaties that banned the use of such gasses. The two sides started attacking each other's ships, threatening the supply of oil from the critical Persian Gulf region. The U.S. started escorting tankers through the Gulf, and made arrangement to store arms and equipment in the nearby Gulf states, just in case.

Reagan didn't just rely on "freedom fighters" to counter the Soviet threat. He had bigger ideas. In 1983, he proposed a space-based missile defense system that would shoot down incoming nuclear missiles. That, in itself, would be a good thing—but Reagan had a deeper reason for proposing it. He knew a race for a working missile shield would force the Soviets spend money they didn't have to keep up, weakening an already struggling Soviet economy.

Reagan's critics attacked this "Strategic Defense Initiative" project. They called it "Star Wars" because it seemed like something out of science fiction; they said it couldn't work, it was too expensive, and it would trigger World War III. None of that stopped Reagan. "Star Wars" eventually paid off—not by shooting down missiles, but by pushing Russia to the brink of financial destitution. The new Soviet leader, Mikhail Gorbachev, recognized the trouble he was in and sought to liberalize the Soviet Union and sign an arms agreement with the United States.

President Reagan stood at the Berlin Wall in 1987, near the end of his presidency, and made a stirring speech about the coming demise of Communism. The wall was, for all, the icon of the Cold War. Reagan's speech included his famous call, "Mr. Gorbachev, open this gate! Mr. Gorbachev, tear down this wall!" In 1989, the wall came down, but by then Reagan's Vice President, George Bush, had been elected and was sitting in the Oval Office.

Reagan had tremendous personal gifts—but he had his weaknesses, too. He was a "hands-off" leader who delegated a lot—too much, in the case of Iran-Contra. He didn't care for details, which made him overly dependent on his staff. His confidence in the power of tax cuts was proven right, in one sense, but he did not or could not keep spending under control, which left America with huge peace-time deficits.

Other modern presidents have followed Reagan, and each year has seen events, small and large, that together have shaped America into what it is today. We are not going to take young children into the labyrinth of detail that would be necessary in order to explain this story adequately. To do that, we invite you to use *Tapestry of Grace* with them as they grow older. If you start with Year 1 of *Tapestry*, your young student will be almost four years older when you return to the complex modern era in which we live, and you will have the same amount of time and perspective on today's events so that you can better guide his understanding of them.

Wrapping Up

Let's look back on what we've covered this year. As you know, *Tapestry Primer* covers the history of the world in twelve mini-units. Throughout these mini-units, we follow the activities of major "characters" on the stage of history. These characters are the Author (God), People, Good, Evil, The Word, God's Creation, and Man's Creation. Let's review some of the highlights from each mini-unit:

- Mini-Unit 1: Eden to Egypt—We studied how God created and chose His people. We reviewed the early history of Mesopotamia, the land between the rivers, and the patriarchs who left that land for Canaan. We finished in Egypt, where Moses grew up. We saw how God established His authority in Creation, but how people rebelled and sought to define good and evil on their own terms, rather than how God defined it. God sent a Flood to re-make Creation and provided people with a way of escape. God revealed Himself to Abraham, a moon-worshipper in Ur, and called him into a land of promise.

- Mini-Unit 2: Tabernacle to Temple—God revealed Himself to Moses as "I AM," and Moses led a nation of slaves into the wilderness, teaching them where they had come from and where they were going. We witnessed the next generation of Israelites conquer the Promised Land and then fall into the same behavior as their neighbors, ultimately asking for a king after generations of a cycle of rebellion and restoration. In Bronze-Age Israel, God established a kingdom under Saul, then gave David a kingdom that would never end. Solomon ruled wisely over David's kingdom until he began to trust in his own wisdom instead of remaining dependent upon God. After Solomon, Israel's story is one of decline.

- ☐ Mini-Unit 3: Daniel's Revelation—We saw how ancient empires rose and fell according to God's plan. After Israel's golden age, Solomon's divided heart led to a divided kingdom. The Jews were buffeted by a series of hostile empires, annihilating Israel and exiling Judah to Babylon. The Persians restored Jerusalem and fought the Greeks, setting the stage for Alexander the Great's conquests, which would spread Greek culture across the Middle East.

- ☐ Mini-Unit 4: Christ and the Church—We marveled at the way God brought Jesus in the fullness of time. Alexander's conquests united the Mediterranean world. We covered Rome and the New Testament. Jesus was born and crucified under Roman emperors and the Church was born, grew, and suffered waves of persecution. Roman rule enforced peace and enabled the gospel message to spread, persecuted though it was until Constantine made Christianity the official religion of Rome.

- ☐ Mini-Unit 5: The Broken Road—We descended from civilization into feudalism, witnessing the fall of Rome and the role that the Church played in preserving learning in Europe. Feudalism was the response to the chaos that followed and led us to the pinnacle of medieval culture: the era of Crusades, Vikings, knights in shining armor, and wandering monks. Although much was lost, God used this time period to establish Christendom and deepen our understanding and application of theology, albeit not without errors. Although life was difficult, great men of character emerged, with their eyes fixed on Heaven, to establish justice and restore order and learning.

- ☐ Mini-Unit 6: Recovery and Discovery—We saw Europeans rediscover God's Word and watched what happened as a result. When Crusaders brought home forgotten works of the classical pagan world, they spurred a new kind of interest in arts and literature in Europe. There was an emphasis on beauty in the south and on truth in the north. Feudalism began to crumble, and the seeds of national identities were sown. Columbus discovered a New World, while Martin Luther turned the Old World upside down with a fresh reading of the Bible. Rulers used the unrest in the Church to advance their own agendas, especially in England.

- ☐ Mini-Unit 7: A New World—We searched for treasure, adventure, and freedom. We followed the new British settlements in the New World. The religious wars that rocked the Old World sent wave after wave of refugees to the New World, shaping the culture and character of thirteen very different colonies. We saw how people who started out to build a sort of Heaven on Earth fell far short of their goals as relationships worsened both at home and overseas.

- ☐ Mini-Unit 8: One Nation—We struggled with Americans for unity as one nation,

MINI-UNIT 12: A SMALLER WORLD

under God. We saw how Britain tried to make America pay for its own defense from the French and Indians. King George's clumsy efforts to tax his subjects led to controversy, conflict, and eventually, war. We watched the conclusion of that war for American independence from Britain, and we saw the bravery and dedication of the patriots who pledged their lives, their fortunes, and their sacred honor to the task of winning that independence.

❑ Mini-Unit 9: Growing Pains—We followed the westward growth of the young nation. We saw how Napoleon's war debts gave the United States the chance to buy the Louisiana territory for a song. We followed the Lewis and Clark Expedition across the new nation, which eventually expanded from thirteen colonies on the Eastern seaboard to a country that stretched from sea to shining sea. Although America gained territory, new lands and pressure to fuel the engines of industrialization served to deepen divisions between North, South, and West. Slavery was supposed to have died out on its own, but industrial demand for cotton made this institutionalized oppression very profitable. Tensions mounted as the balance of power between slave states and free states shifted back and forth.

❑ Mini-Unit 10: A House Divided—We saw how the sectionalism and industrialization of the young nation finally ripened into the bitter fruits of Civil War. Sometimes called the first Modern War, this conflict pitted brother against brother, fueled by the rapid transportation of railroads, communications of telegraphs, and lethality of mass-produced weapons. Photography captured the images of war in America for the first time, leaving an indelible imprint on our national identity. The Civil War split America, and the country sought to heal in the aftermath of the war as the *United* States, not *these* United States.

❑ Mini-Unit 11: Engines of Empires—As America tried and failed to weather Reconstruction, we learned how technology continued to change the world. In the United States, Americans filled the West at the cost of promises they had made to Native Americans. People sought to redefine good and evil, applying concepts of Social Darwinism and the Gospel of Wealth in the place of the idea that all men are created in the image of God and are called to spread the Gospel of Peace. This was the Gilded Age, featuring both immigrants and Captains of Industry. America seemed to be a shining, golden land of opportunity and opened its doors to the huddled masses of the world, only to have many of them huddle in dark places and work in dangerous factories. The airplane and the automobile changed the way that people moved, shrinking the world and (along with other innovations in medicine and communications) giving rise to terrific expectations for a new century. Almost immediately in that new century, however, we saw the optimism of the modern world stagger under the horrendous burdens of World War I.

- ❏ Mini-Unit 12: A Smaller World—We learned how closely we are connected by inventions that have bridged distance and time, bringing us close enough to help and also to hurt one another. World War I was followed by the silliness of the Roaring Twenties, the suffering of the Depression, and another—more devastating—world war. As people cast off the moorings of faith in God, they cast about for something else in which to believe. Germany had barely surrendered in the second war before the Allies turned on one another in tensions that led into a whole new "Cold War." The Space Race and proxy wars were the battlegrounds of this new kind of war between superpowers who were now armed with city-shattering weapons. We saw how Reagan's decisions drove the Soviet Union to the point of collapse, and the Internet, GPS, and other tools were unleashed, triggering new opportunities and concerns.

Throughout it all, though we have looked at the story of mankind from many different viewpoints, it has remained the same story—one of a battle waged in a garden. God created people in His image for His glory. Human beings, in our arrogance and desire to be like God, have consistently rebelled and sought to define good and evil on our own terms, rather than accept His Authority, definitions, and sovereignty over us.

God has given us His Word, in the incarnate Jesus Christ and in the pages of the Bible, in order to make it very plain who He is and what our response to Him should be. Ultimately, as the Author, God has told us that He will redeem and renew His creation. His plan is for His people to be restored to a full, unbroken relationship with Himself. Through Jesus Christ, that can begin now for those who accept His salvation and His assessment of our condition. The story of history points to Jesus.

There are two places in the Bible where the expression "the fullness of time" is used. Galatians 4:4-5 says, "But when the fullness of time had come, God sent forth his Son, born of woman, born under the law, to redeem those who were under the law, so that we might receive adoption as sons." Ephesians 1:7-10 describes how, "In him we have redemption through his blood, the forgiveness of our trespasses, according to the riches of his grace, which he lavished upon us, in all wisdom and insight making known to us the mystery of his will, according to his purpose, which he set forth in Christ as a plan for the fullness of time, to unite all things in him, things in heaven and things on earth." This will be the ultimate end of the story, and it will be to the glorious praise of God, not men, when all is said and done.